Contents

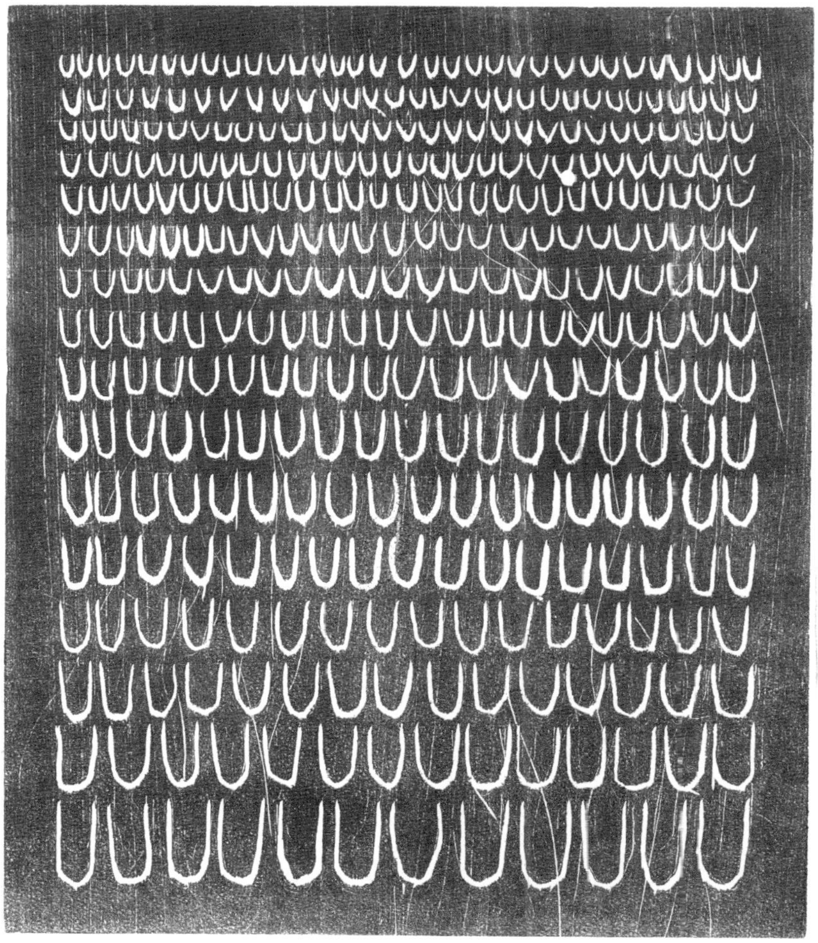

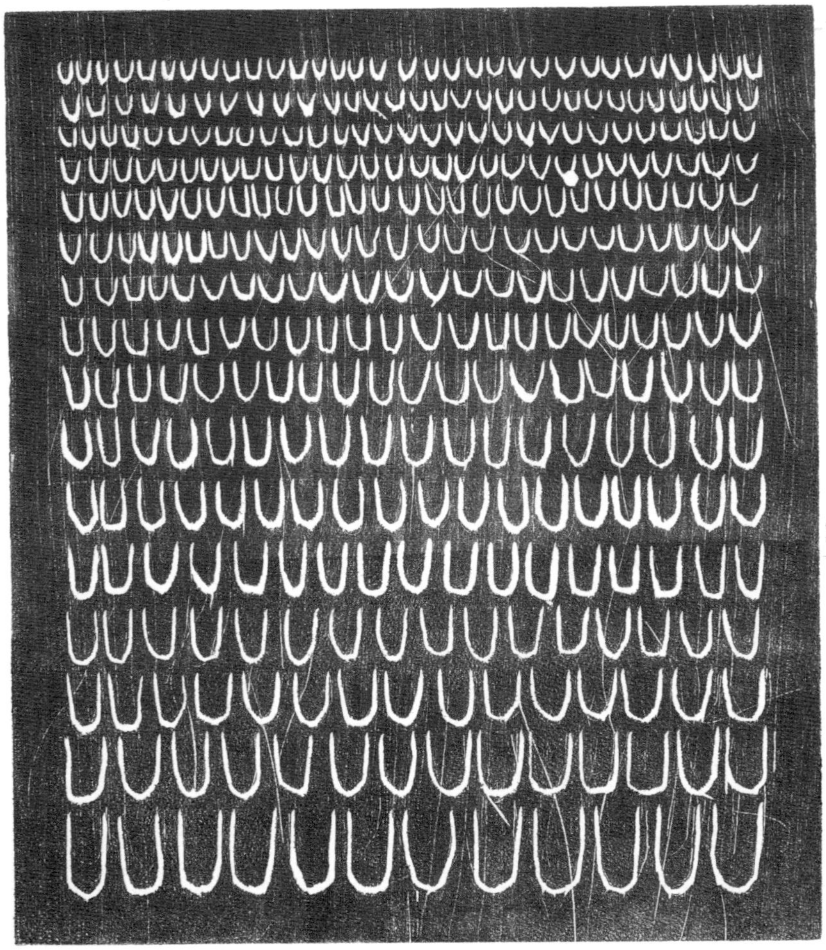

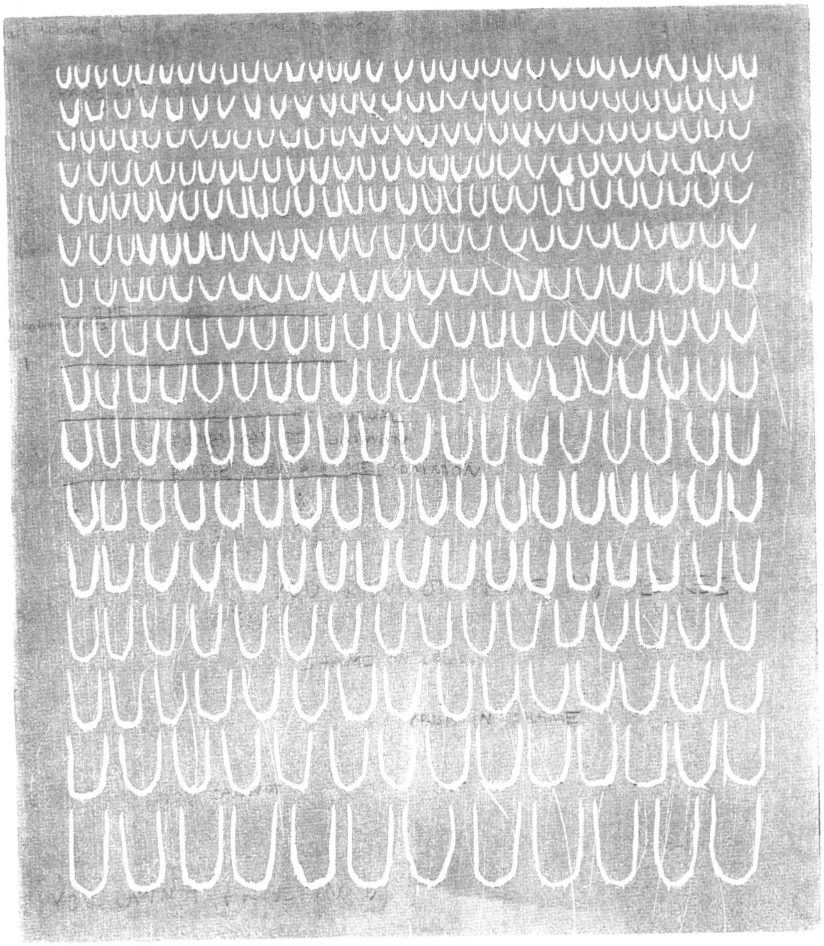

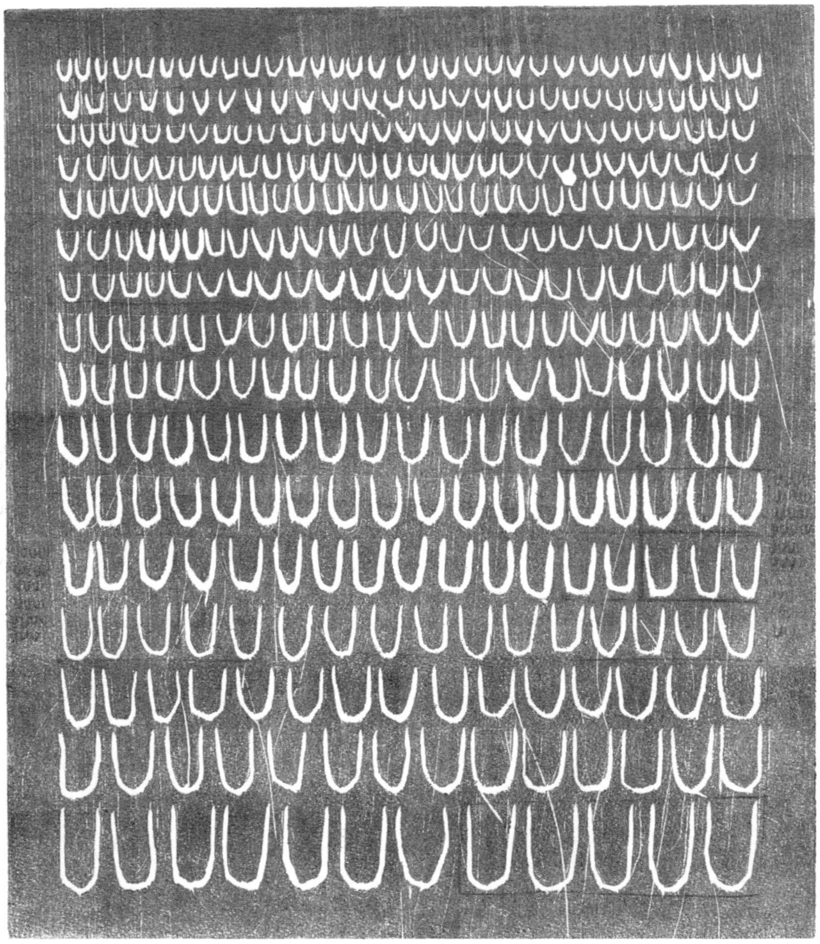

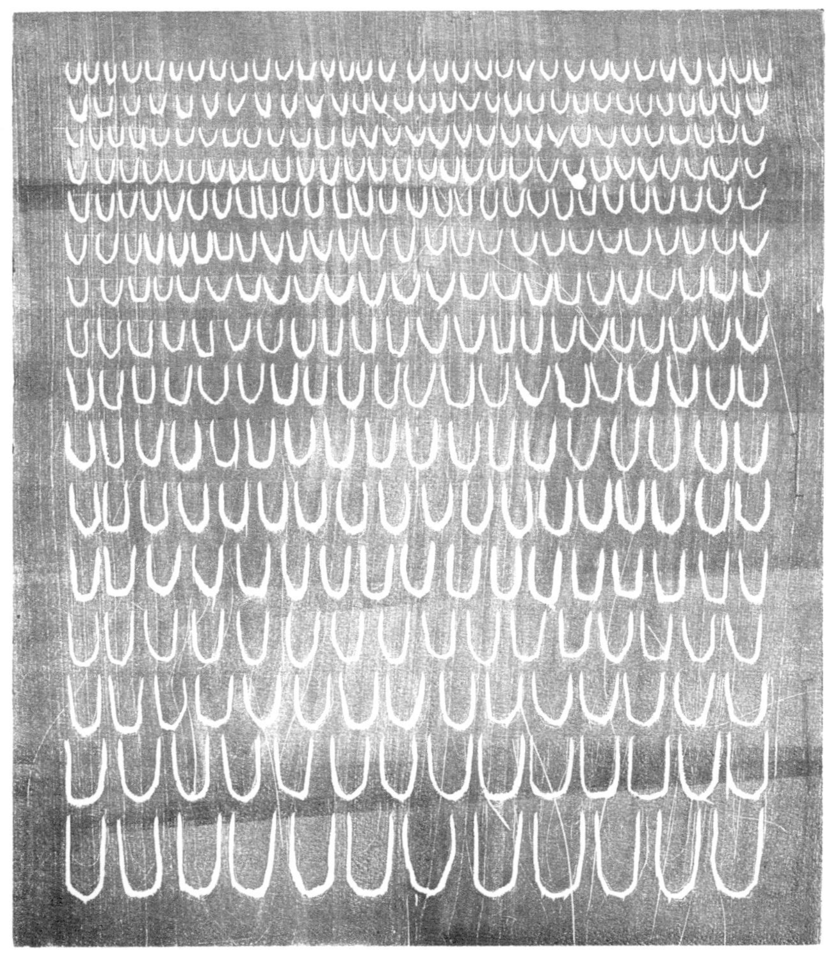

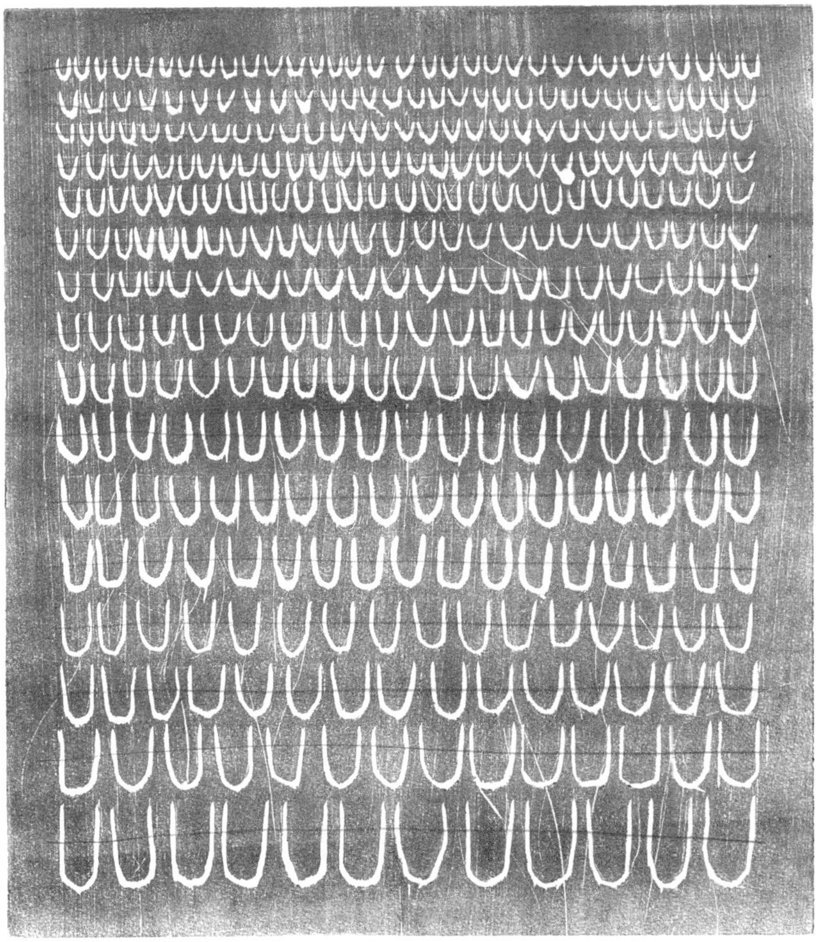

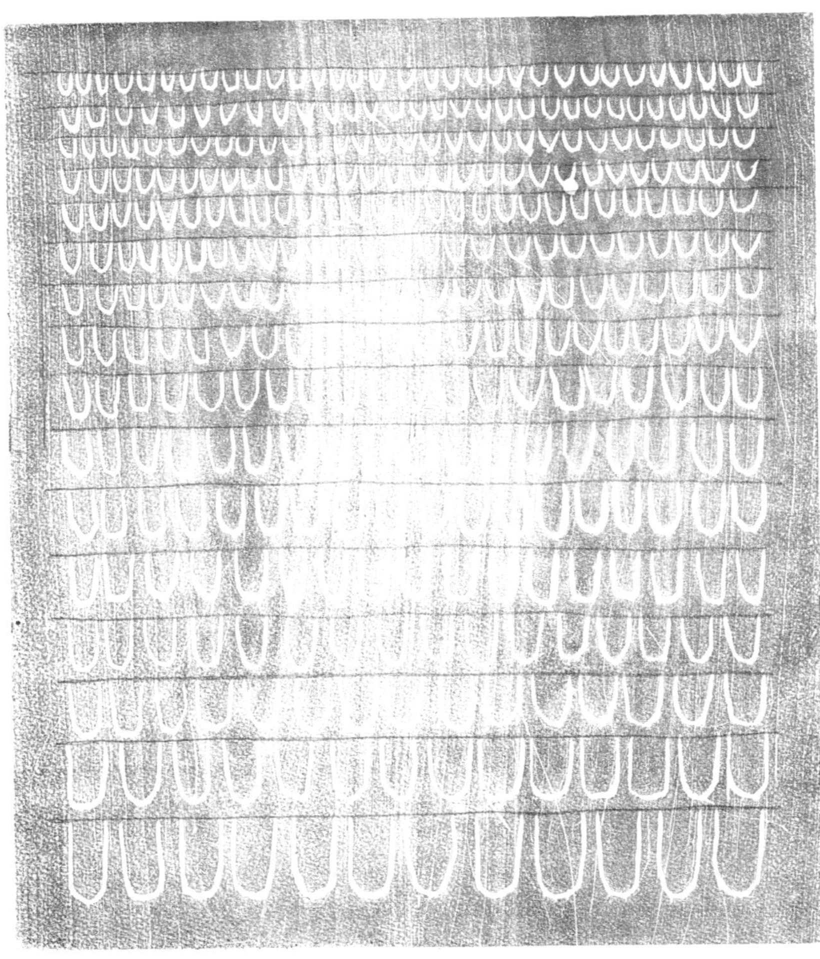

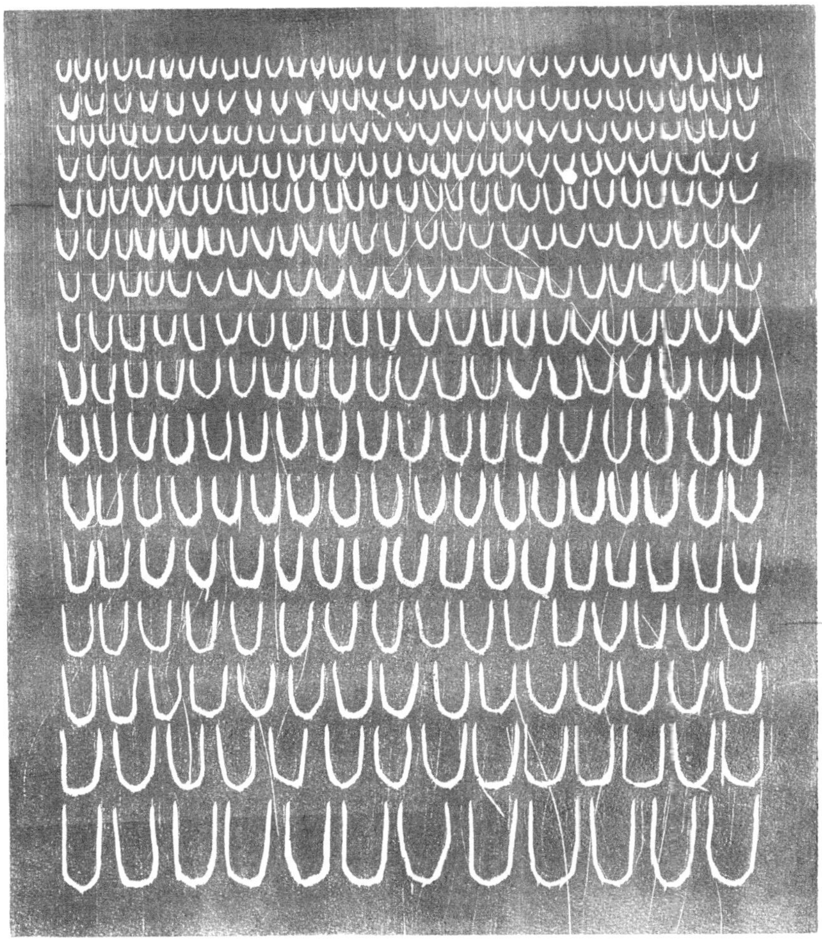

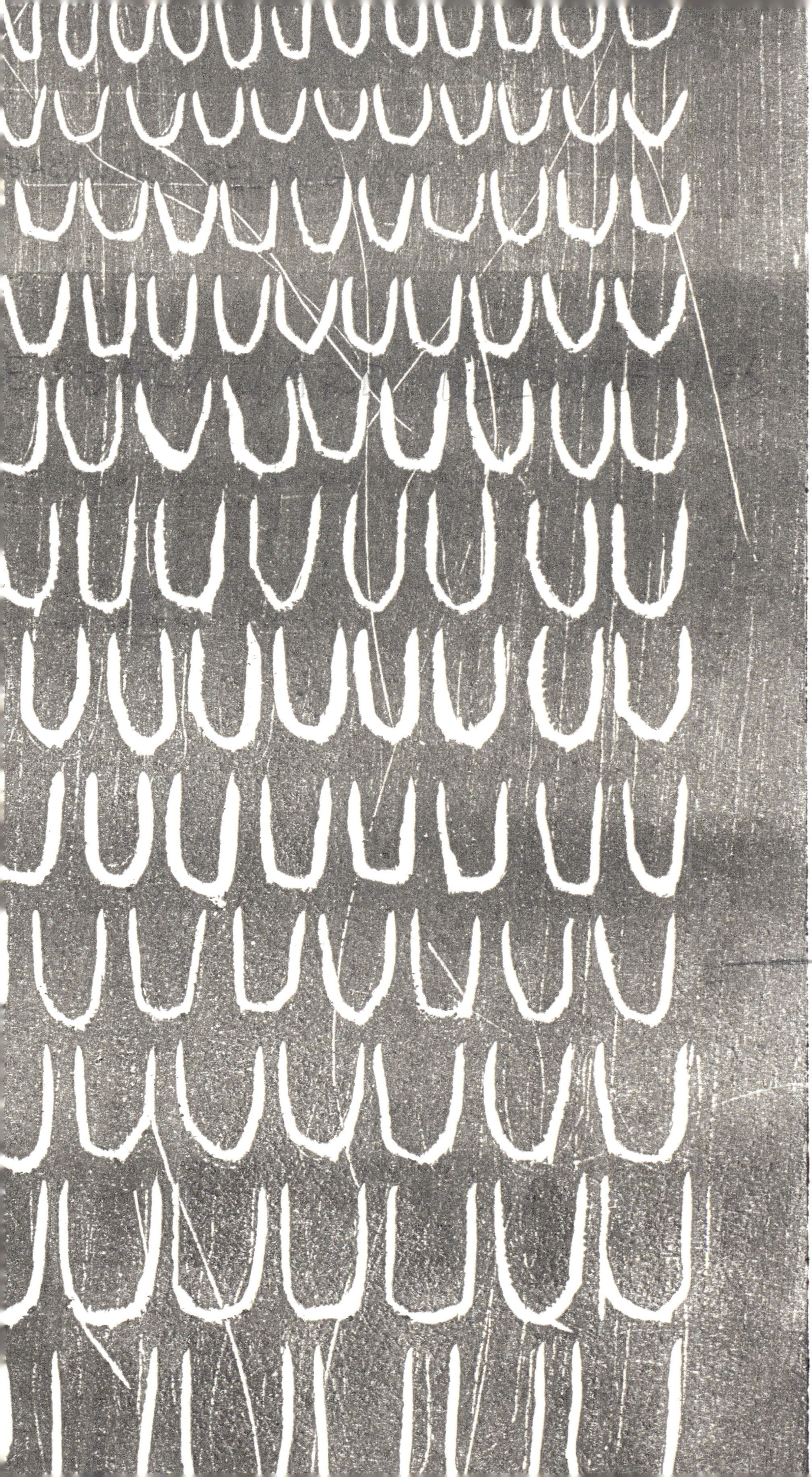

about what is physical
about what is coincidental
about what is vulnerable
about what is economic
about what is subjective
I RECOGNISE MYSELF
I DONT RECOGNISE MYSELF
I HAVE NO PLAN

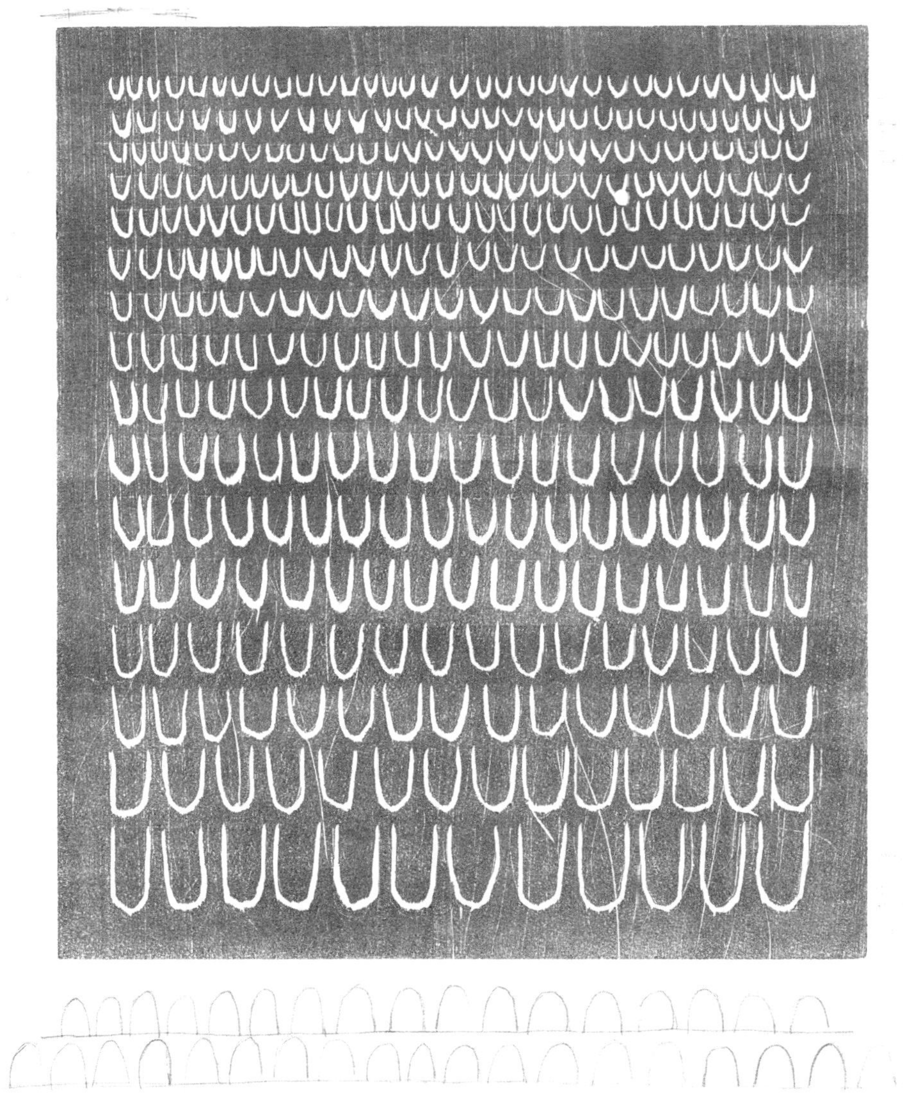

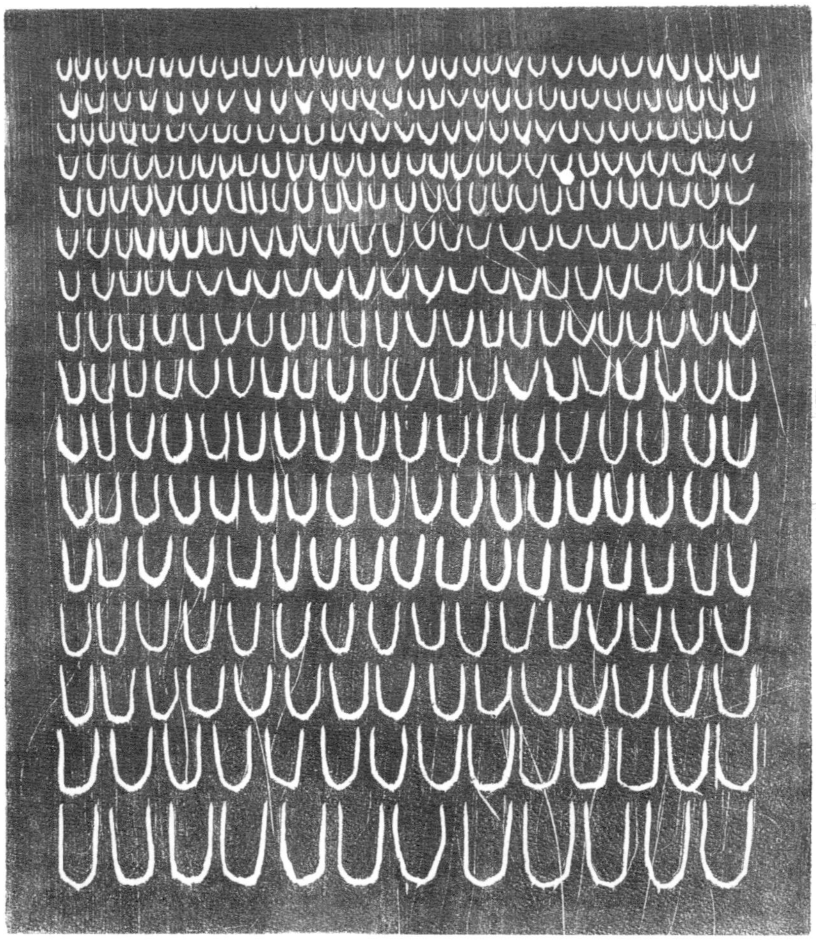

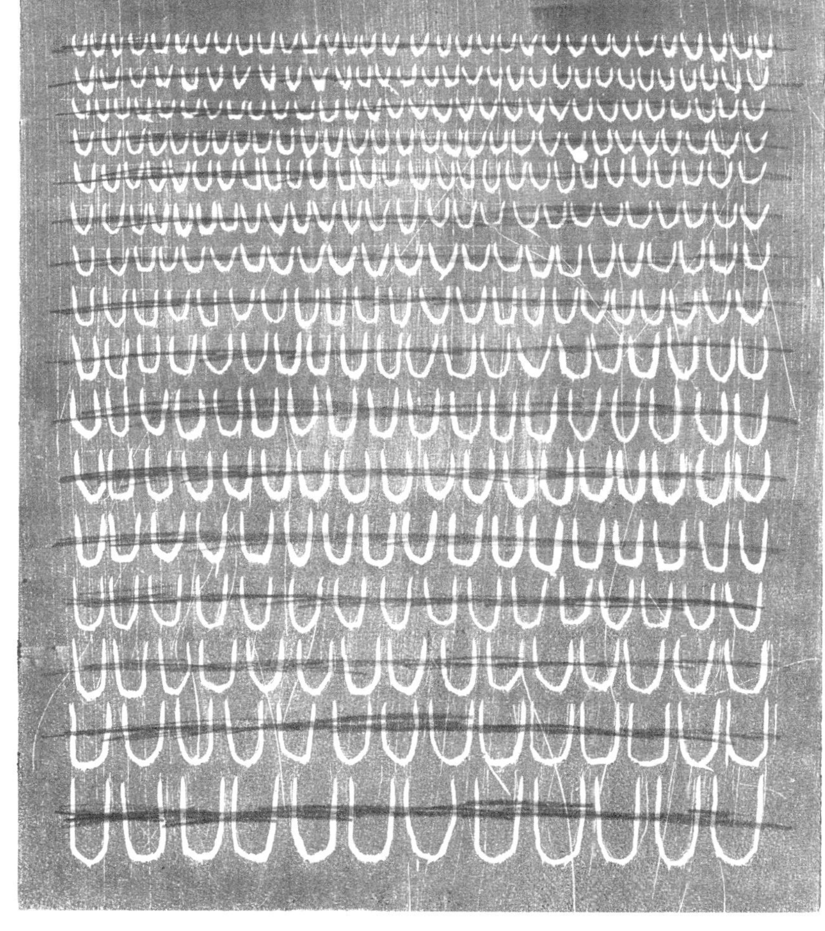

I am the wooden body

THE BODY AS A LAND OF WONDER

The measurement of transitions have grown out of language.

THE BODY AS A LAND OF WONDER

...N I WANT TO KNOW you
UNTIL I DON'T KNOW you ANY MORE

Public:
but it was never said

IMAGINE THE BODY AS A SENTENCE
IN A ... VERY ... PARA...

The body as a land of wonder

the body has grown out
the ... and ... signs

are not coordinate

The lovers

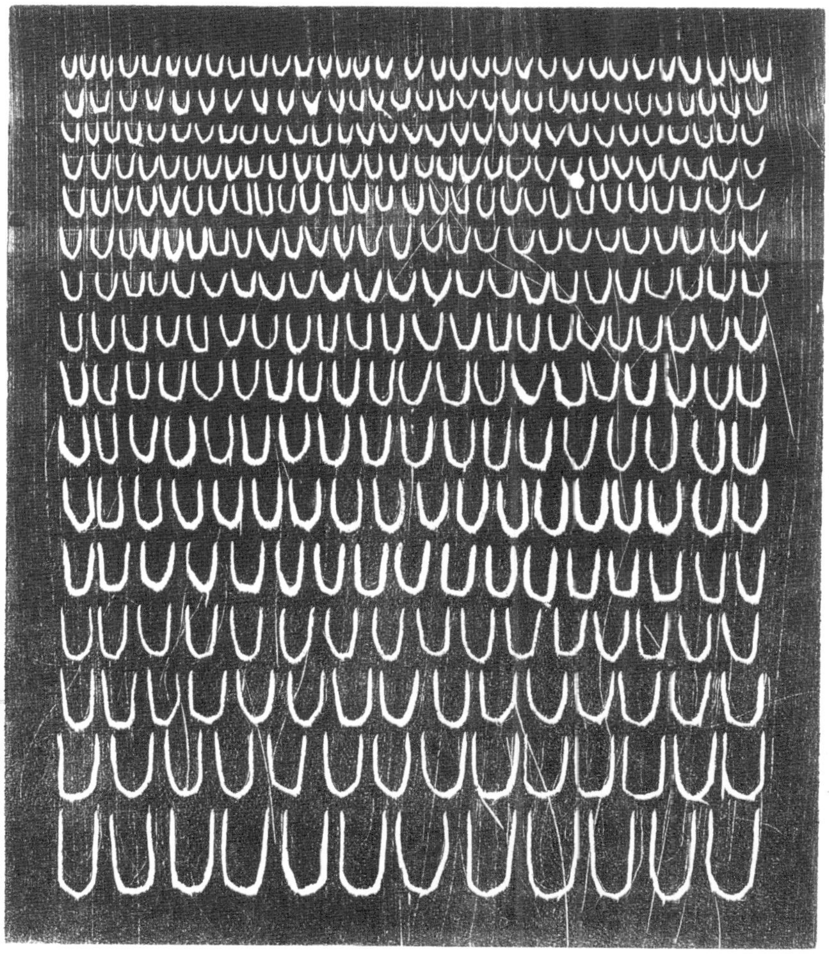

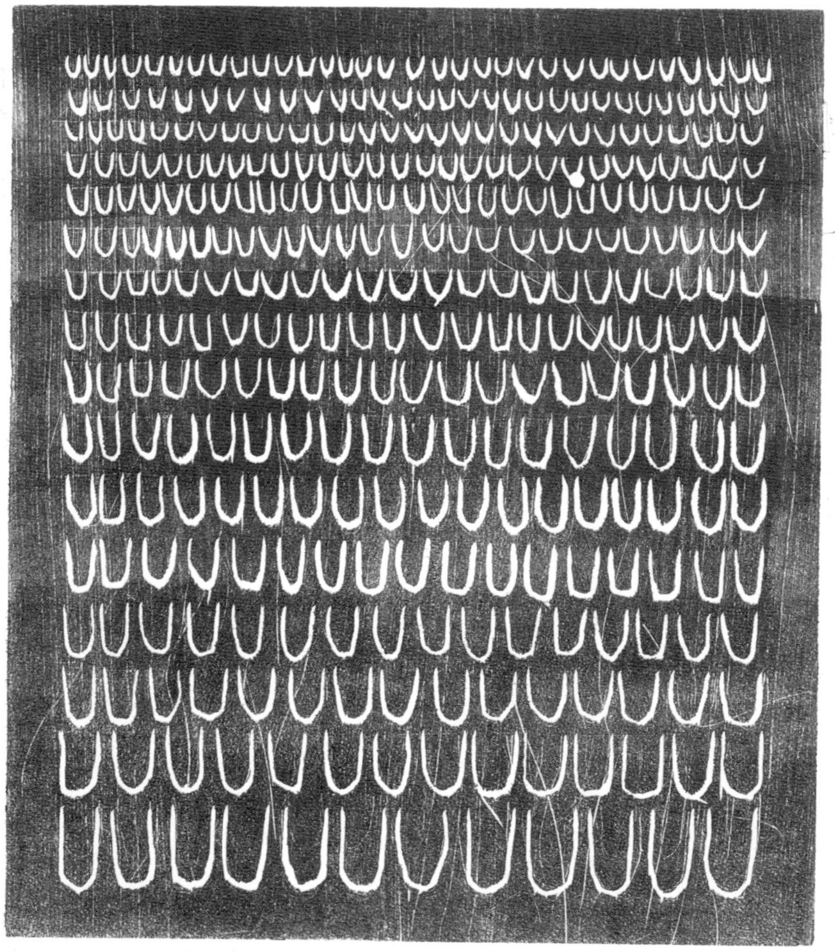

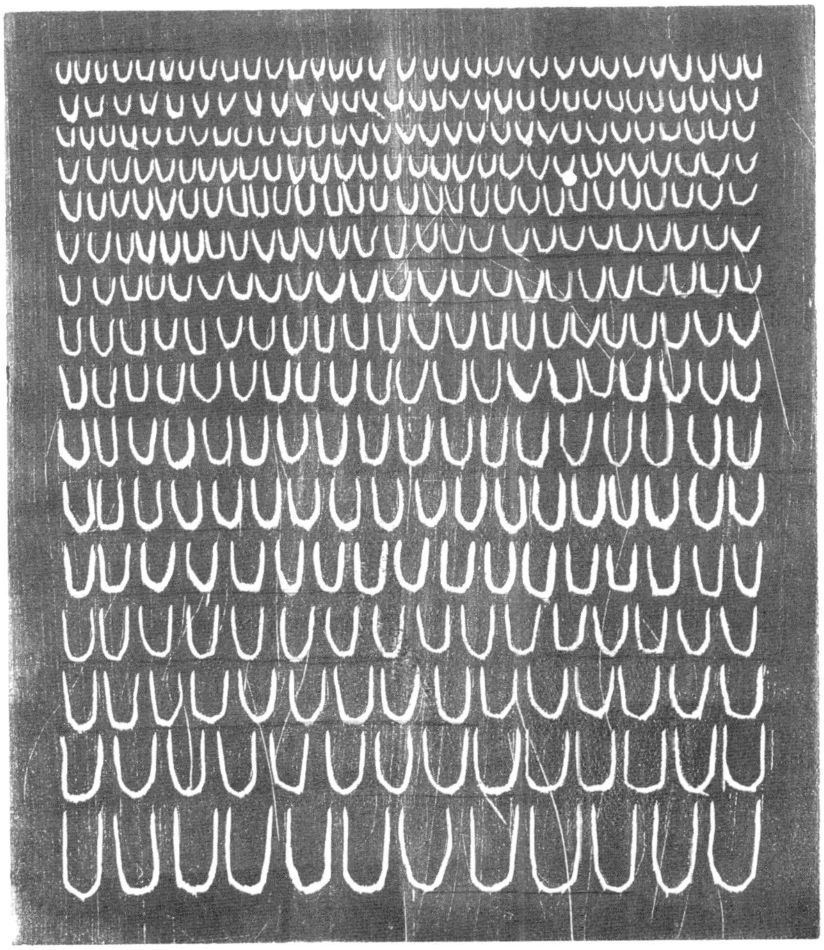

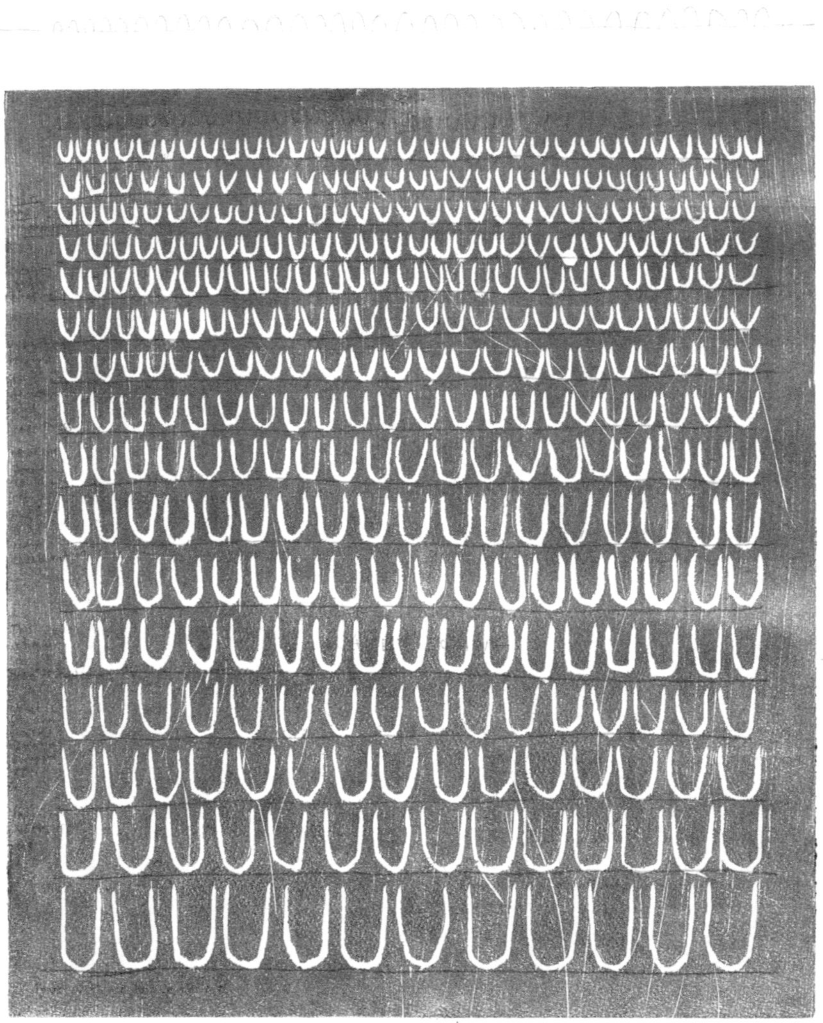

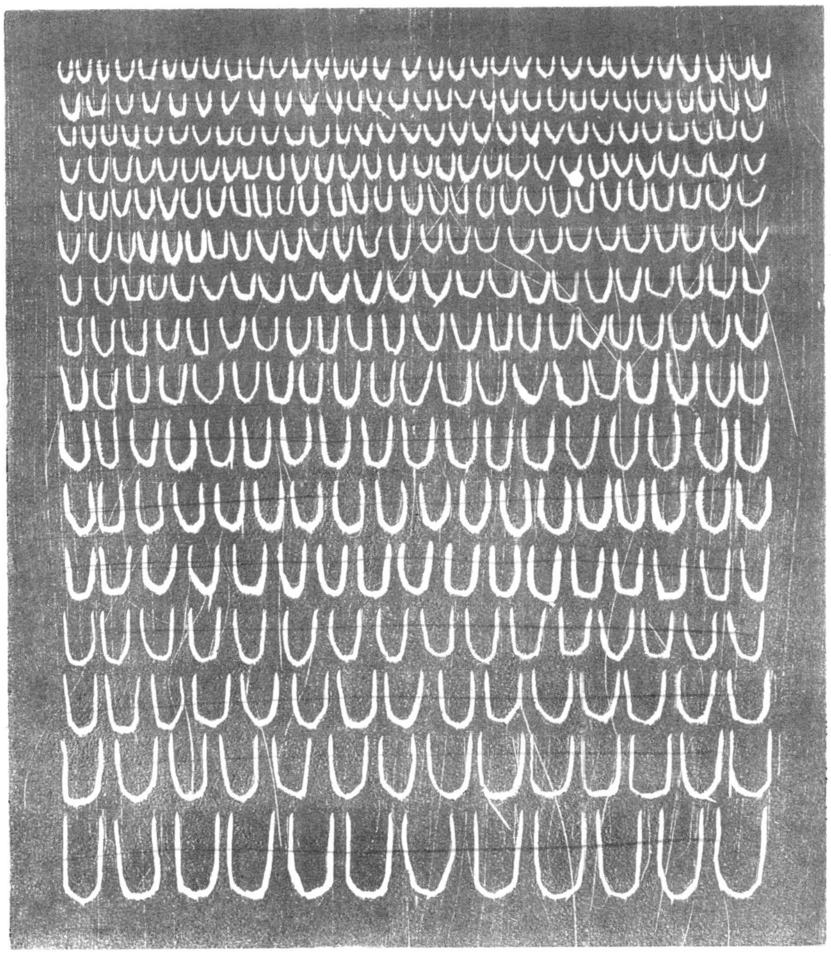

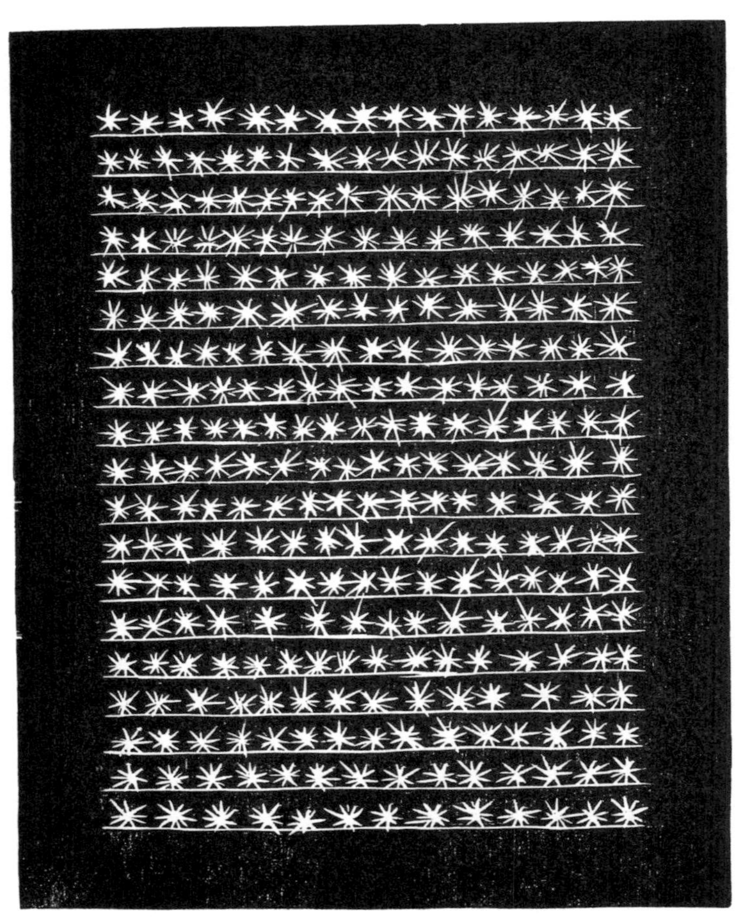

Argumenter for begær (Arguments for desire), 2013–2015

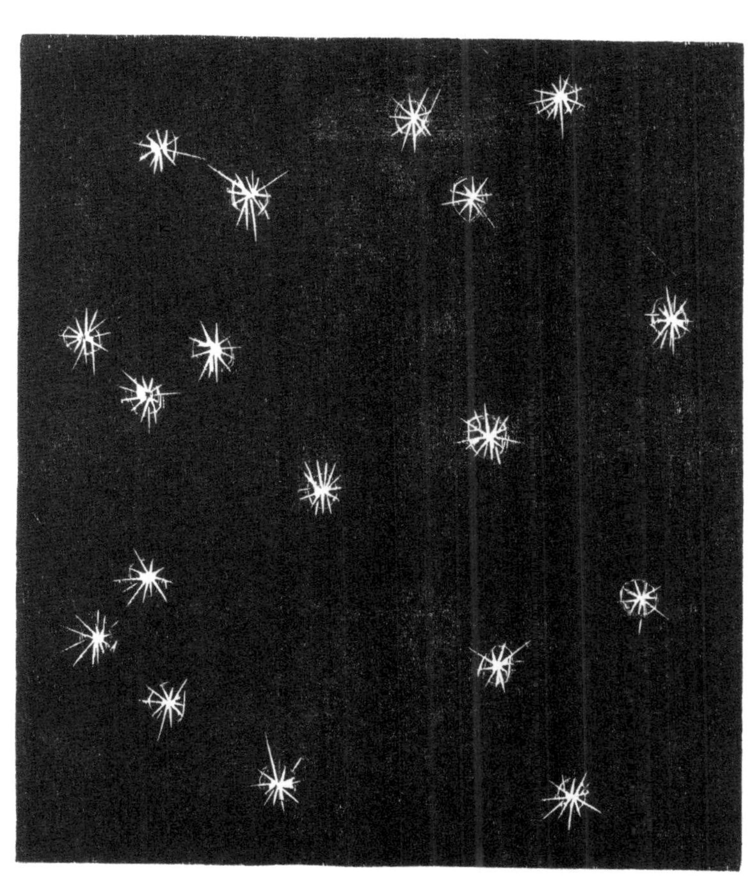

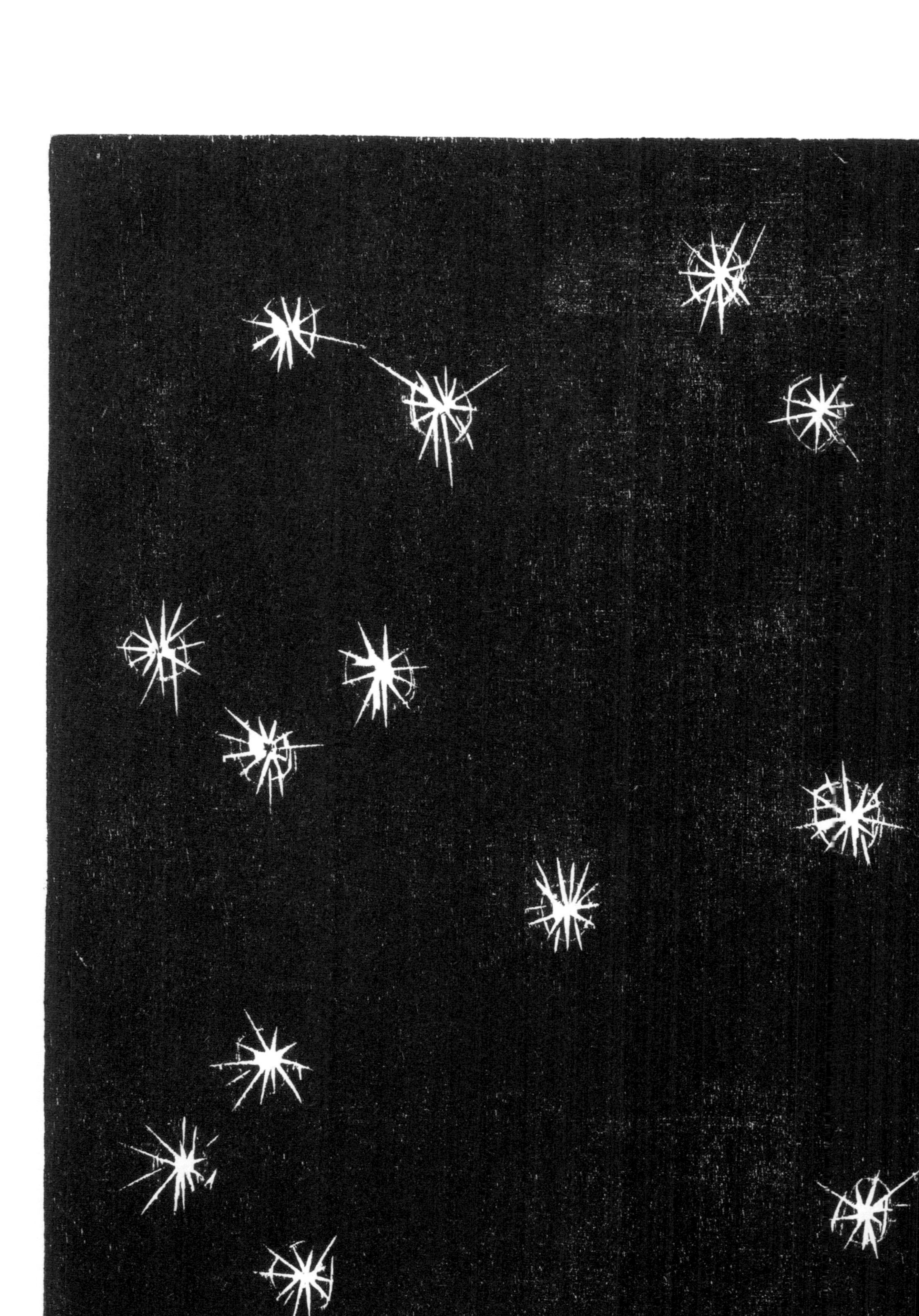

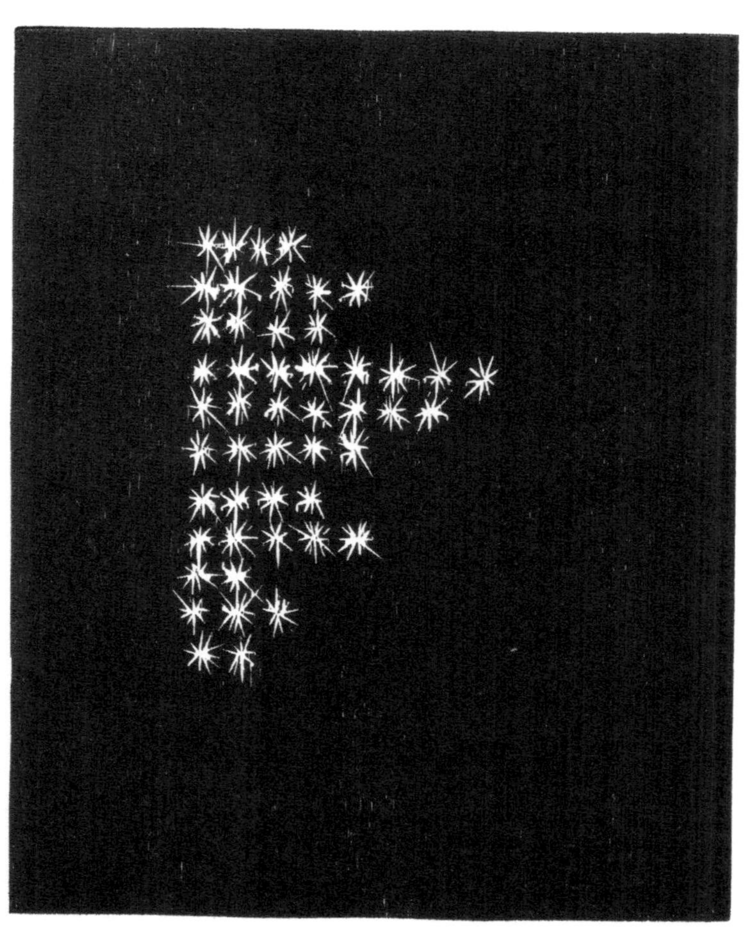

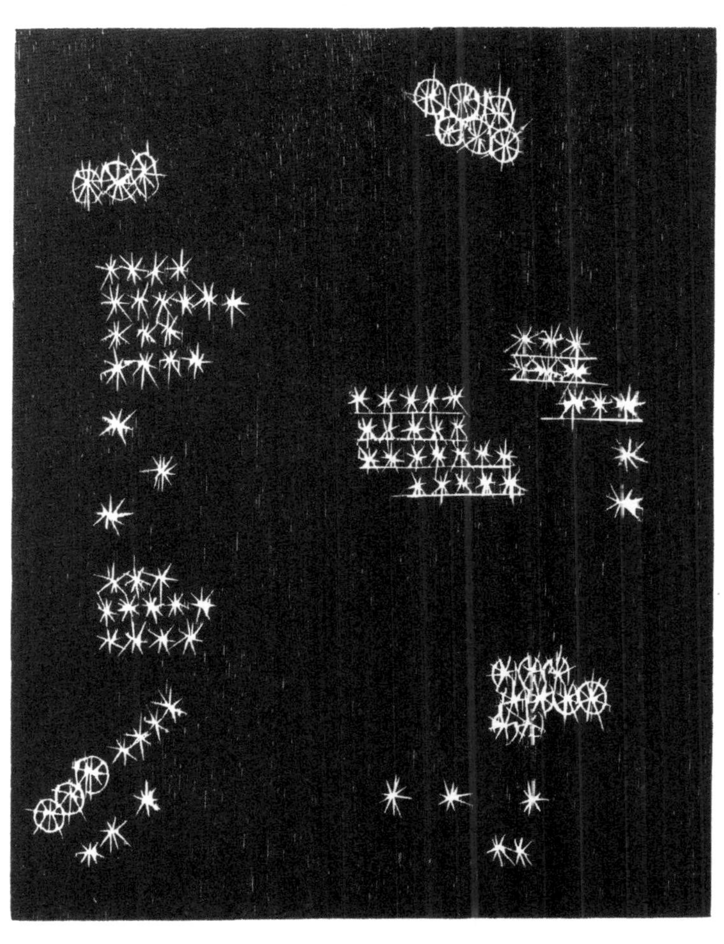

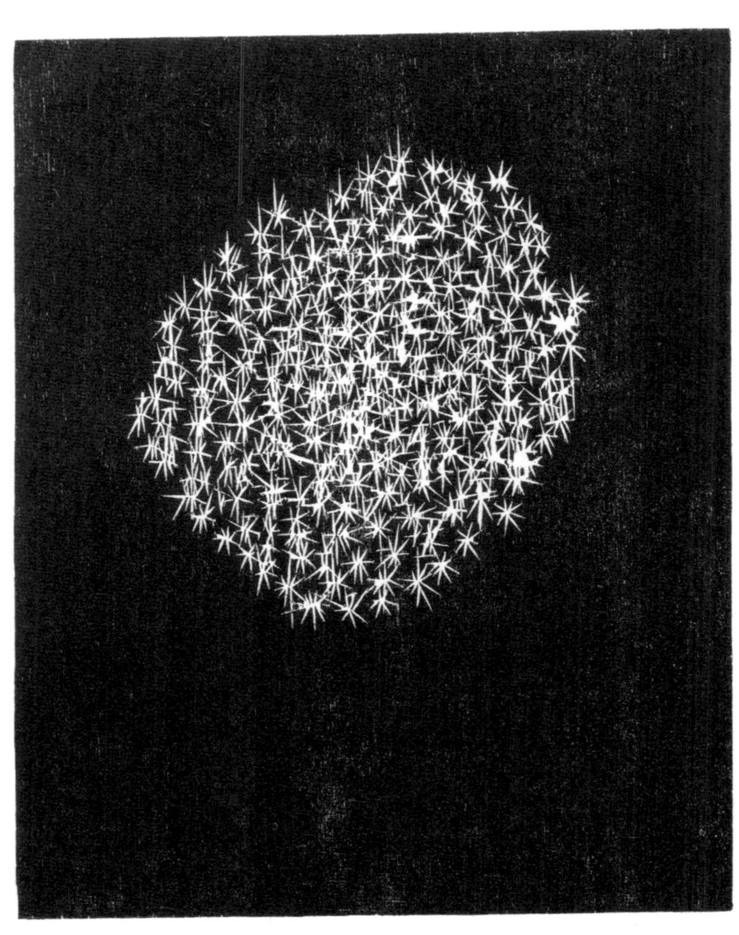

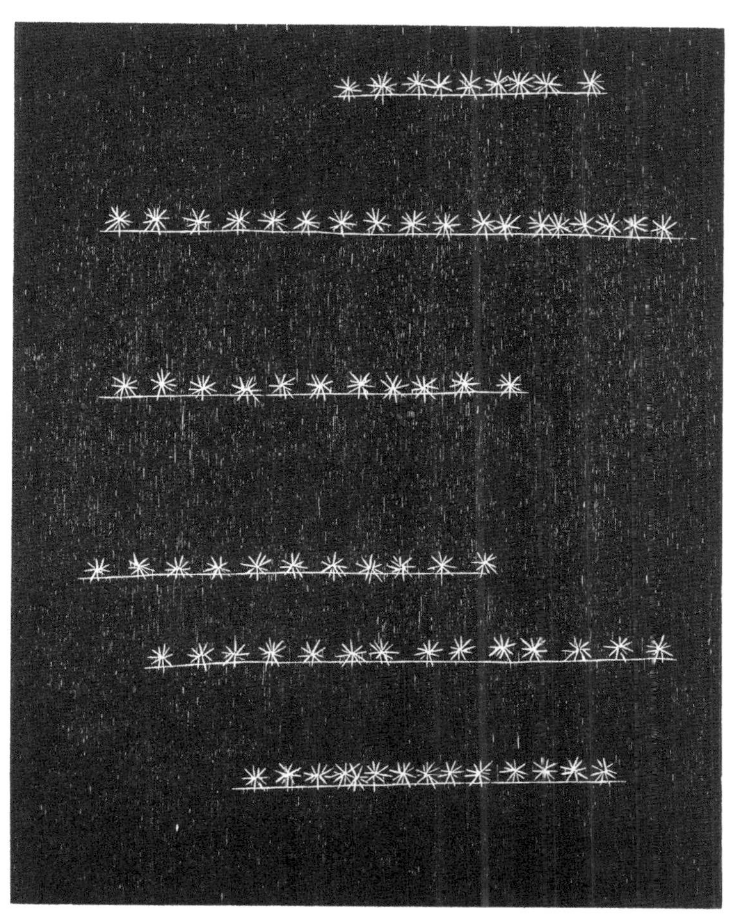

Arguments for desire (encore, encore), 2018

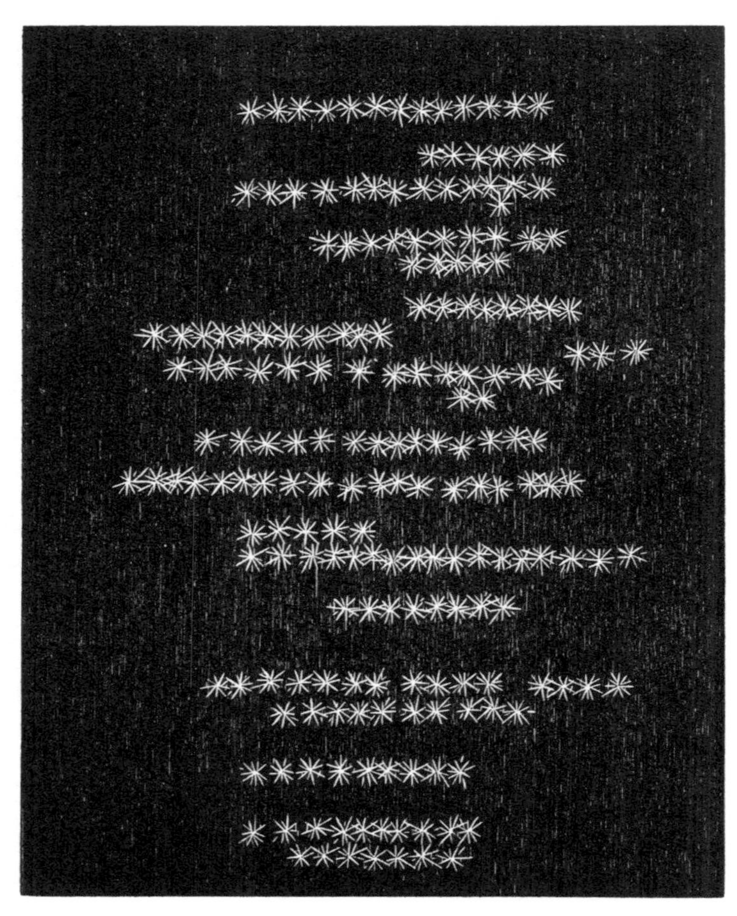

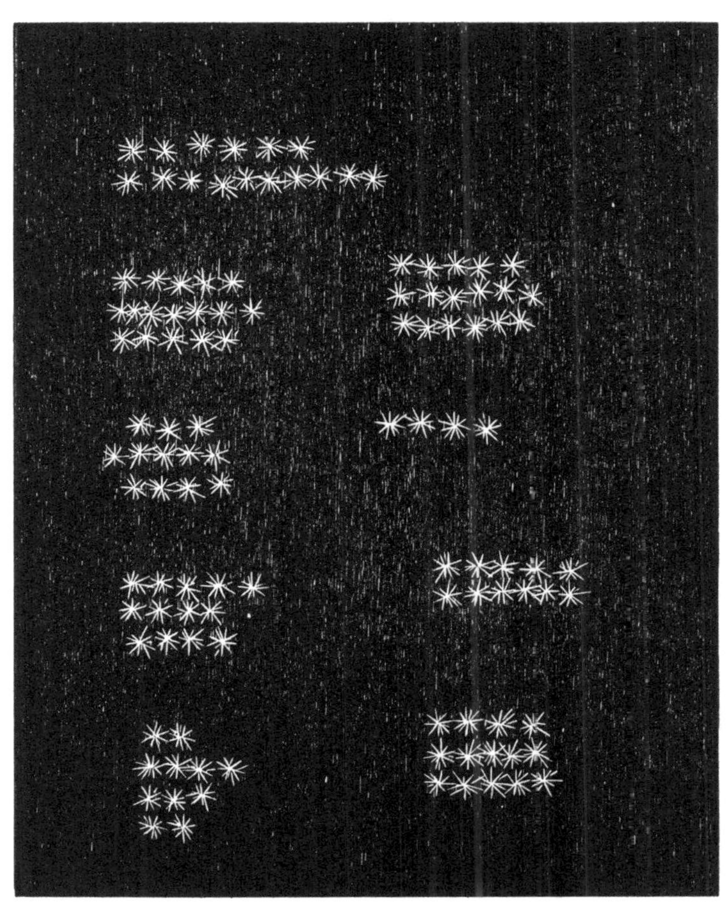

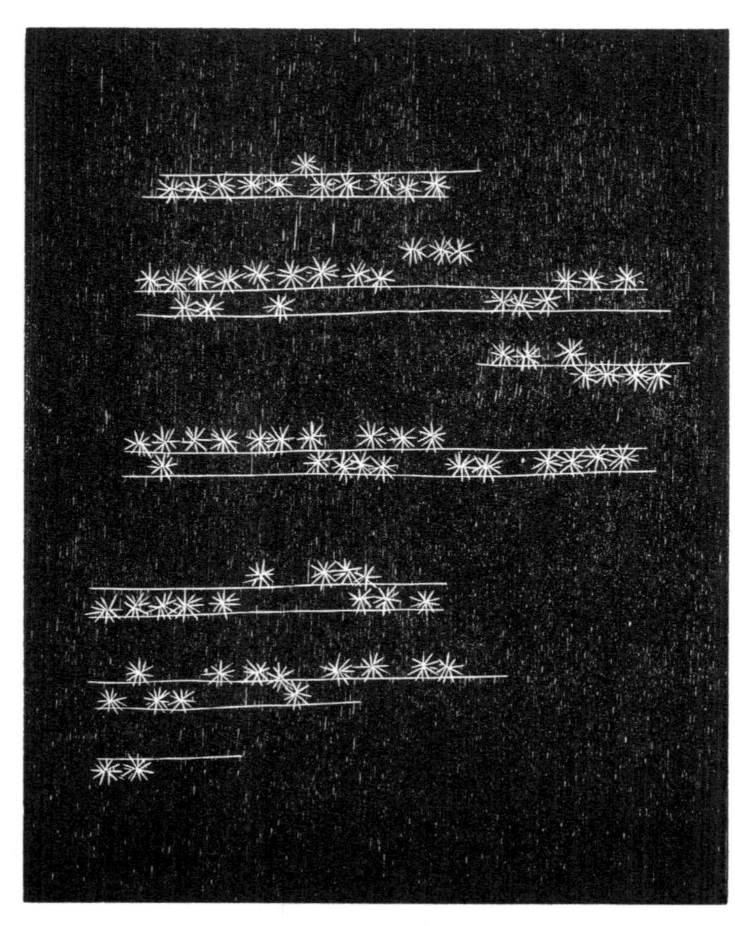

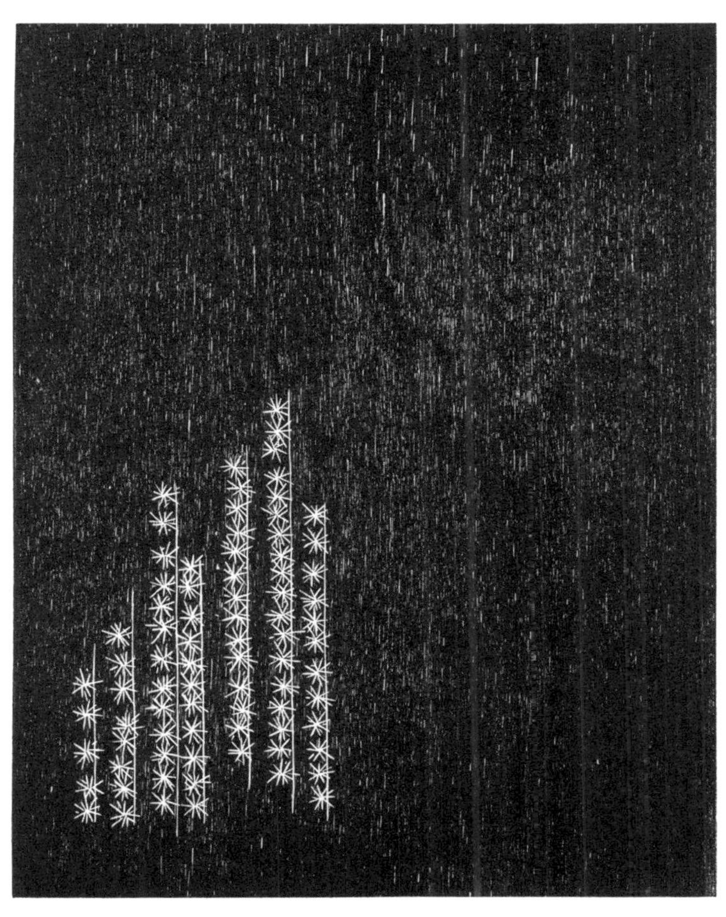

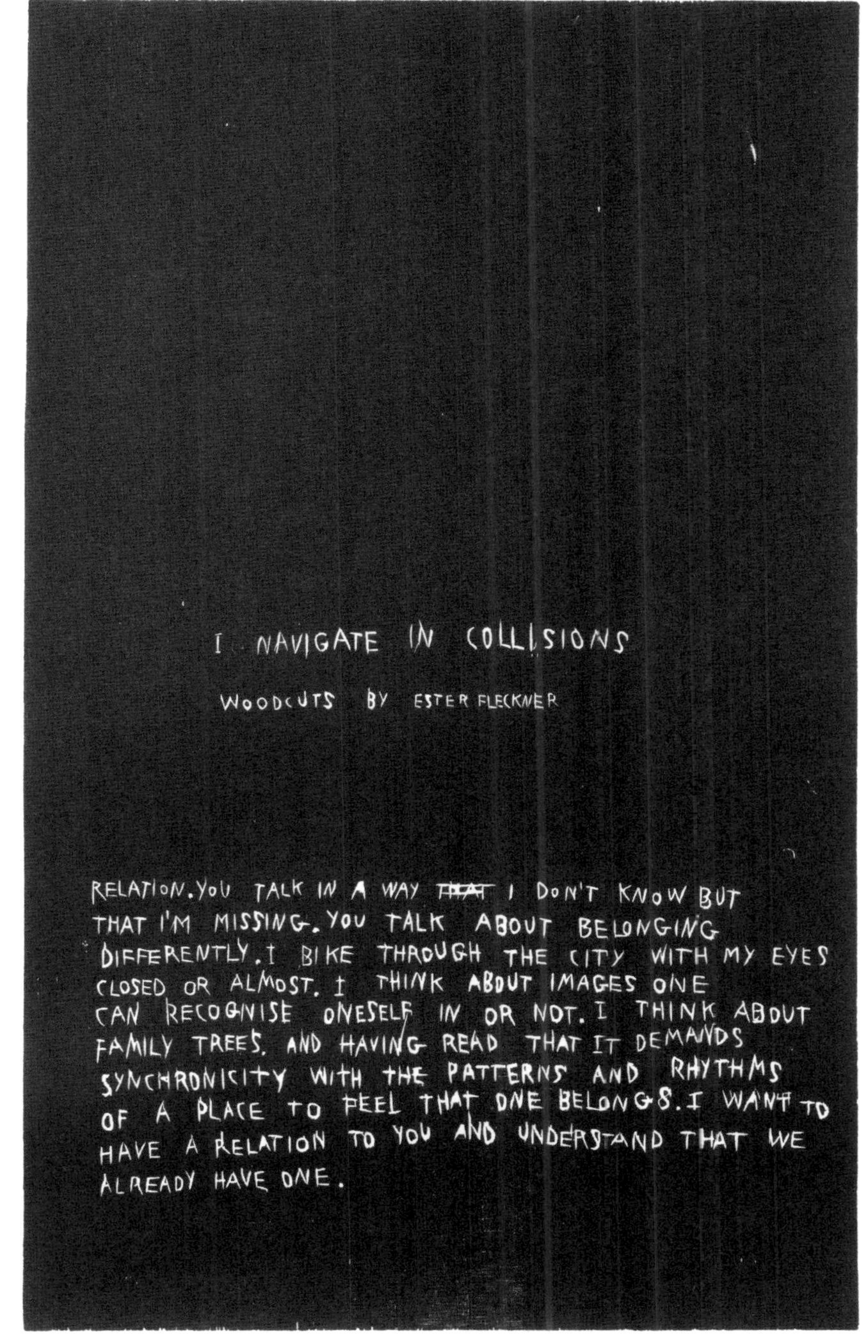

I navigate in collisions, flyer (English version), 2014–2015

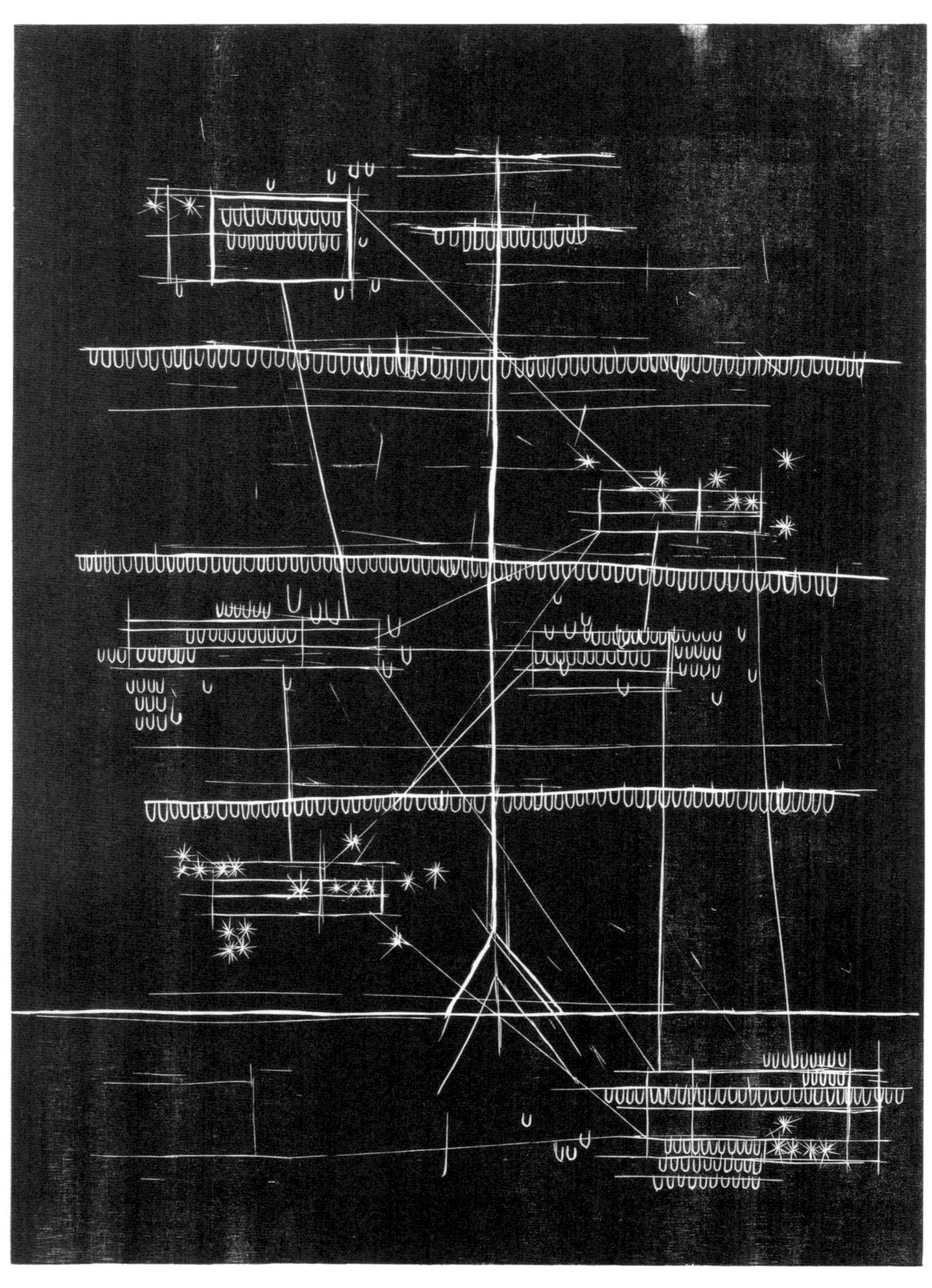

Jeg navigerer i kollisioner (I navigate in collisions), 2014–2015

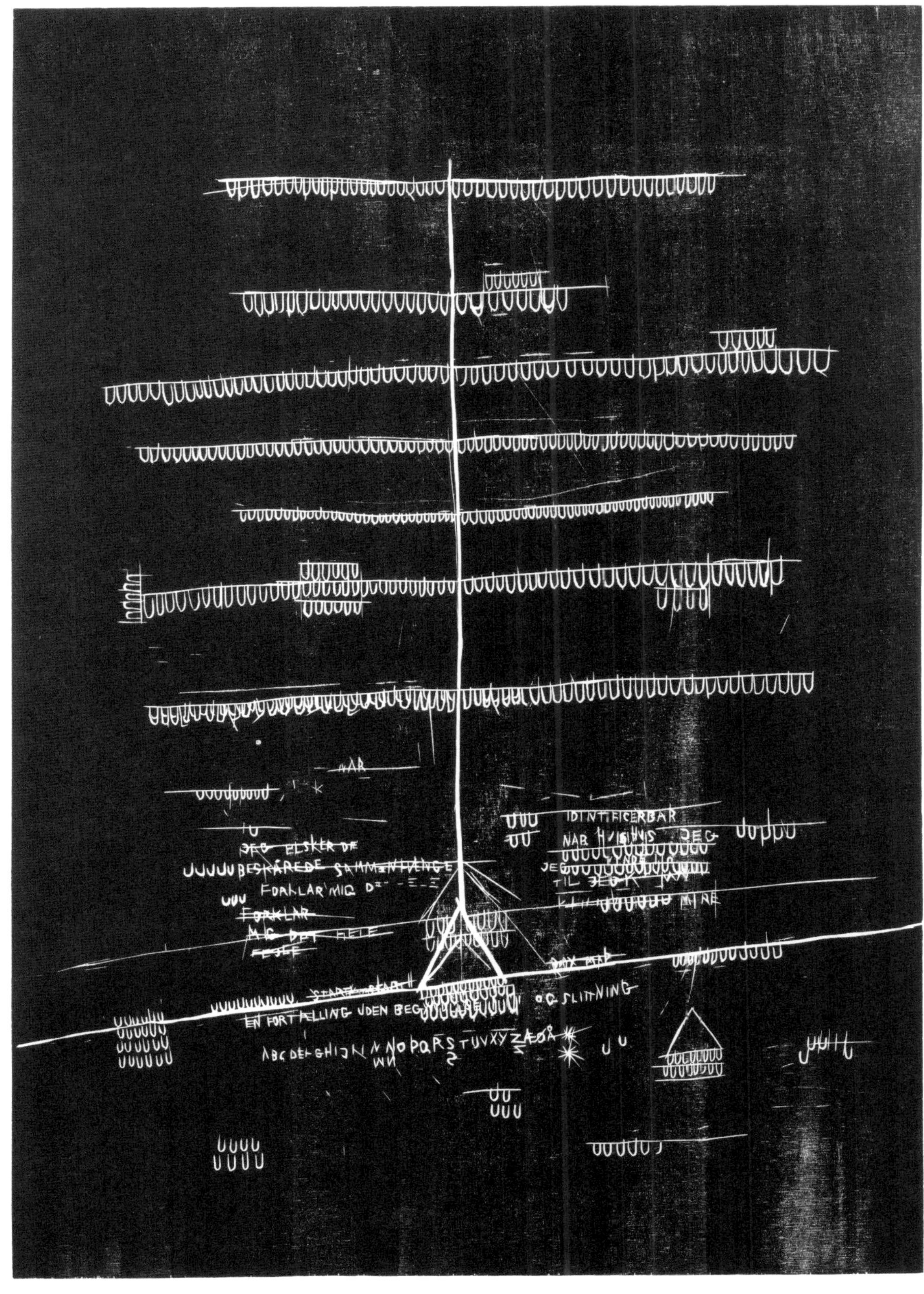

AAR
IDENTIFICERBAR
JEG ELSKER DE NÅR HVIS/HVIS JEG
BESKÅREDE SAMMENHÆNGE JEG
FORKLAR MIG D TIL JEG
FORKLAR MINE
MIG DET HELE
HELE
EN FORTÆLLING UDEN BEGYNDELSE OG SLUTNING
ABCDEFGHIJKLMNOPQRSTUVXYZÆØÅ

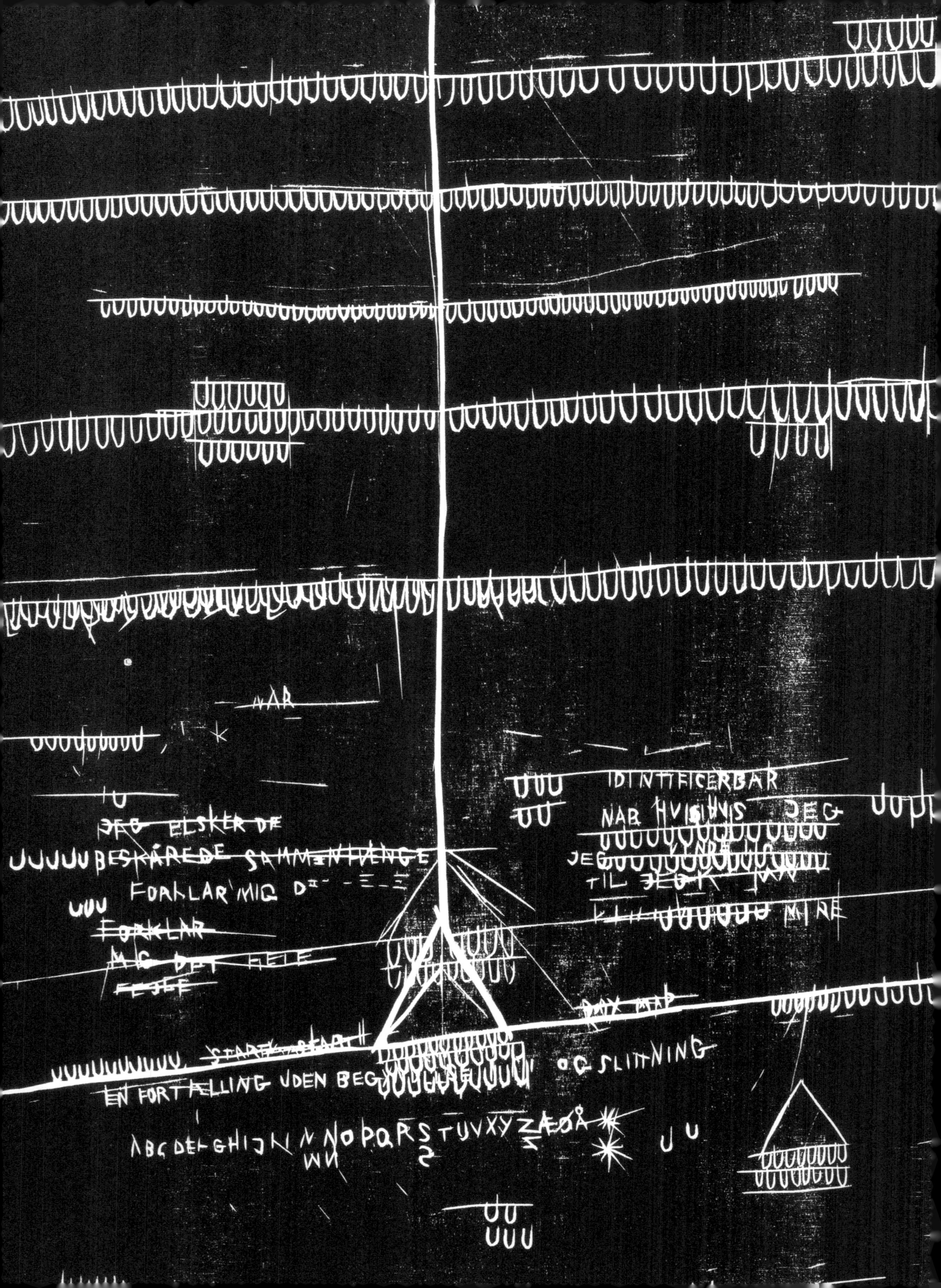

NÅR

JEG ELSKER DE
UBESKÅREDE SAMMENHÆNGE
FORKLAR MIG D
FORKLAR
MIG DET HELE
FEJLE

IDINTIFICERBAR
NÅR HVIS/HVIS DEG
JEG
TIL FEJL
MINE

BLIV MAD

START START
EN FORTÆLLING UDEN BEG
OG SLITNING

ABCDEFGHIJ N NOPQRSTUVXYZÆØÅ
WM
JU

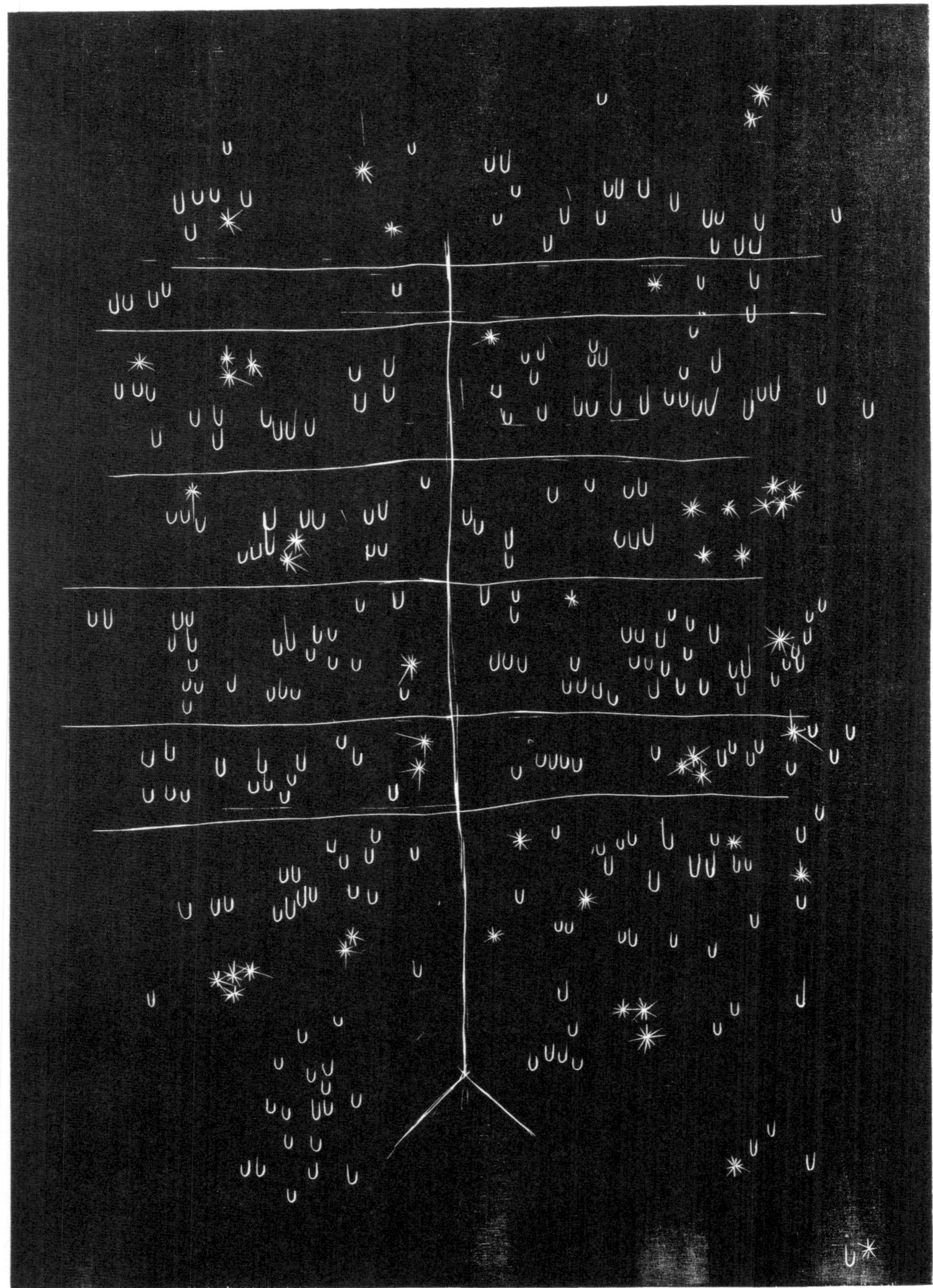

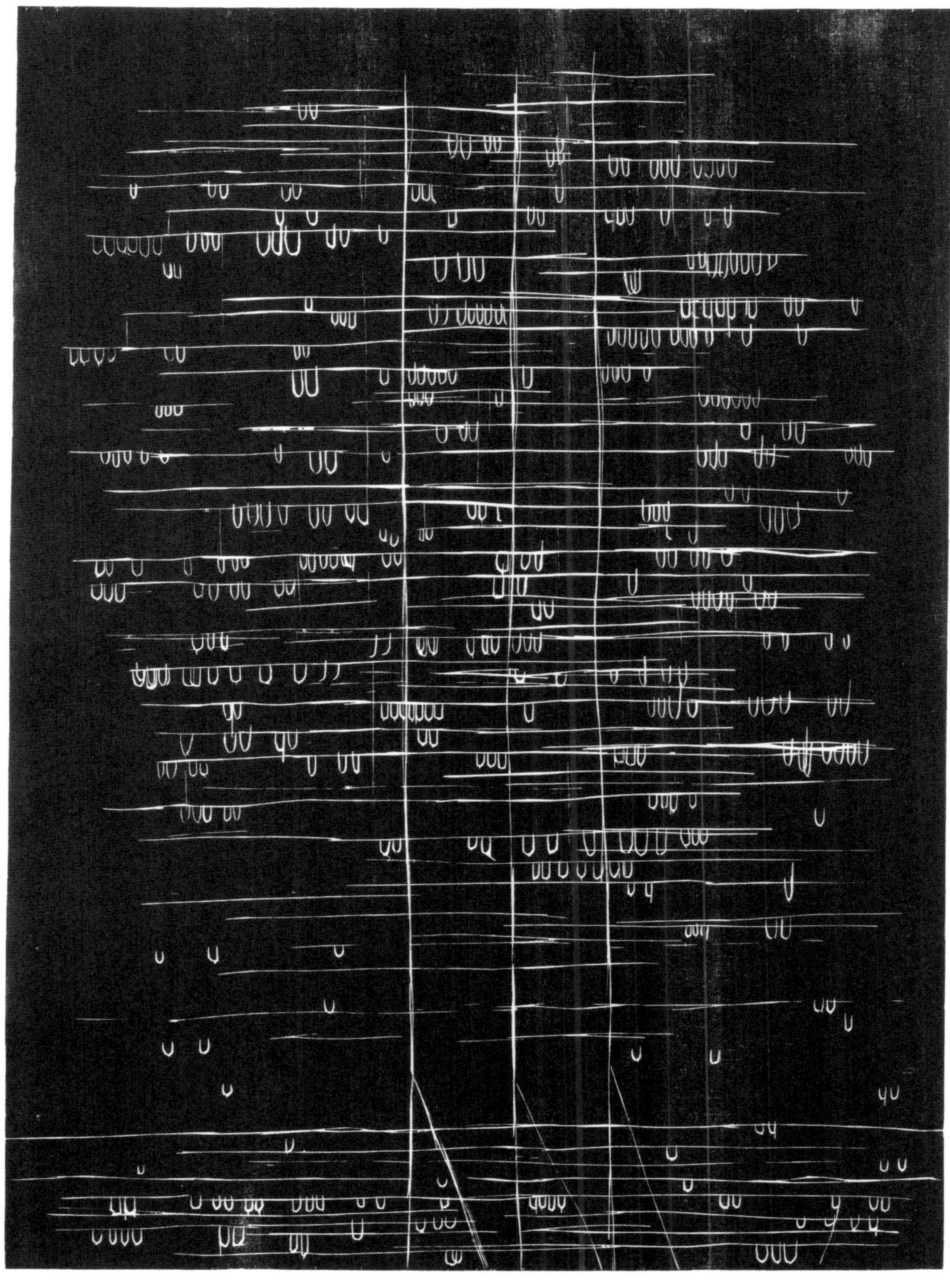

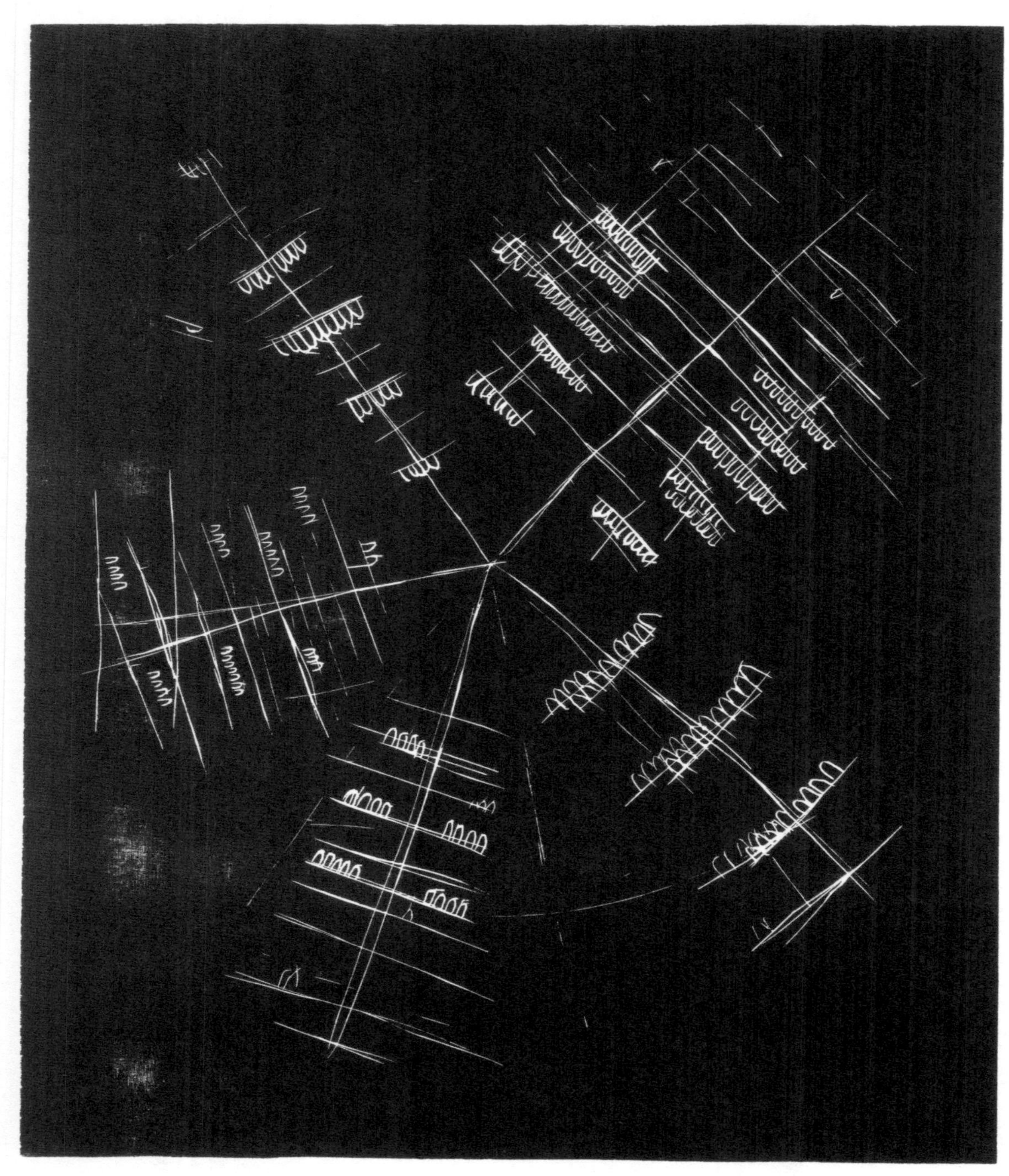

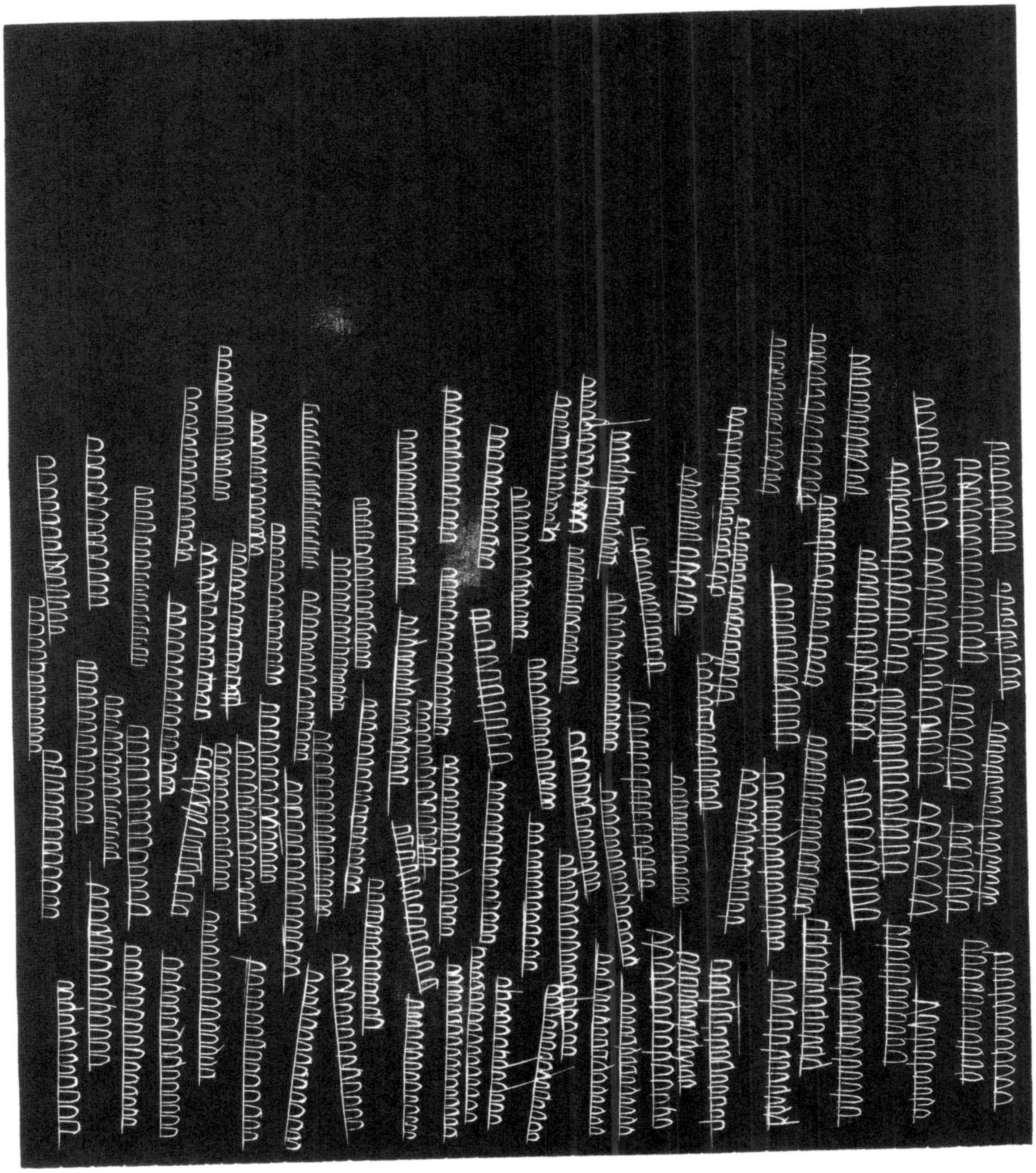

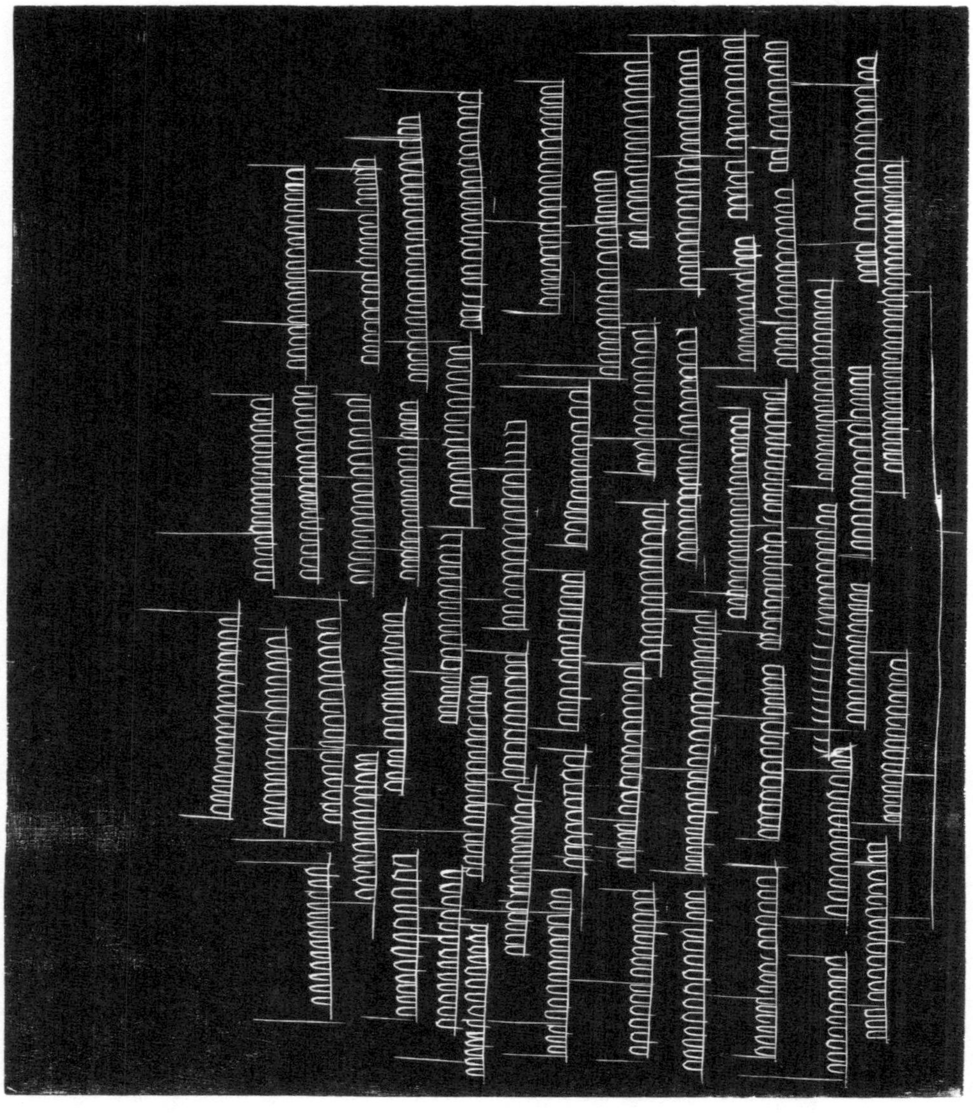

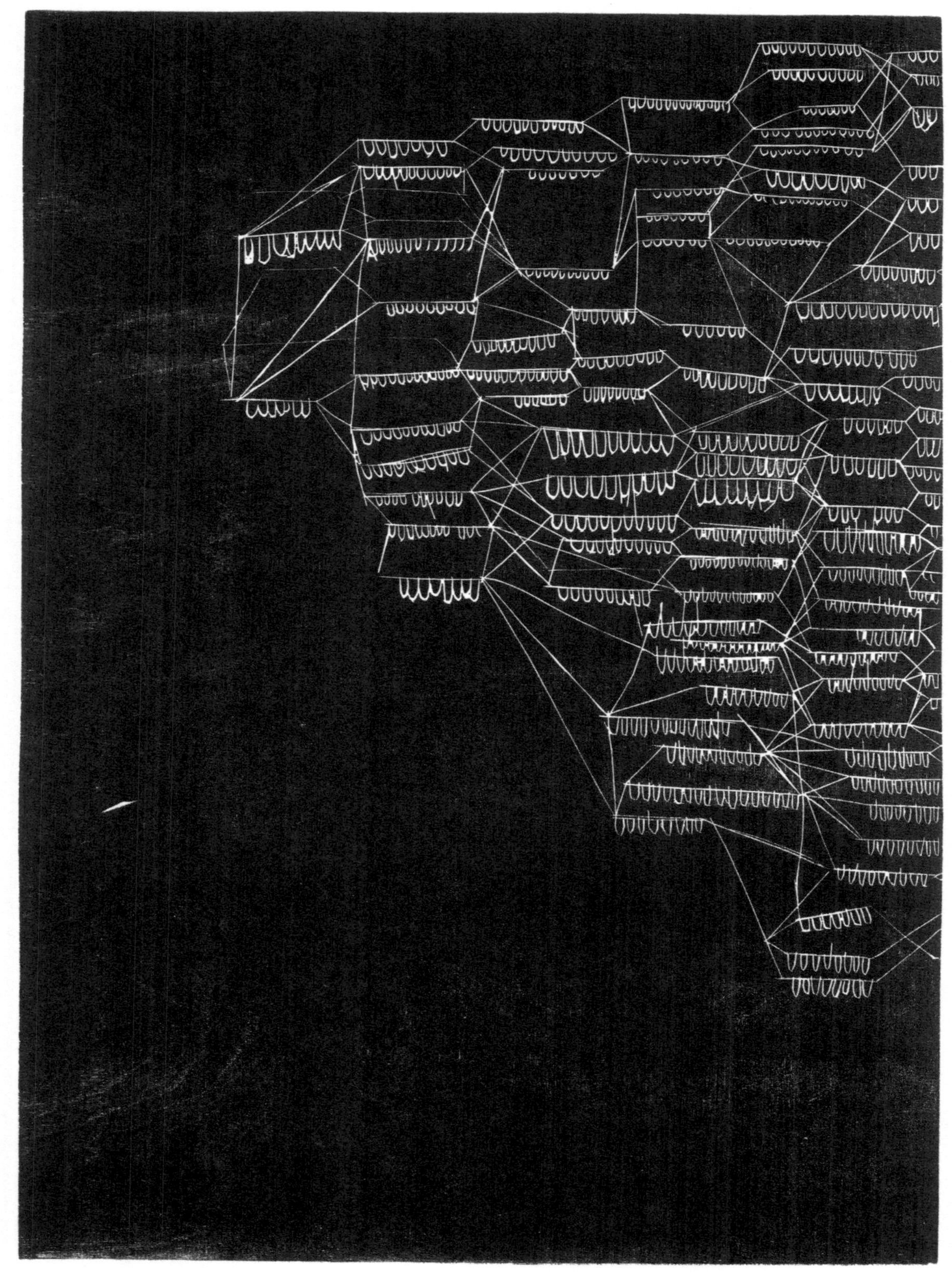

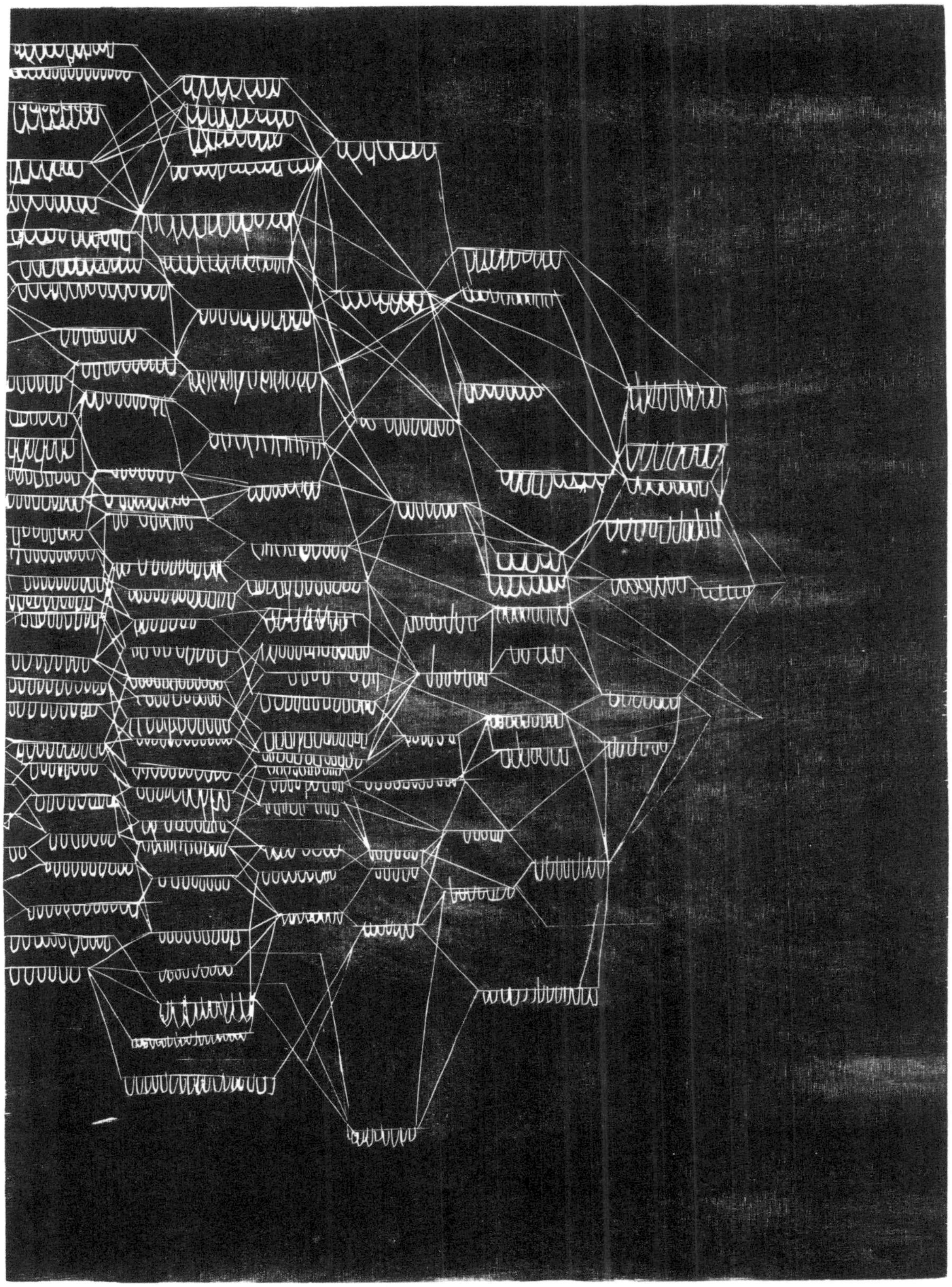

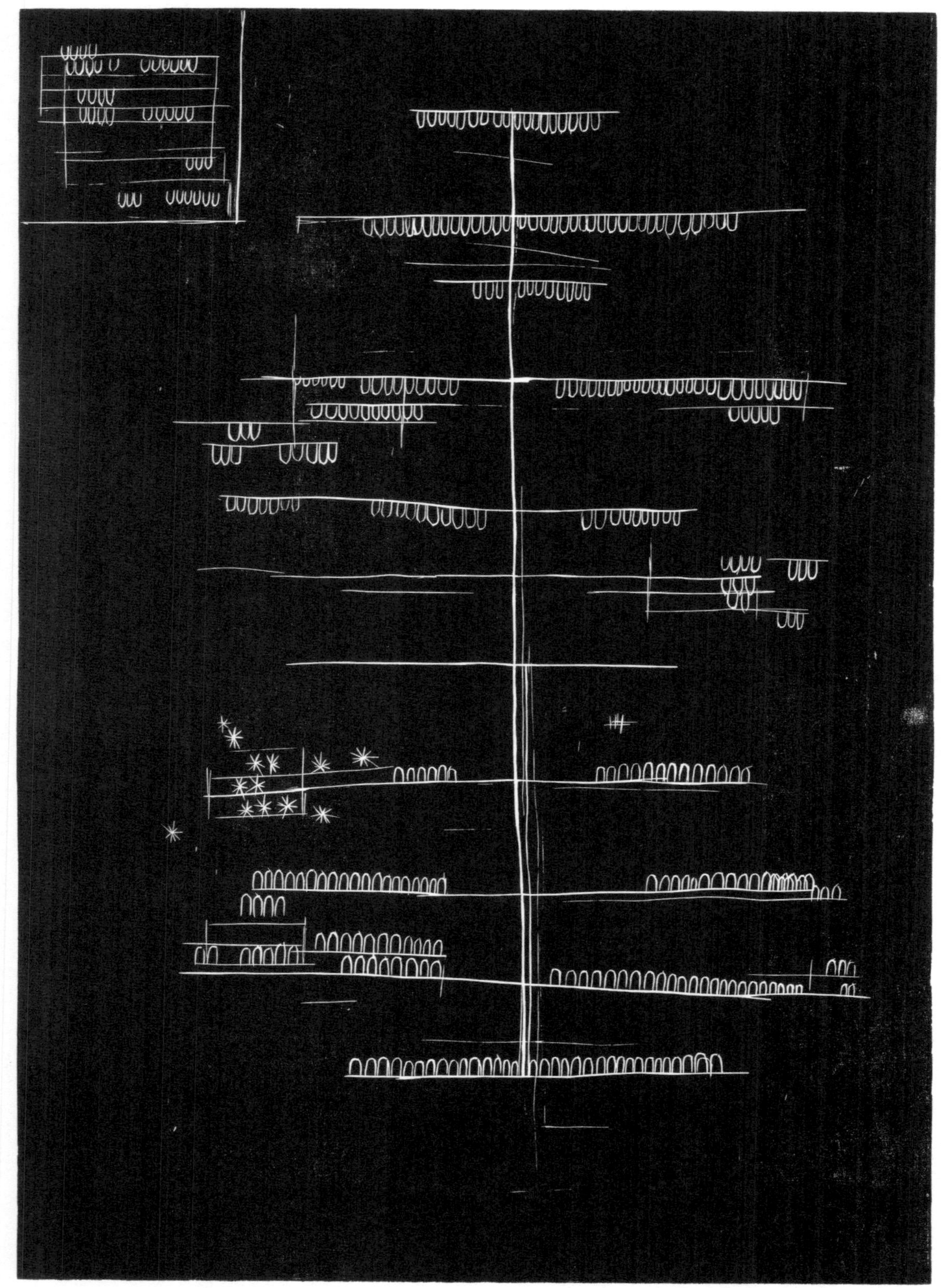

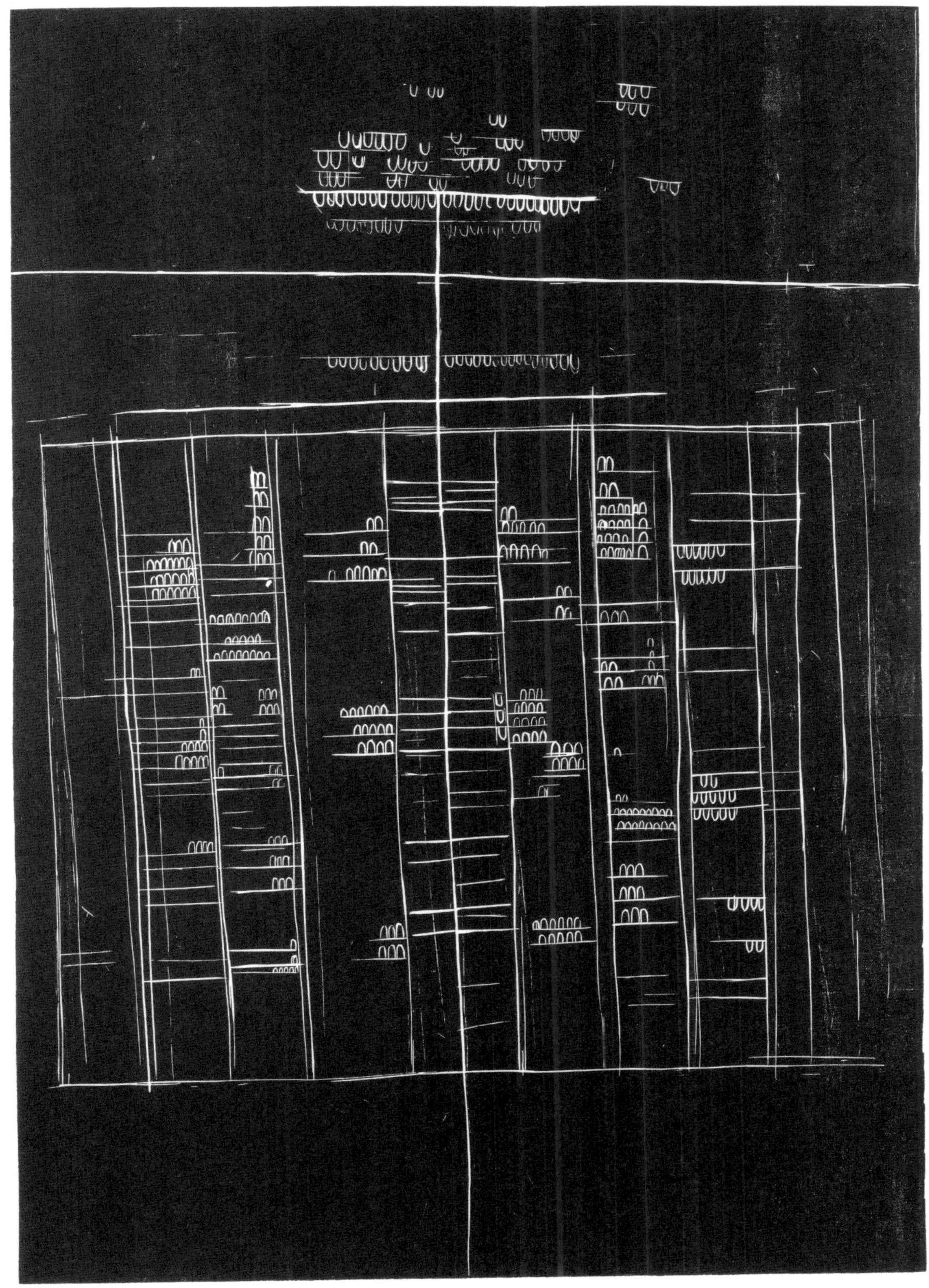

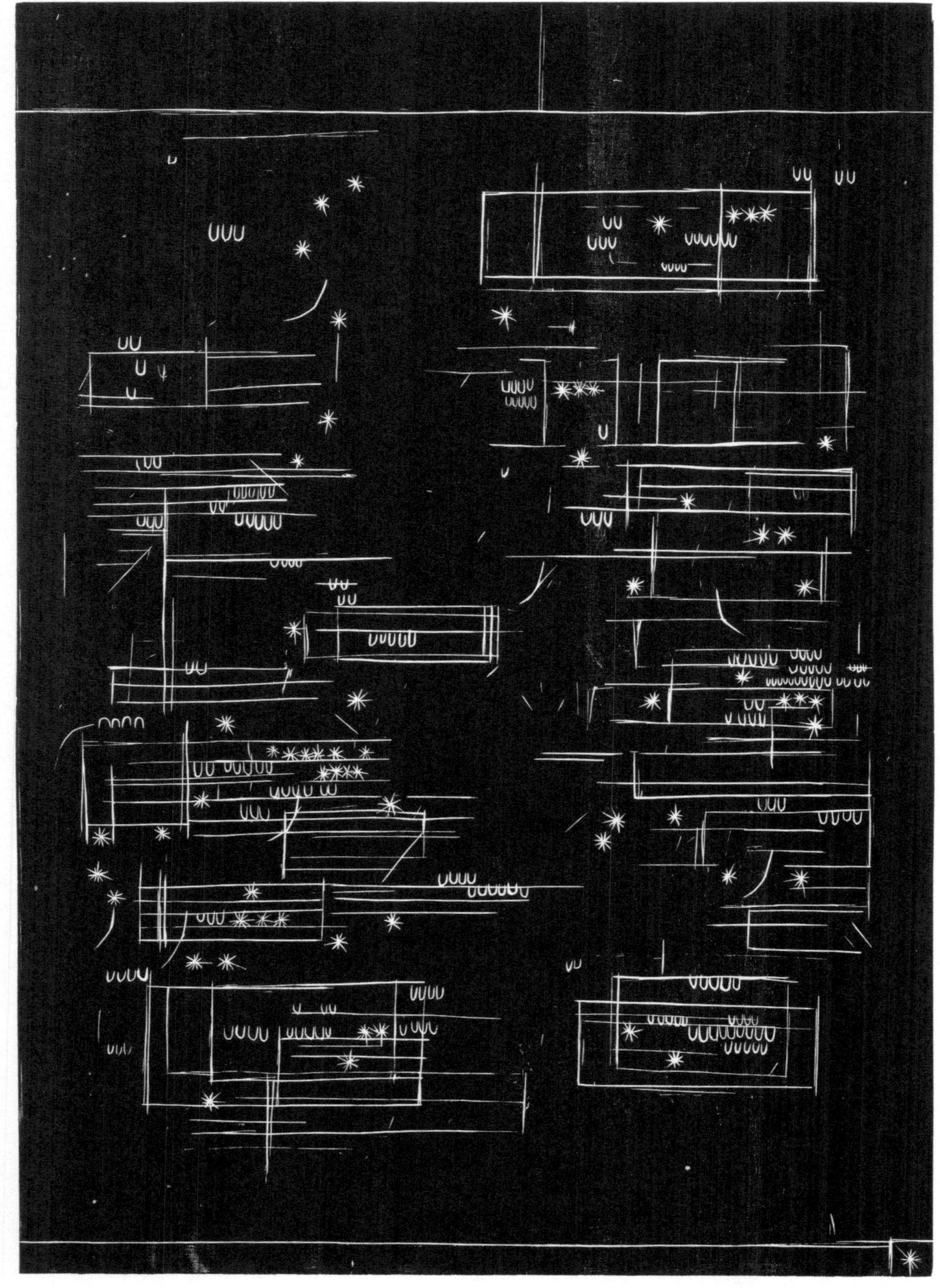

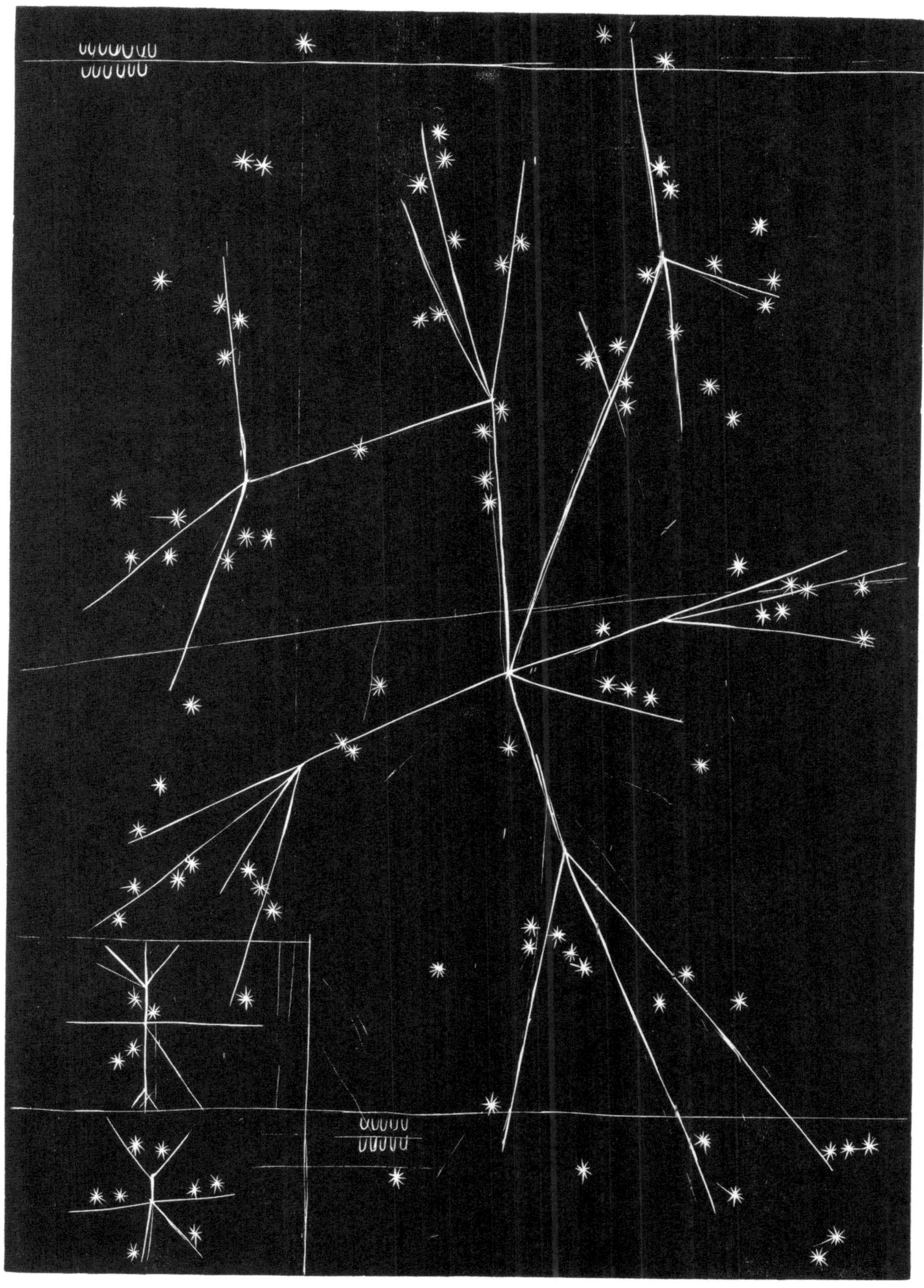

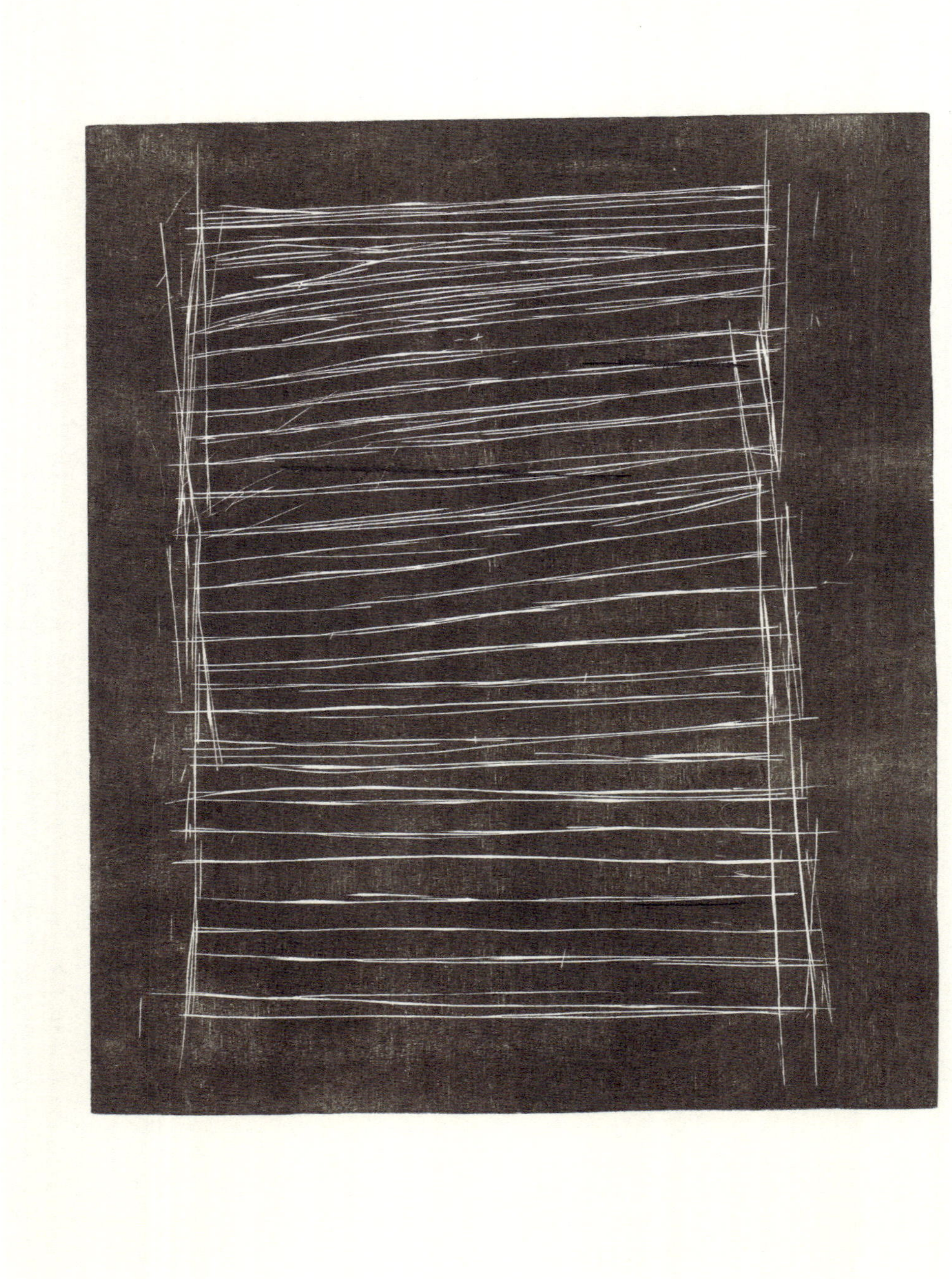

How to spell a sound that is physical, 2014

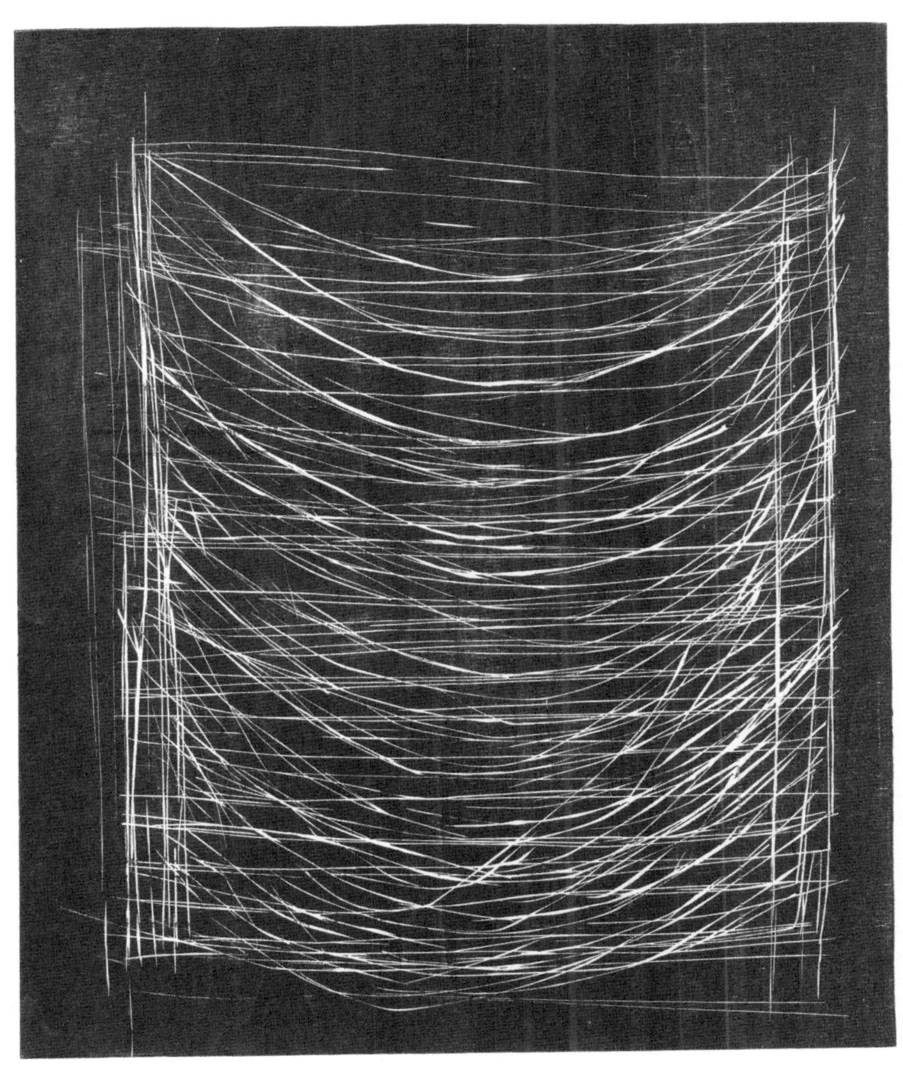

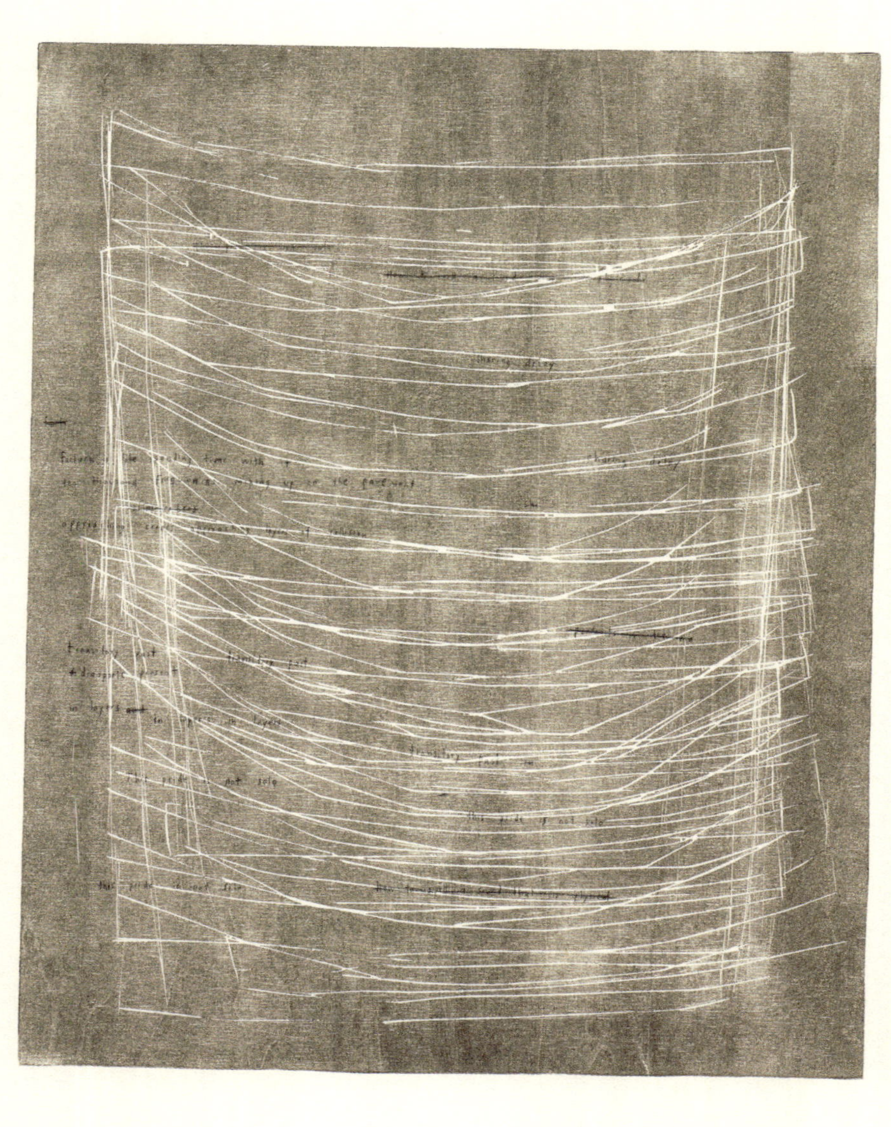

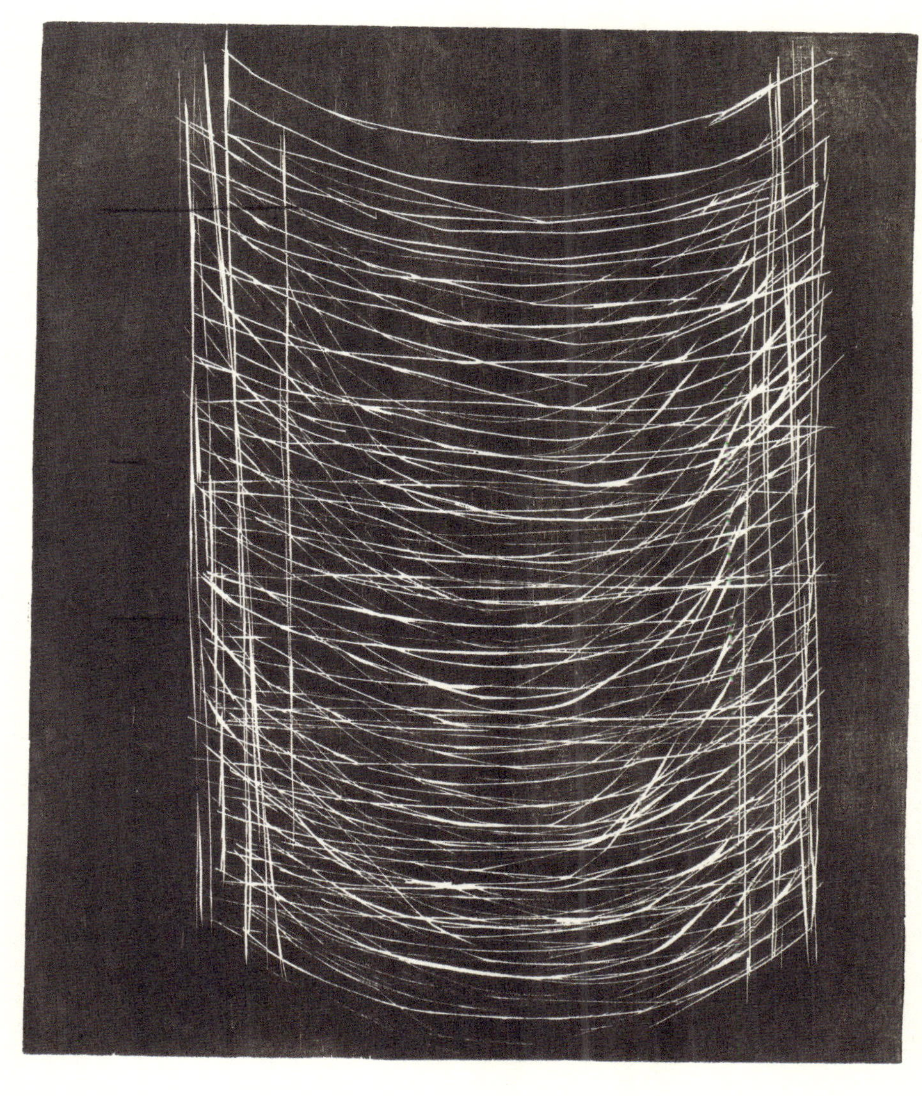

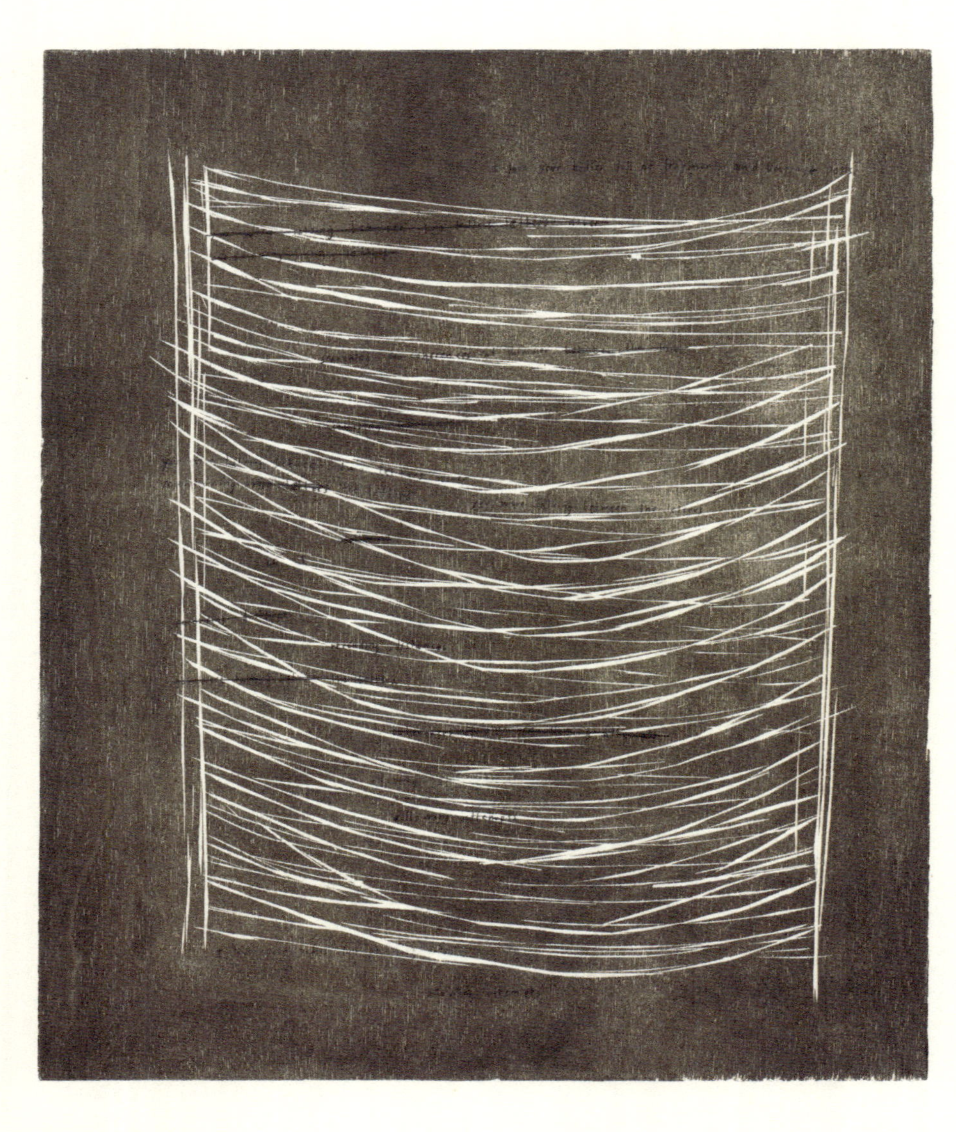

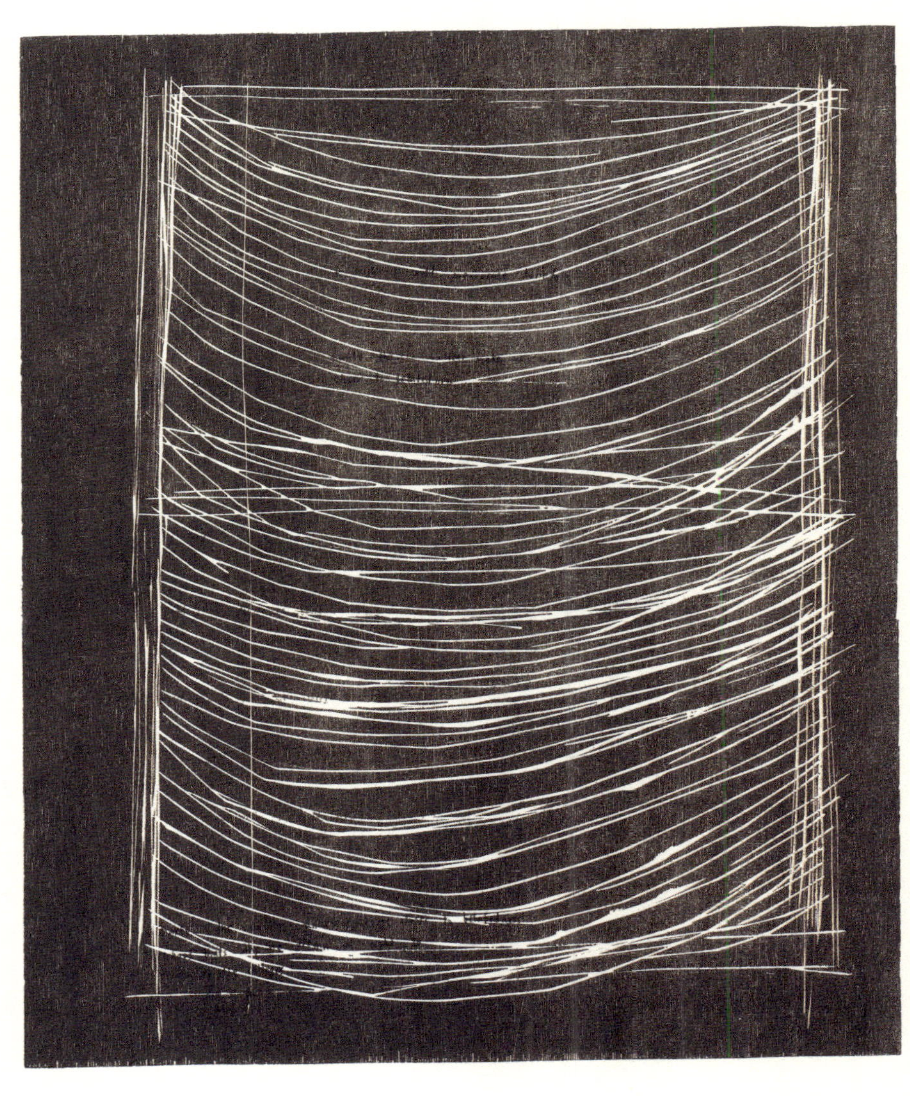

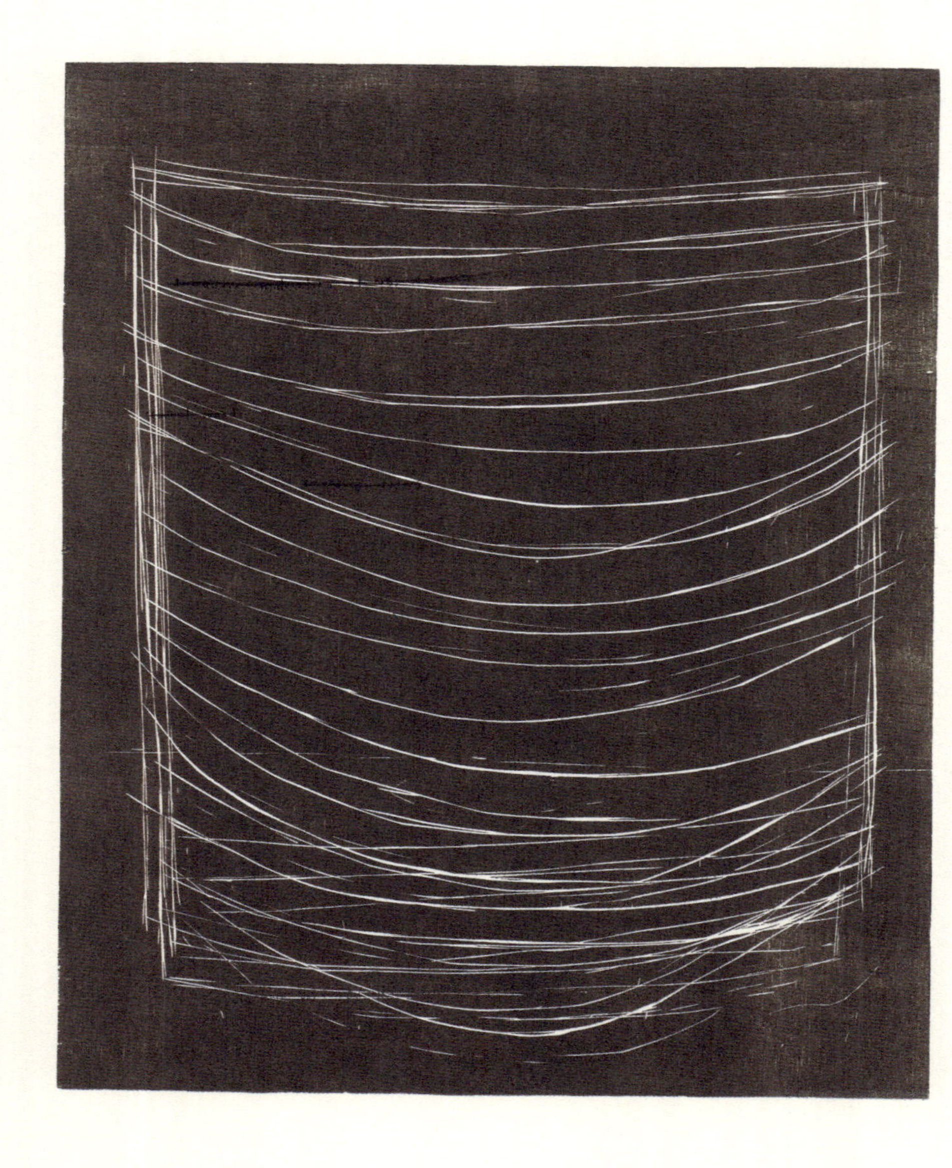

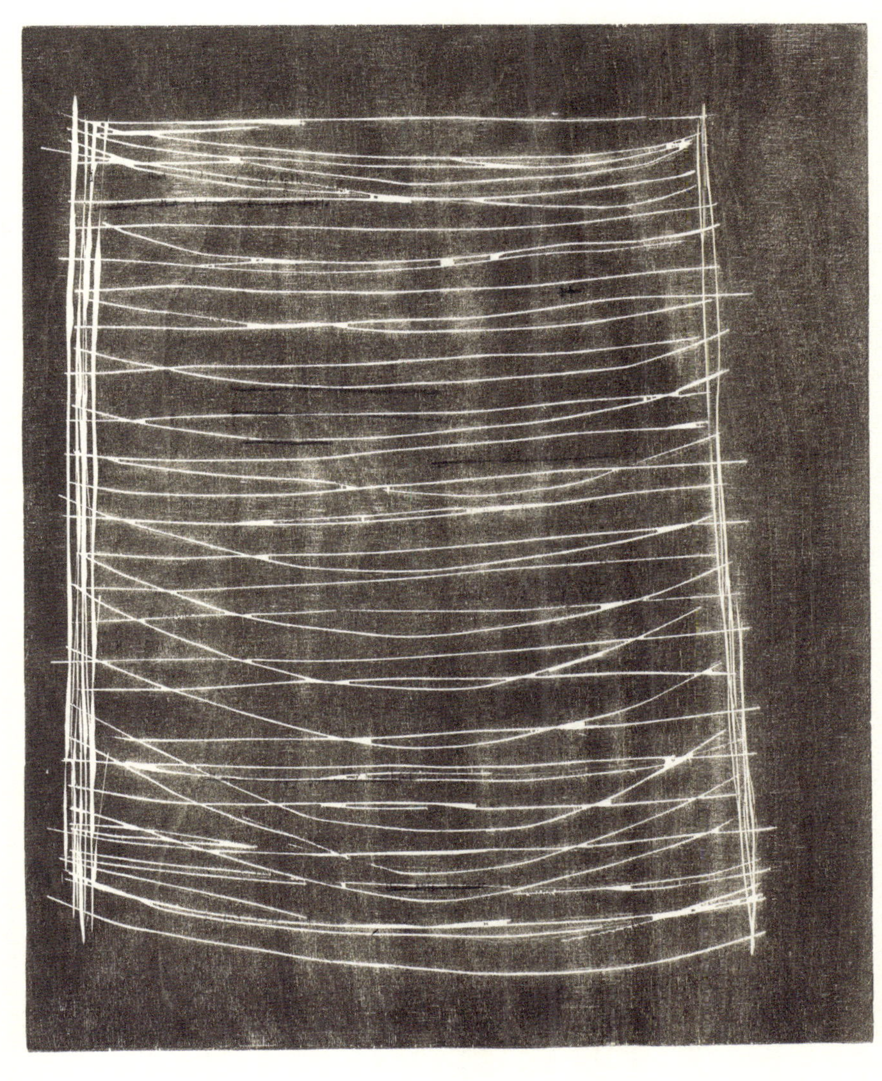

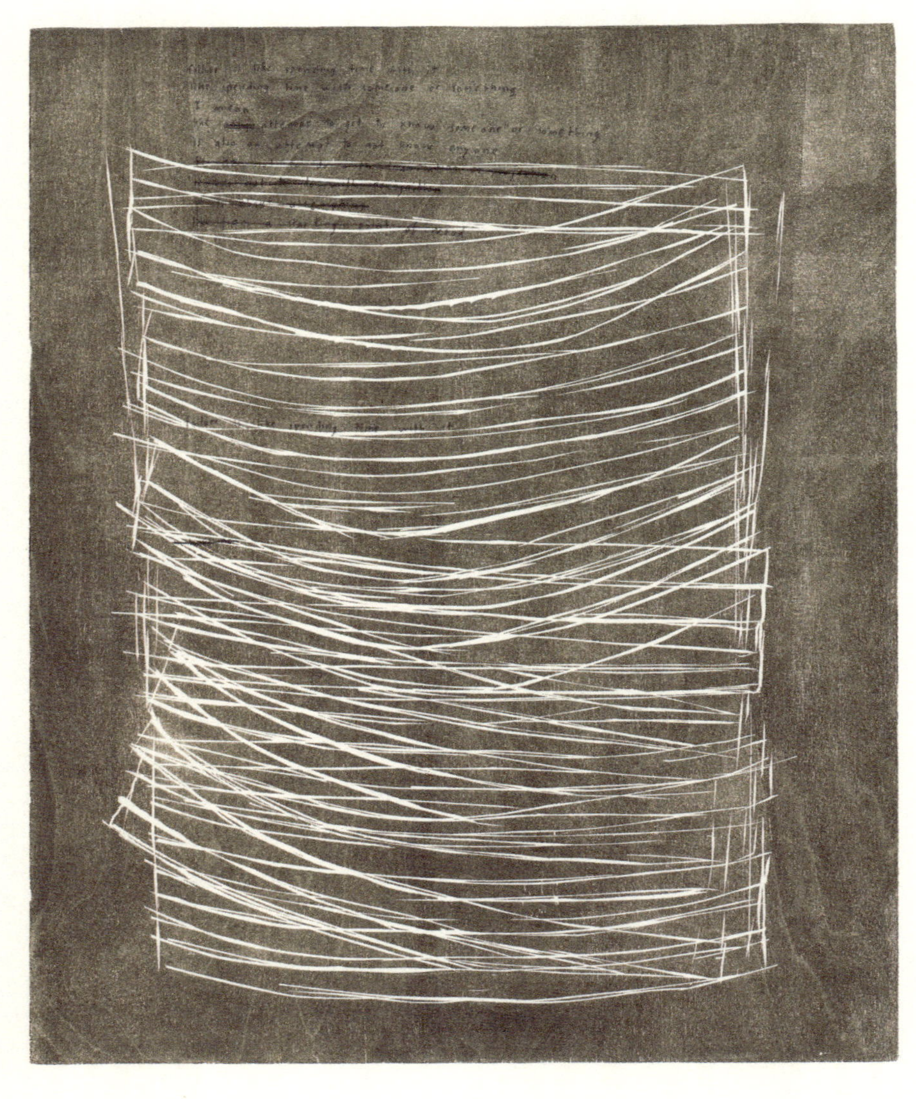

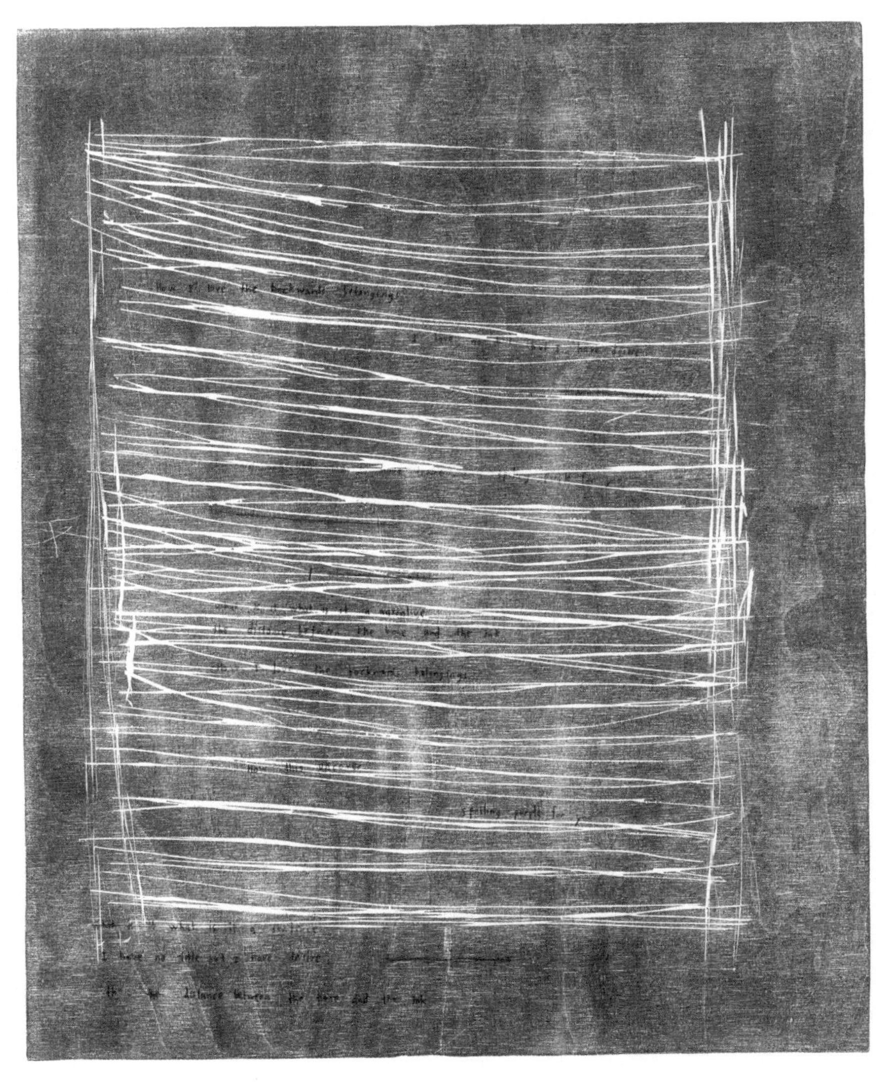

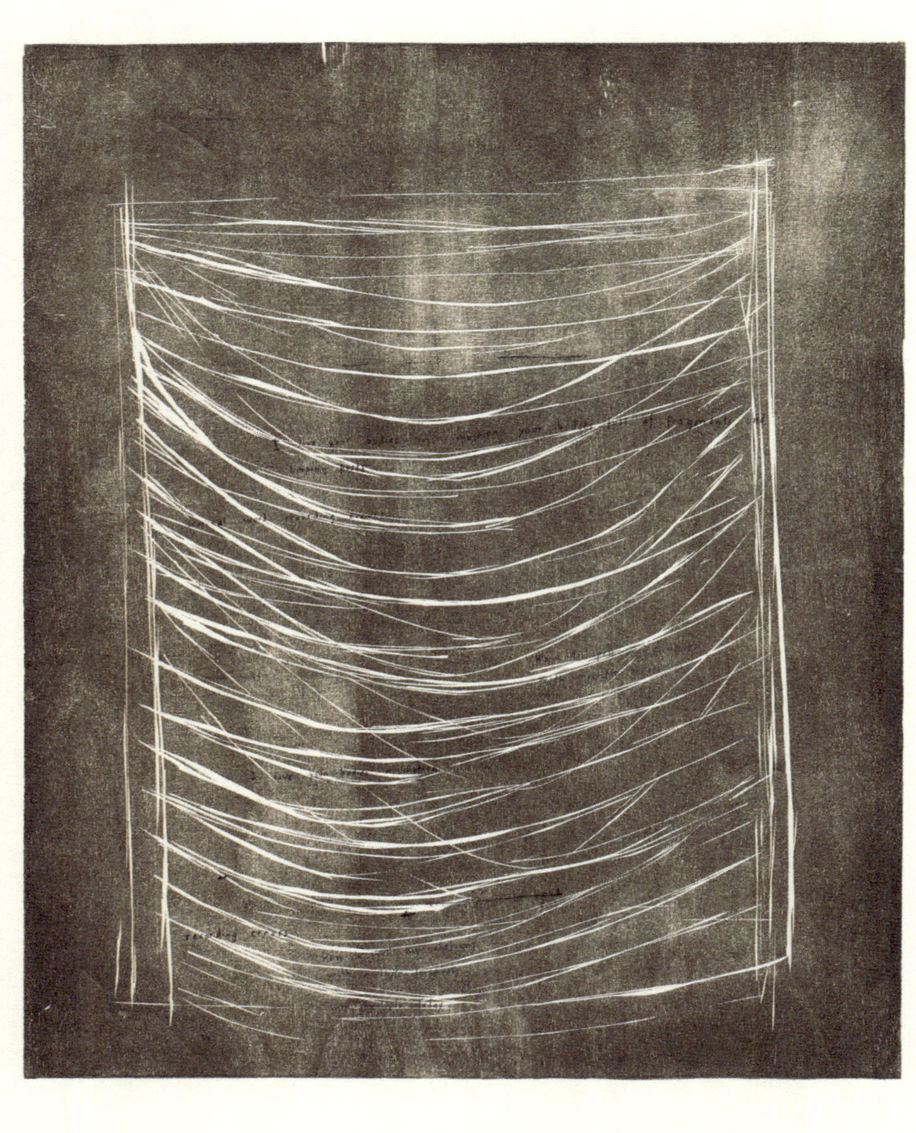

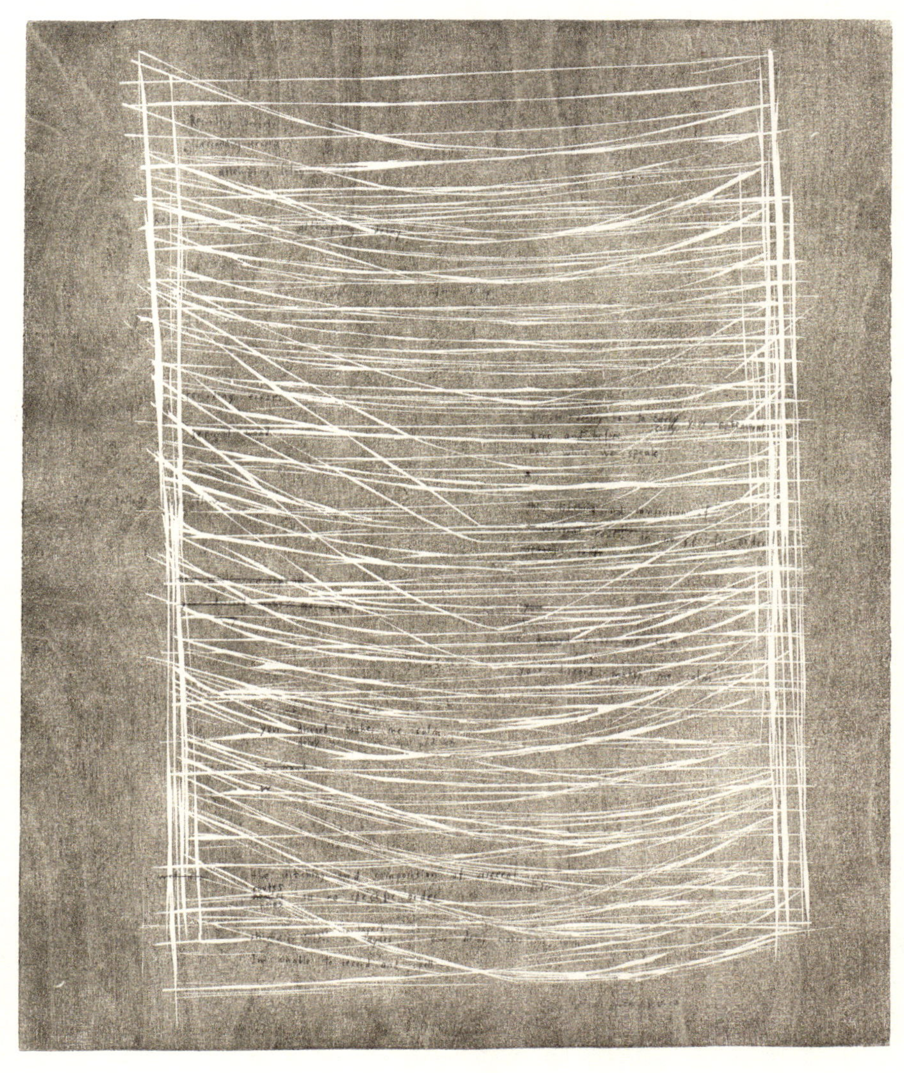

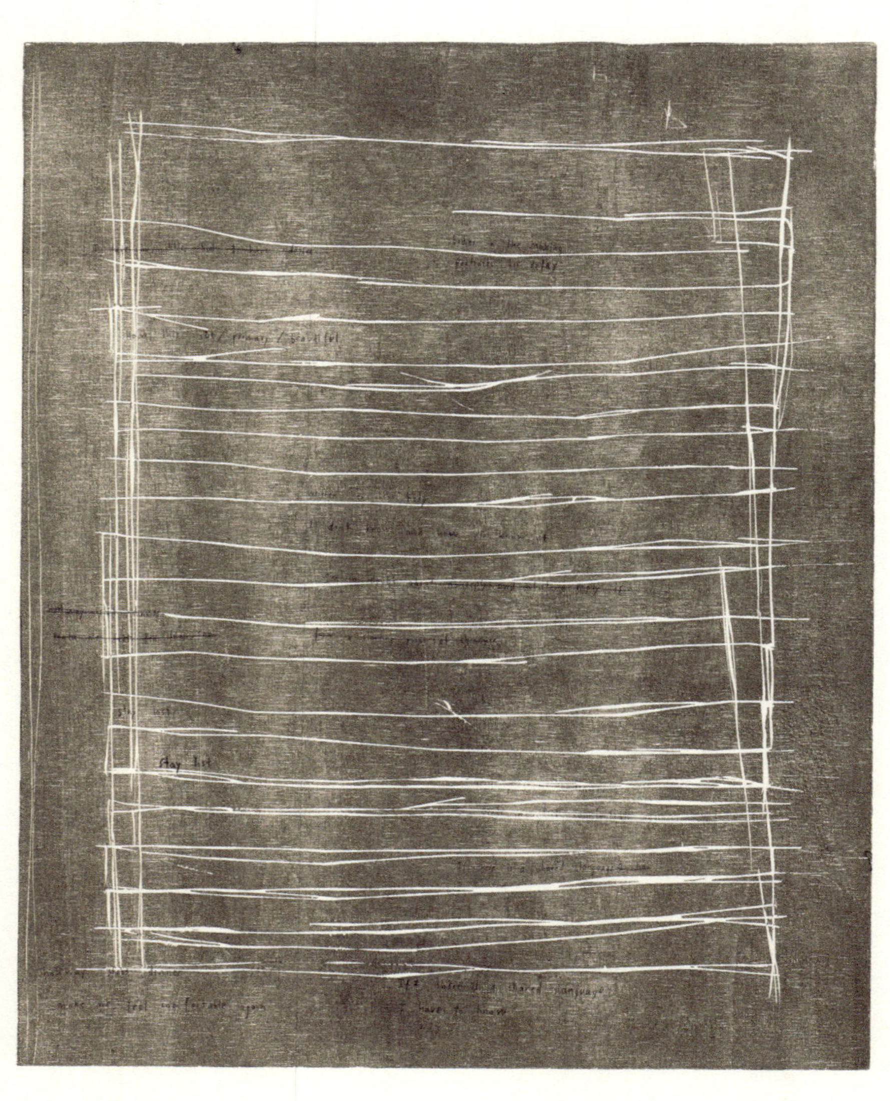

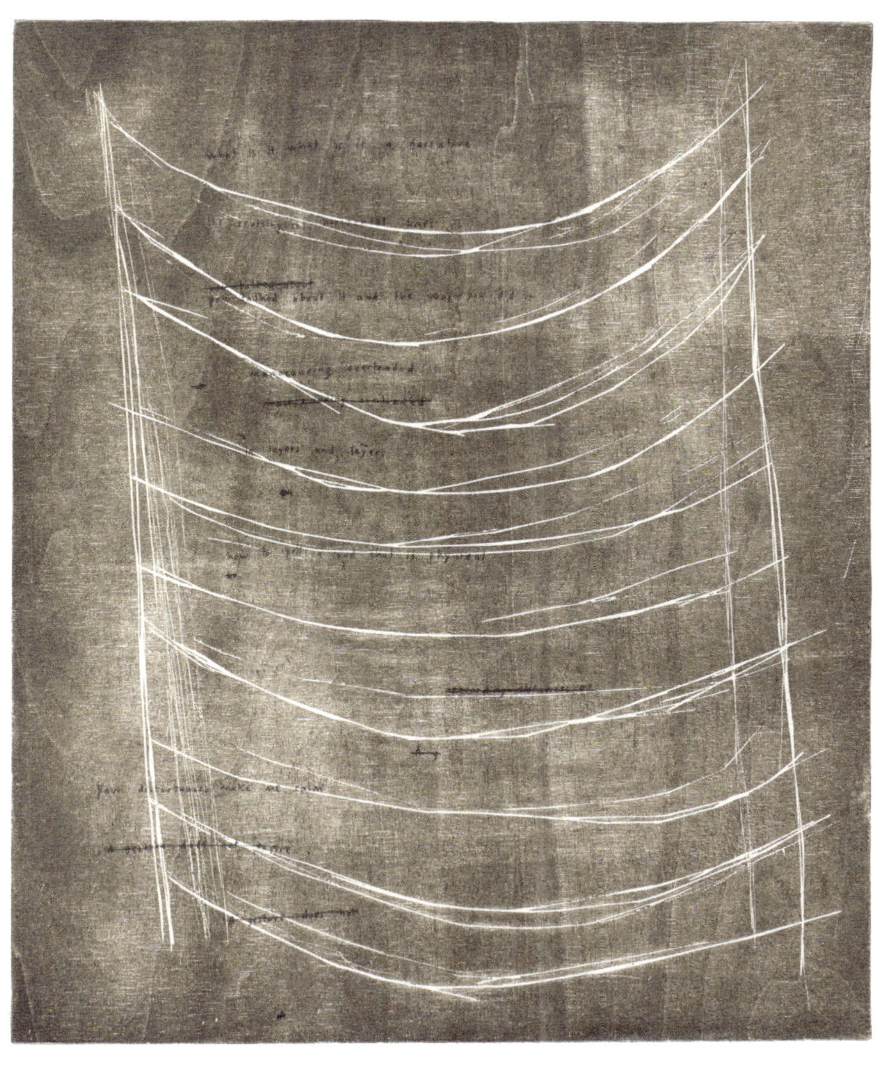

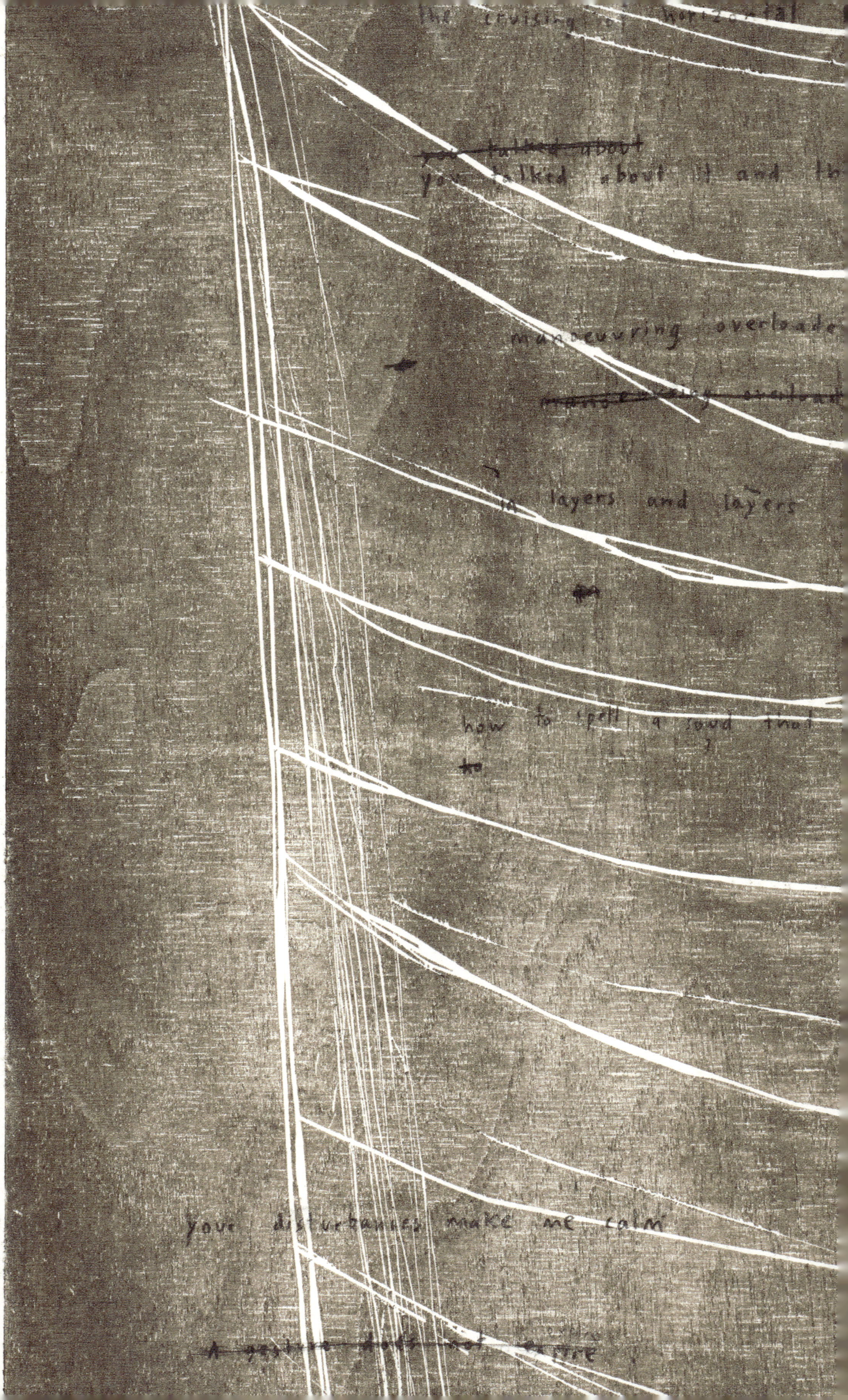

the cruising of horizontal

talked about

you talked about it and th

manoeuvring overloade

layers and layers

how to spell a sound that
to

your disturbances make me calm

A gesture does not gesture

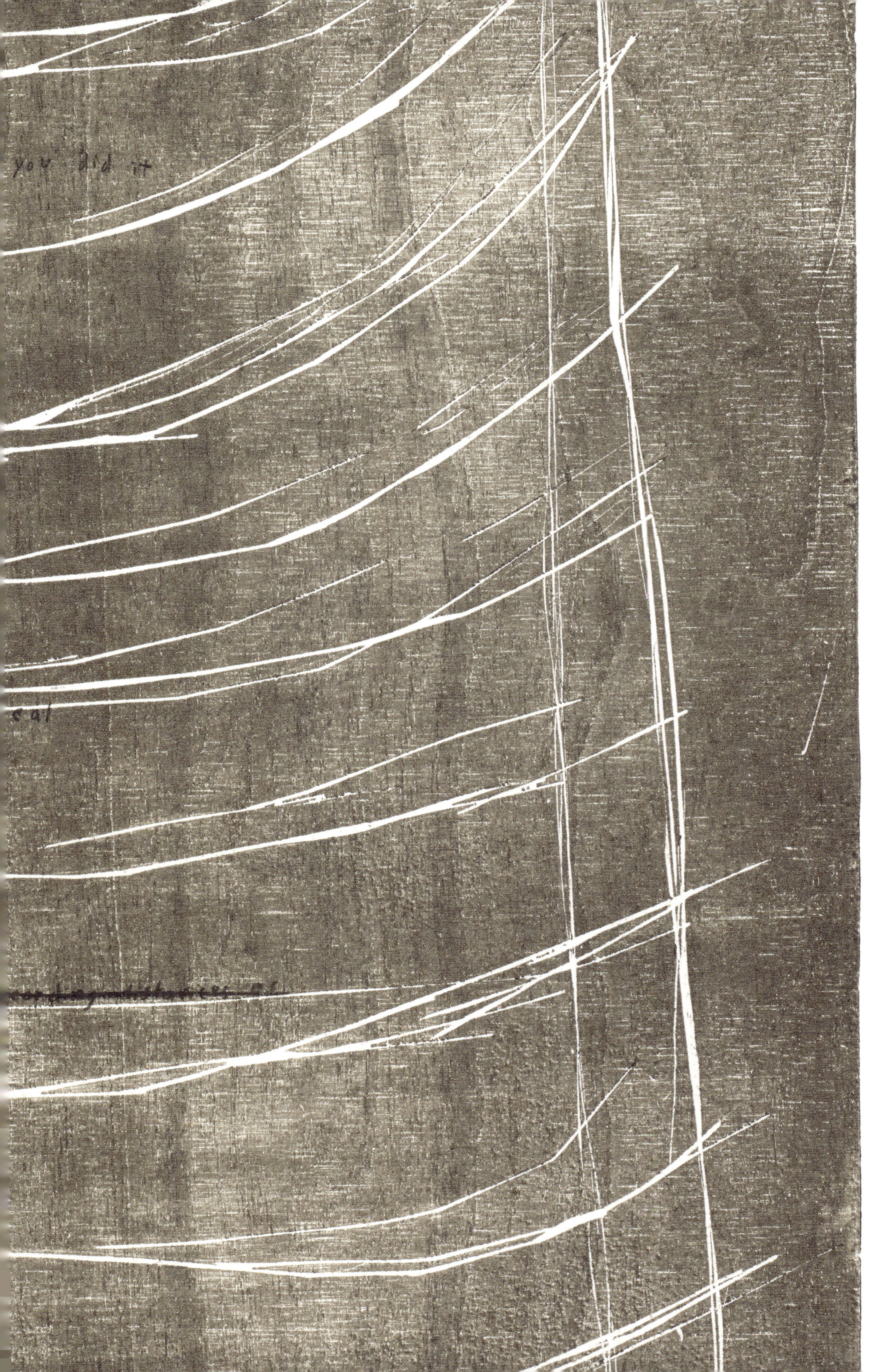

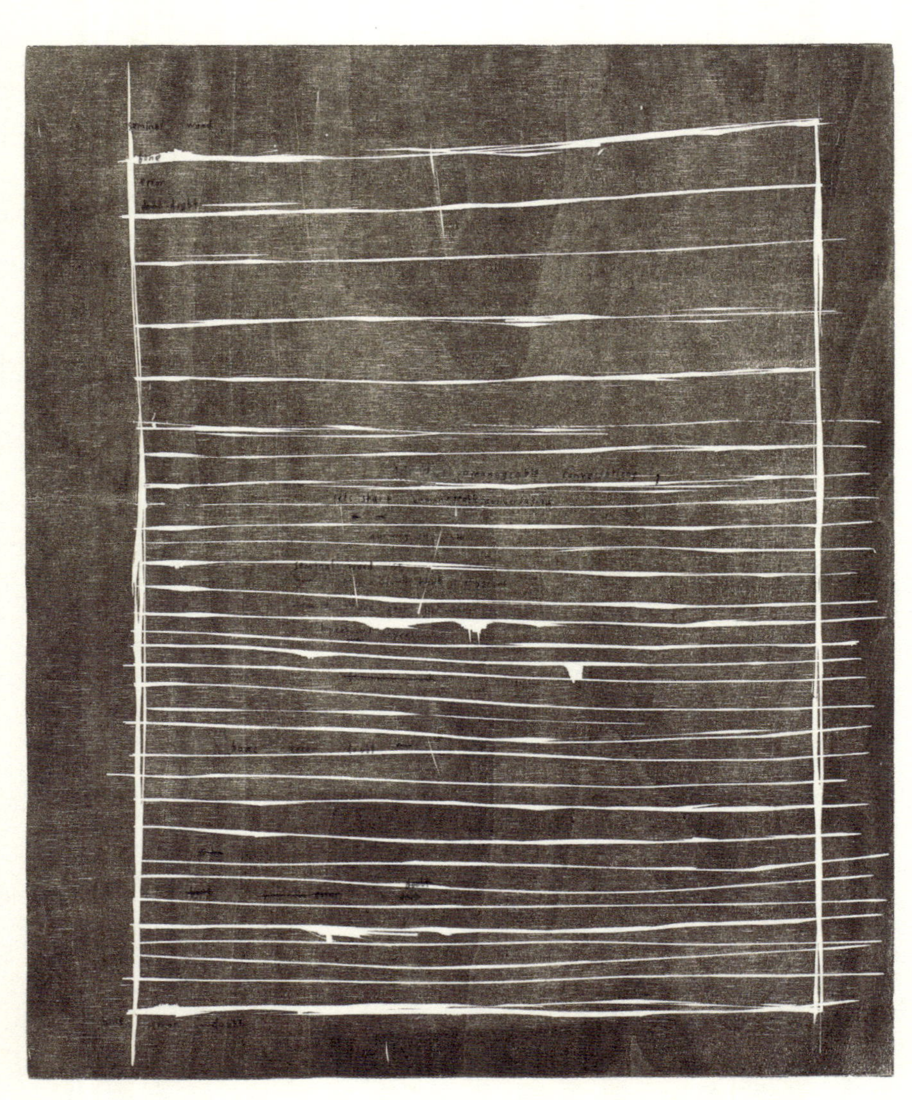

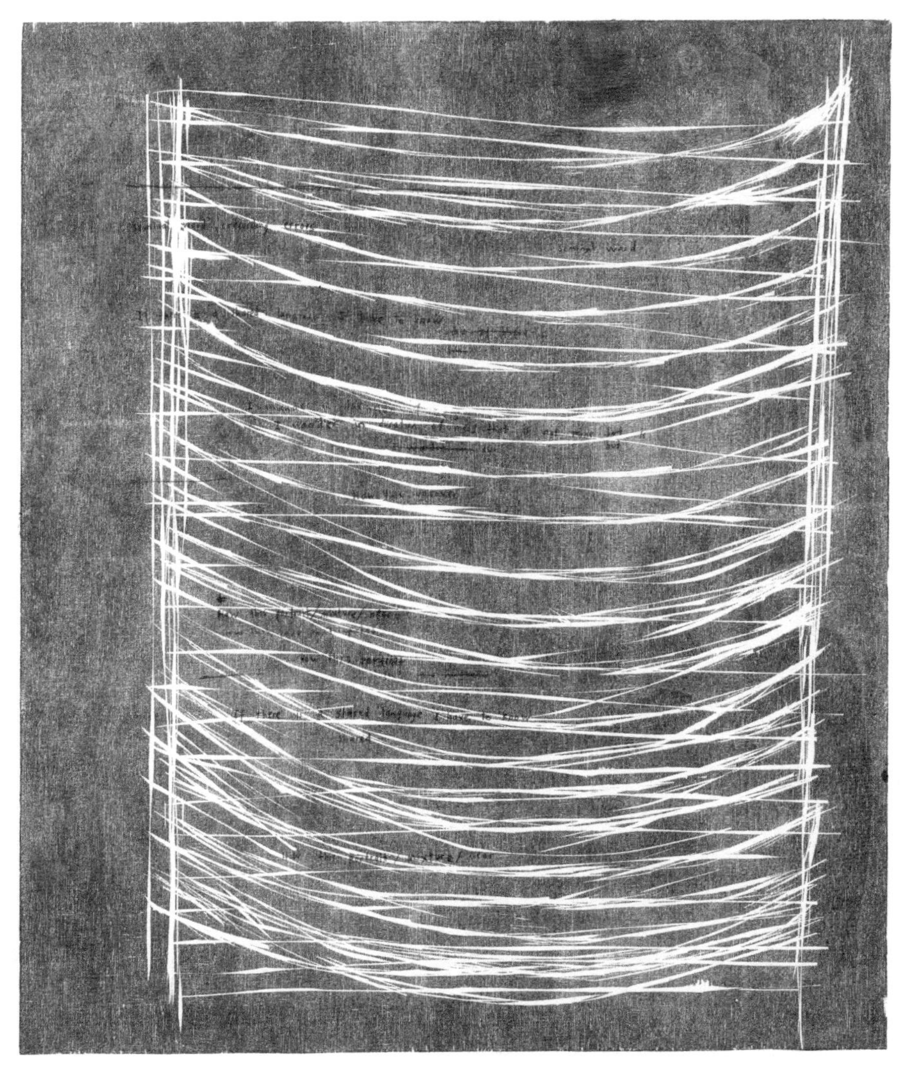

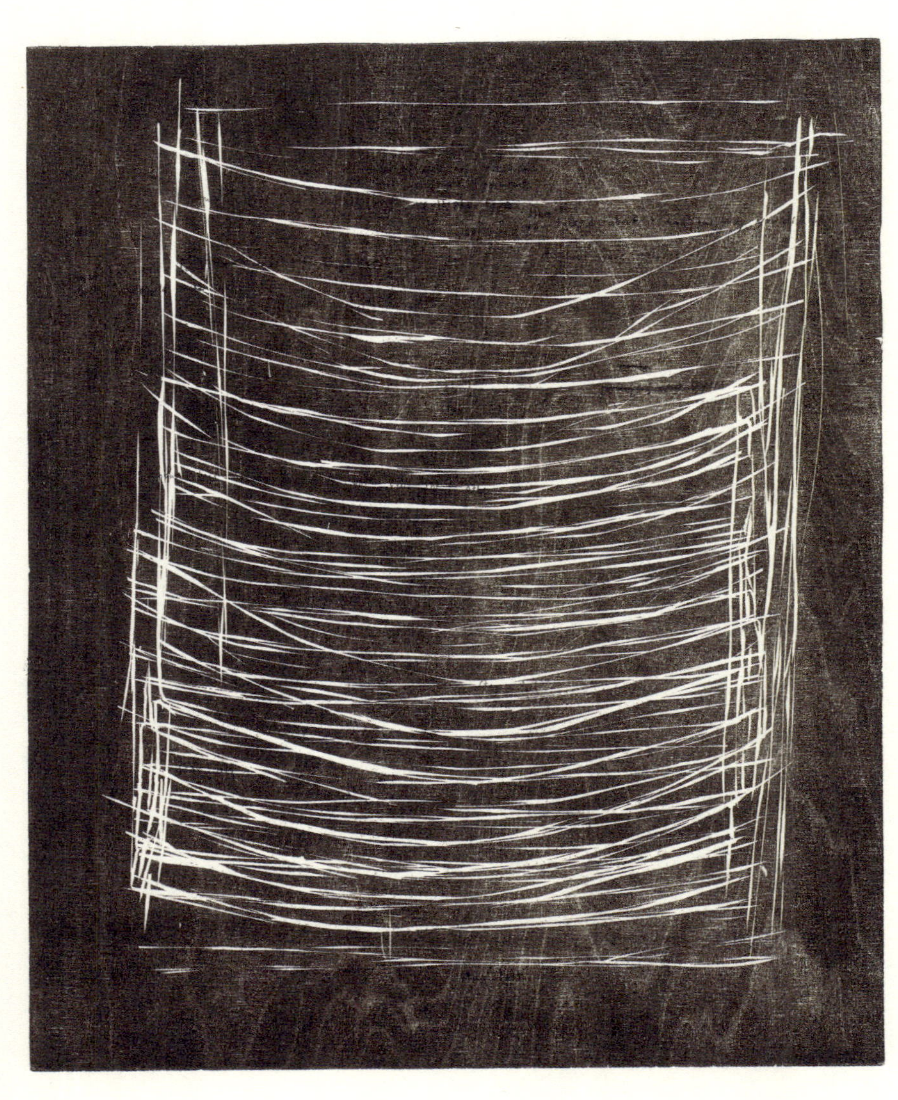

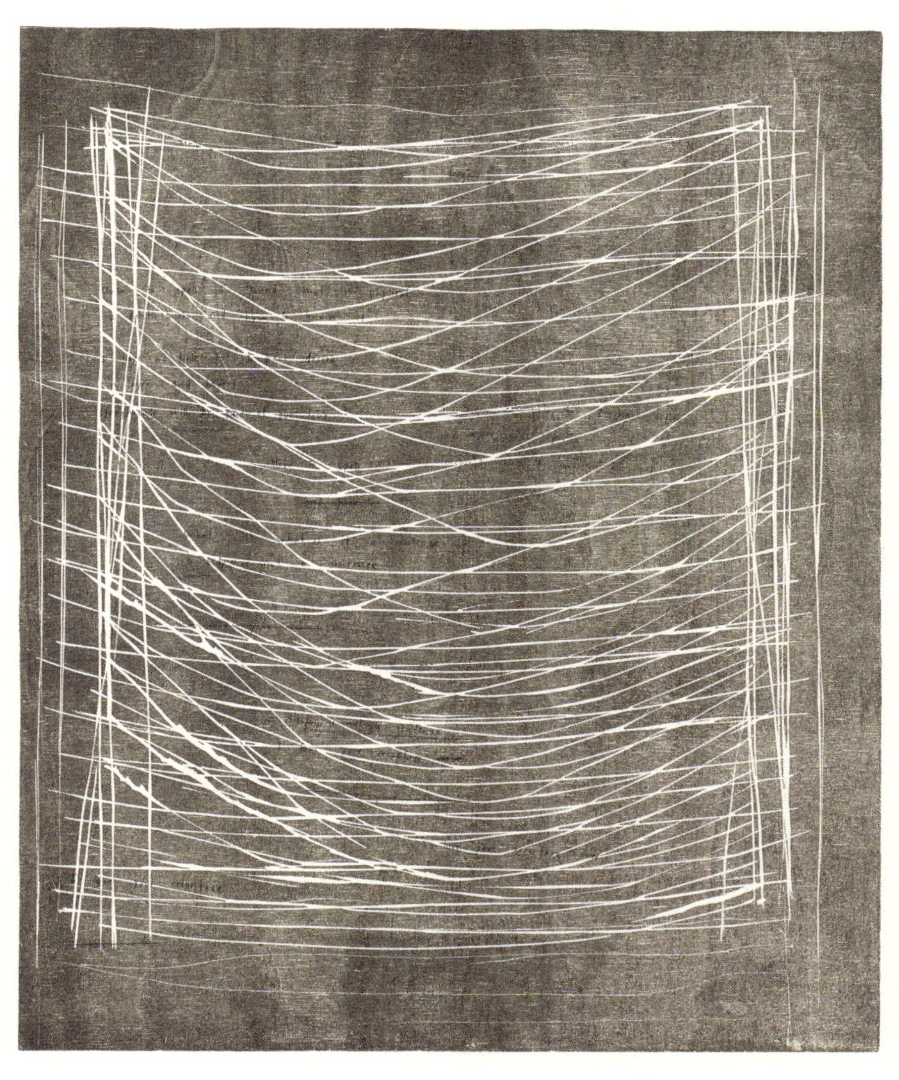

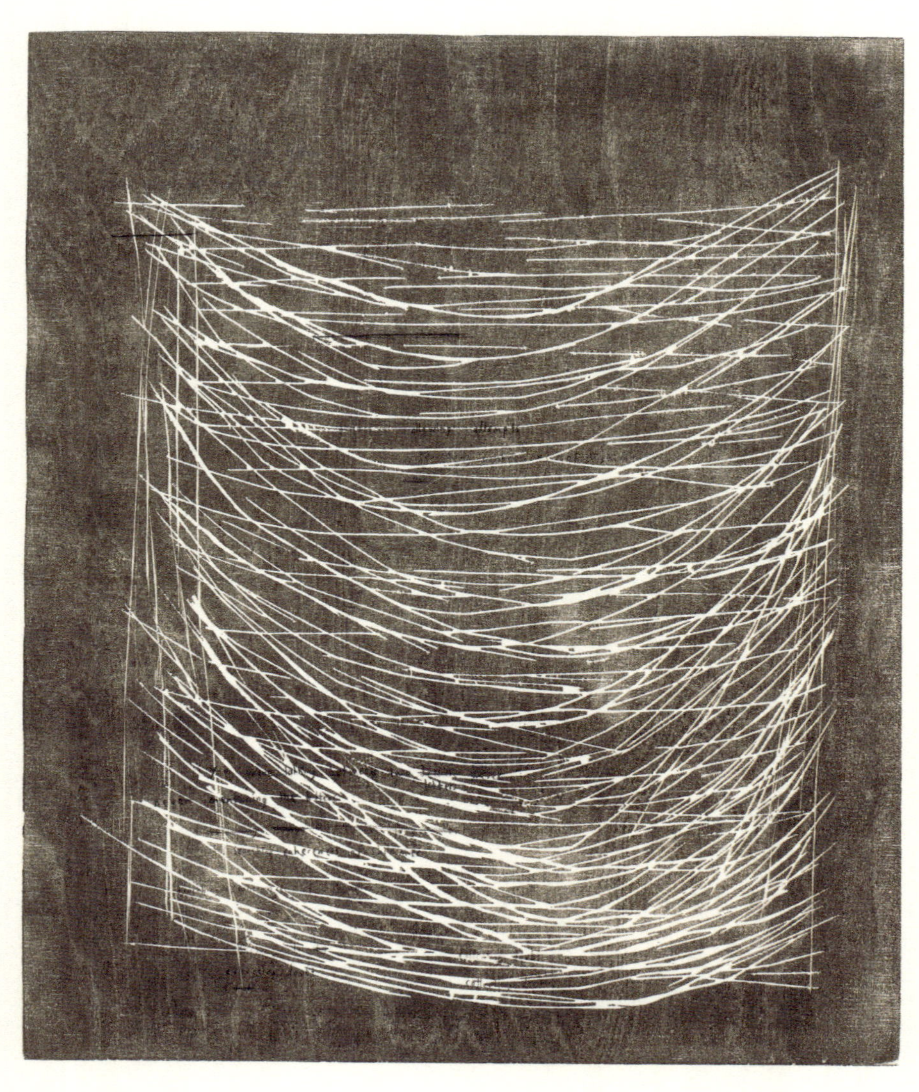

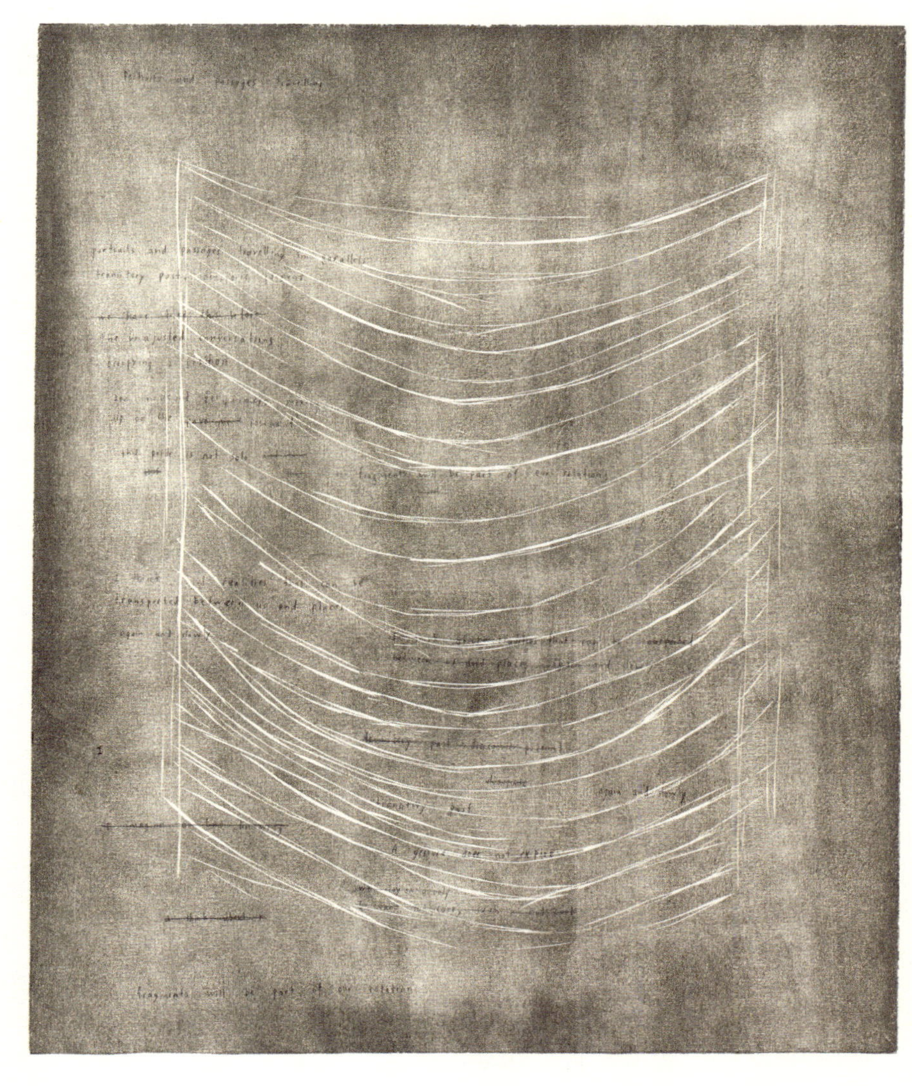

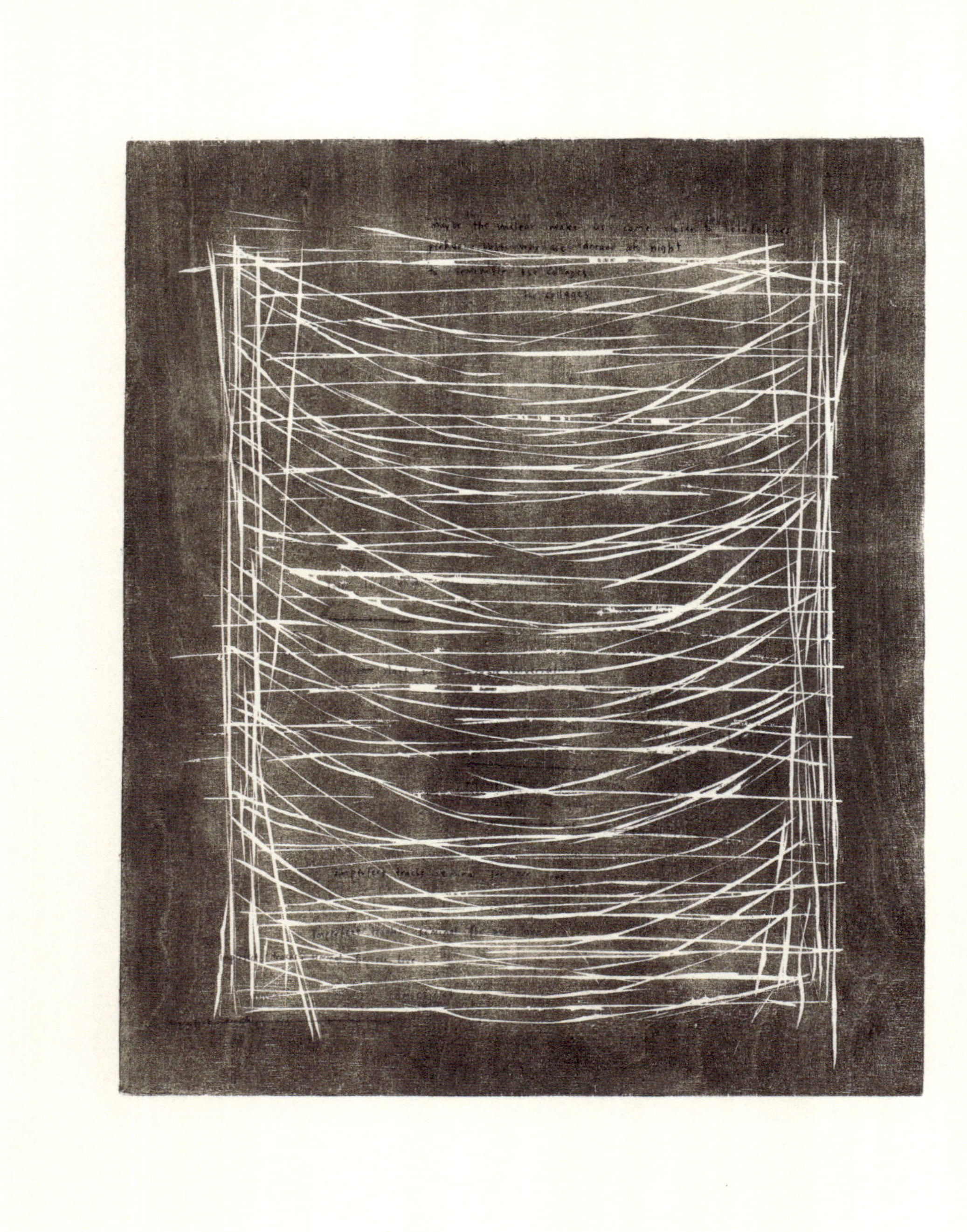

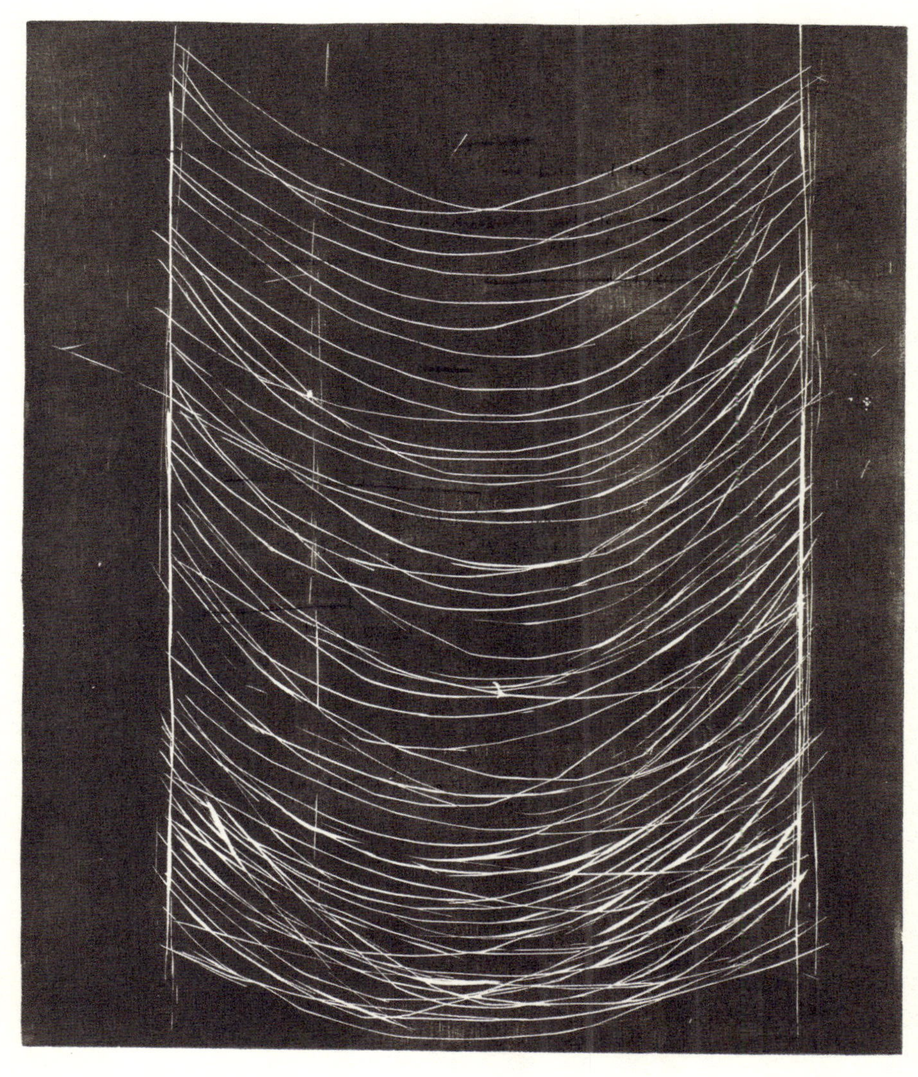

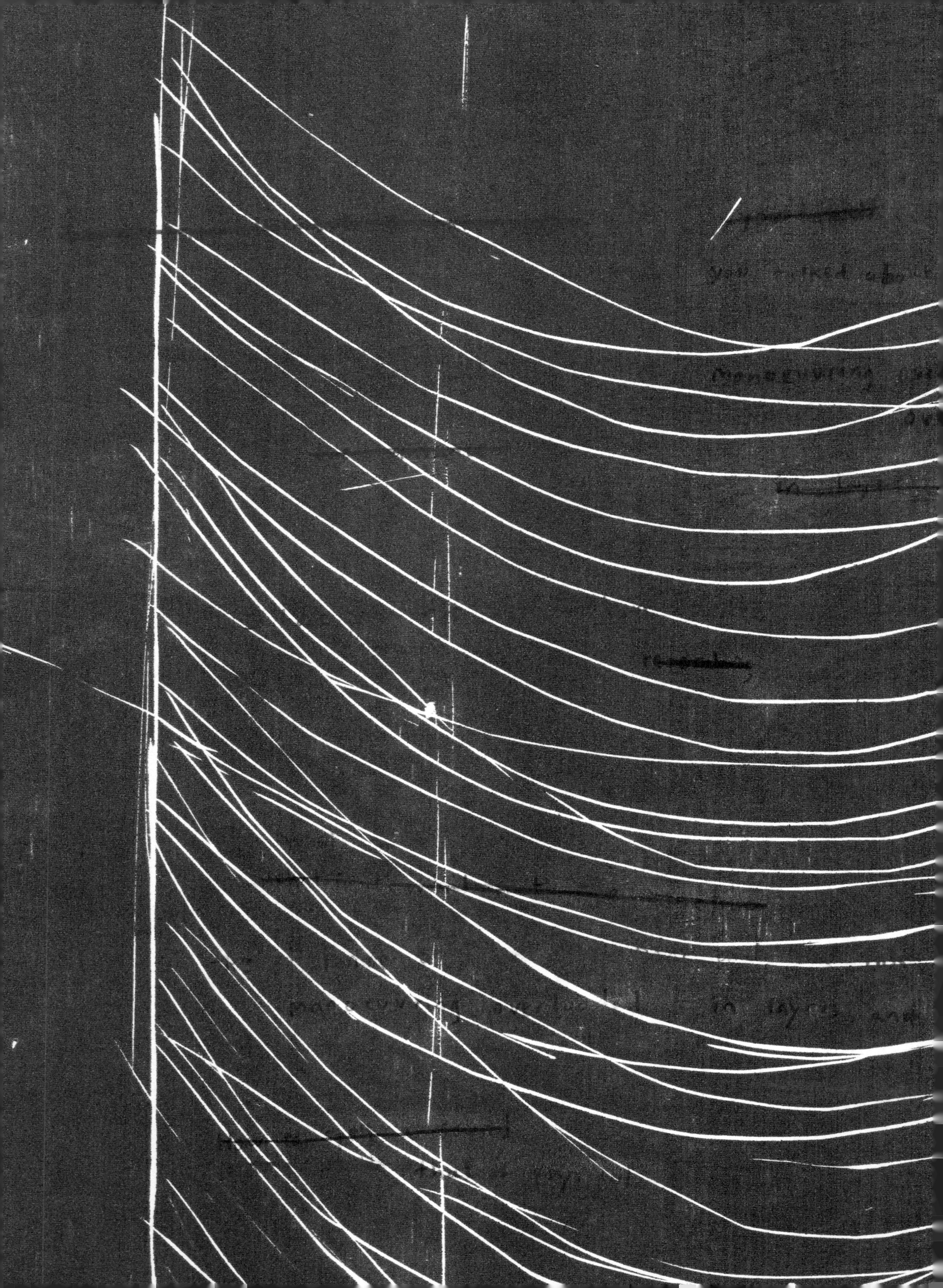

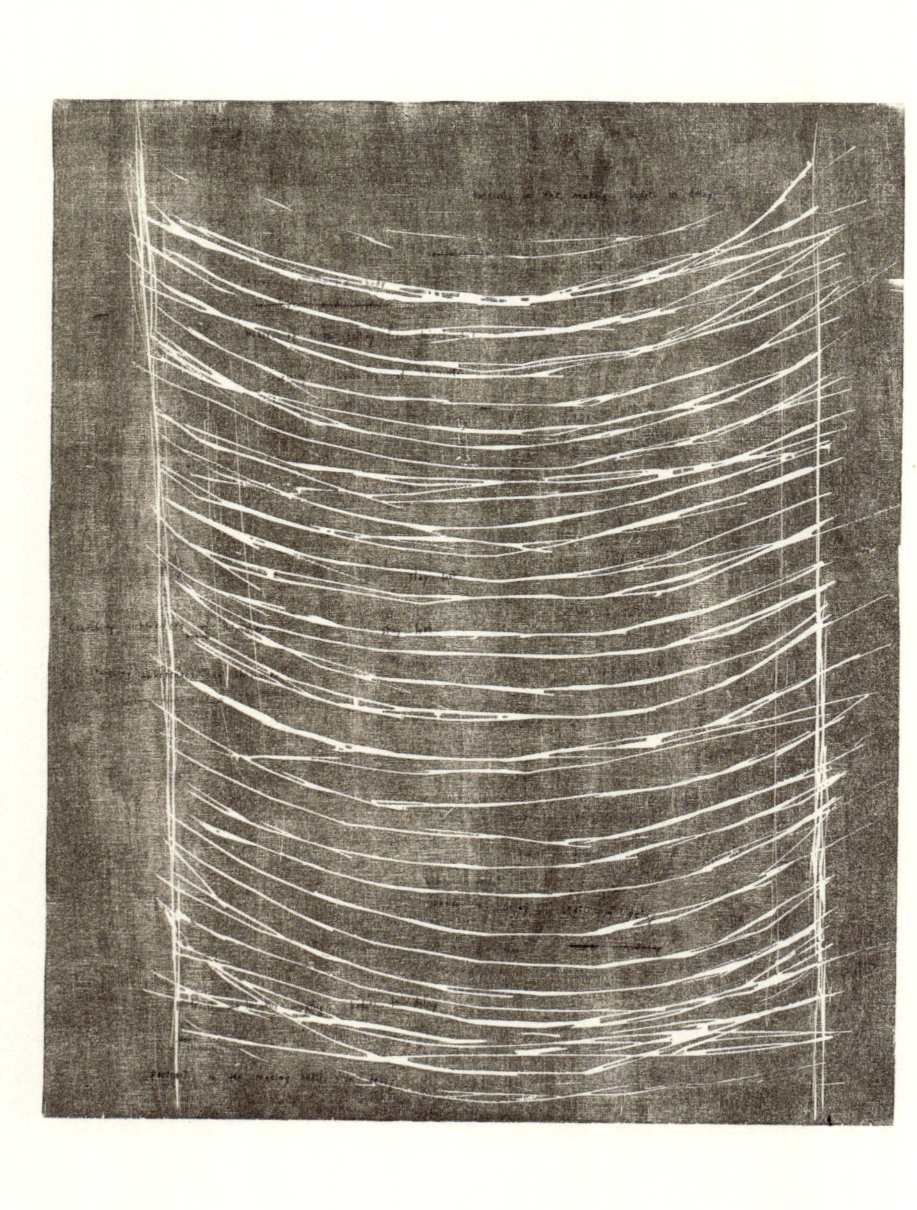

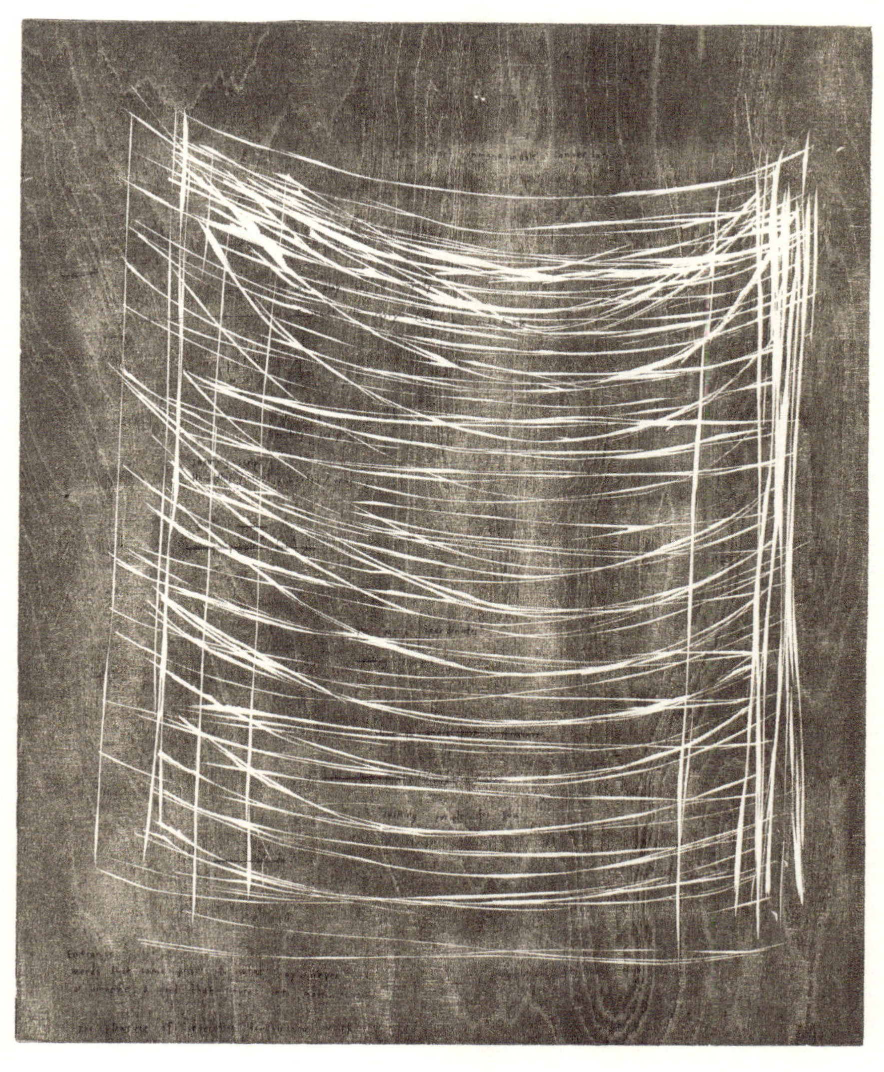

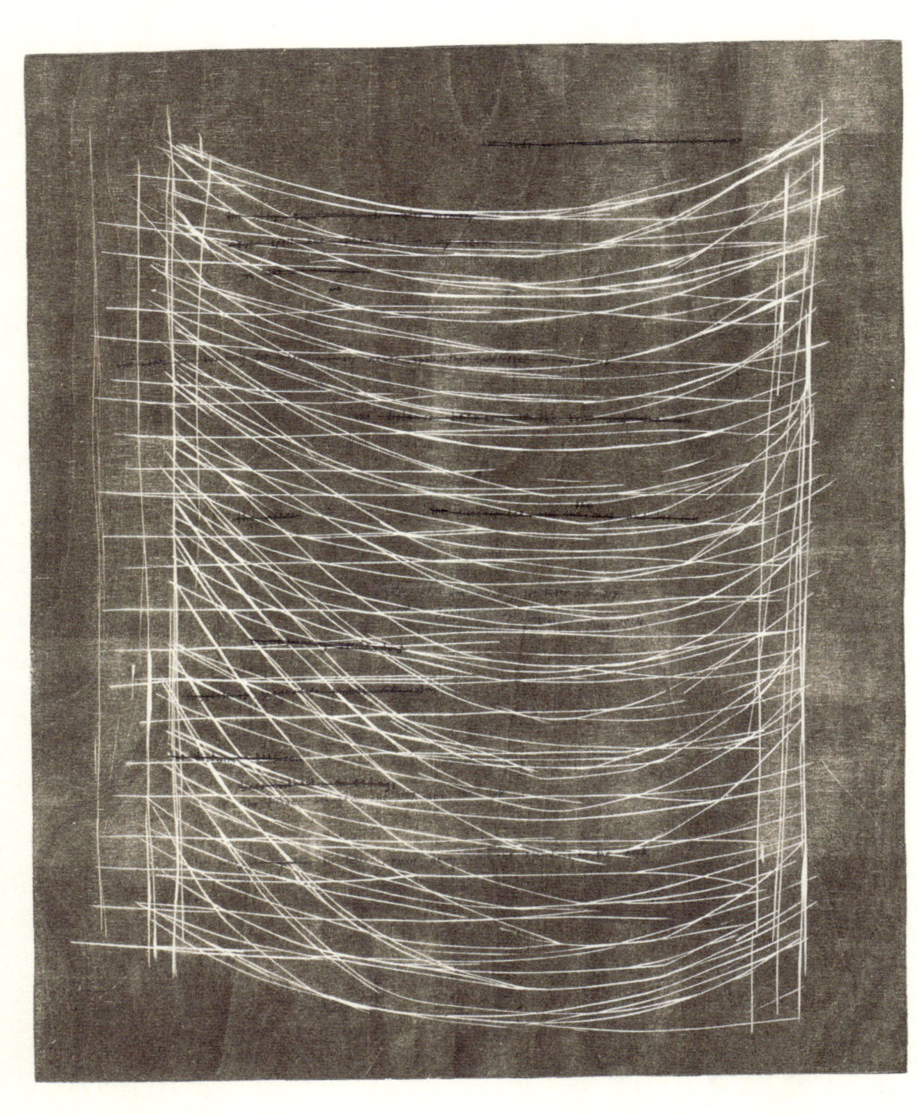

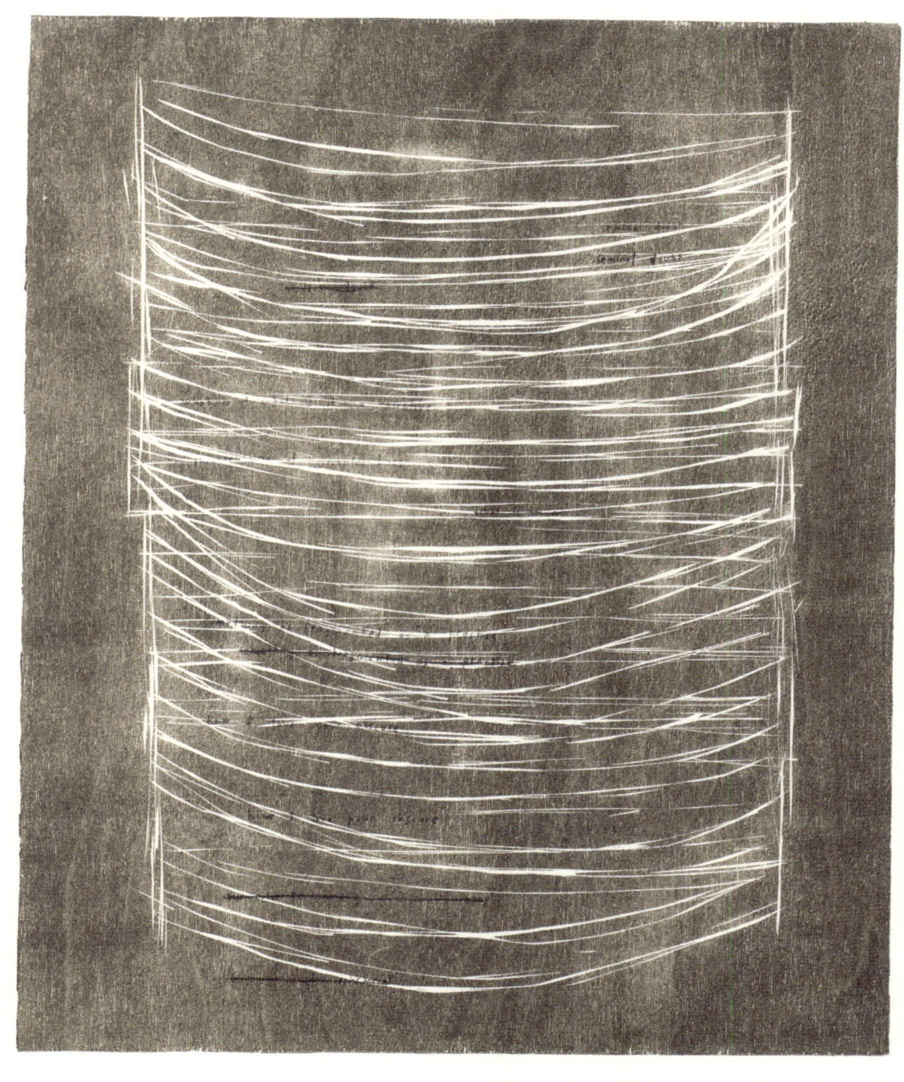

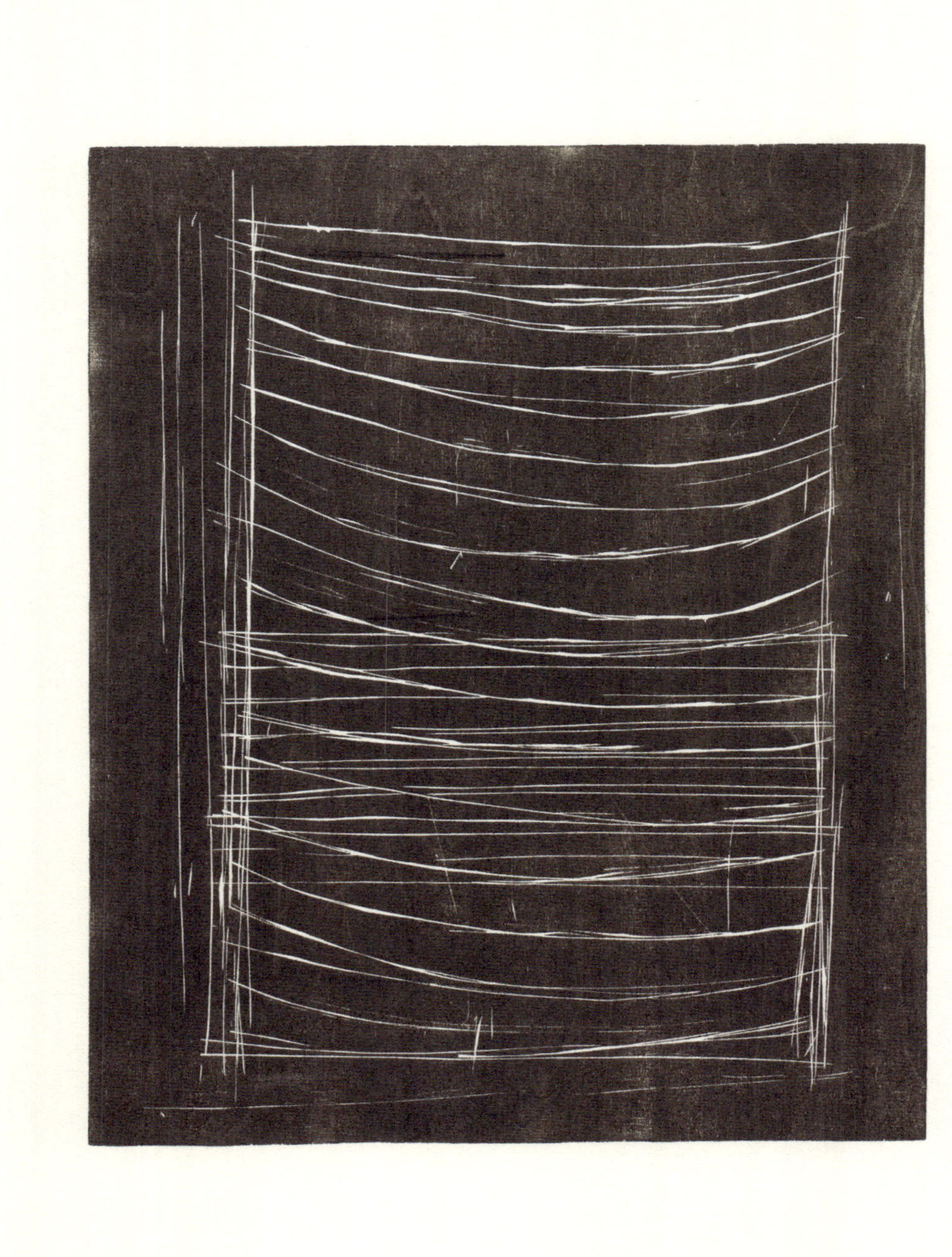

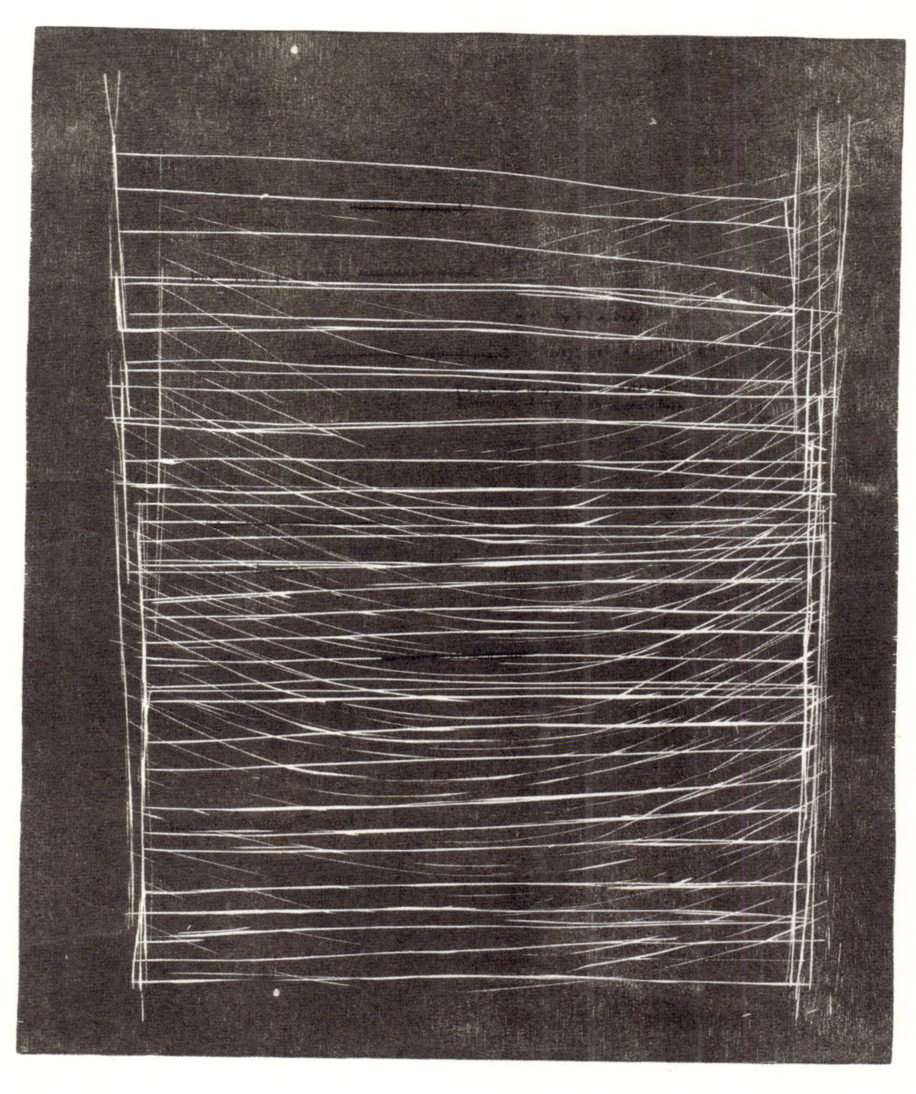

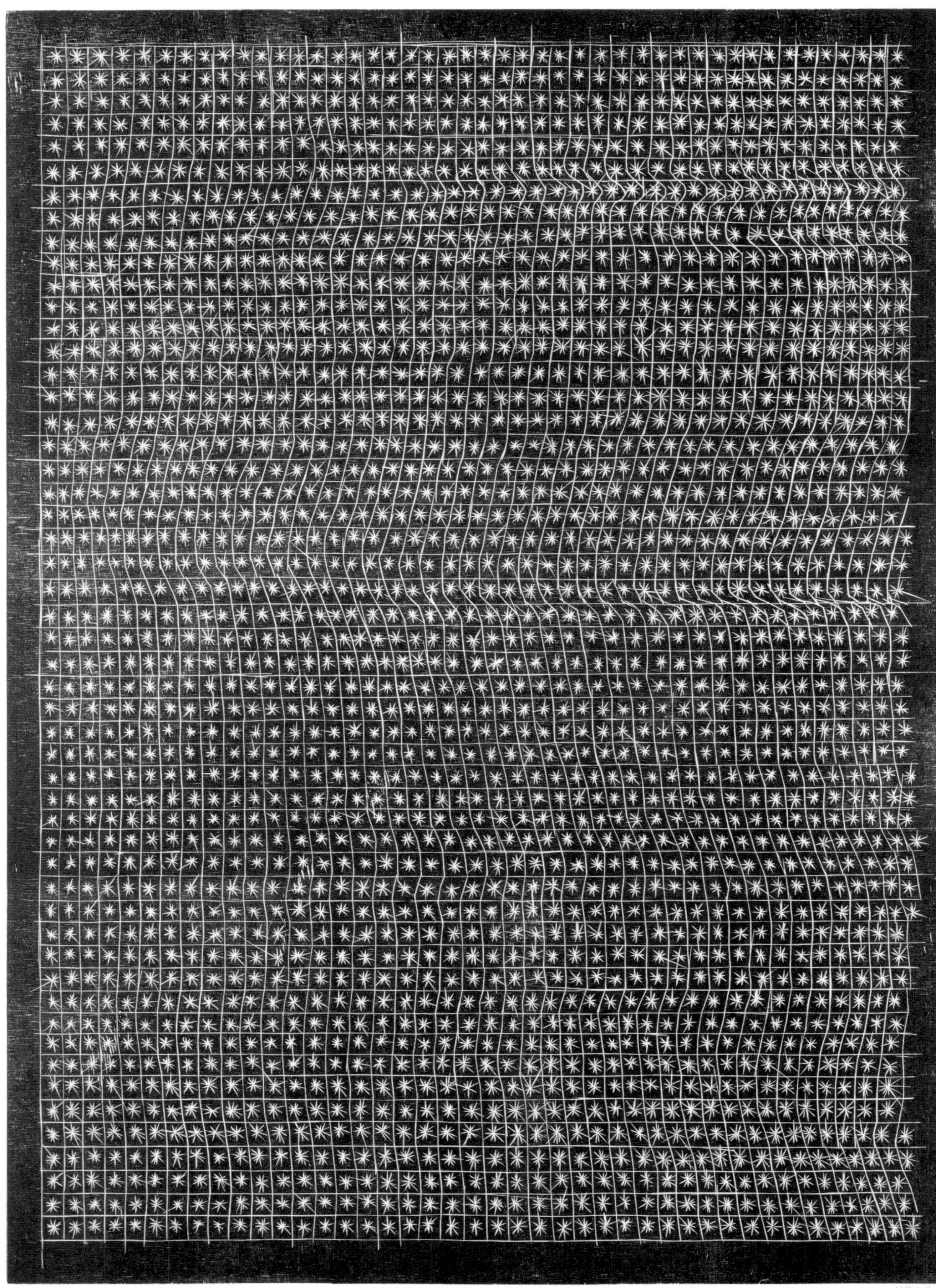

Wooden scripts (How I love your obscure), 2015

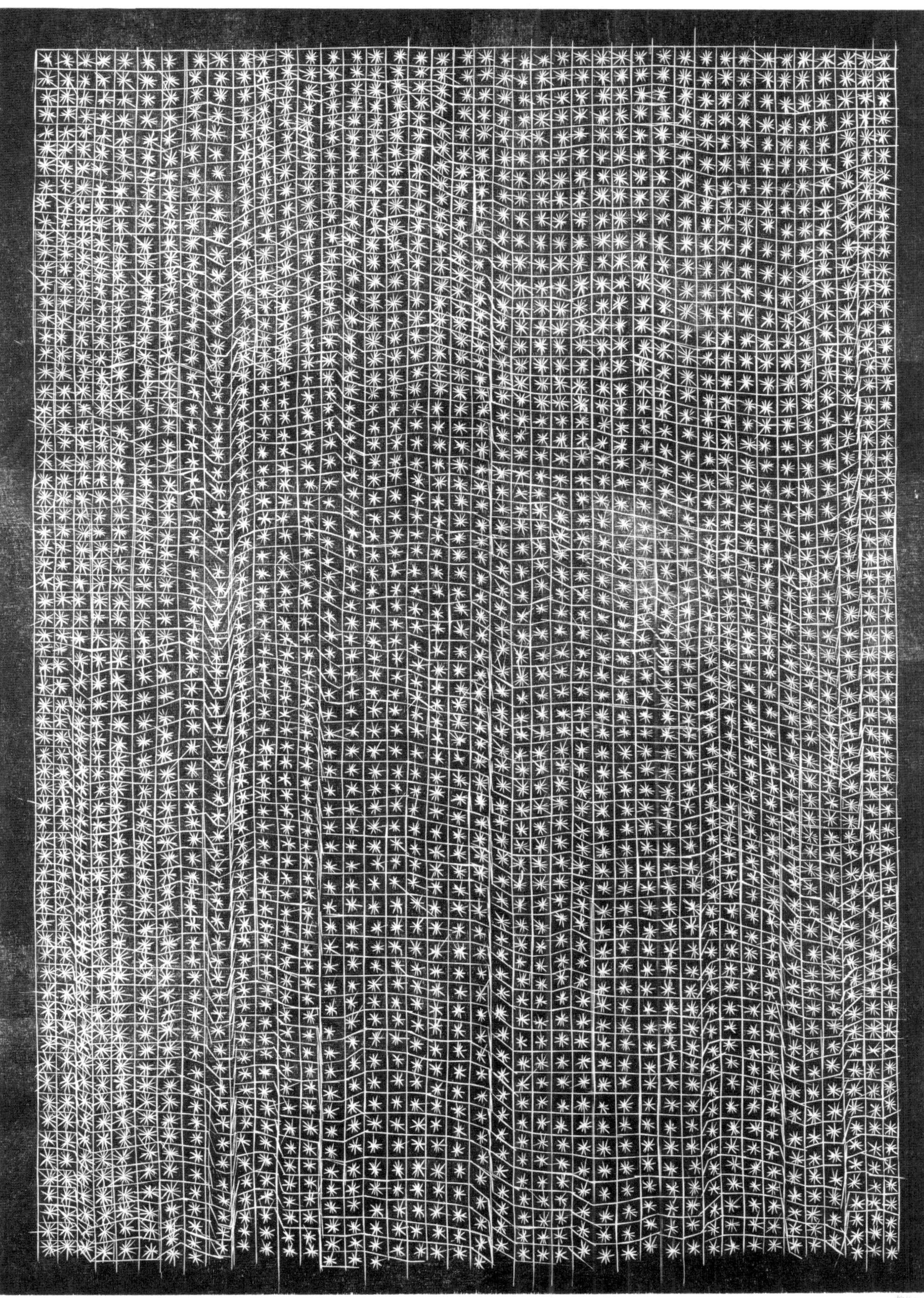

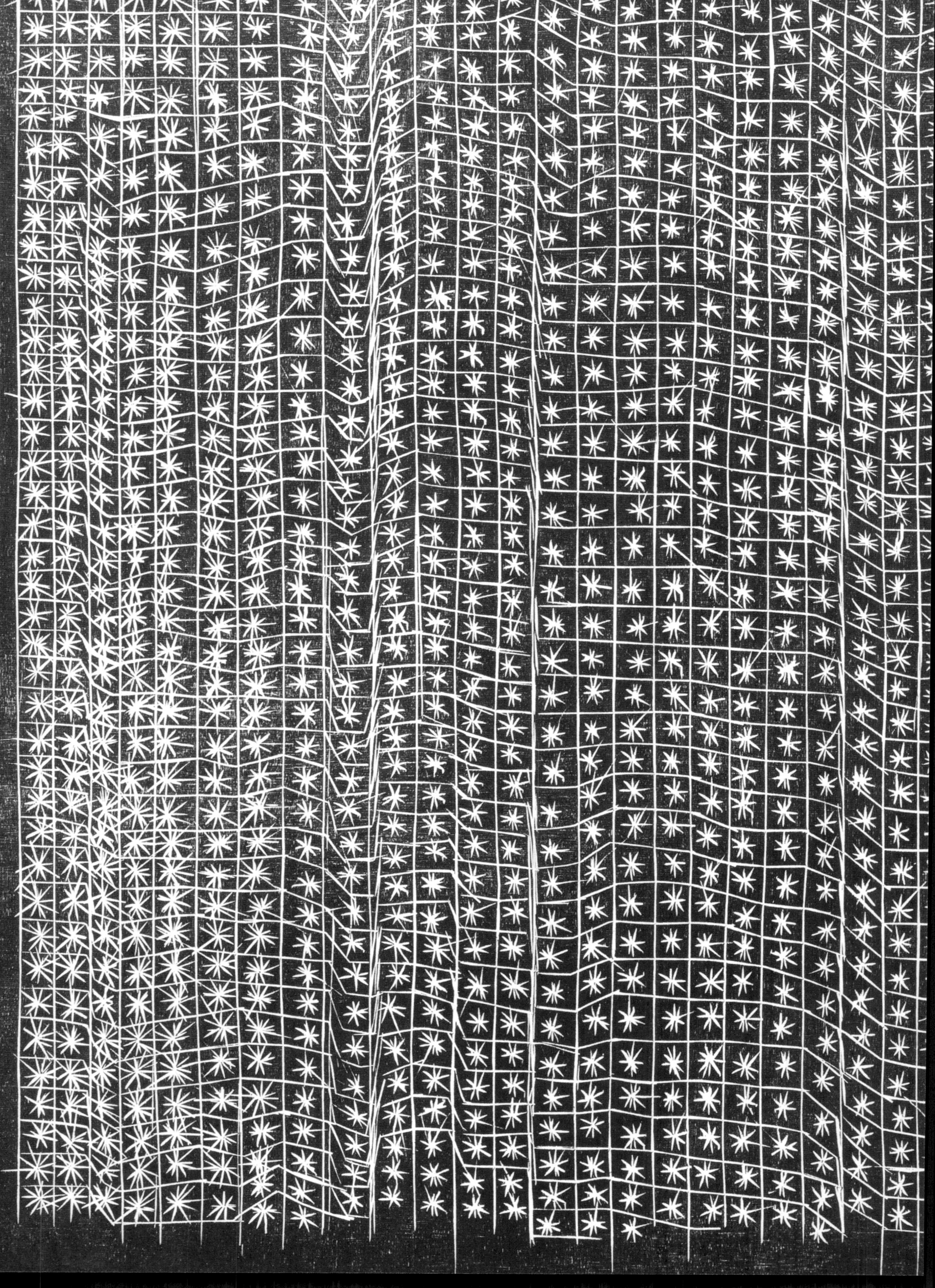

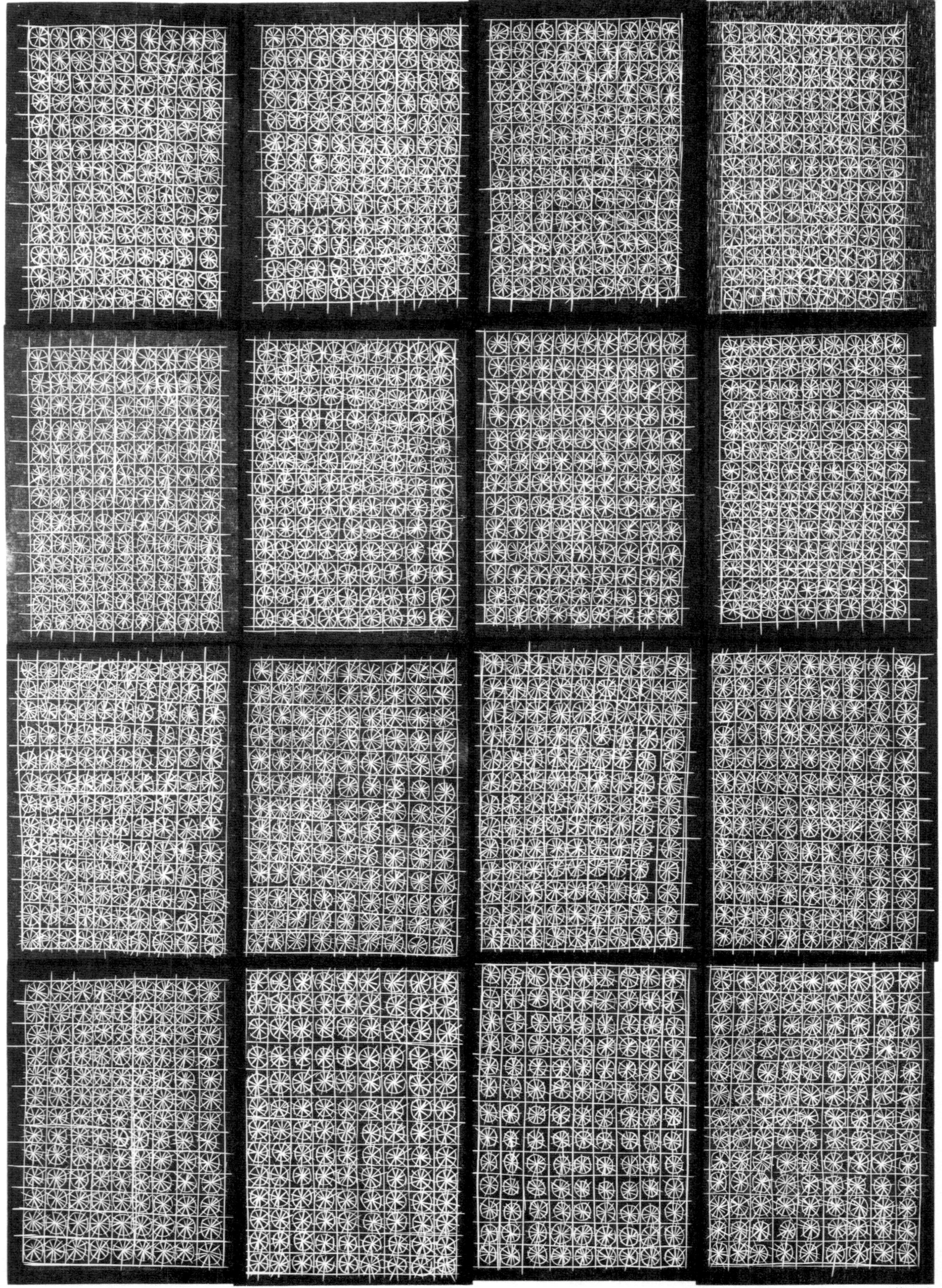

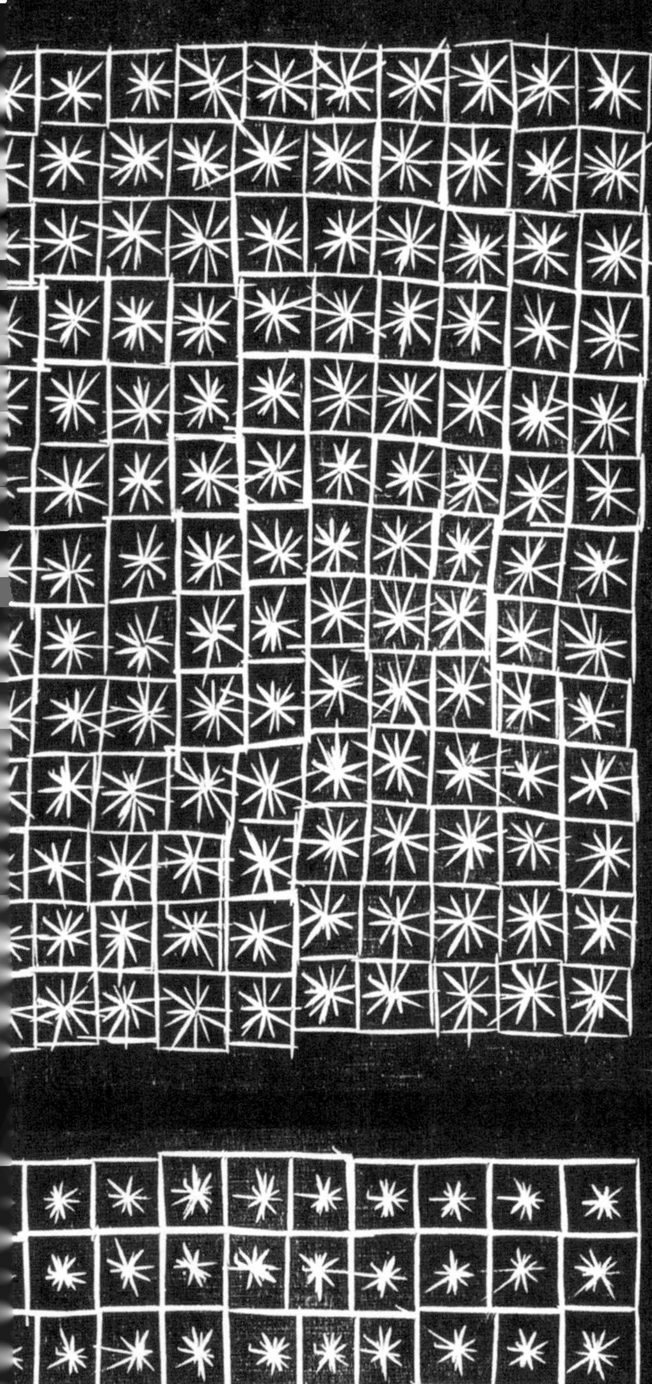
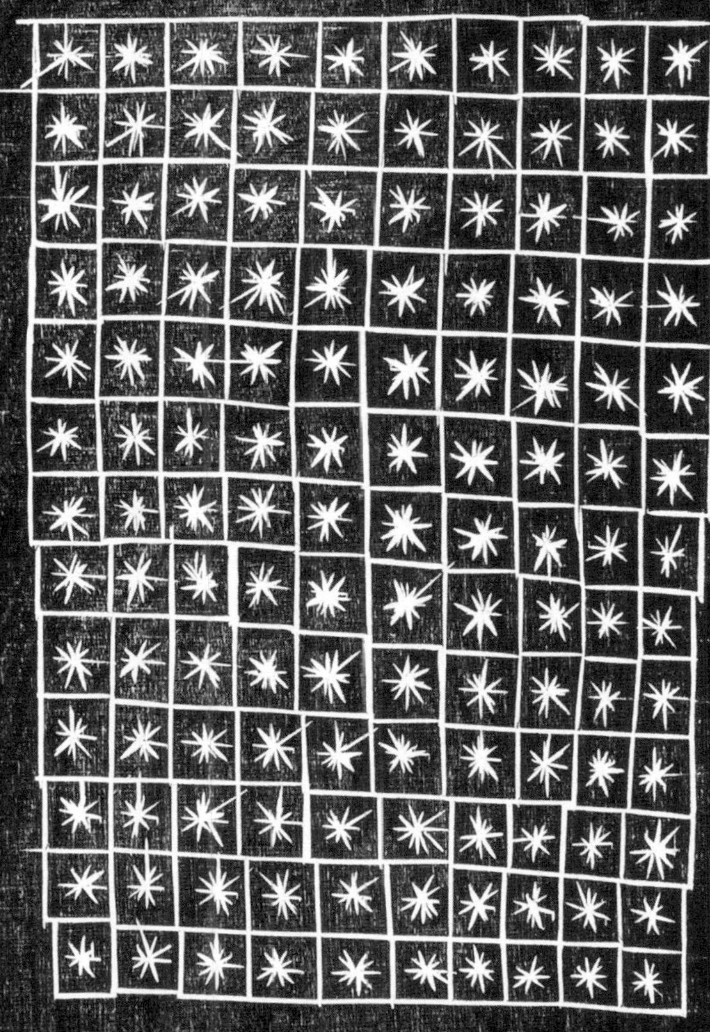
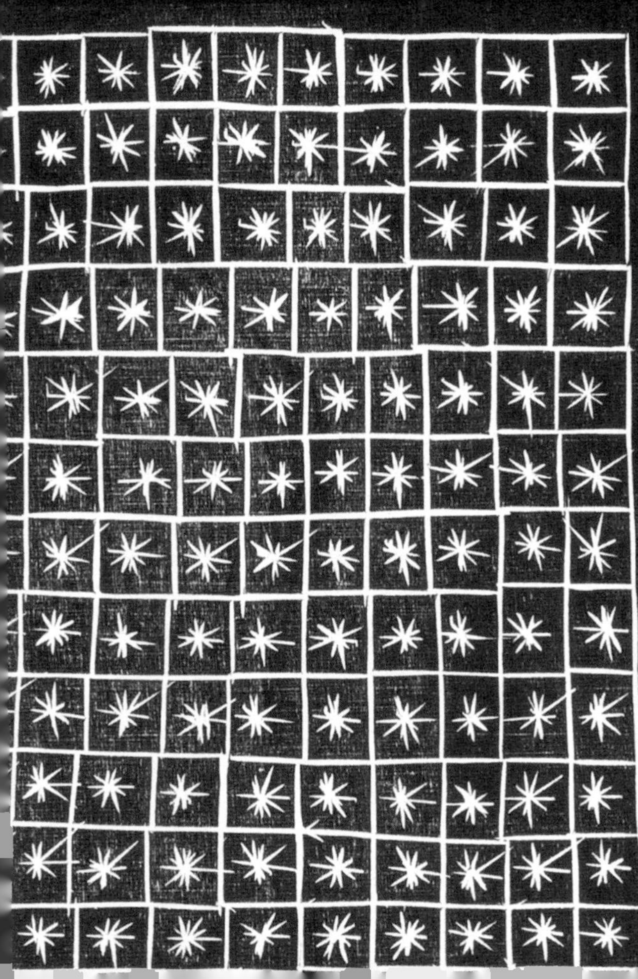
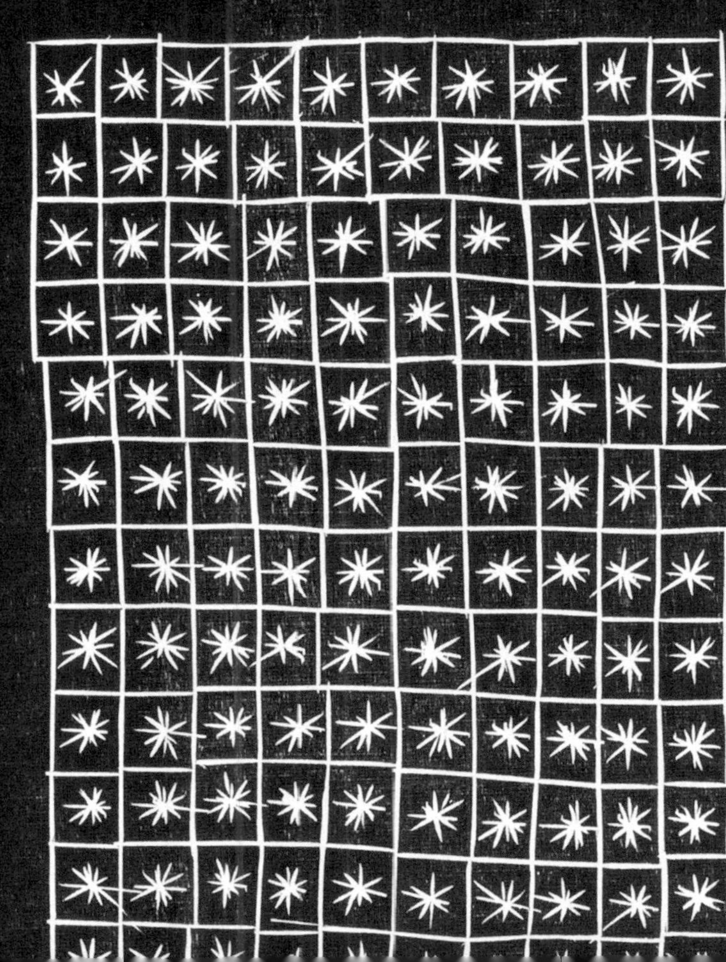

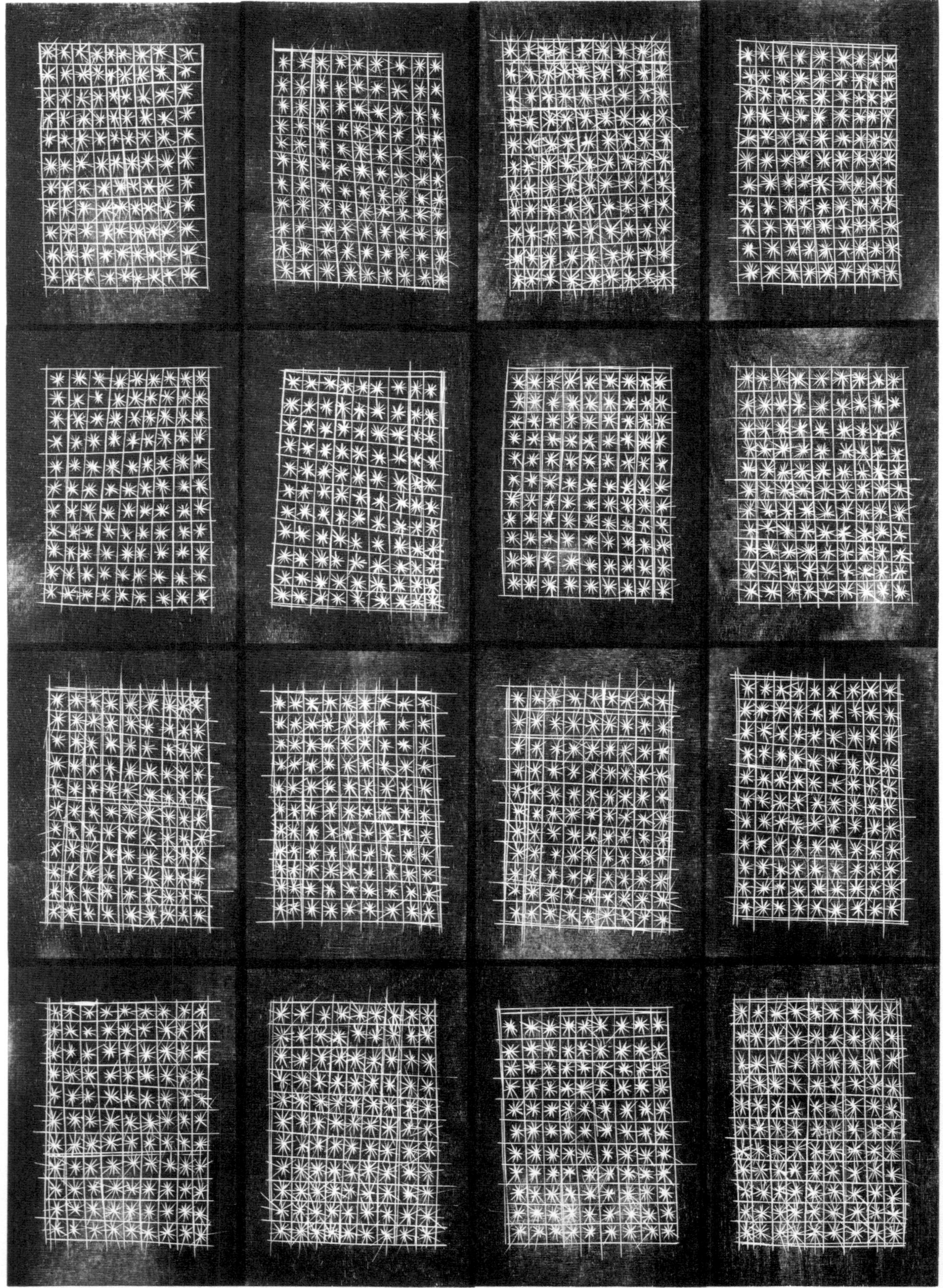

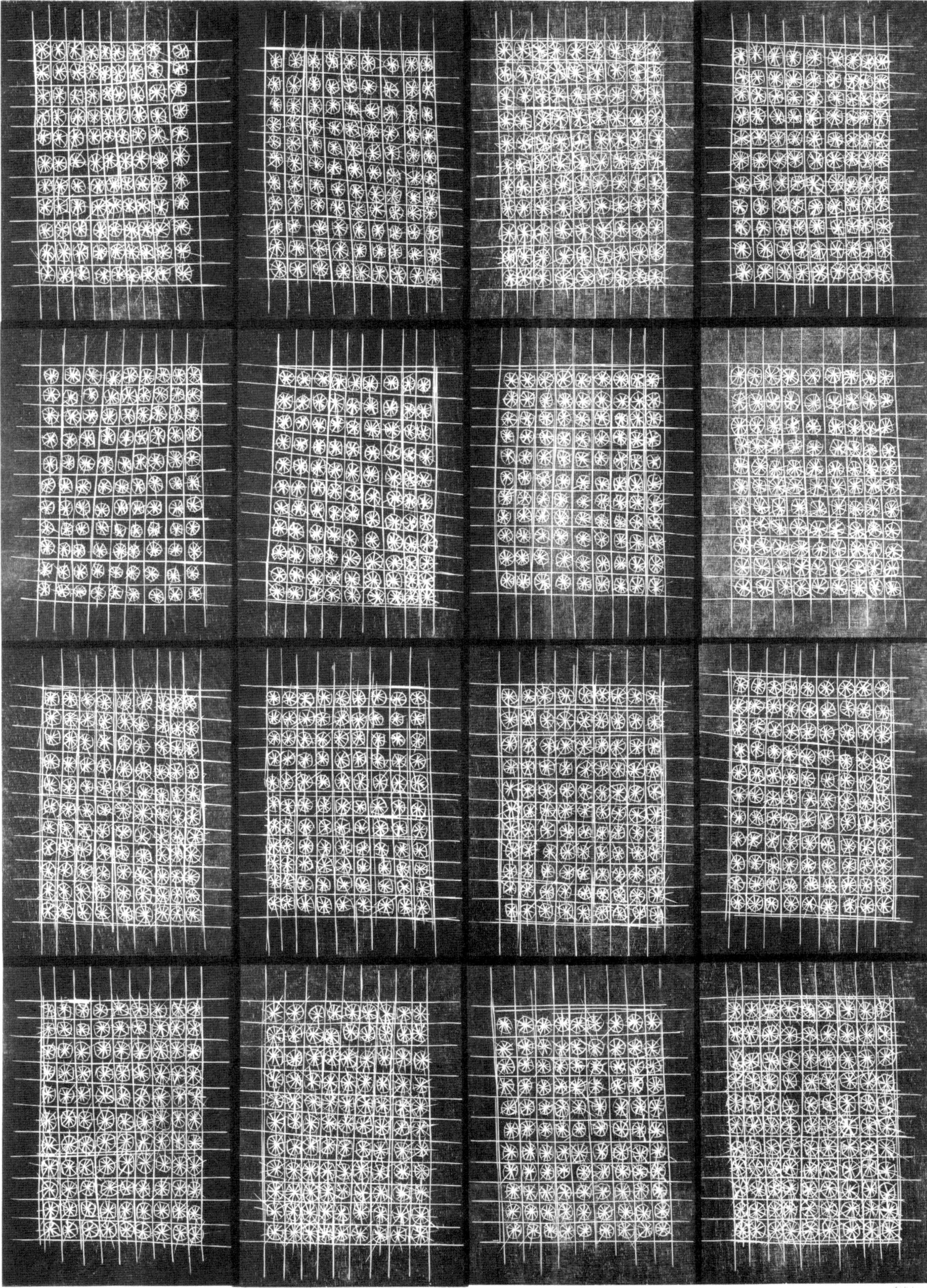

A closet does not connect under the bed, 2016

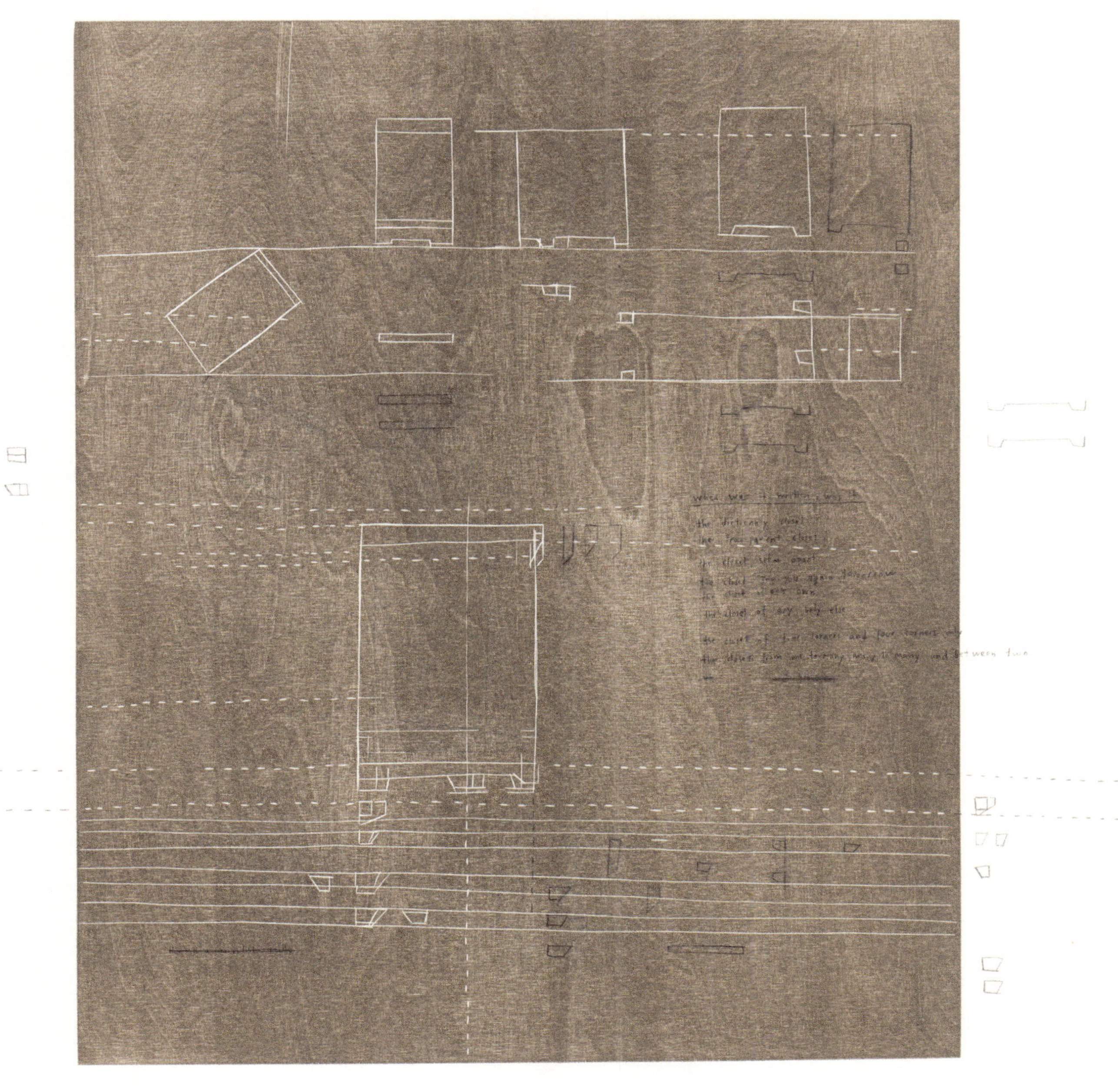

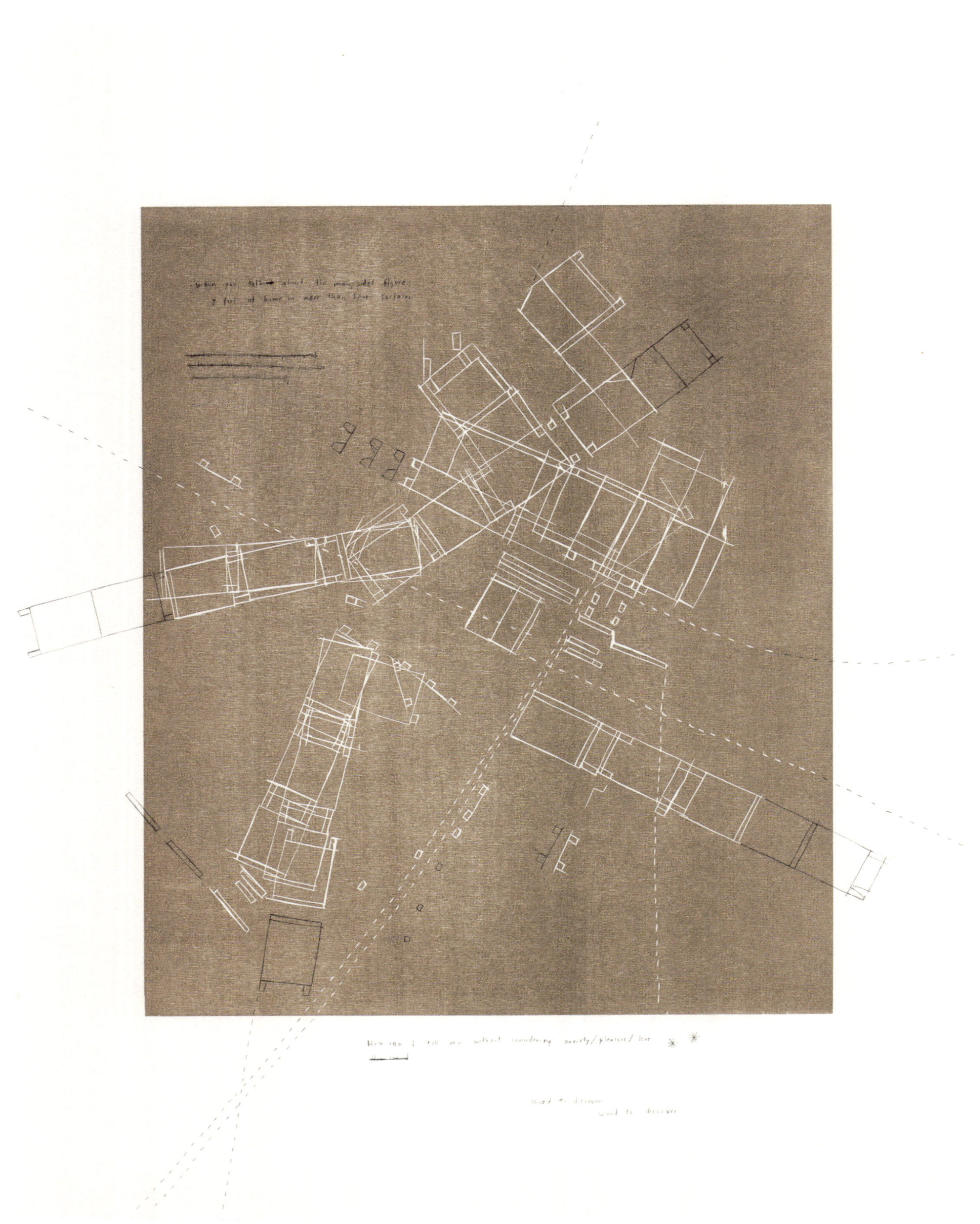

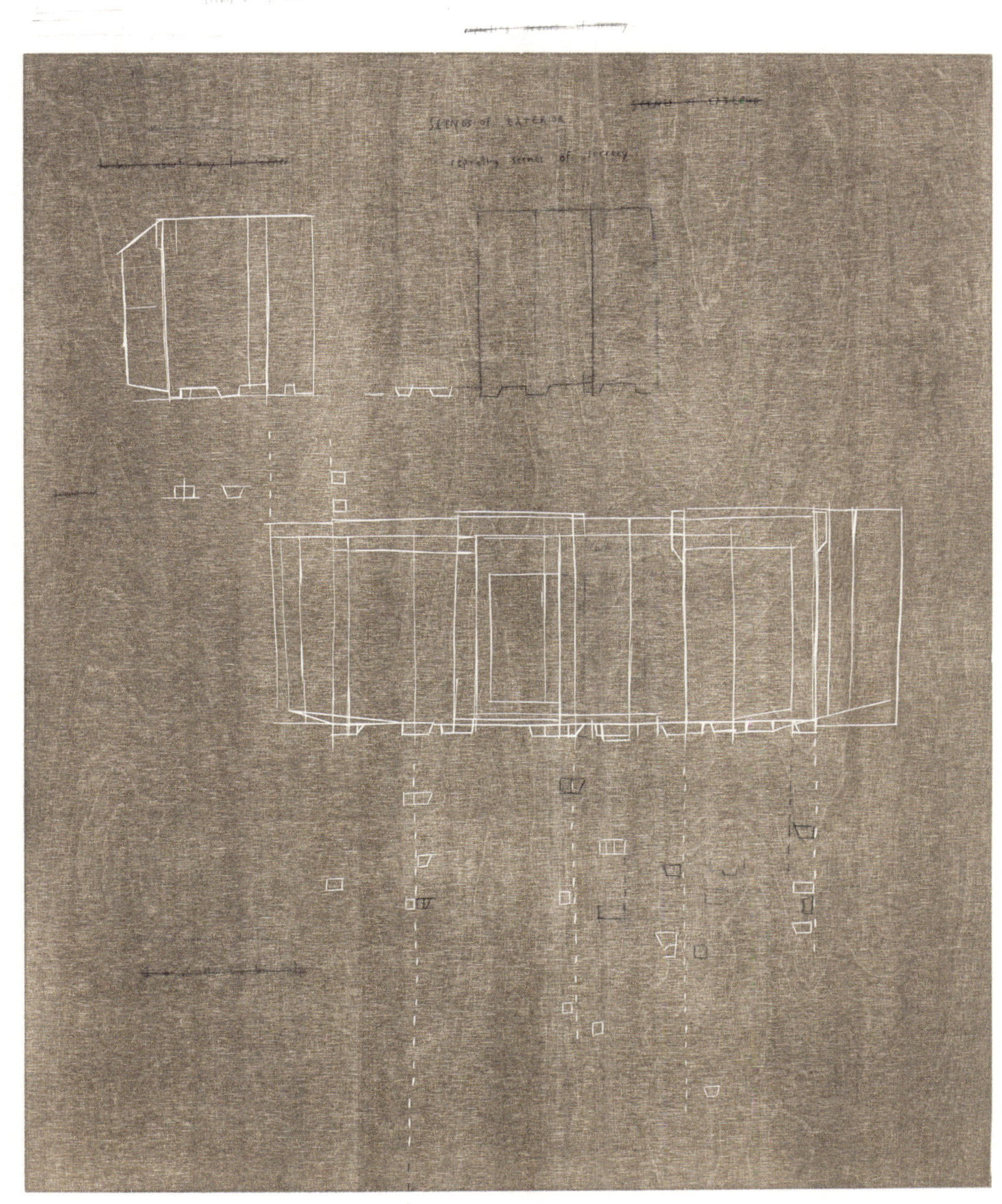

SCENES of EXTERIOR
repeating scenes of scenery

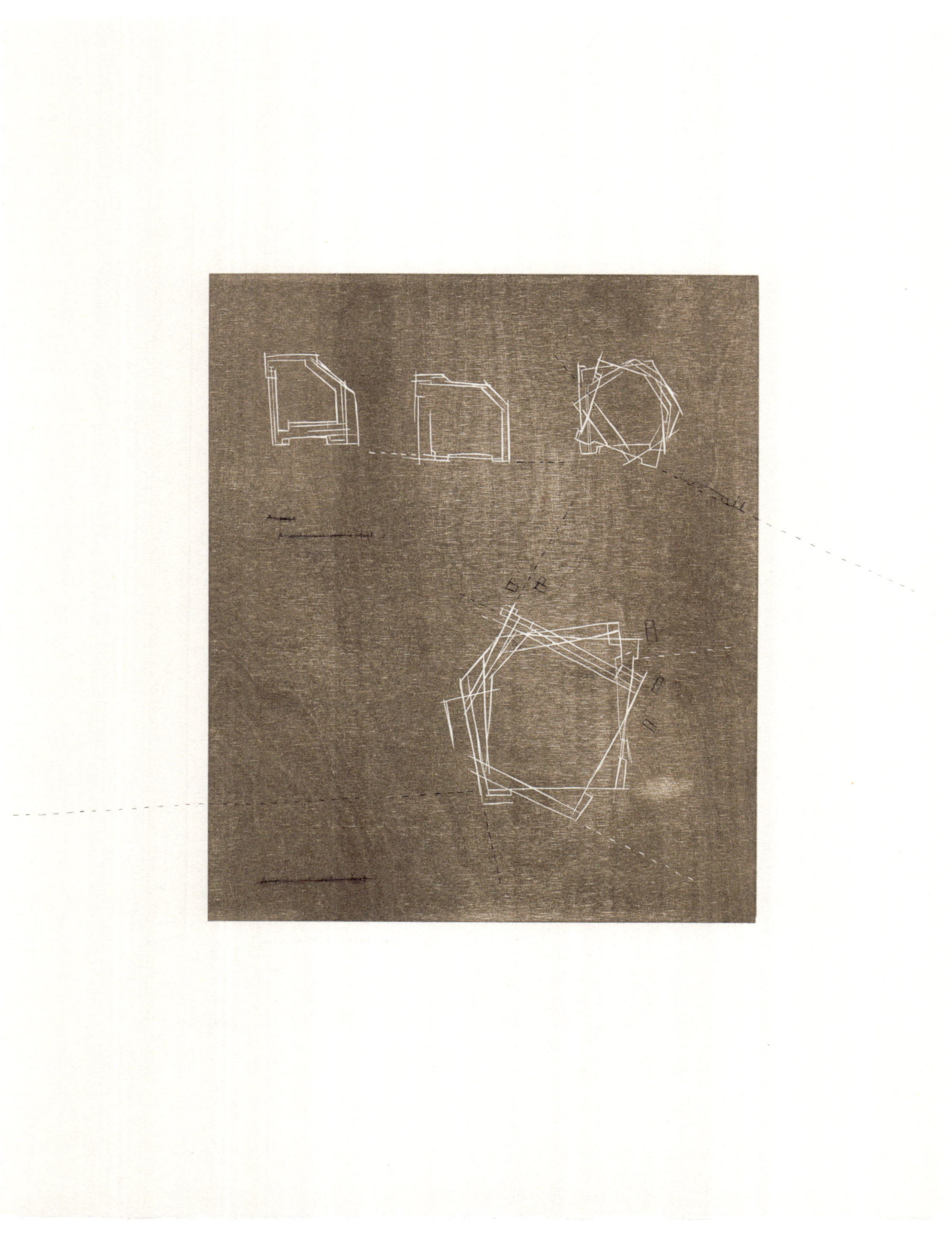

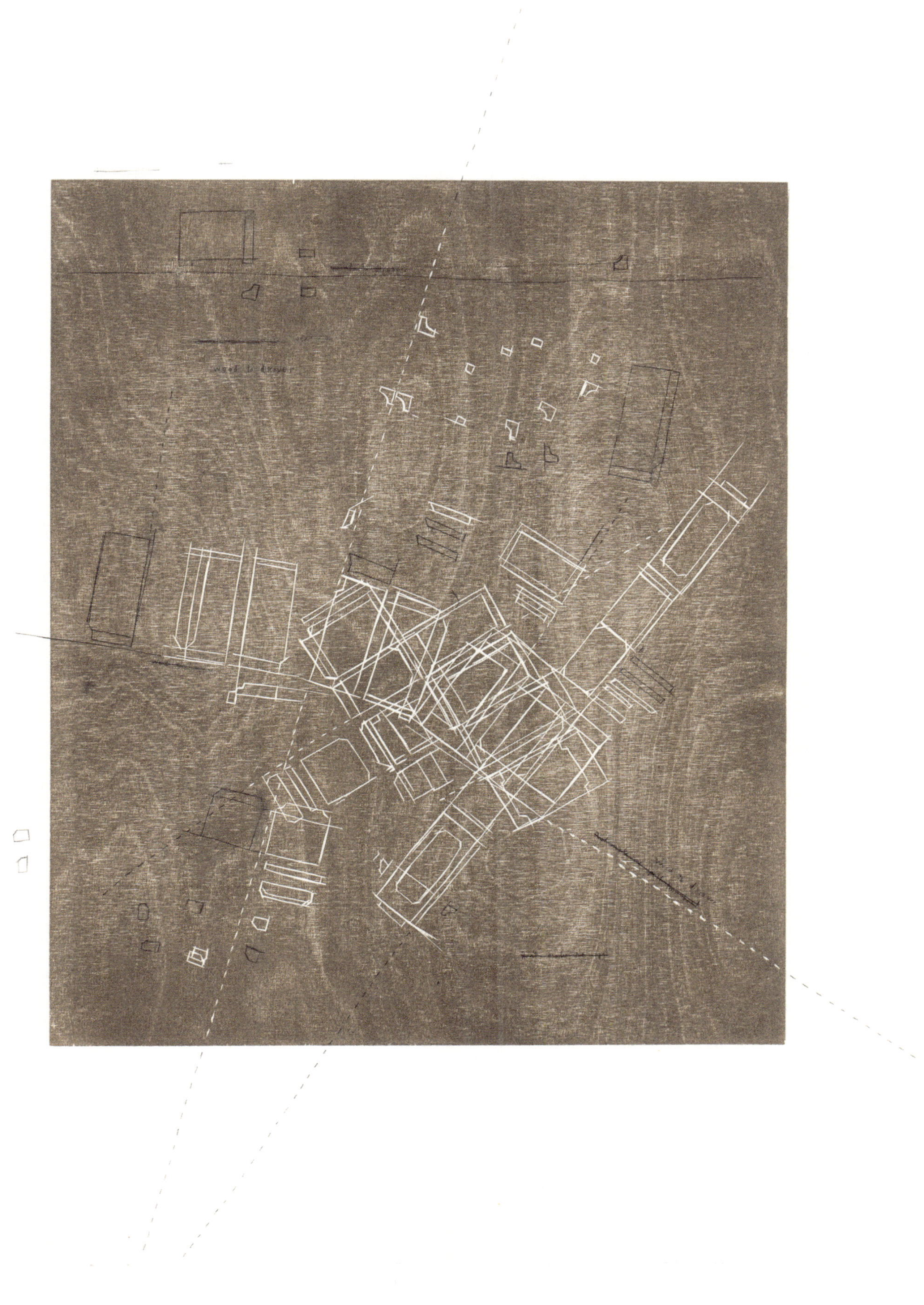

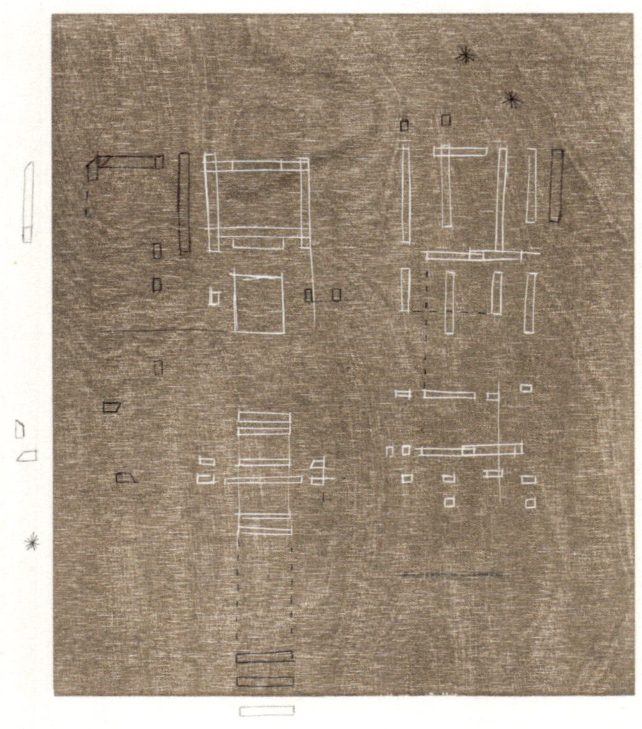

A metaphor is not bald and bald about it

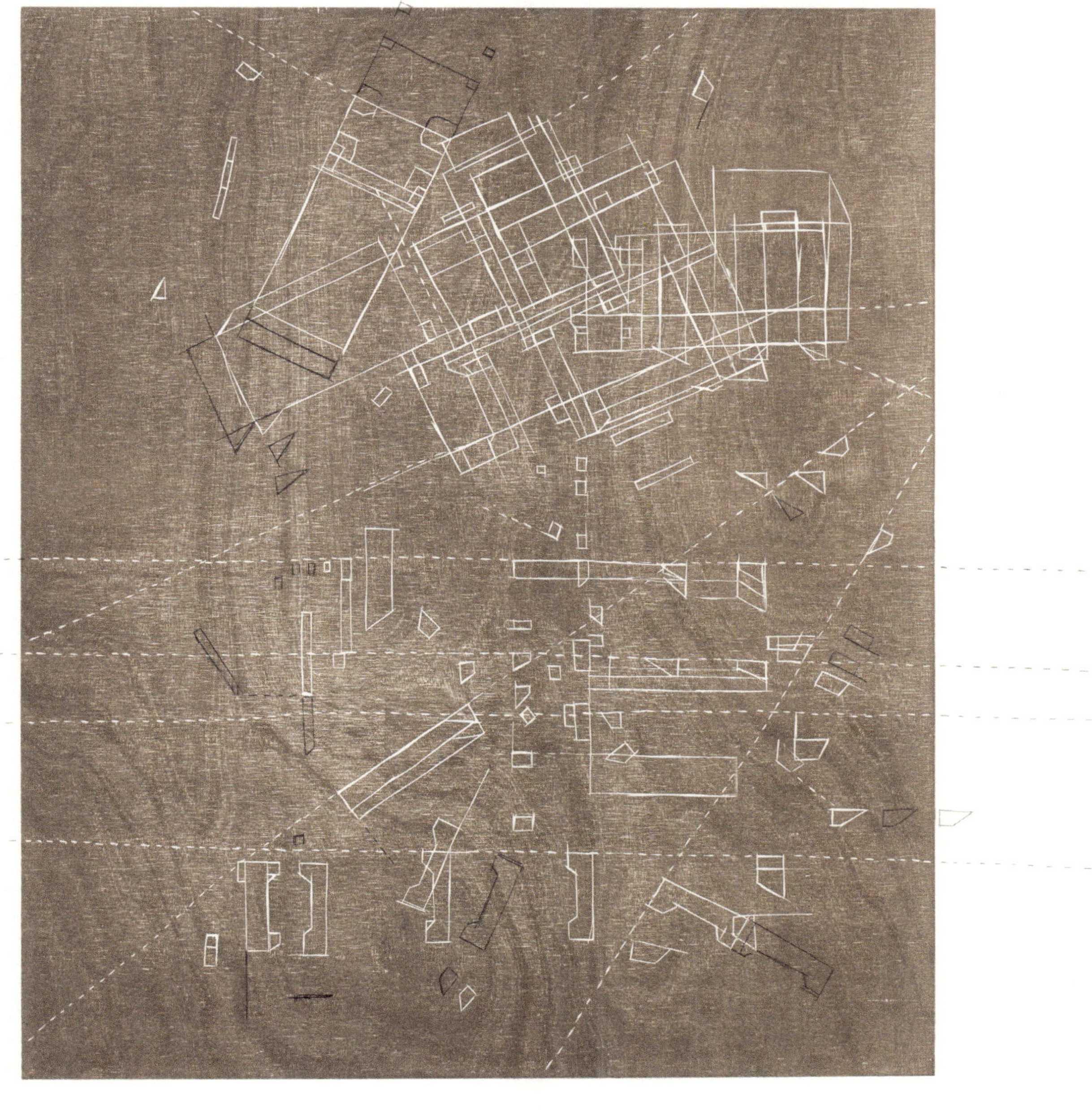

a metaphor has no desire
a metaphor has no anus
a metaphor has no closet
a metaphor has no desire no closet
a metaphor doesn't know about it

COPY OF AN ENTRY, piece by piece
A frame an entry
However
From one to many, many to many and between two

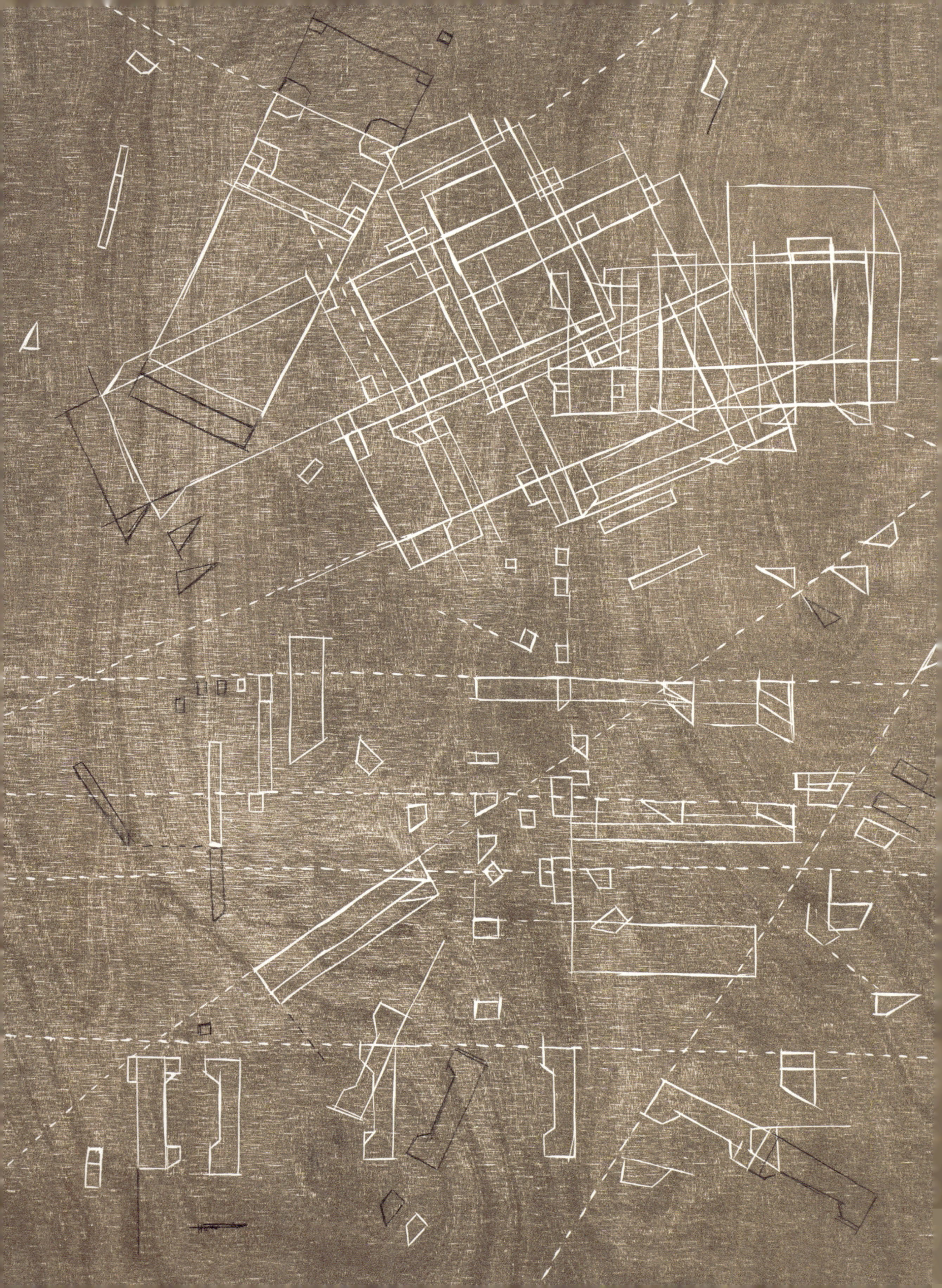

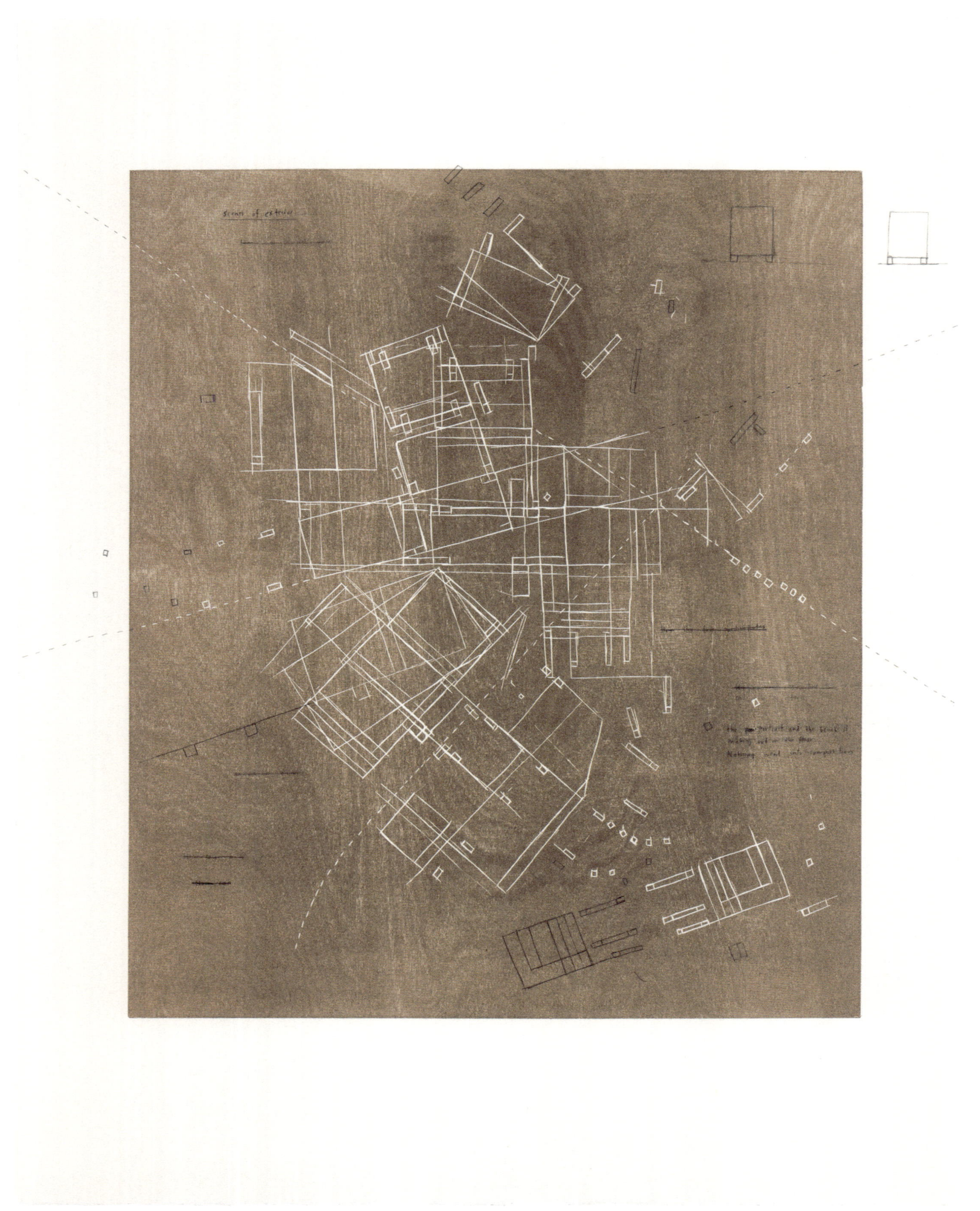

the closet I told you so

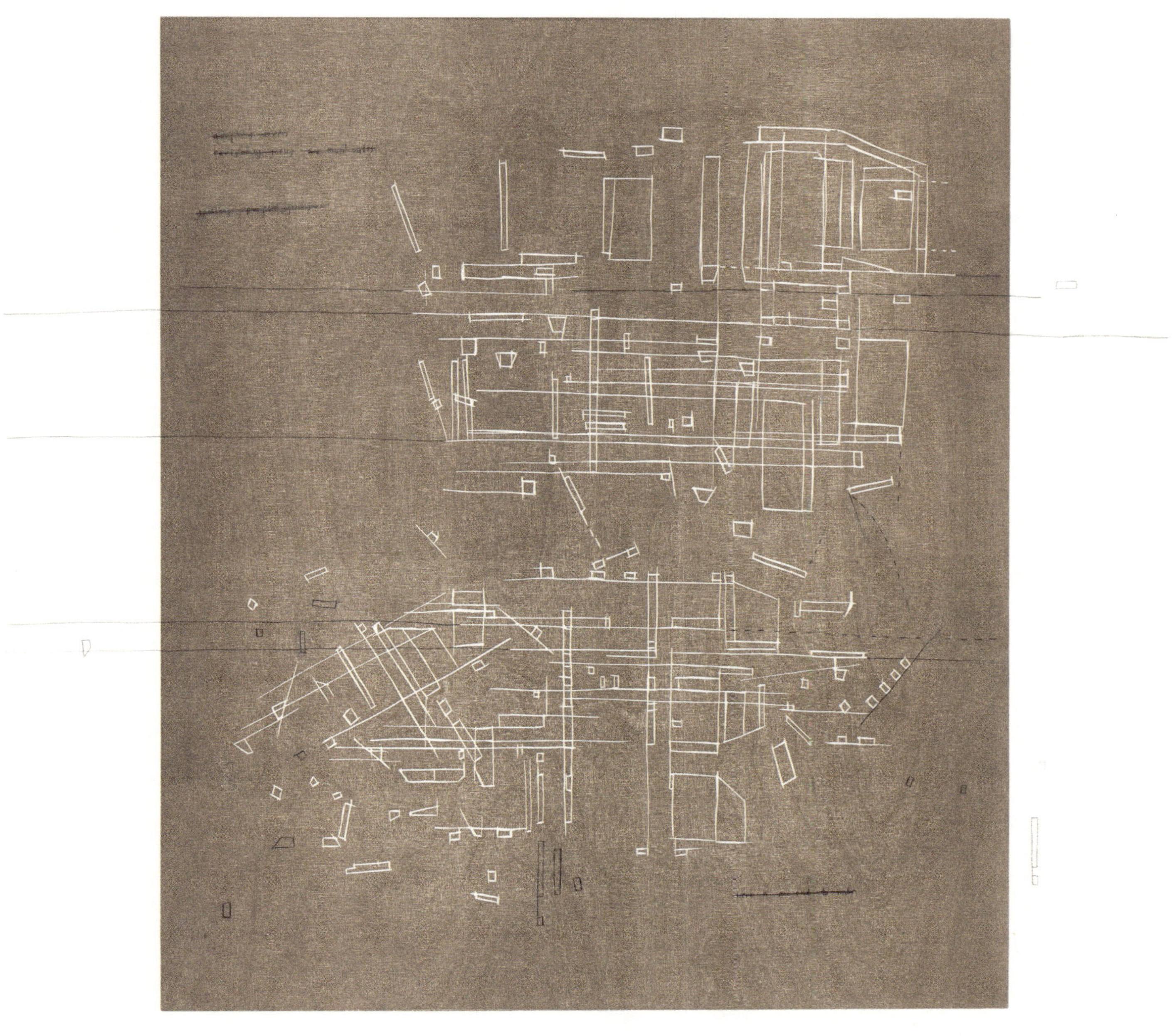

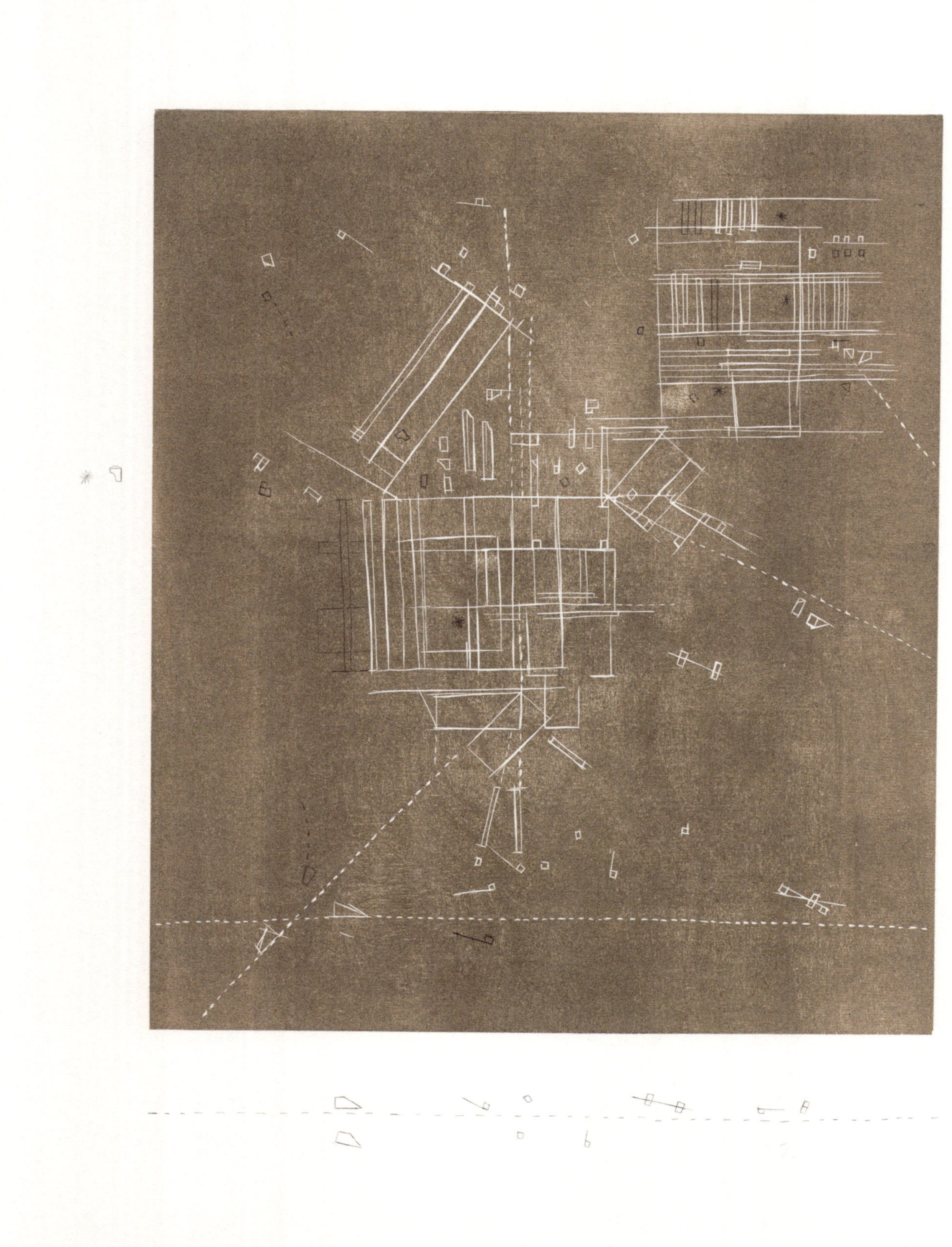

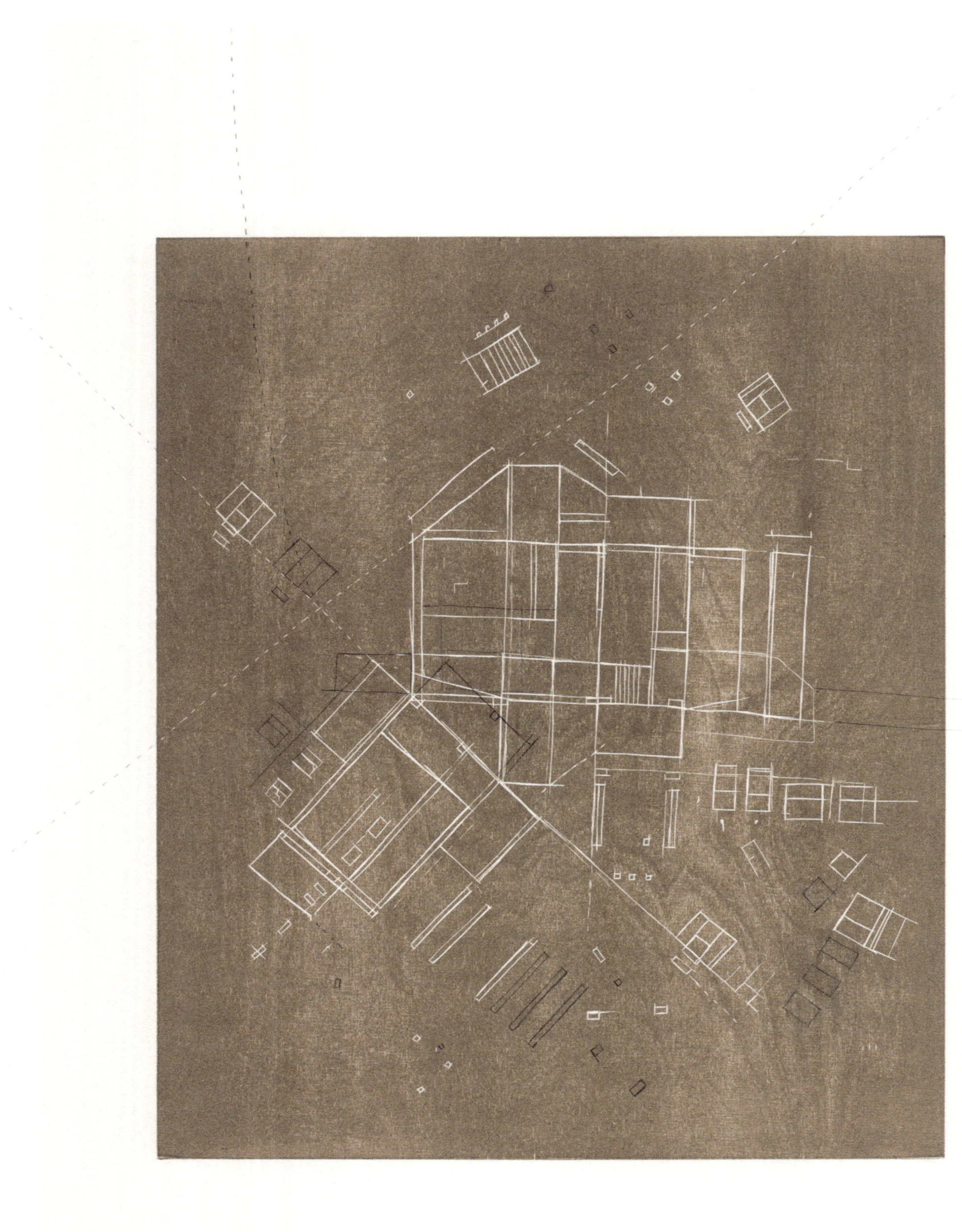

A closet does not connect under the bed
a closet does not know about it
Everything I know about closets

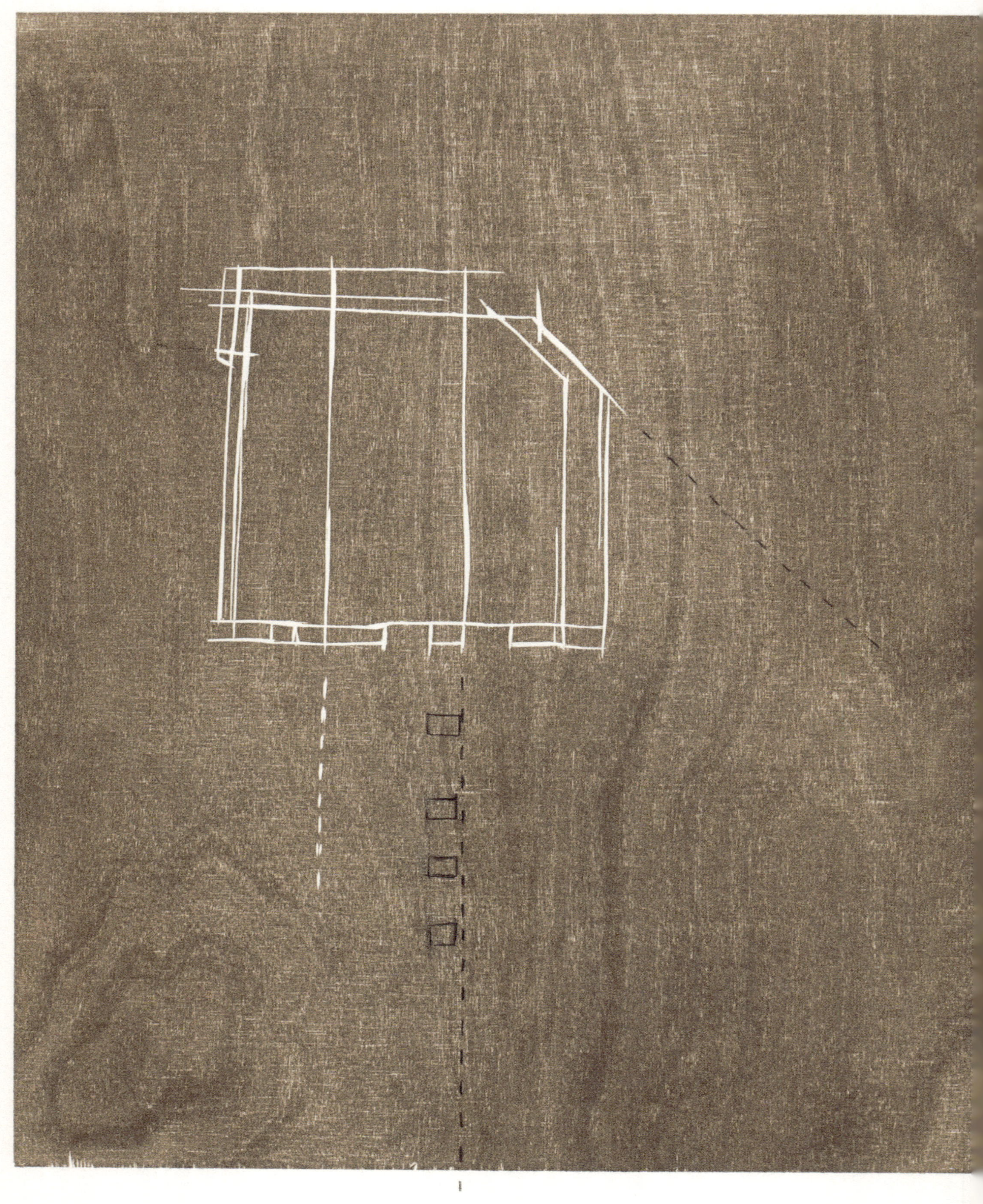

A closet does not connect under the bed
a closet does not know about it
Everything I know about closets

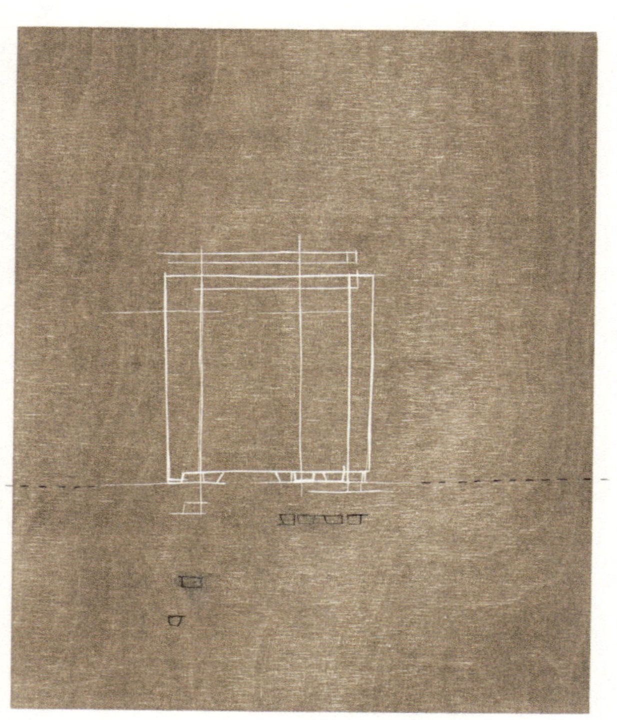

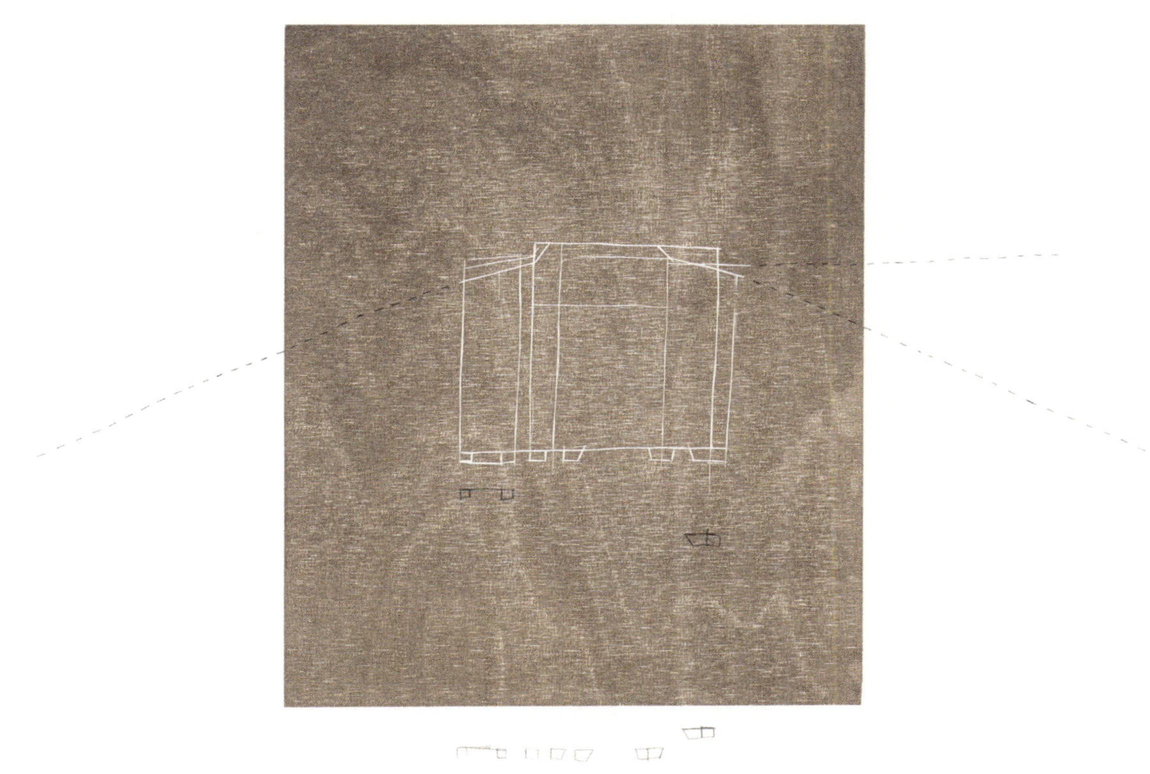

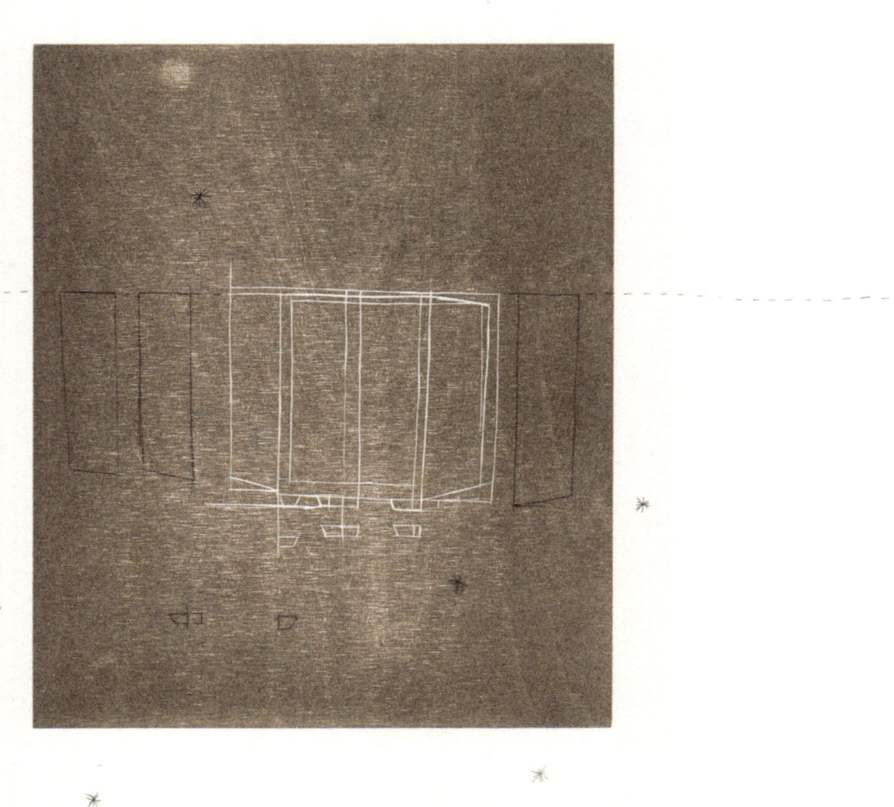

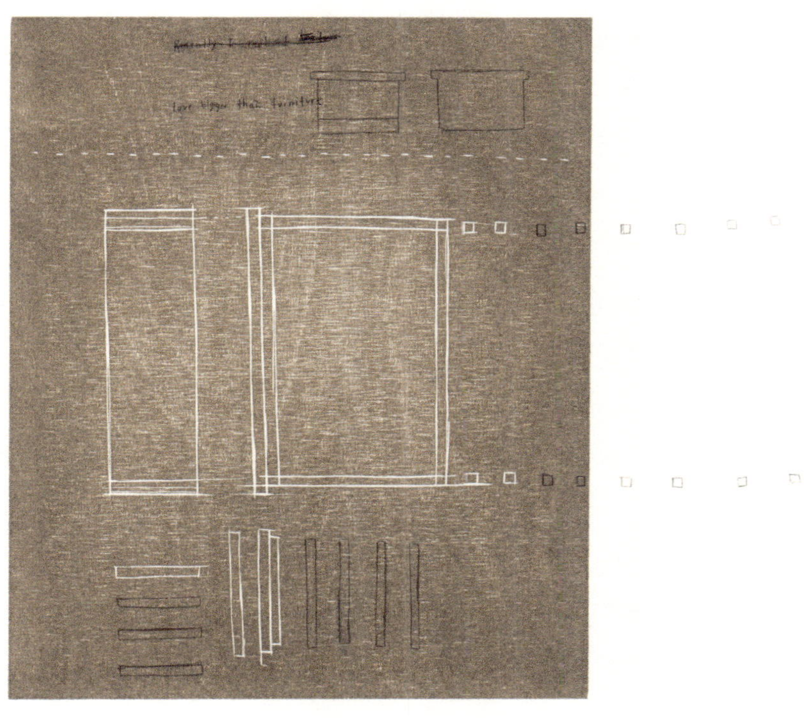

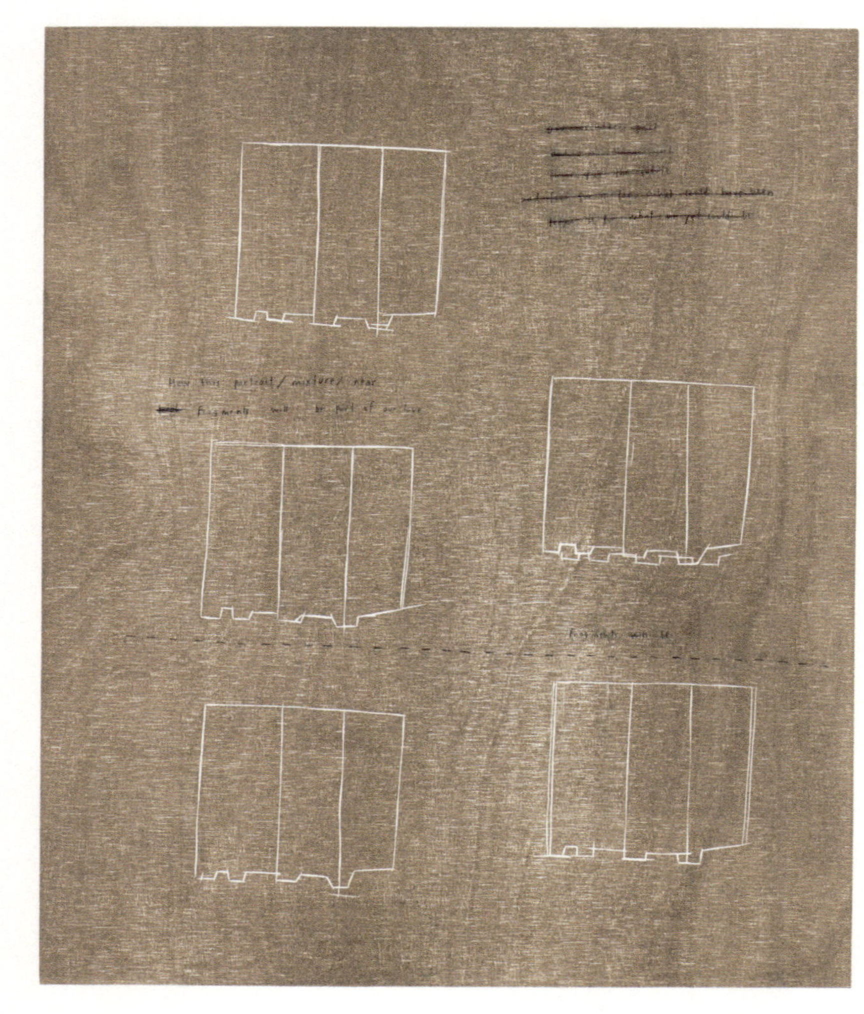

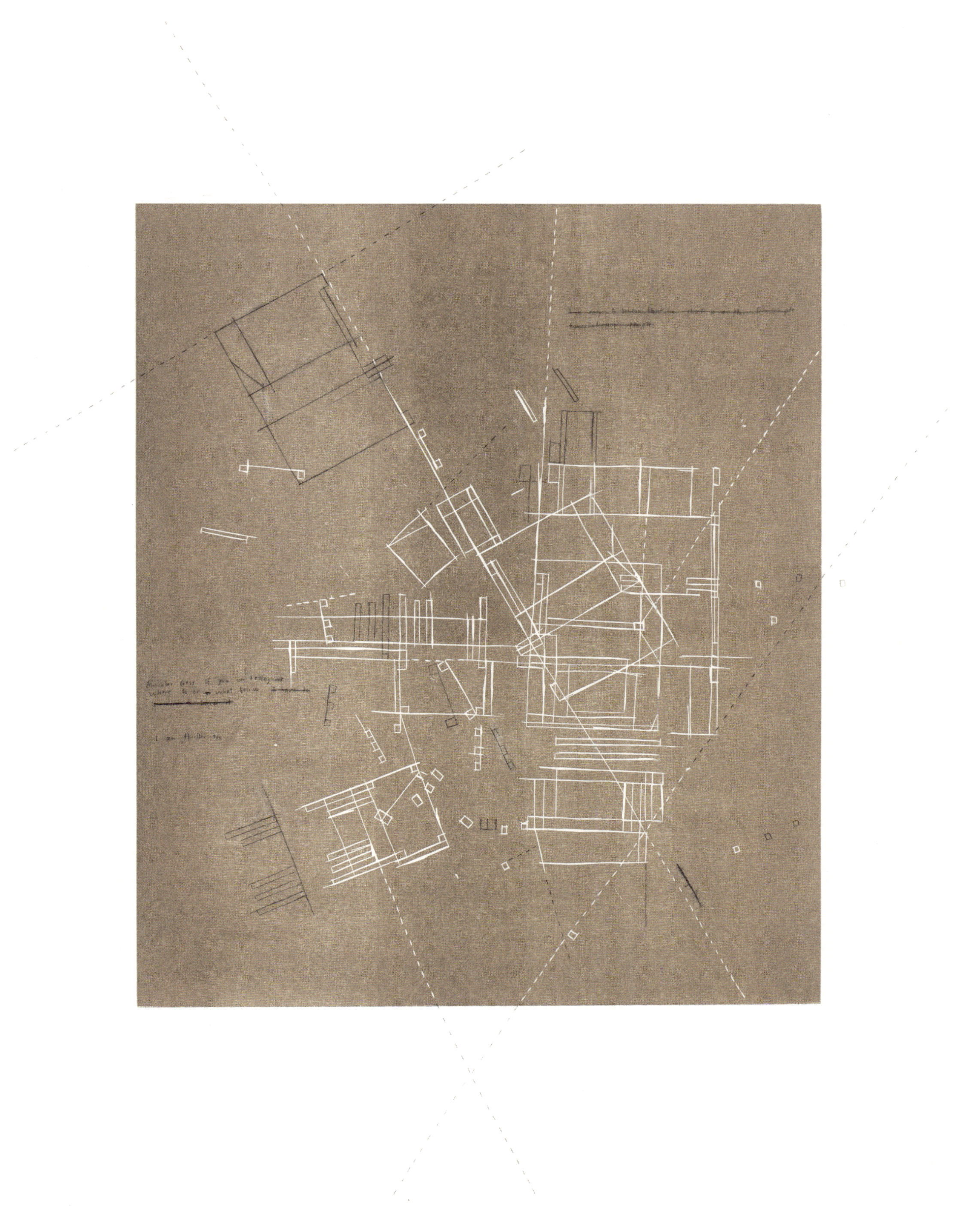

Compounds of convictions, 2017

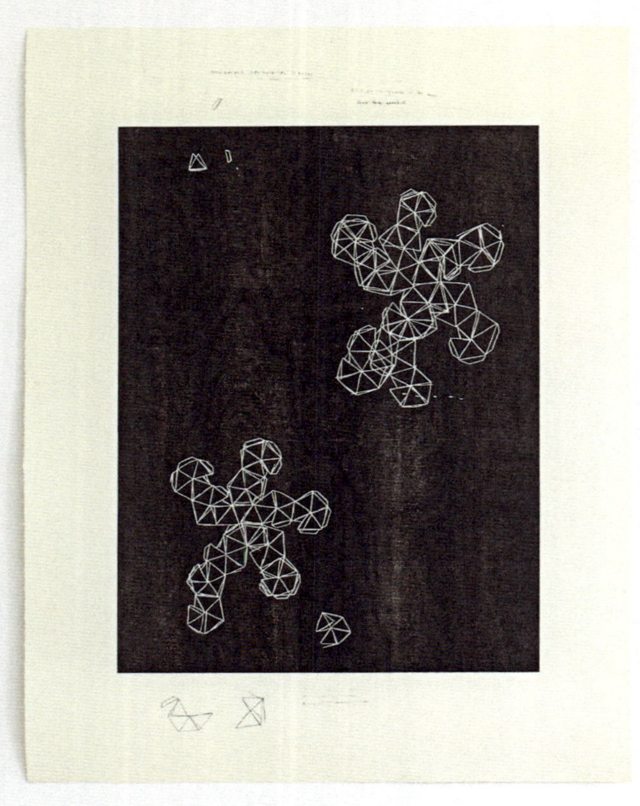

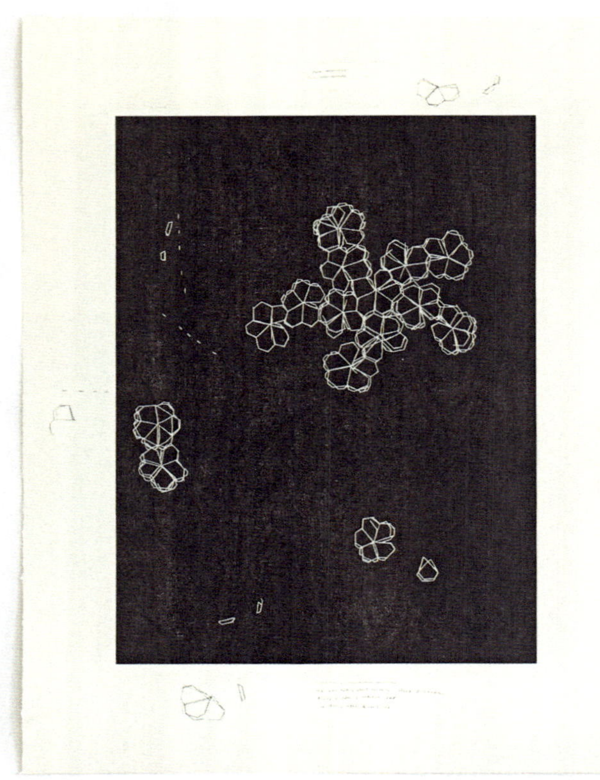

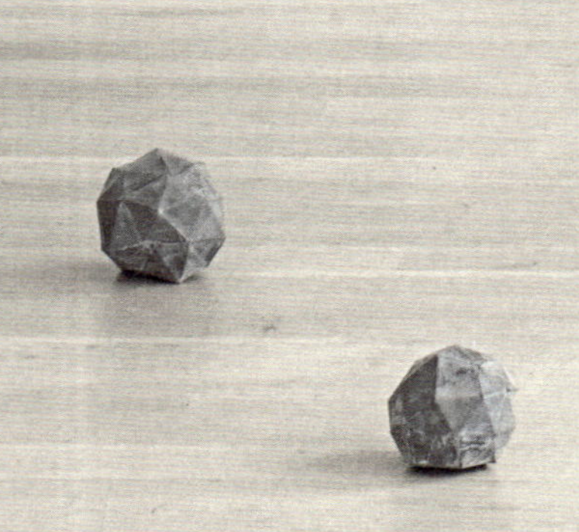

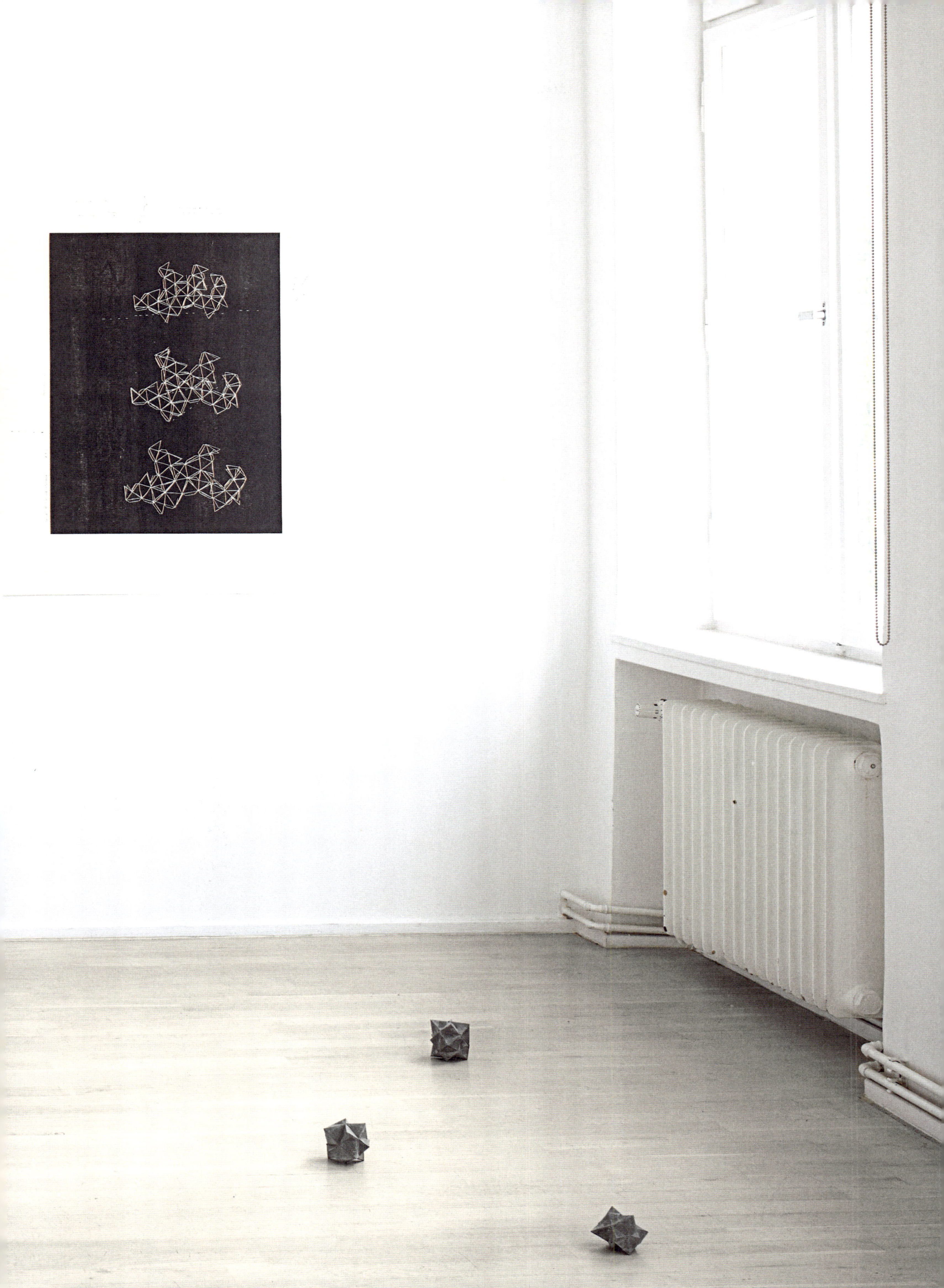

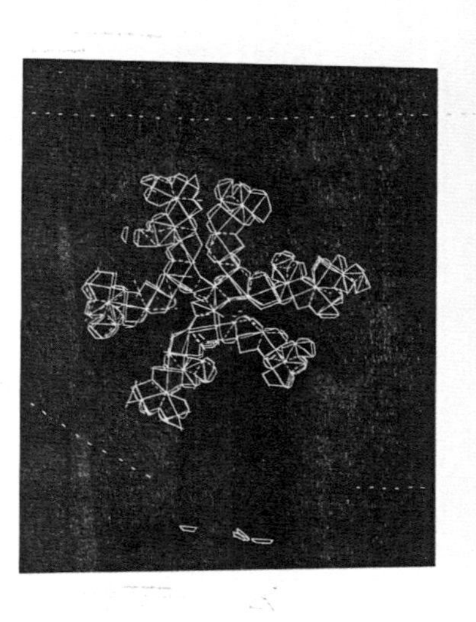
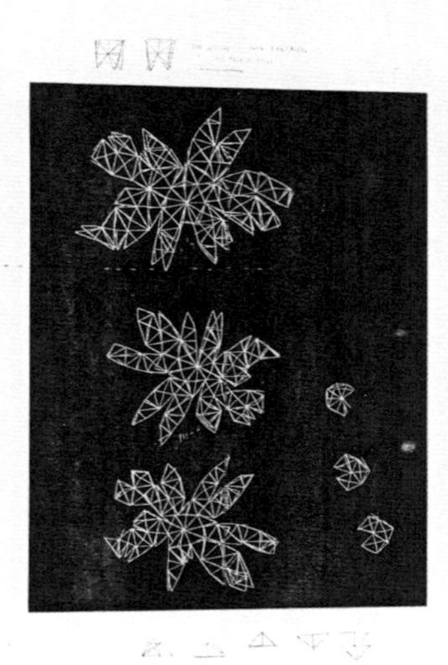
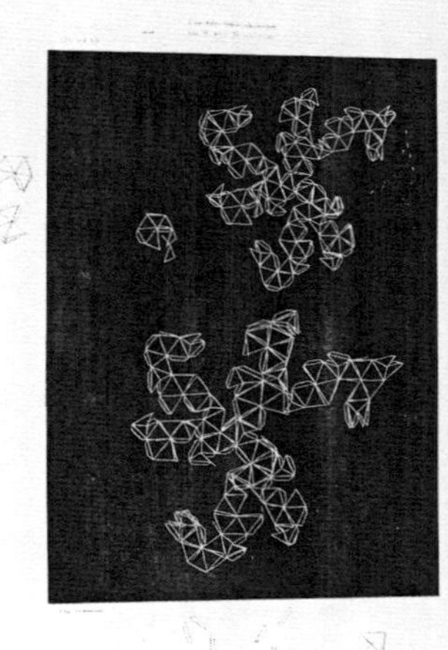
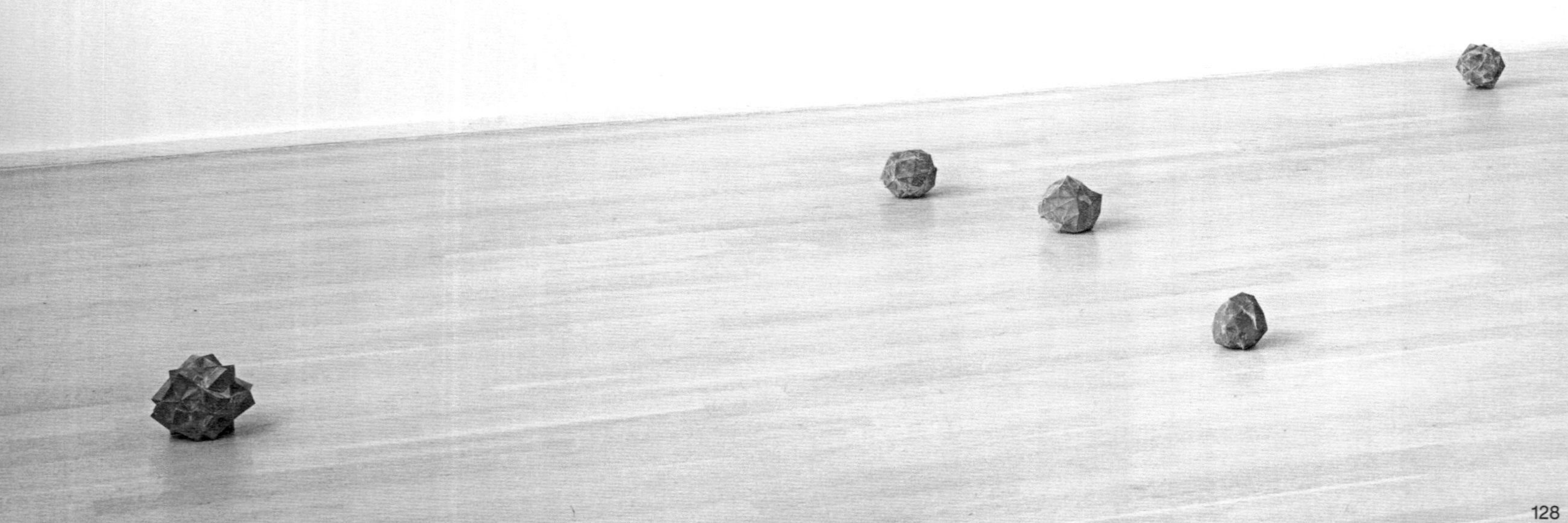

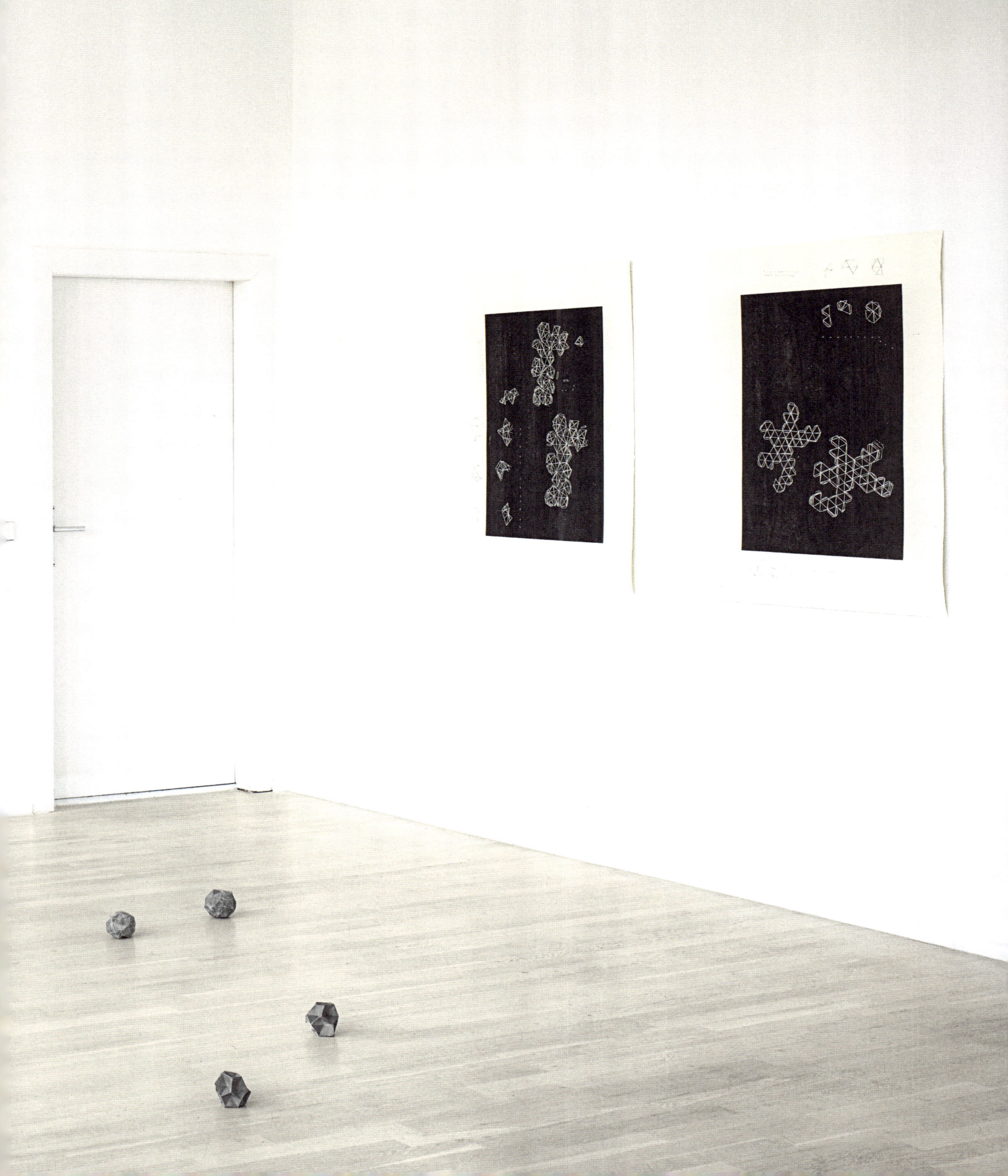

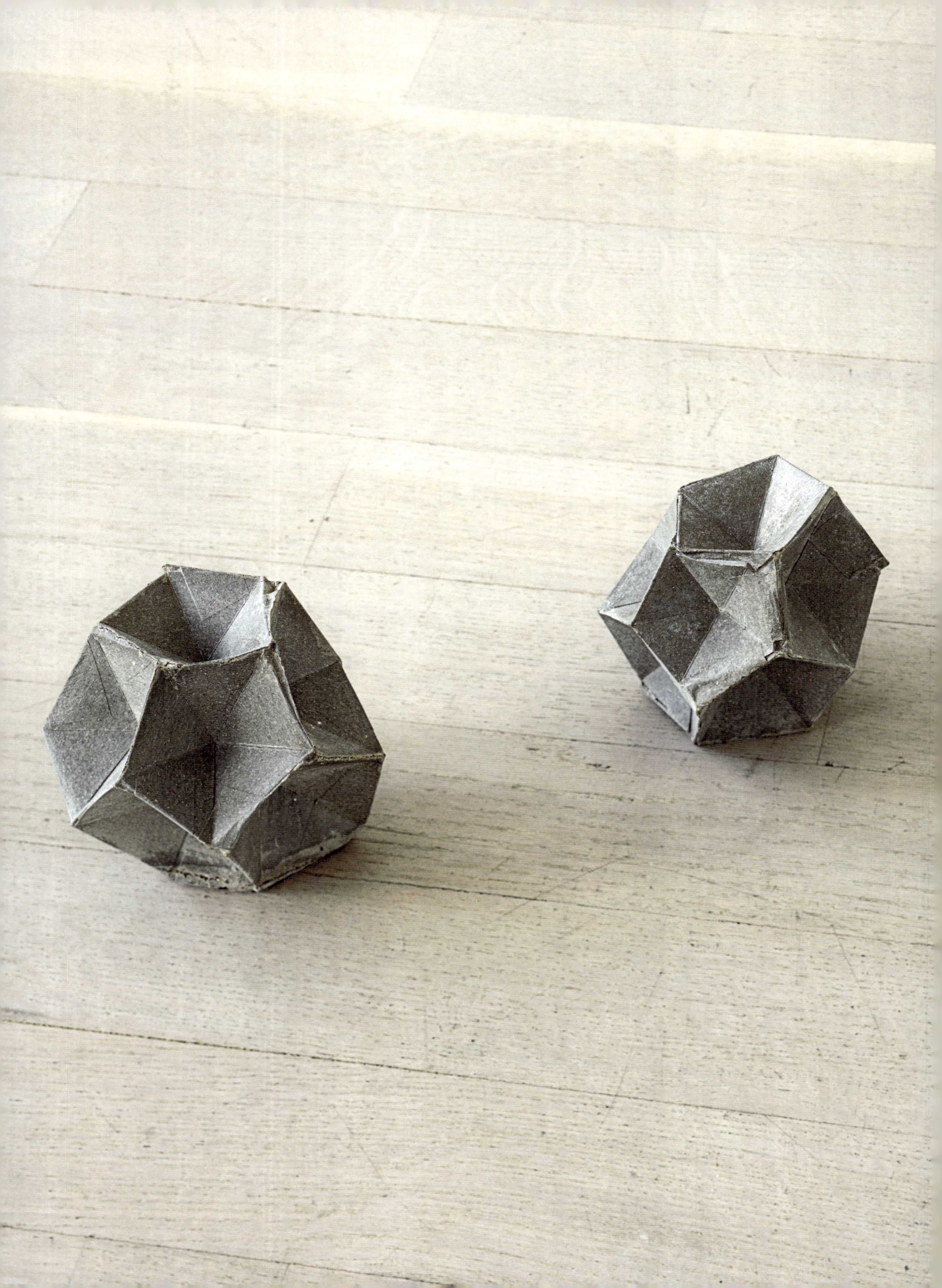

There are no squares in the snow

Some facts about it

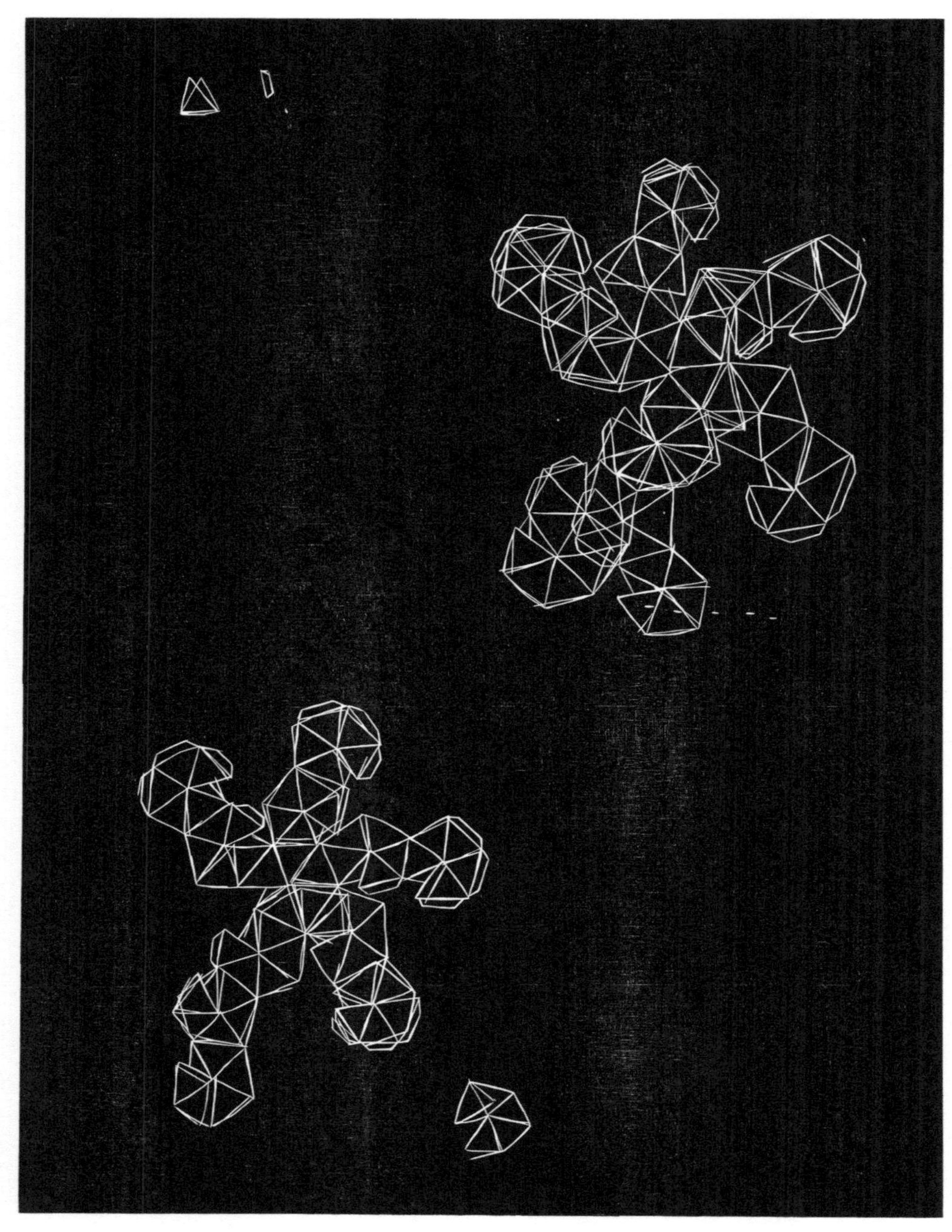

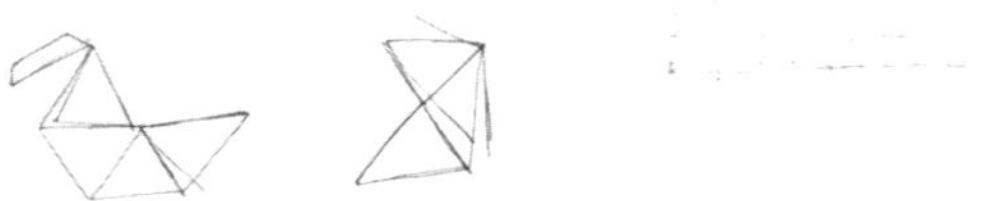

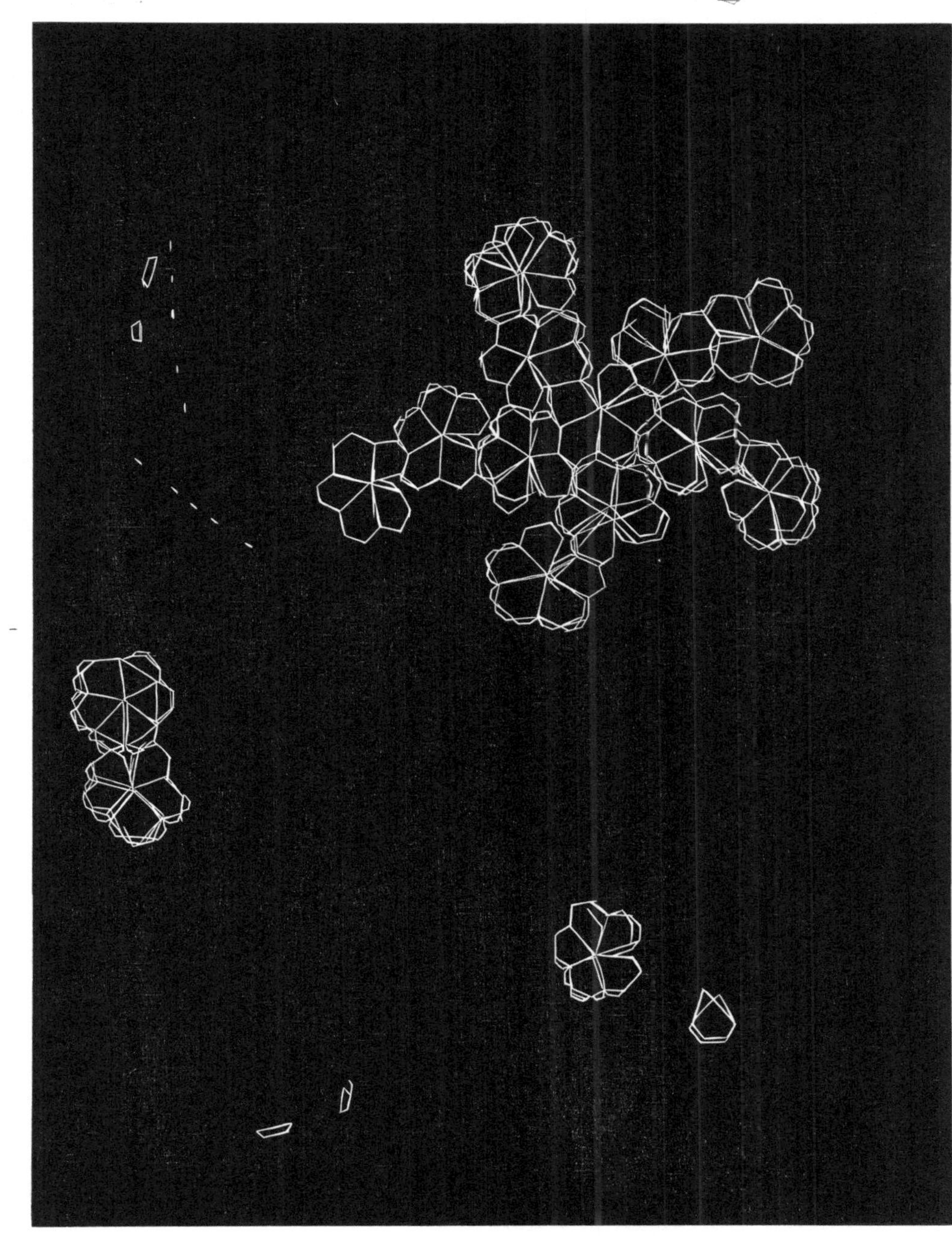

You were talking about appearing about polyhedrons
turning on sides to structure, and
to find other dimensions

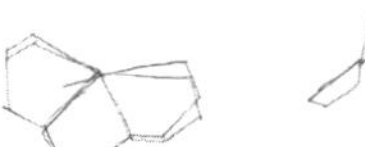

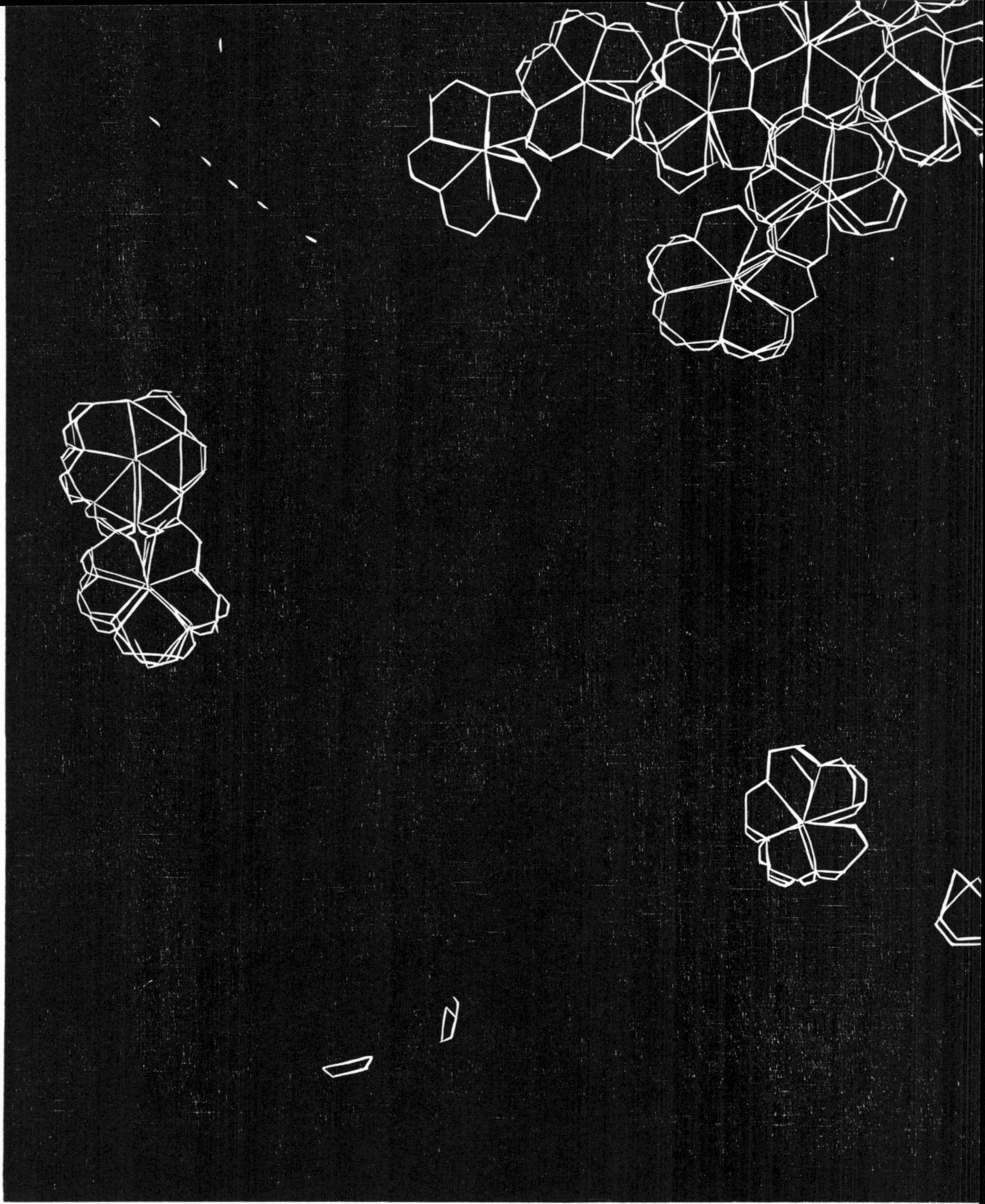

You were talking about appearing, abo
turning on sides to orientate, rest
in four_ other dimensions

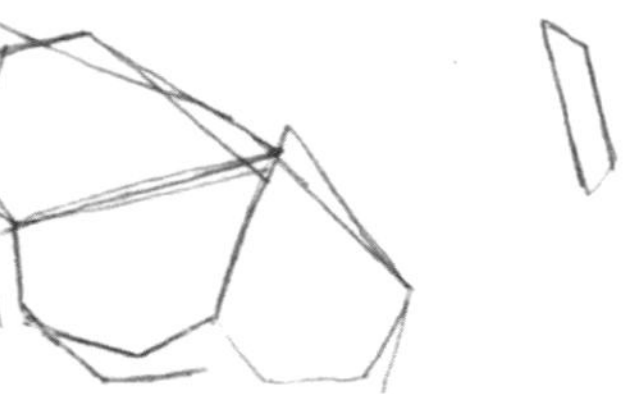

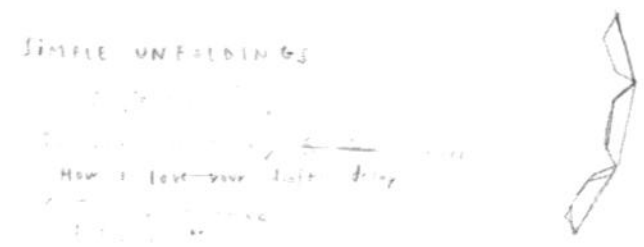

SIMPLE UNFOLDINGS

How i love your luit ...

There are ~~no~~ Rhombs in the spine
there are rhombs in the spine

Compound of cube and octahedron   A B C

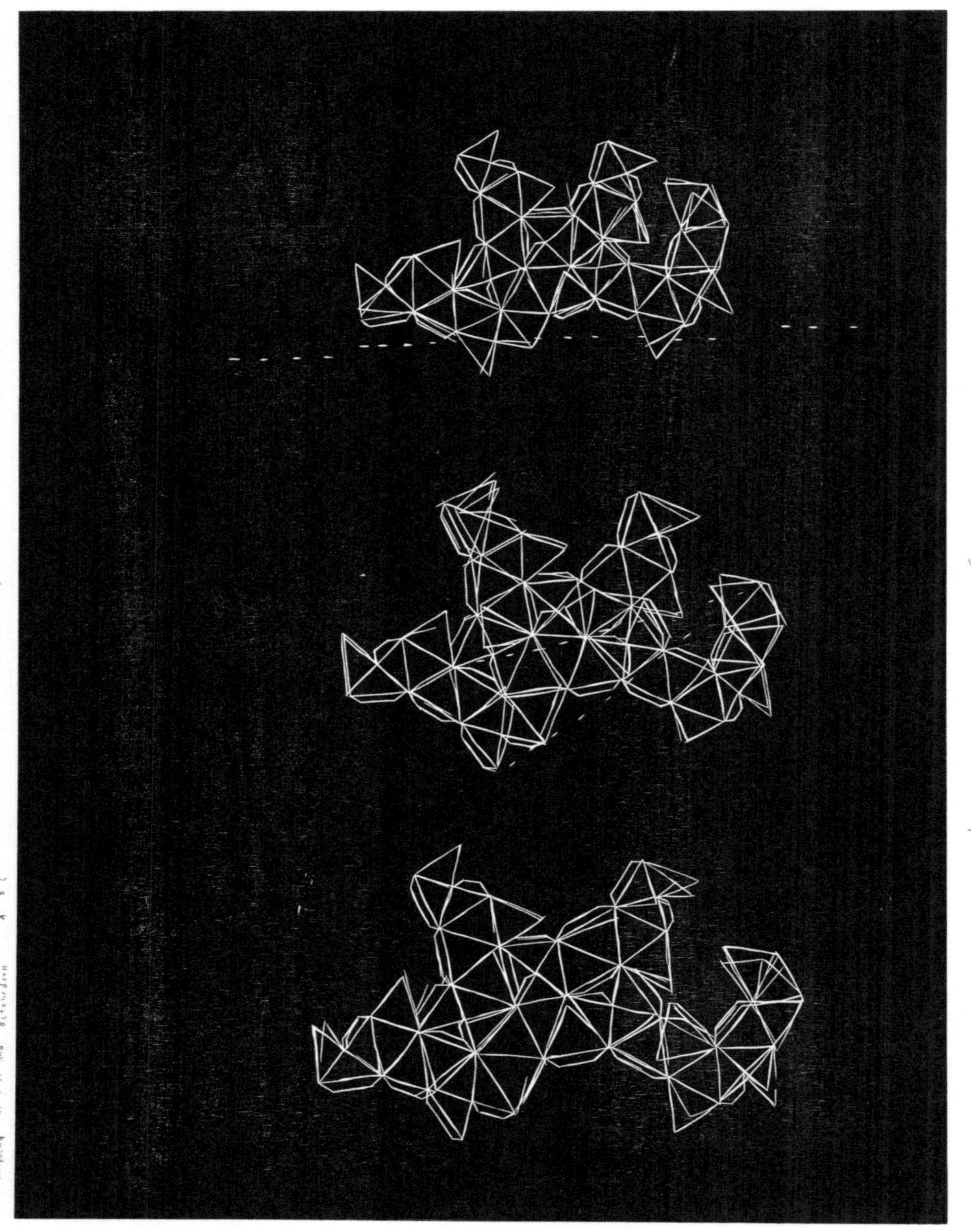

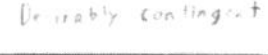
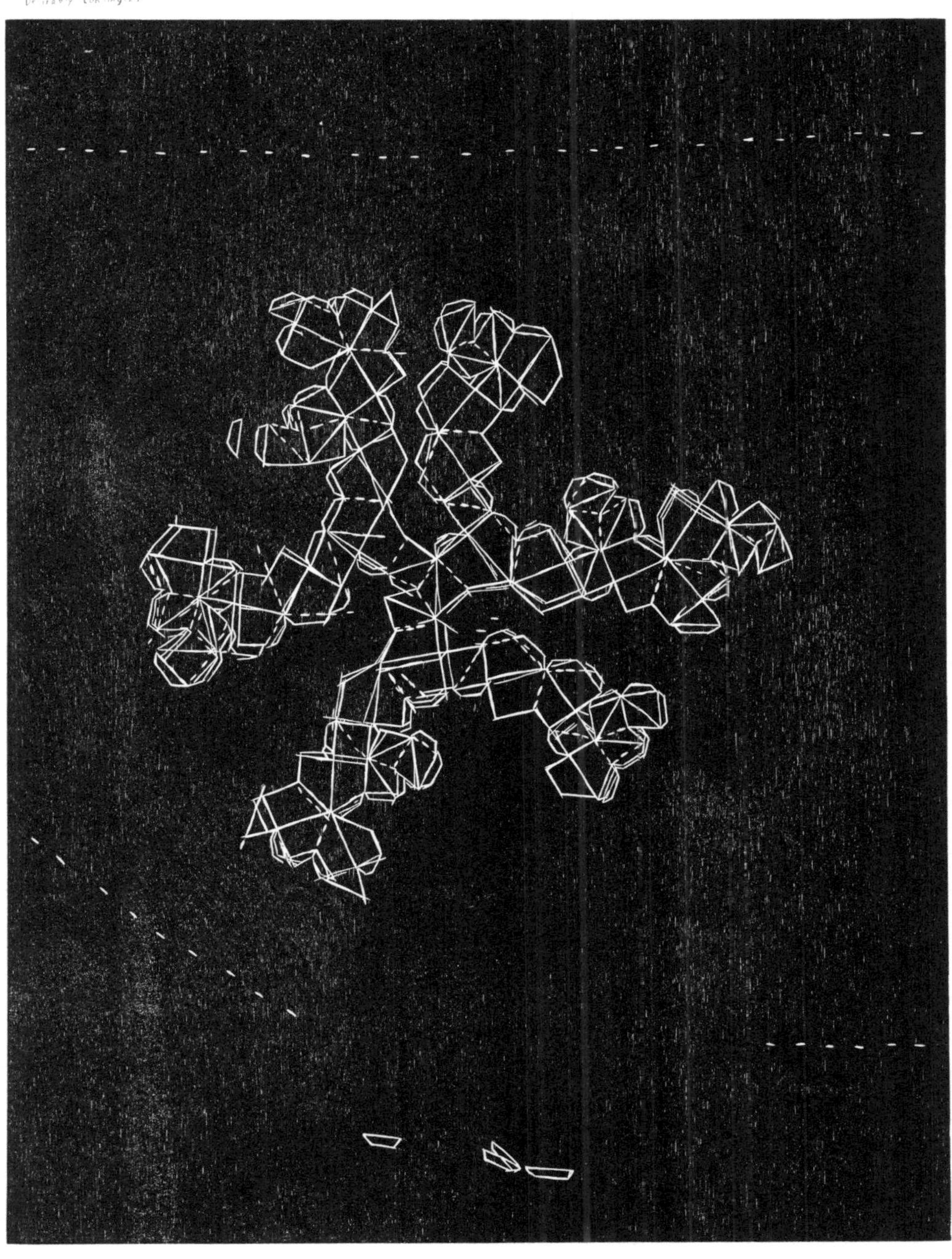
Desirably contingent

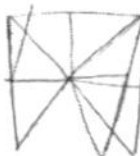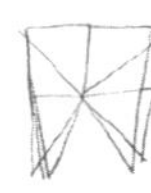
Solid fantasies   SOLID FANTASIES
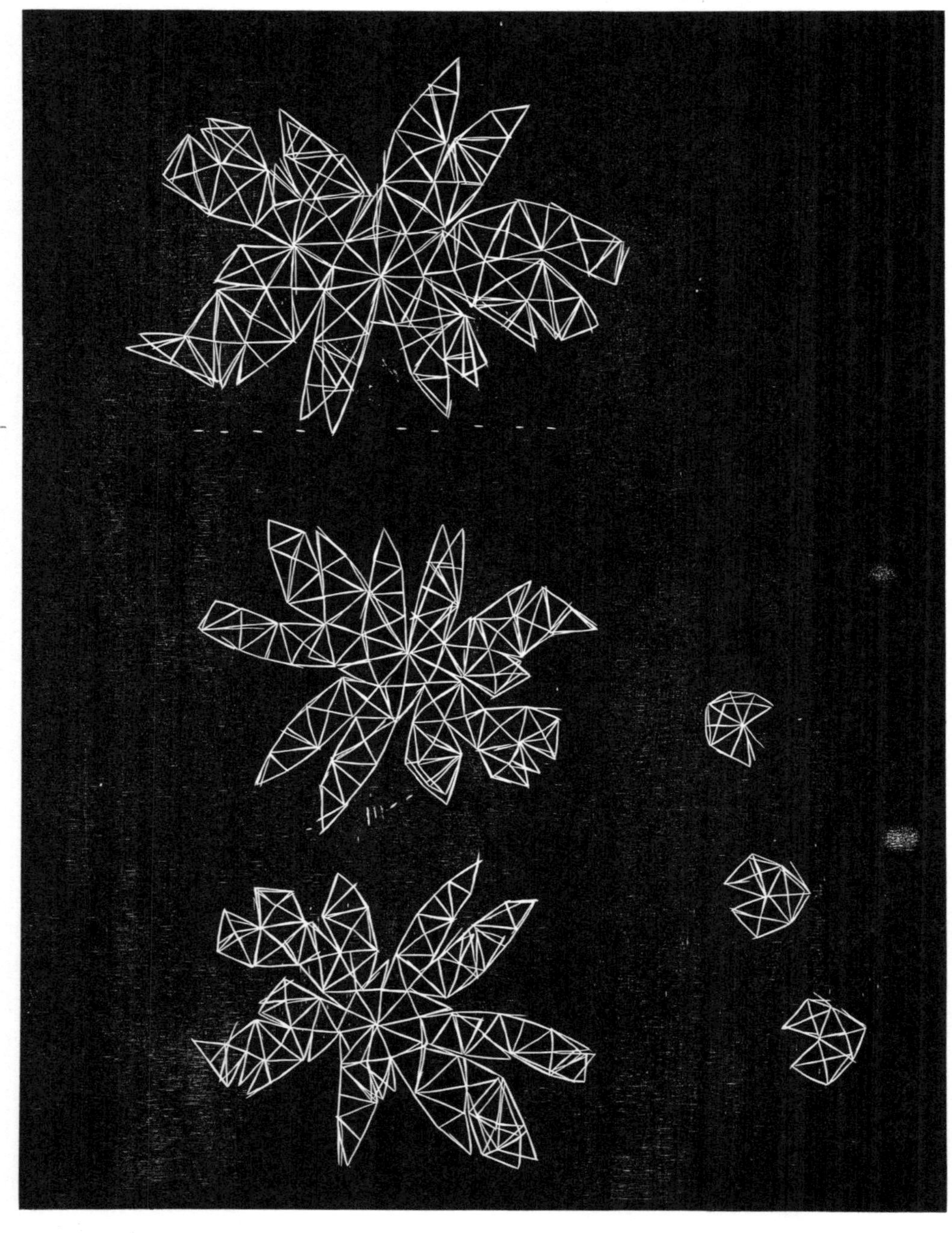
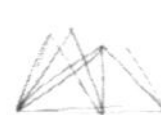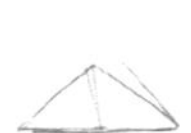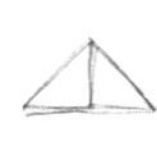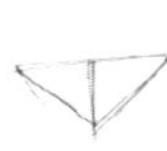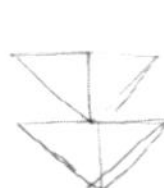

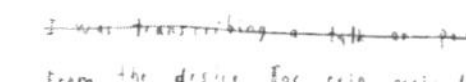

I was transcribing a talk on poem
that   from the desire for reip arrivals

(ut and fold

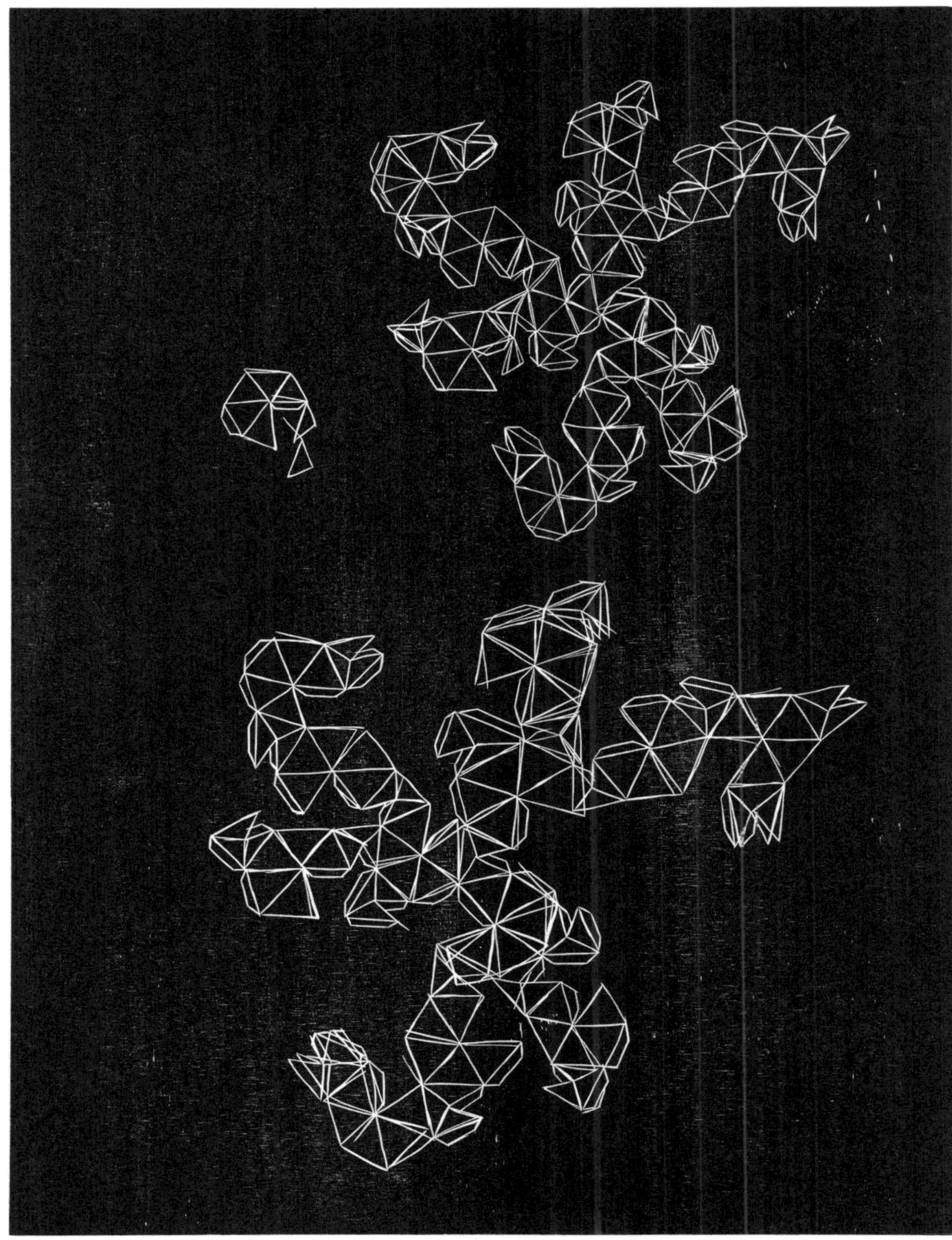

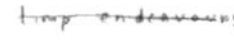

tiny endeavours

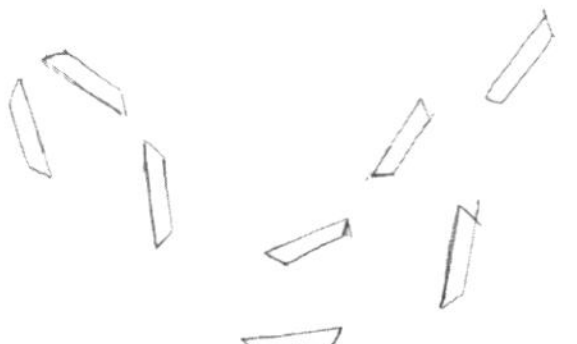

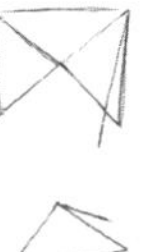

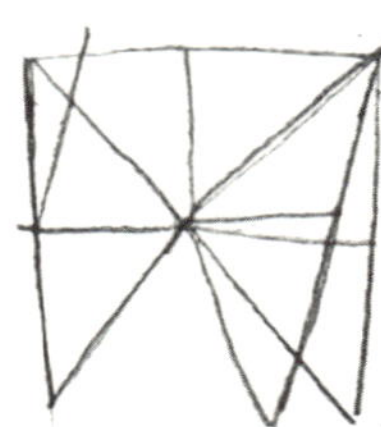
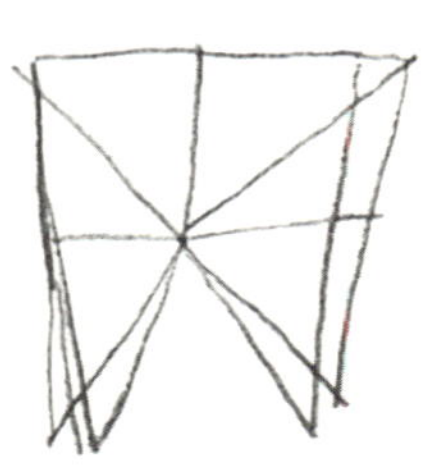

Solid fan
in

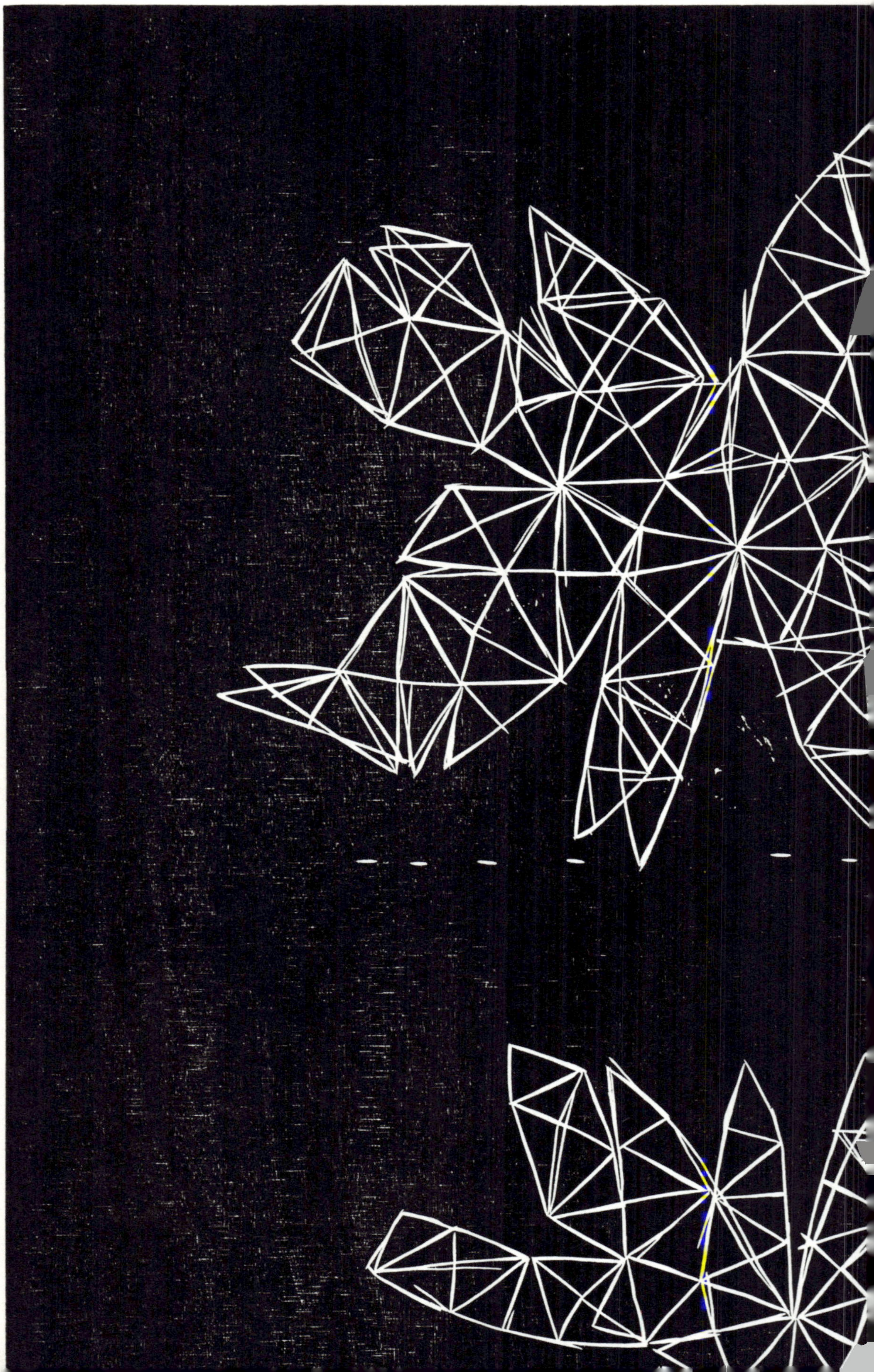

SOLID FANTASIES

for Strings

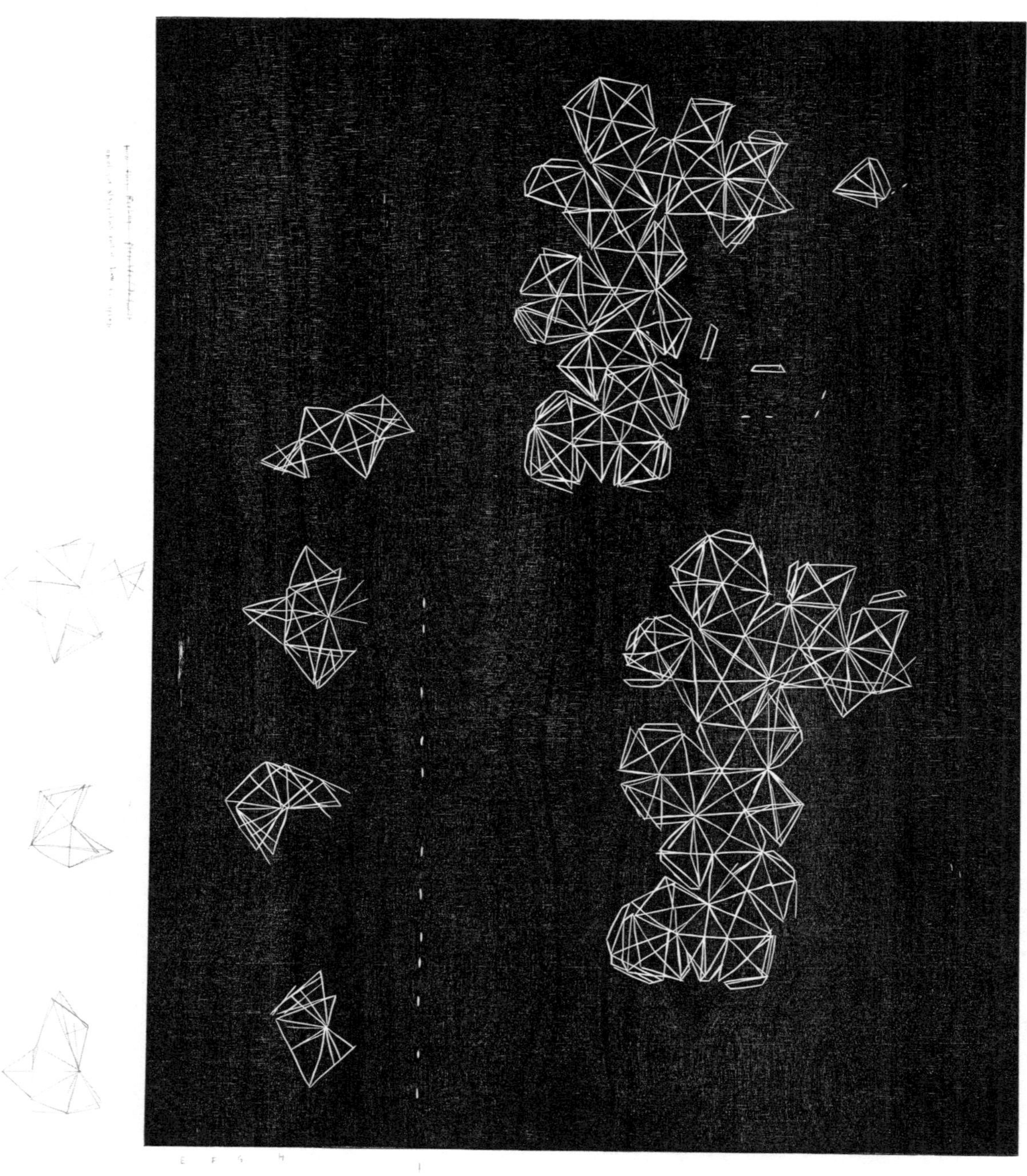

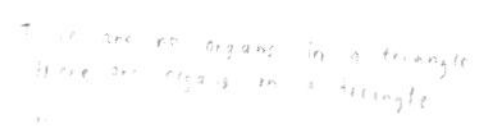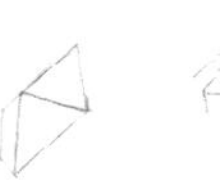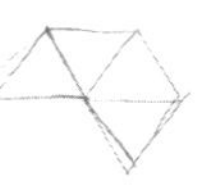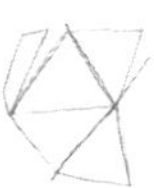

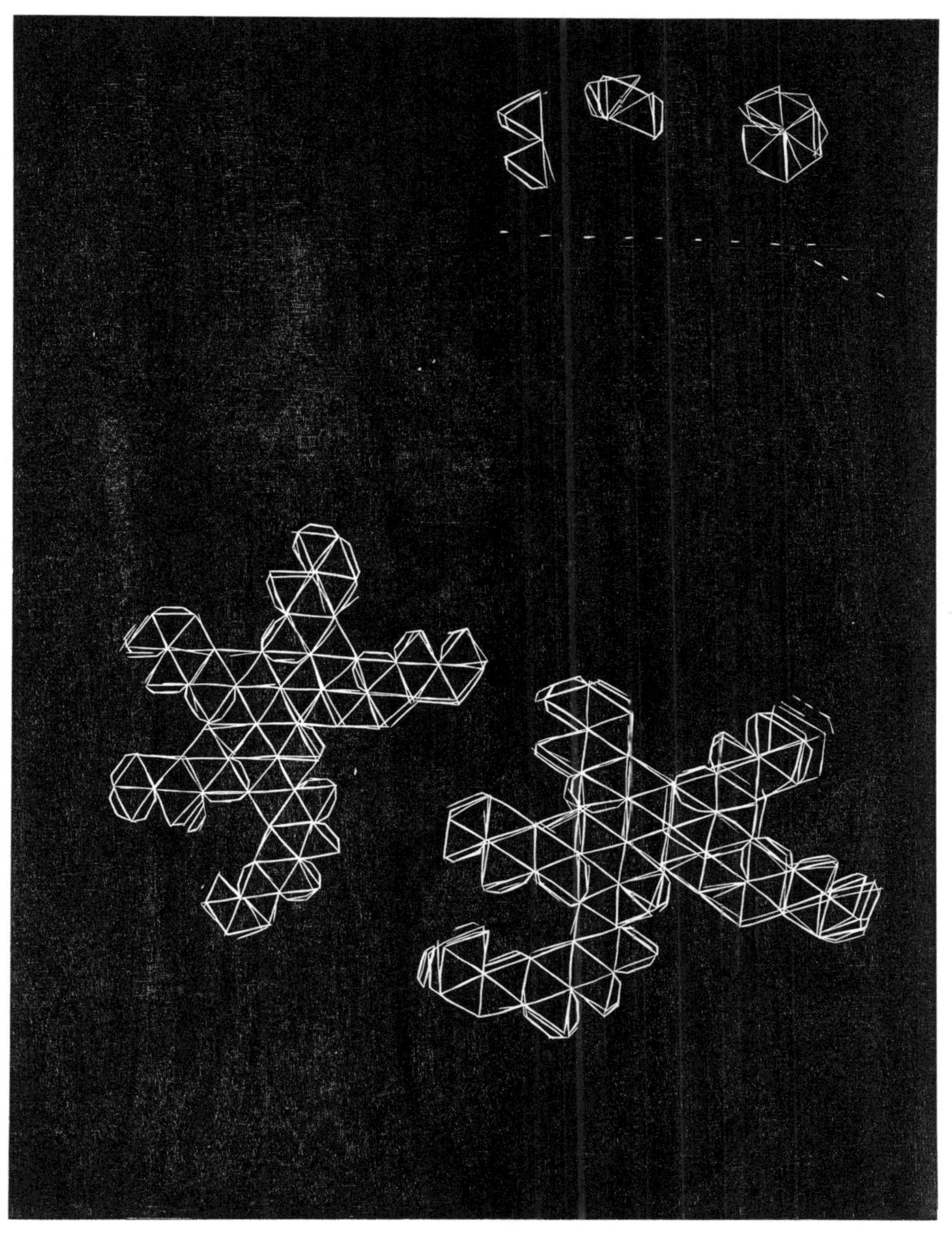

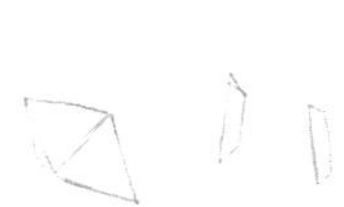

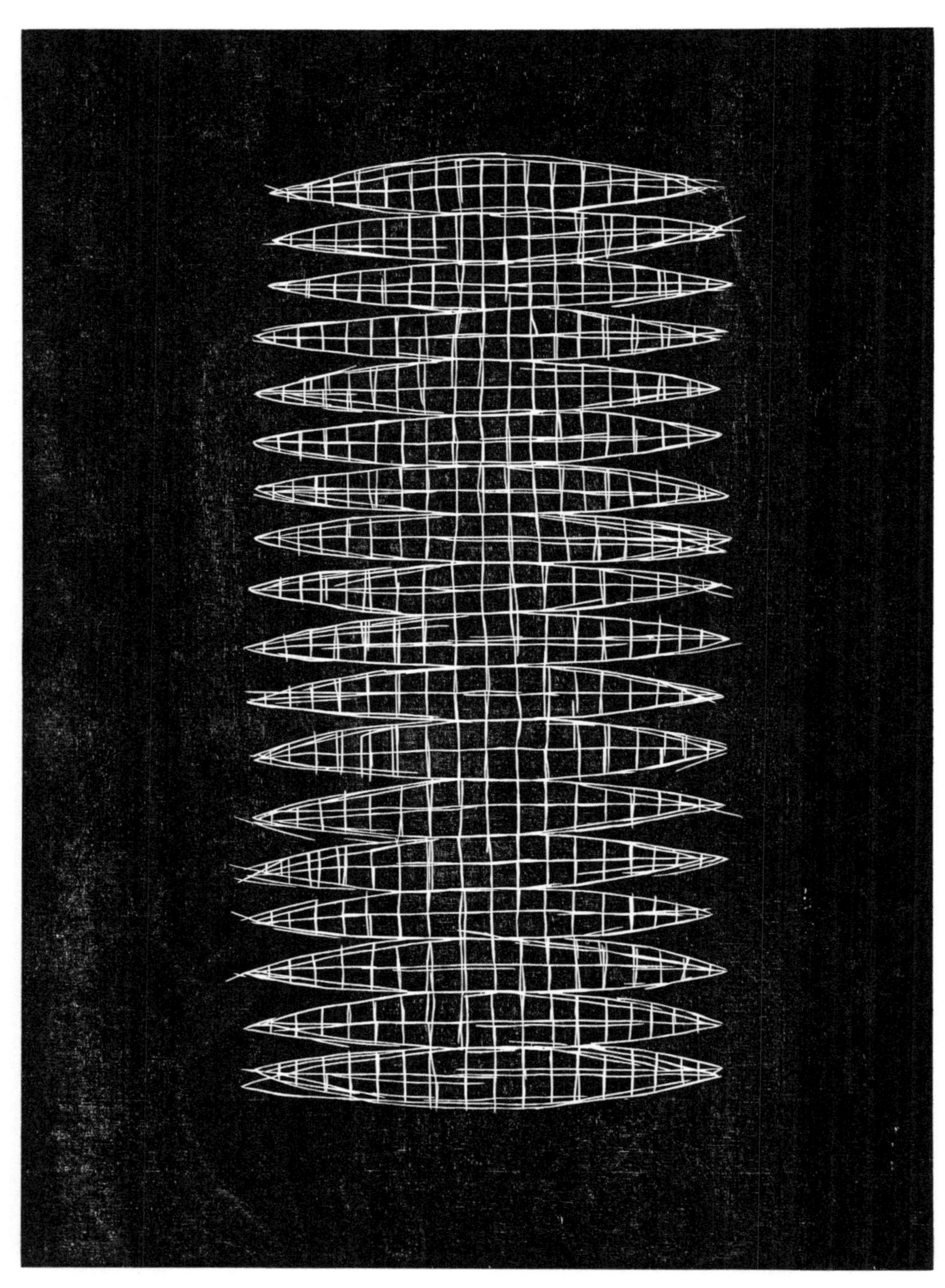

Companions, 2017

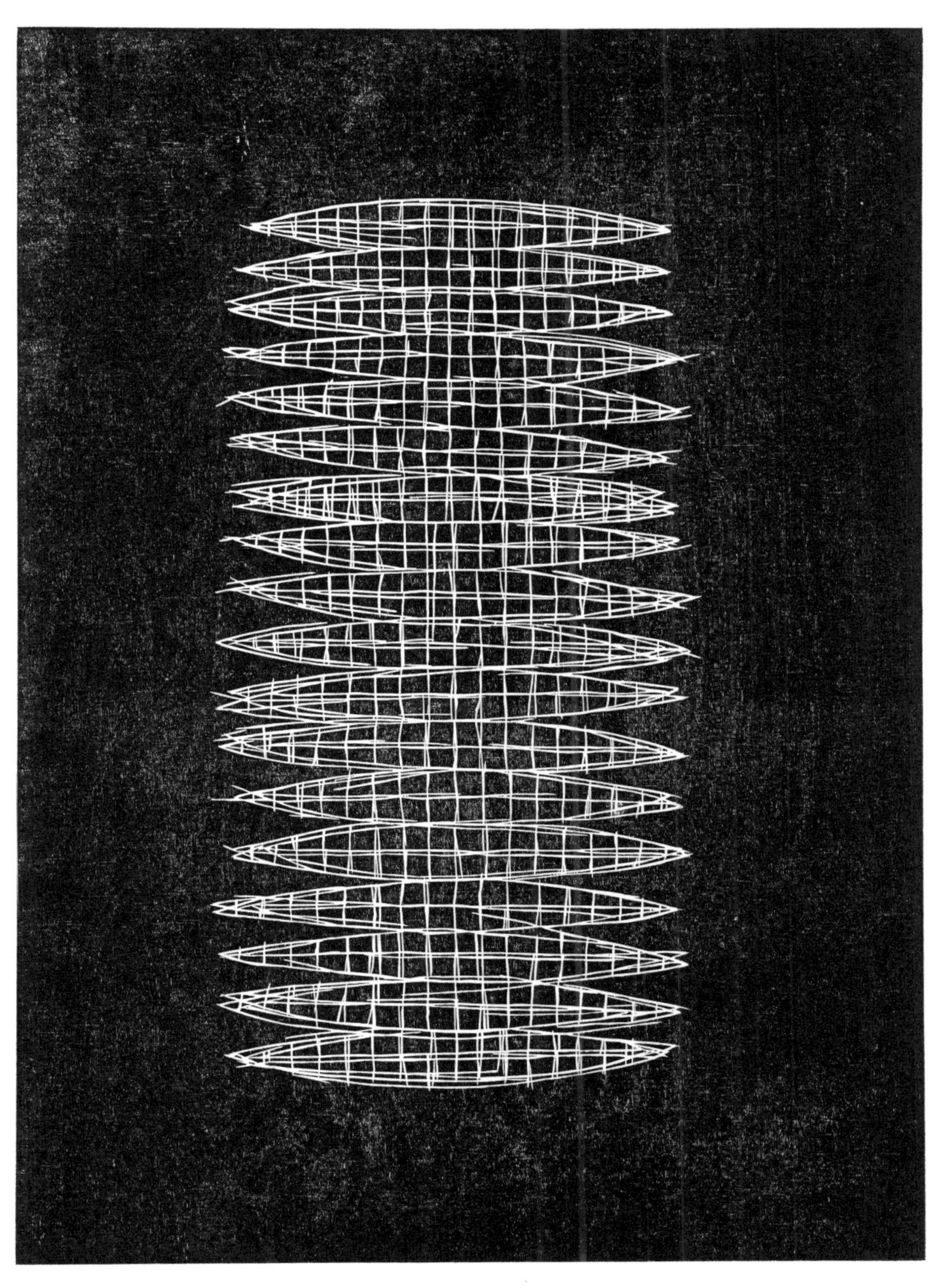

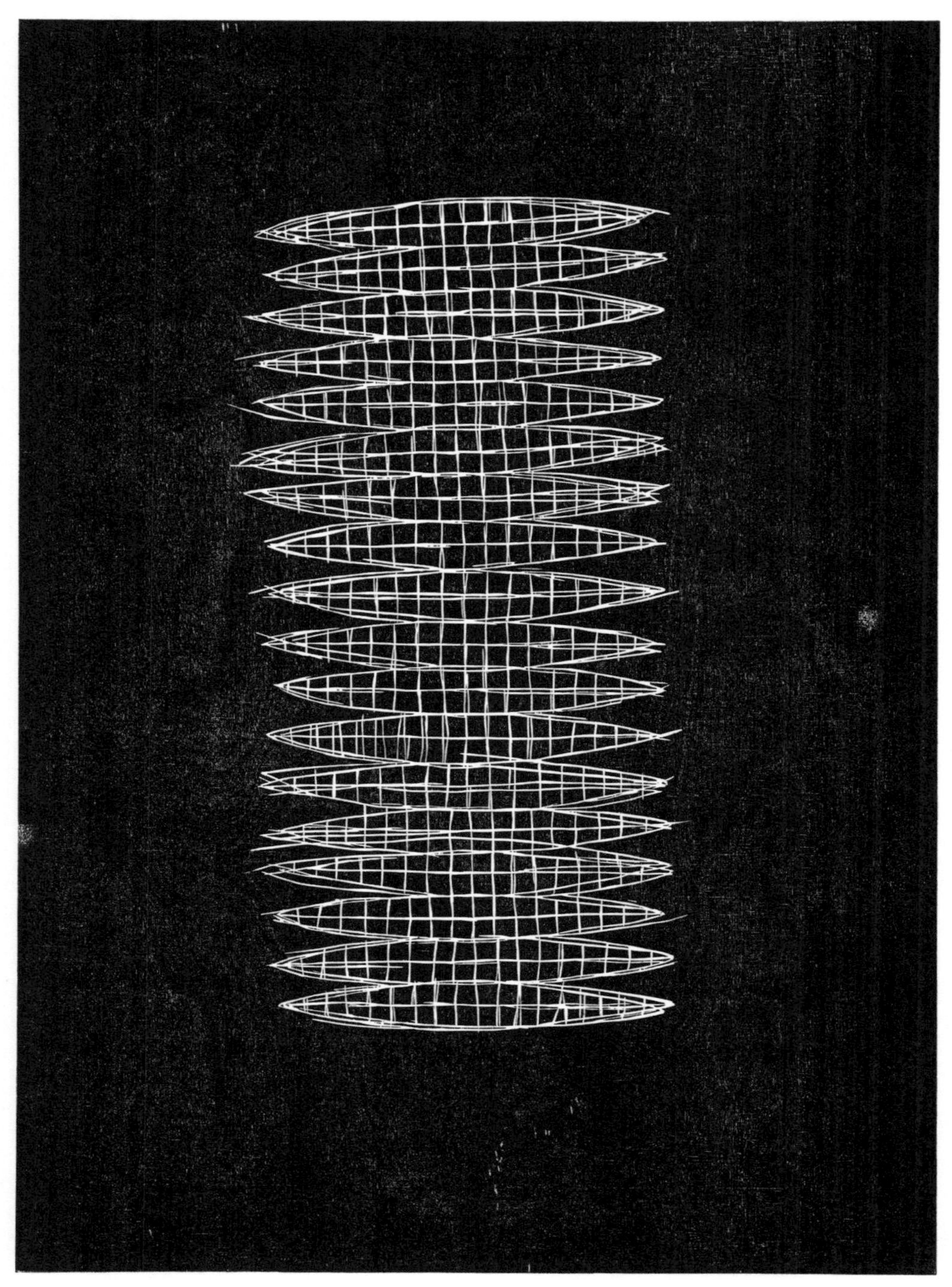

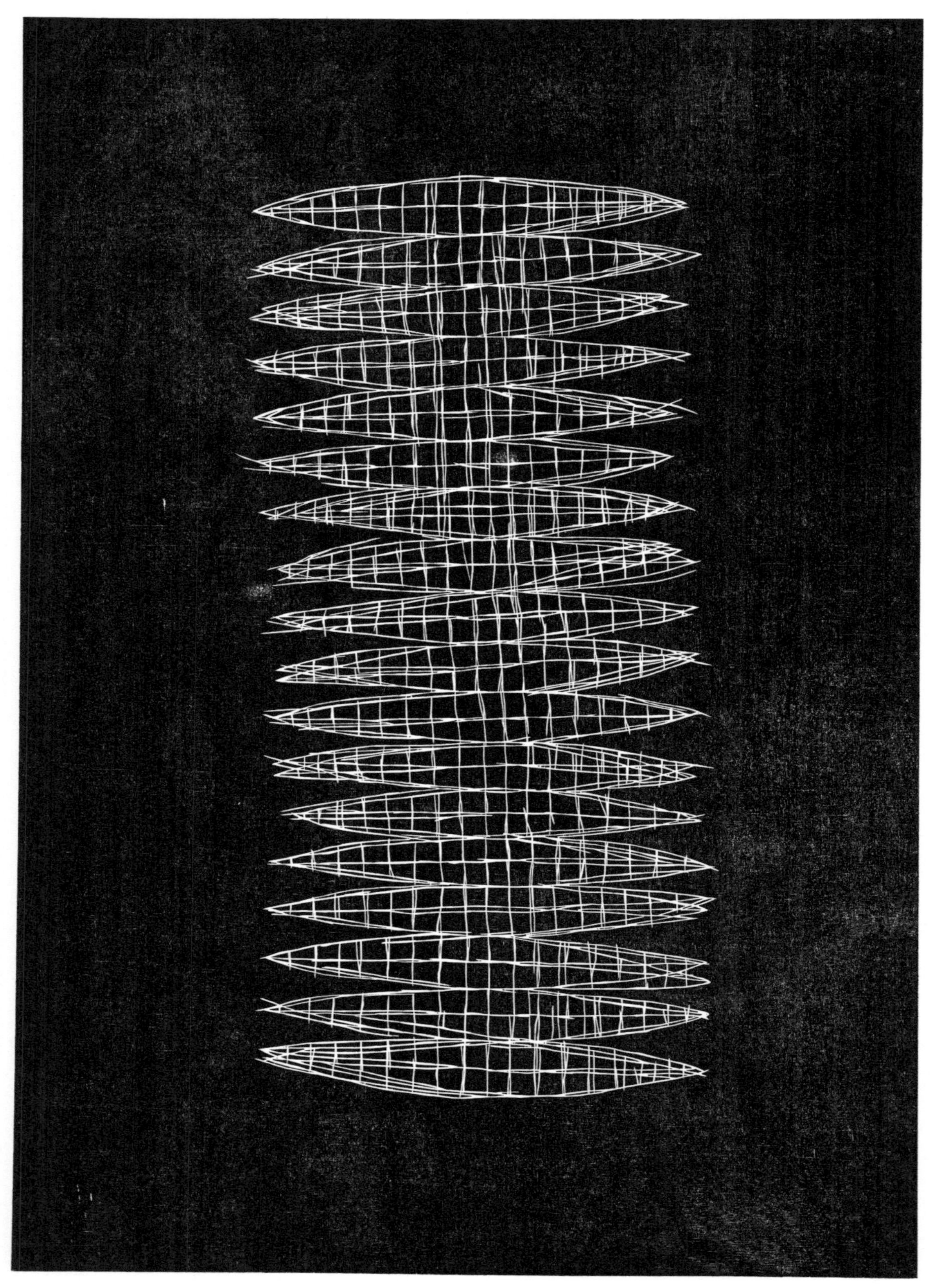

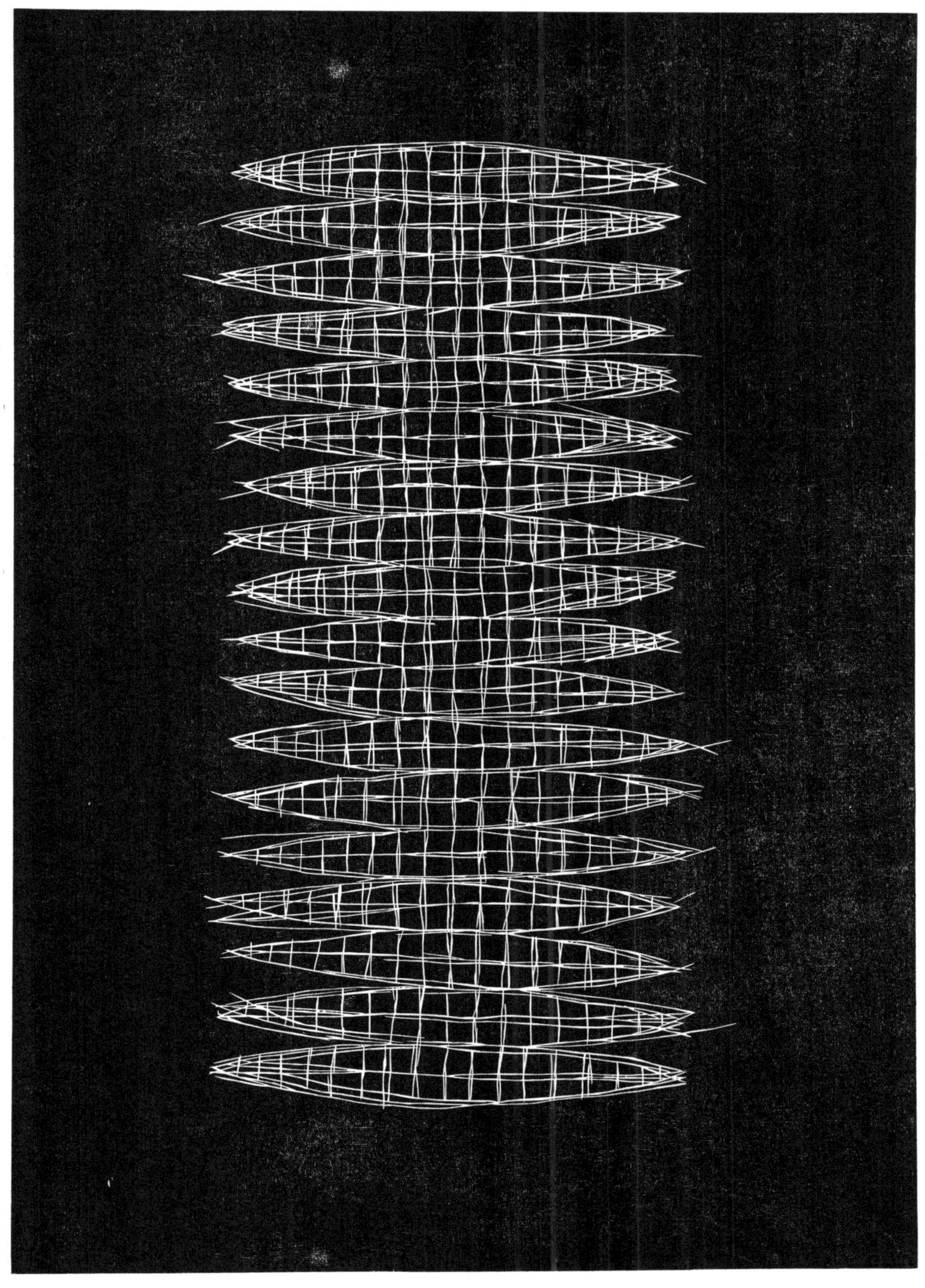

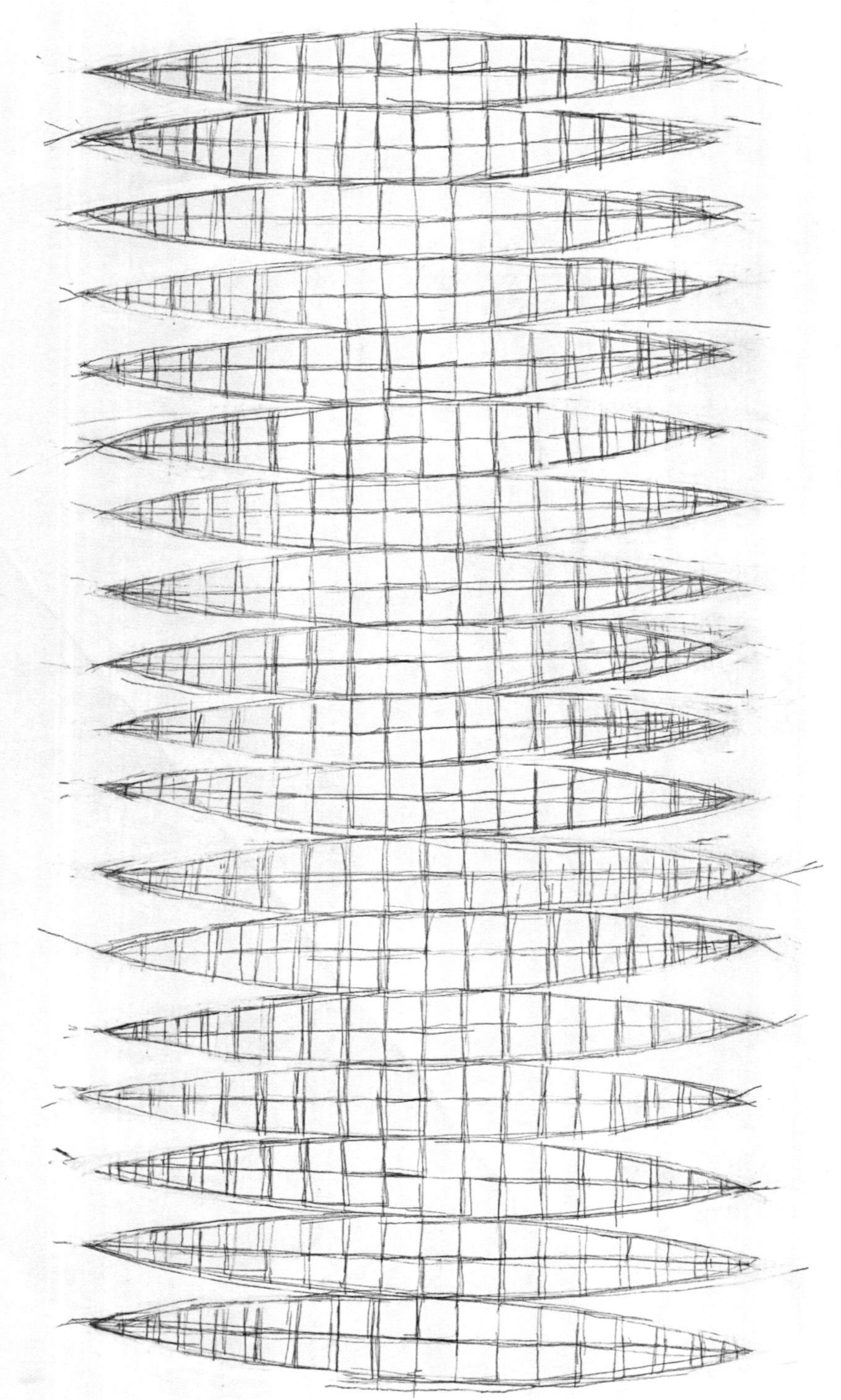

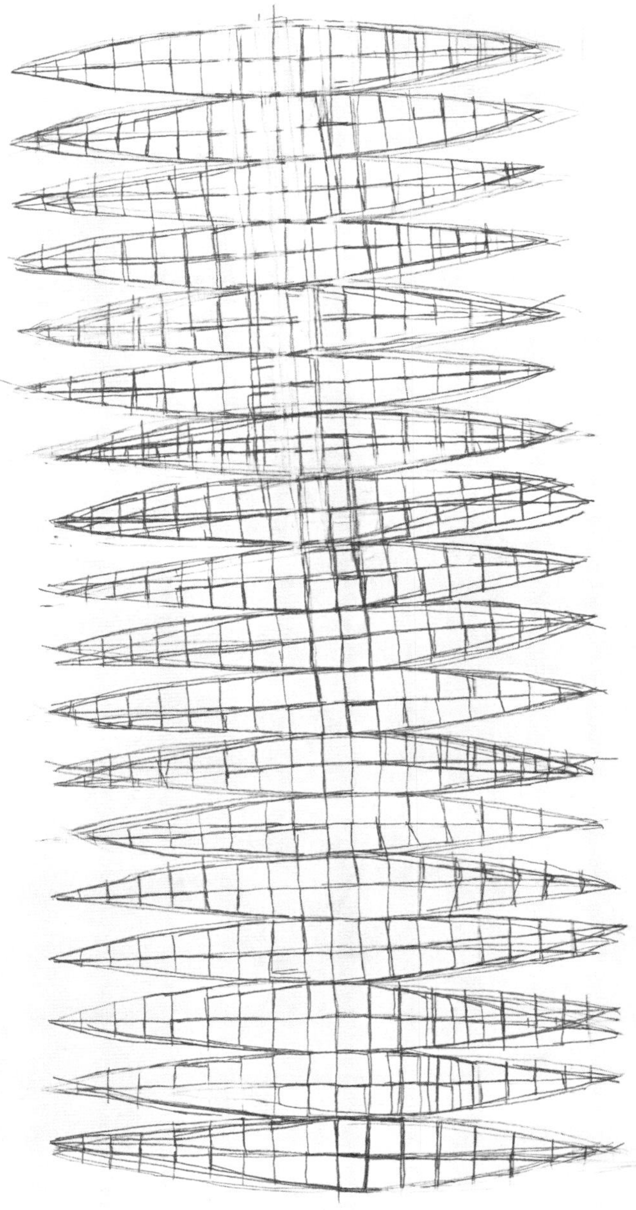

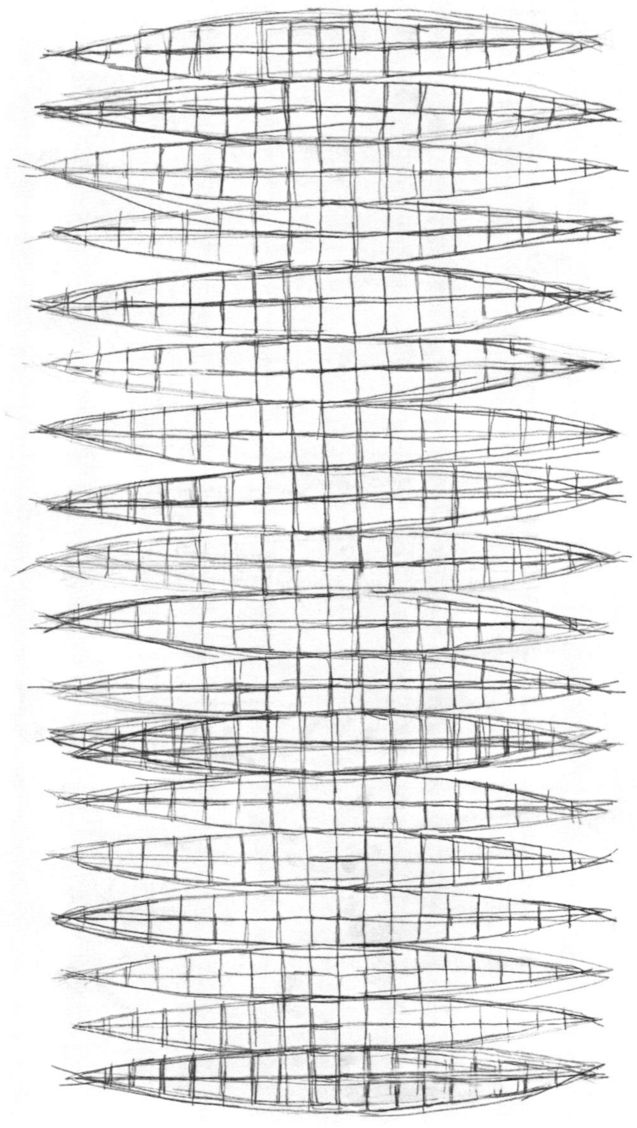

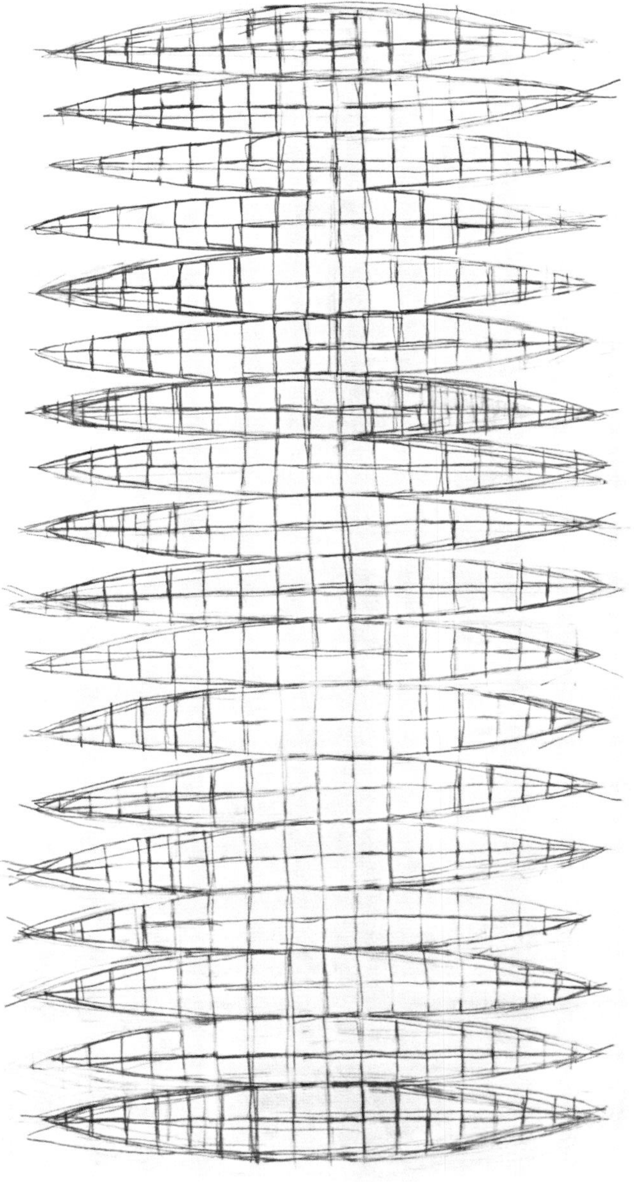

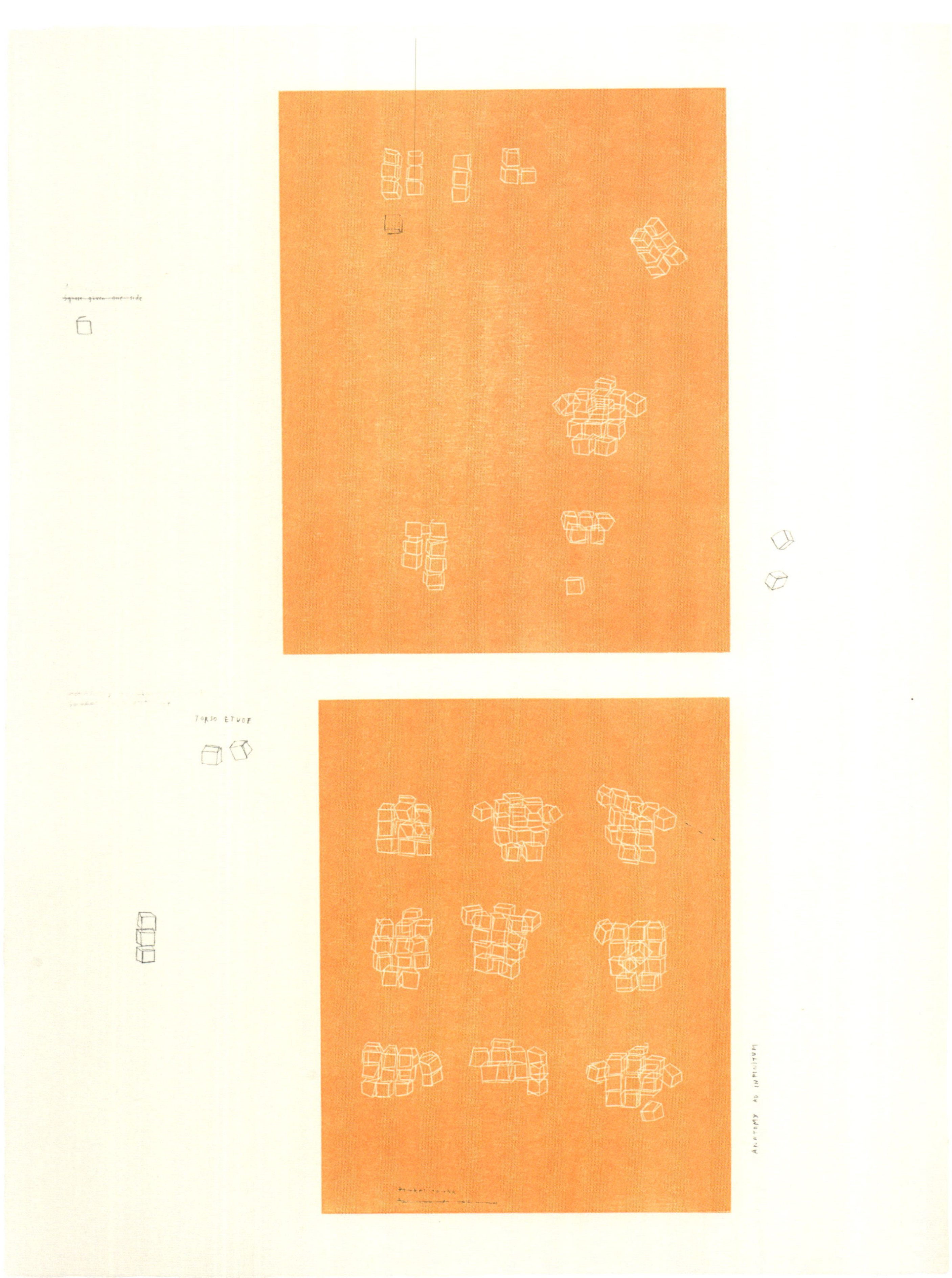

Contraposer (Torso Etude), 2018

Contraposer (Back-facing), 2018

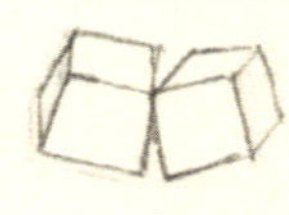
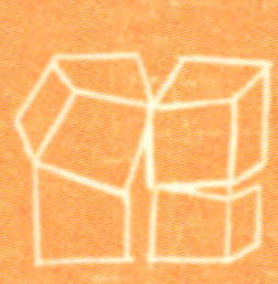
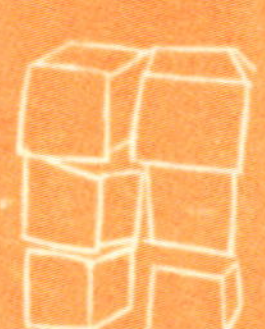
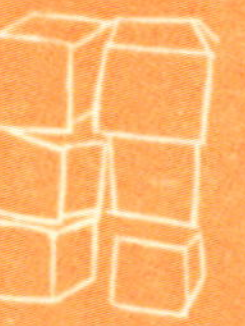
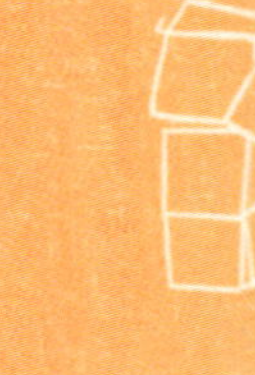
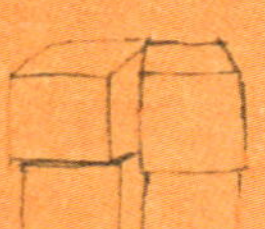

ANATOMY AS EXPLANATION
ANATOMY IS NOT THERE

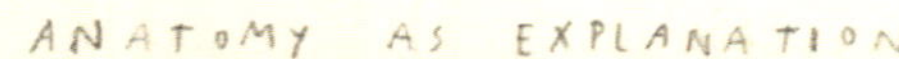
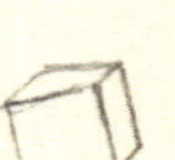
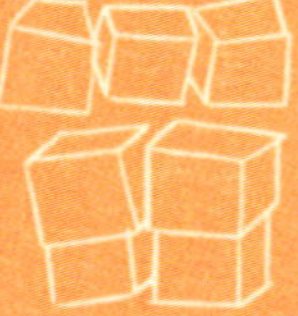
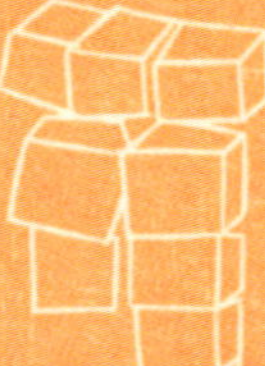
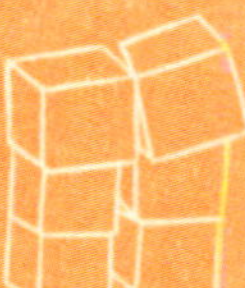
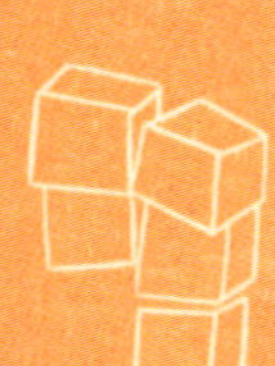
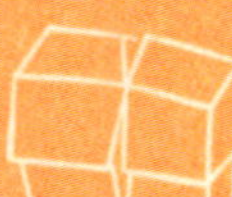

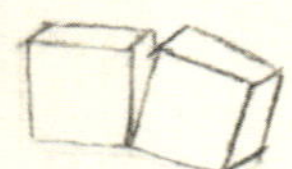

Slow BUTT NO CONTRAPOSER

A   B

Back-facing

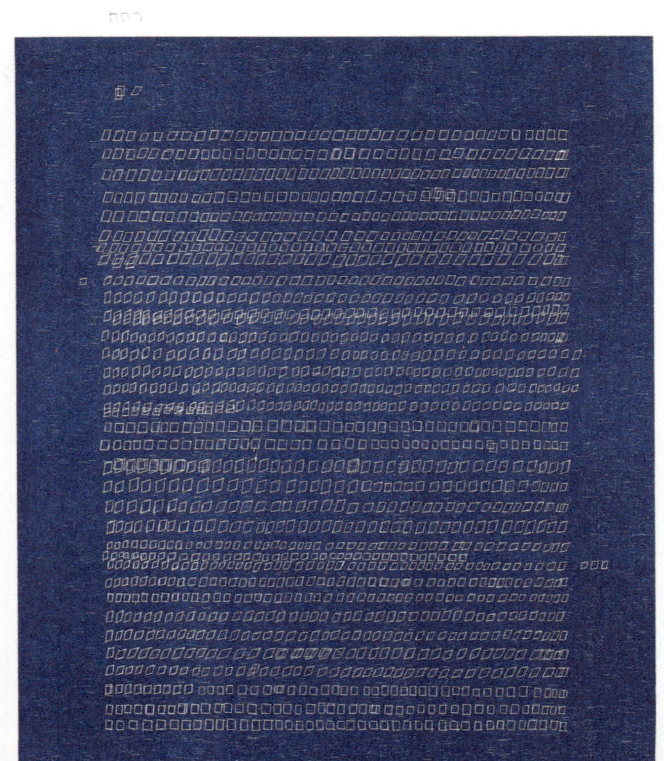

Woodbeds, brimming, 2019

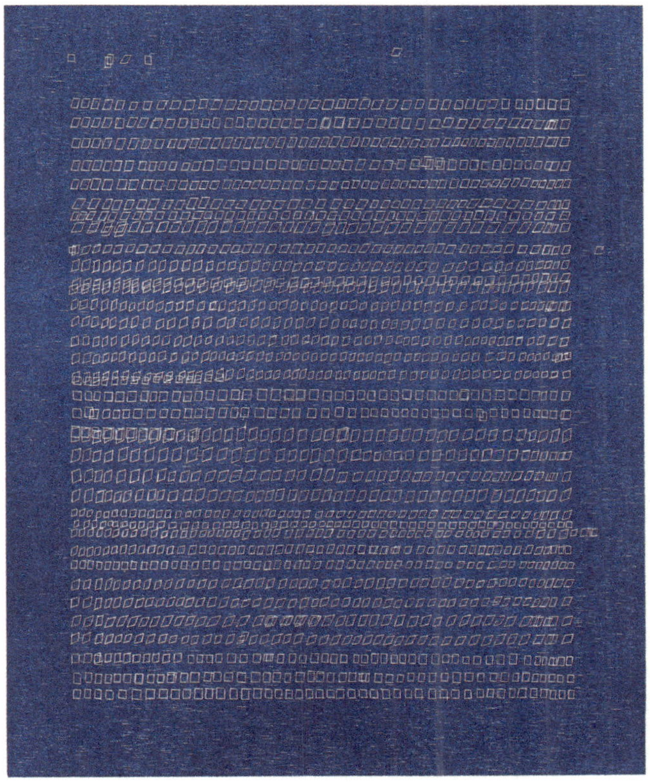

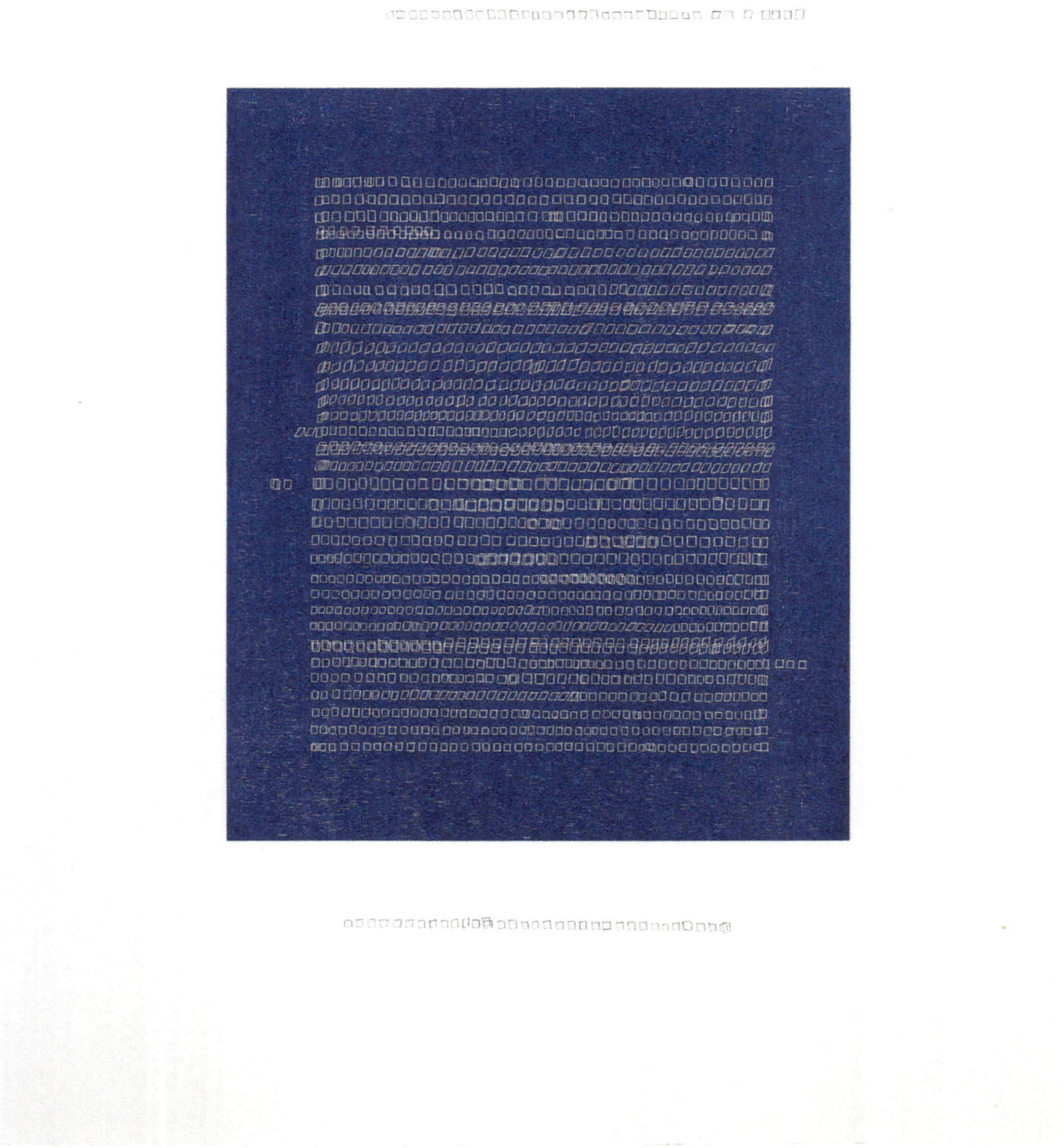

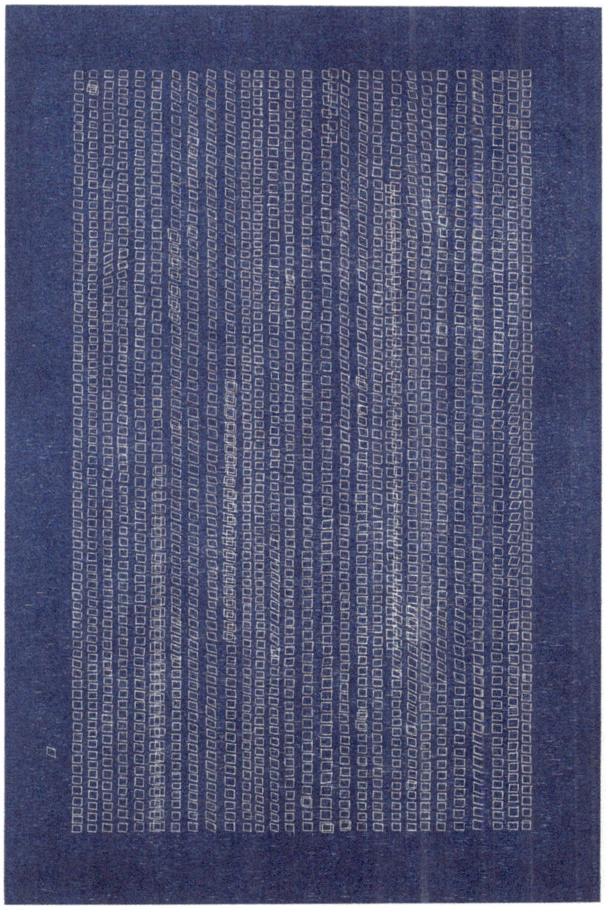

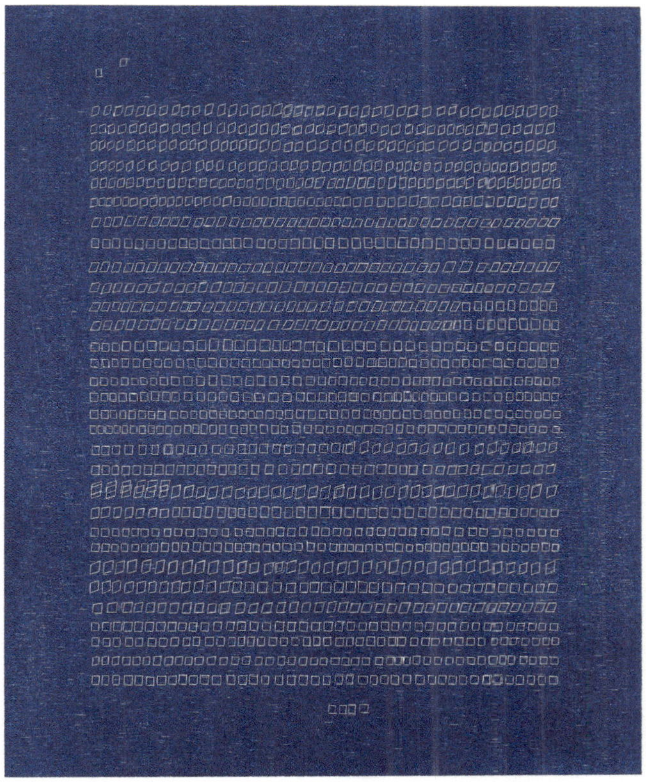

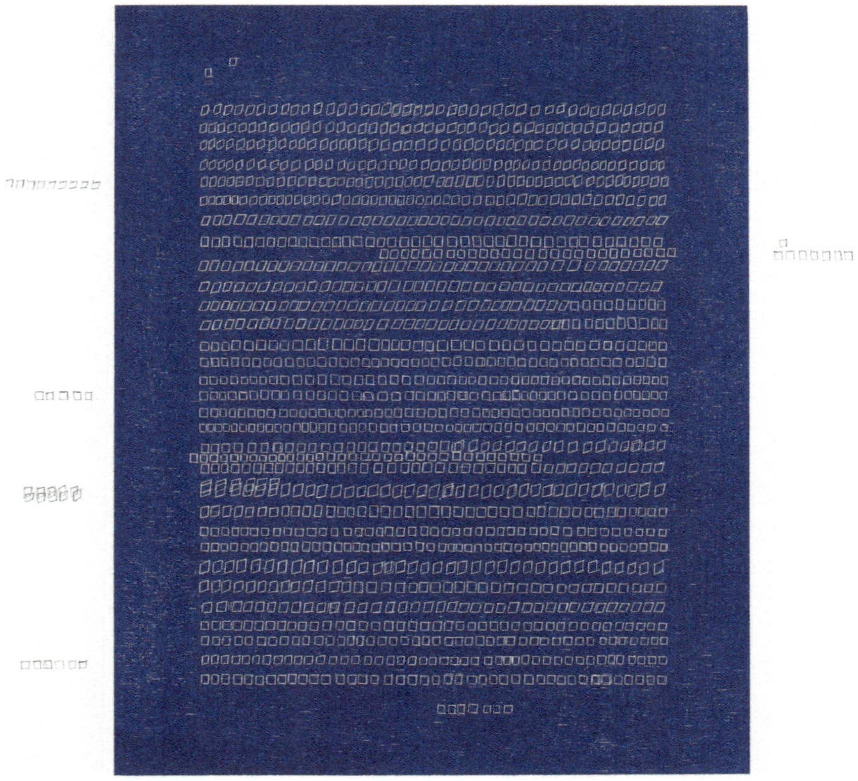

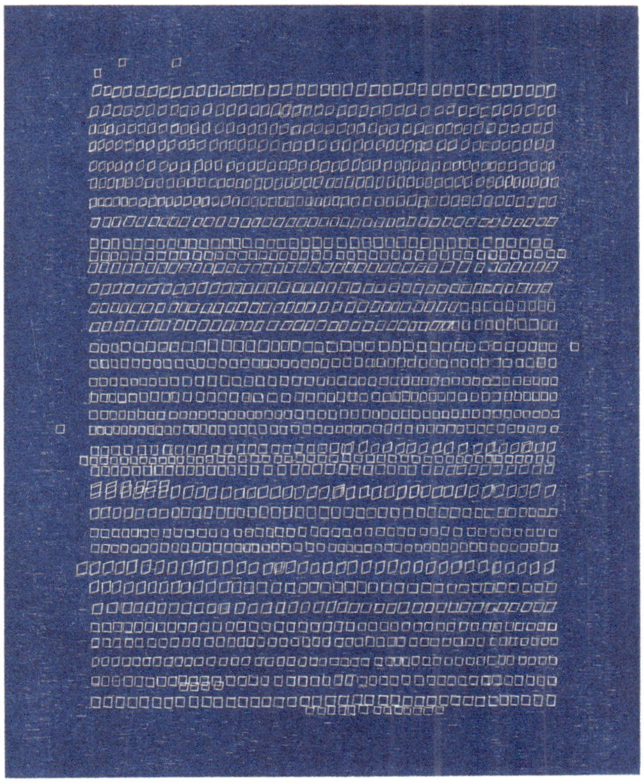

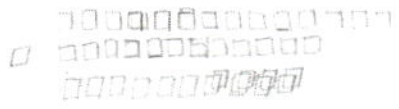

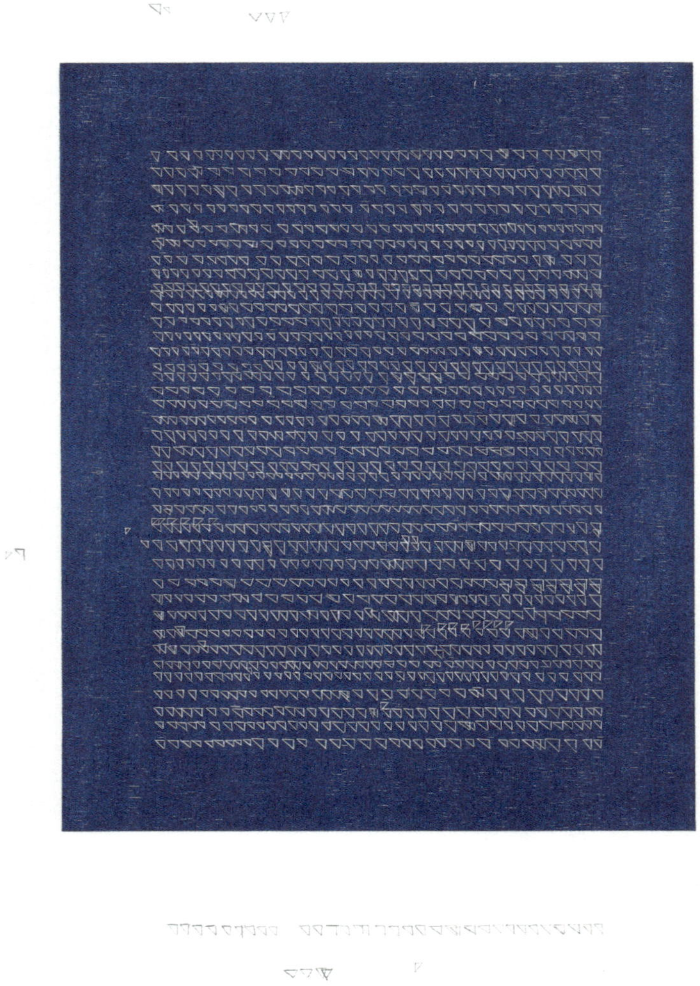

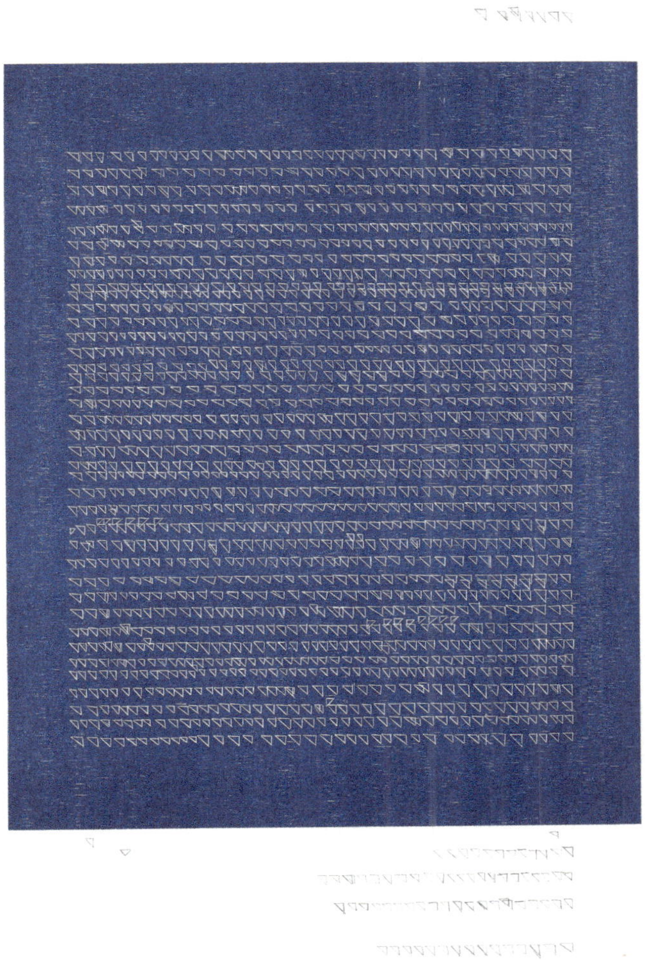

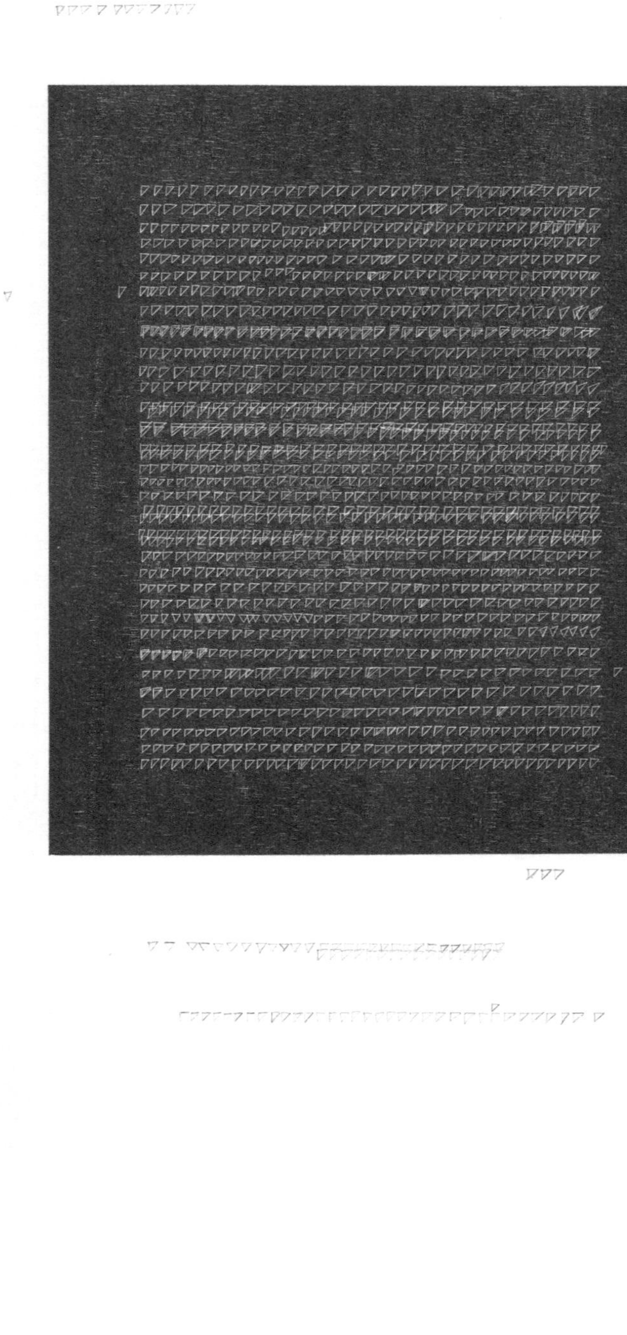

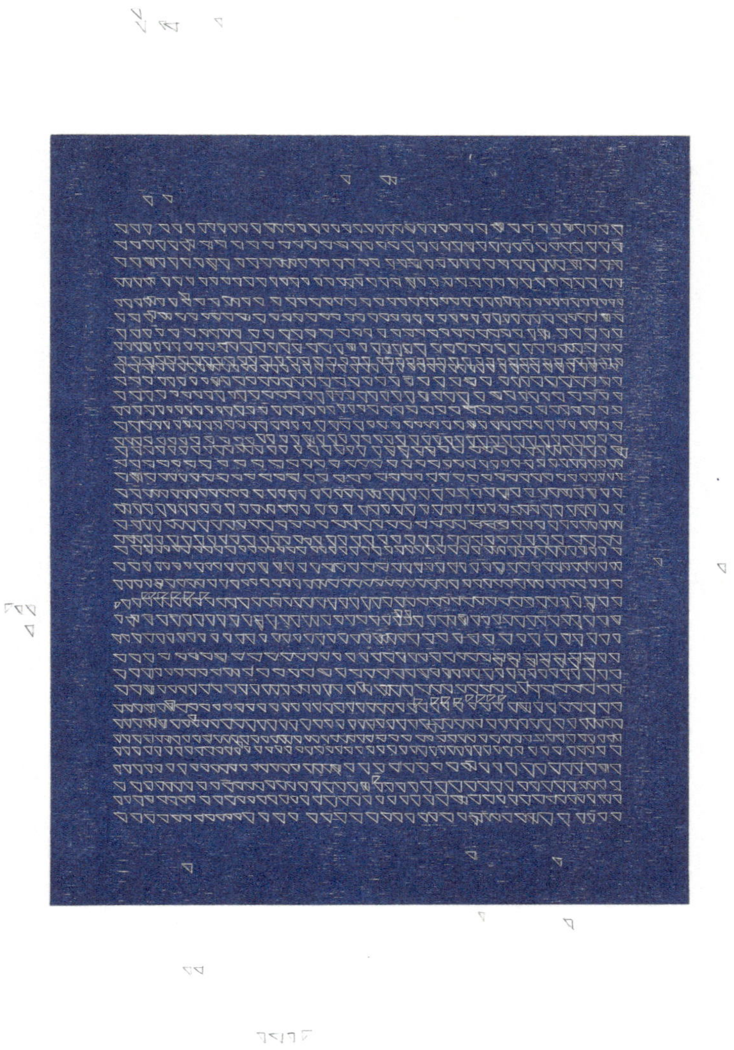

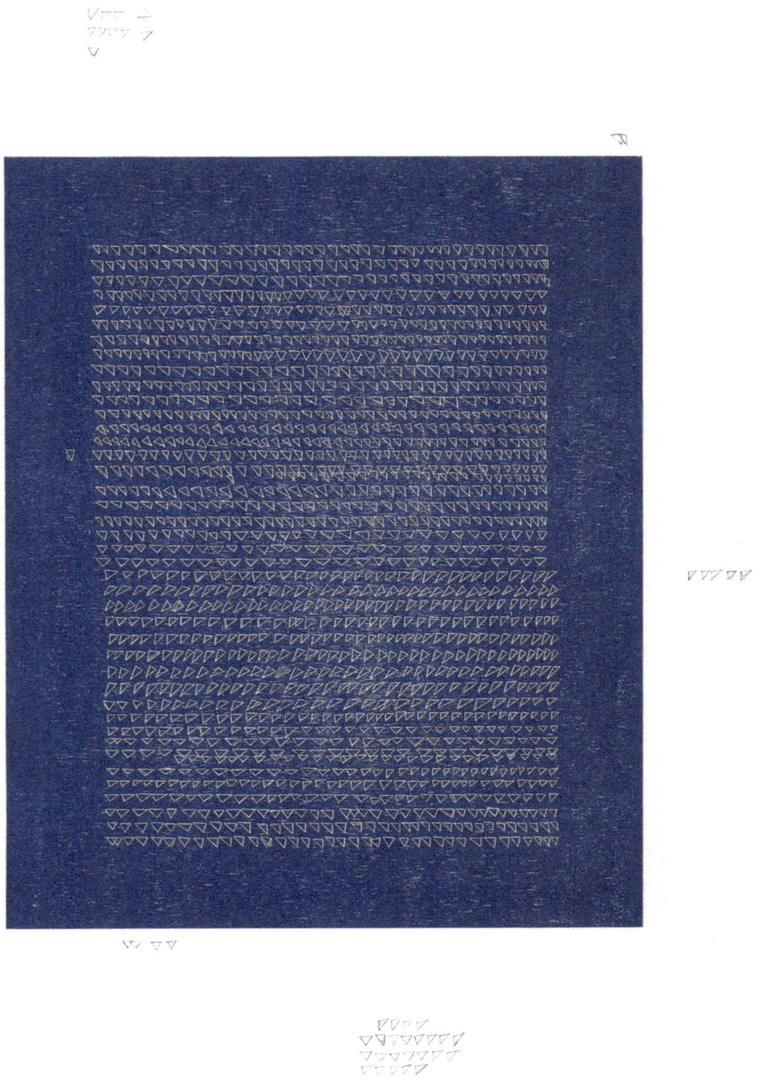

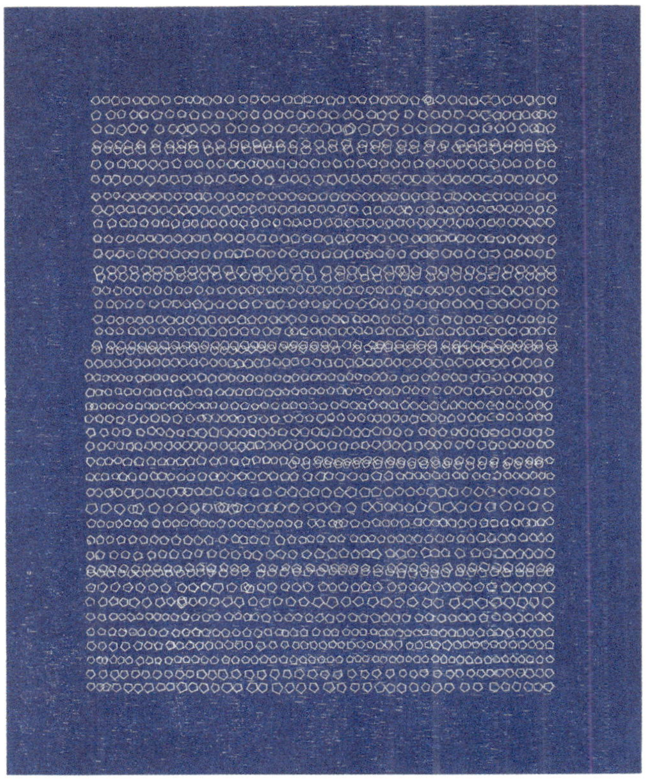

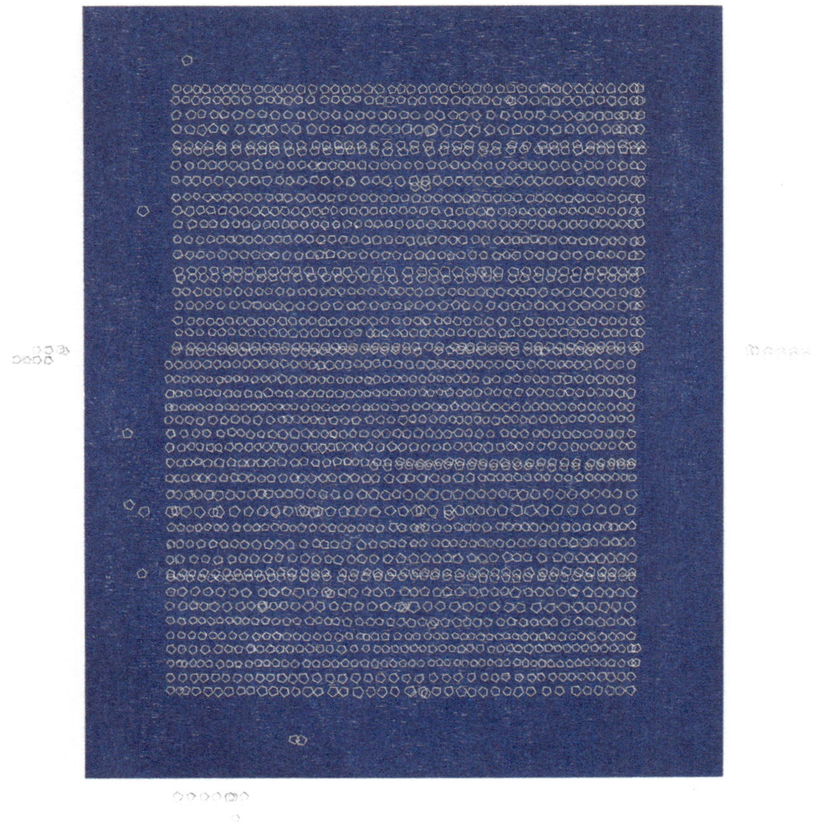

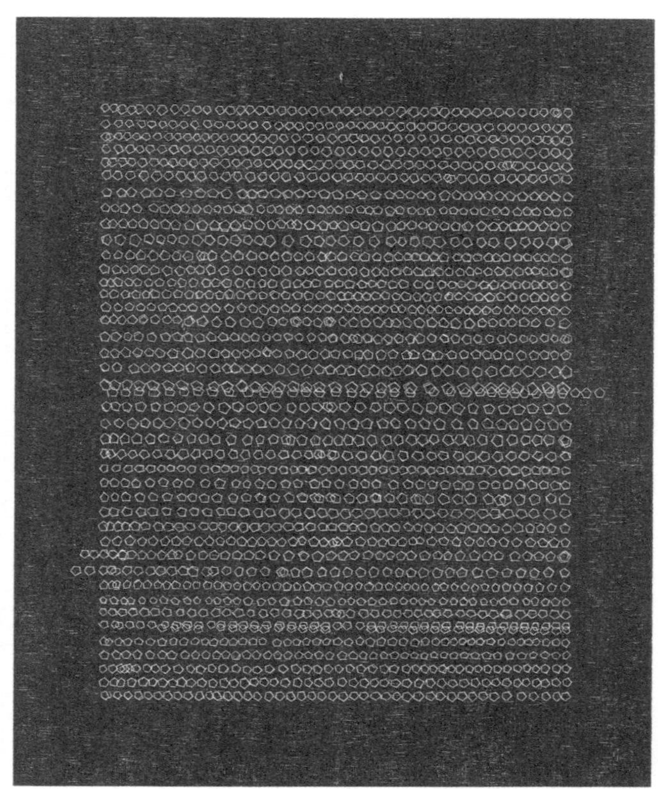

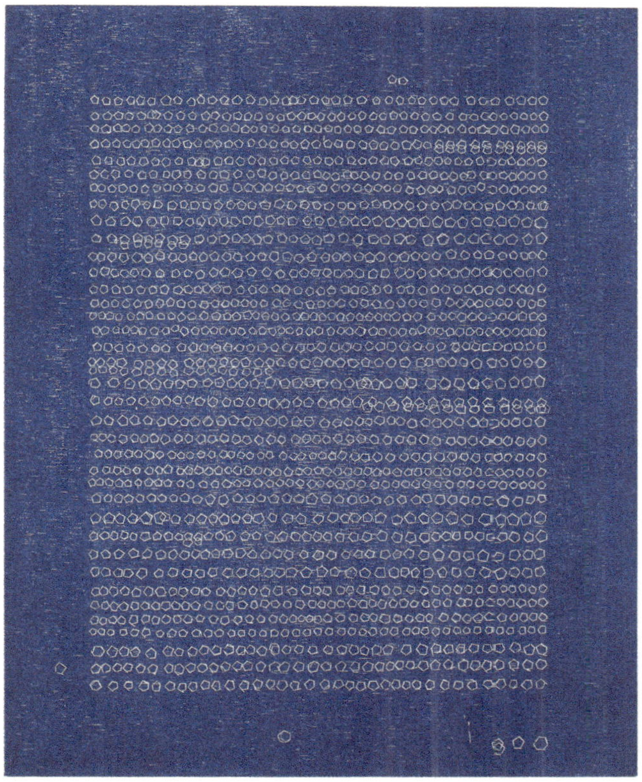

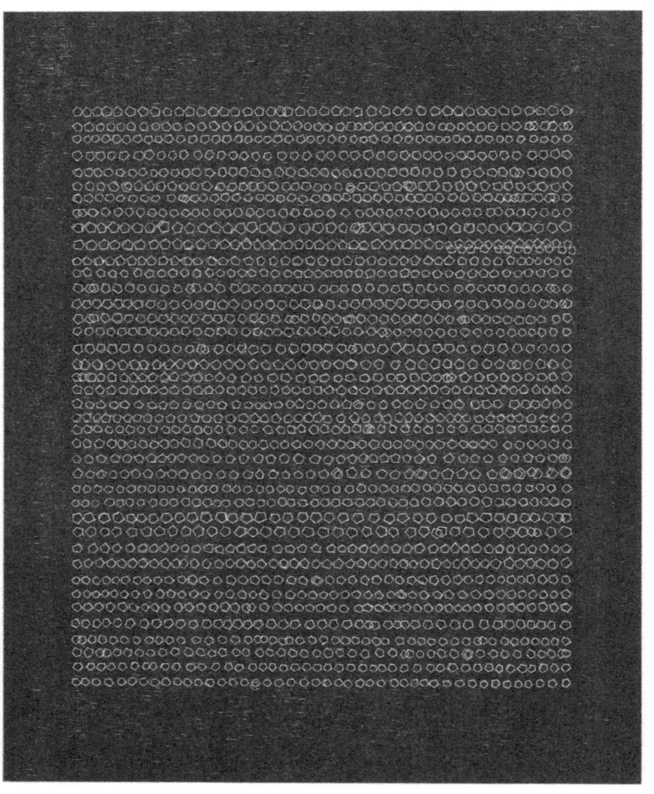

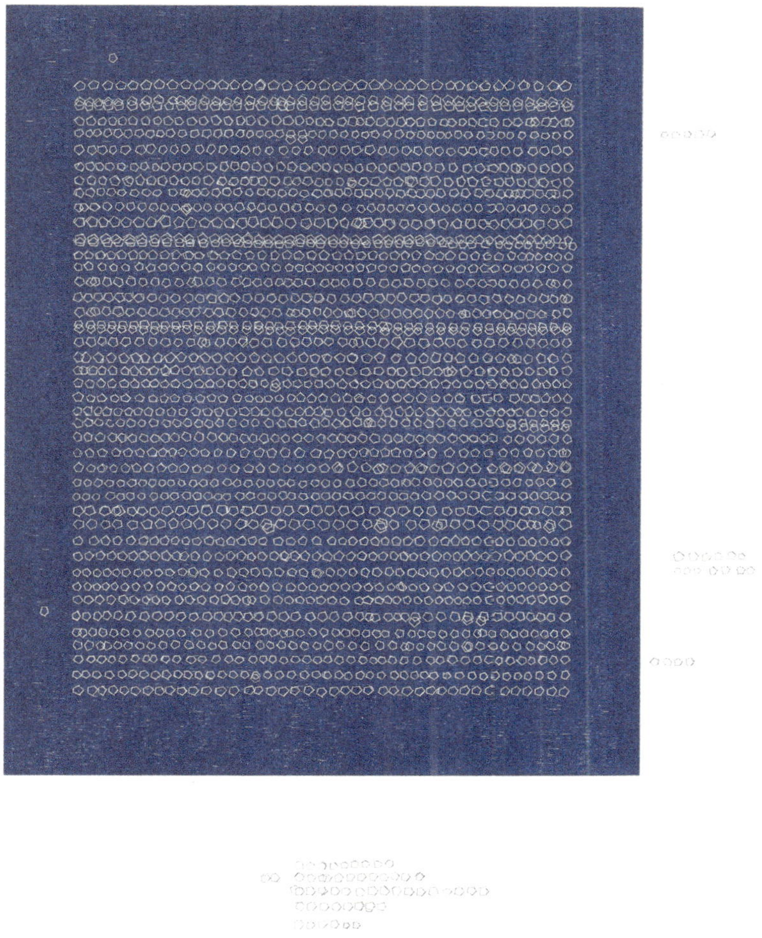

Woodbeds, brimming, 2019

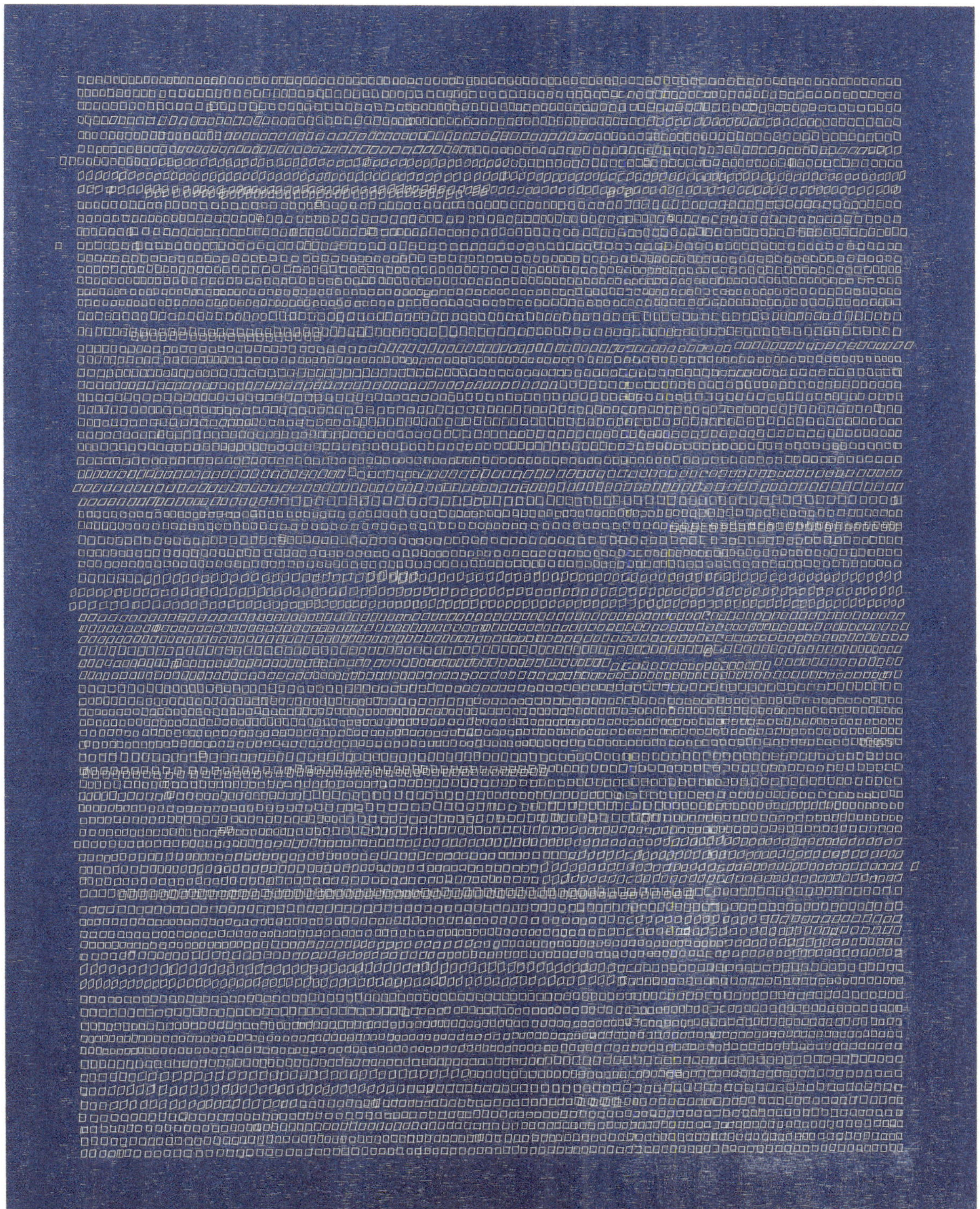

Woodbeds, brimming (on), 2020

Woodbeds, brimming (more), 2020

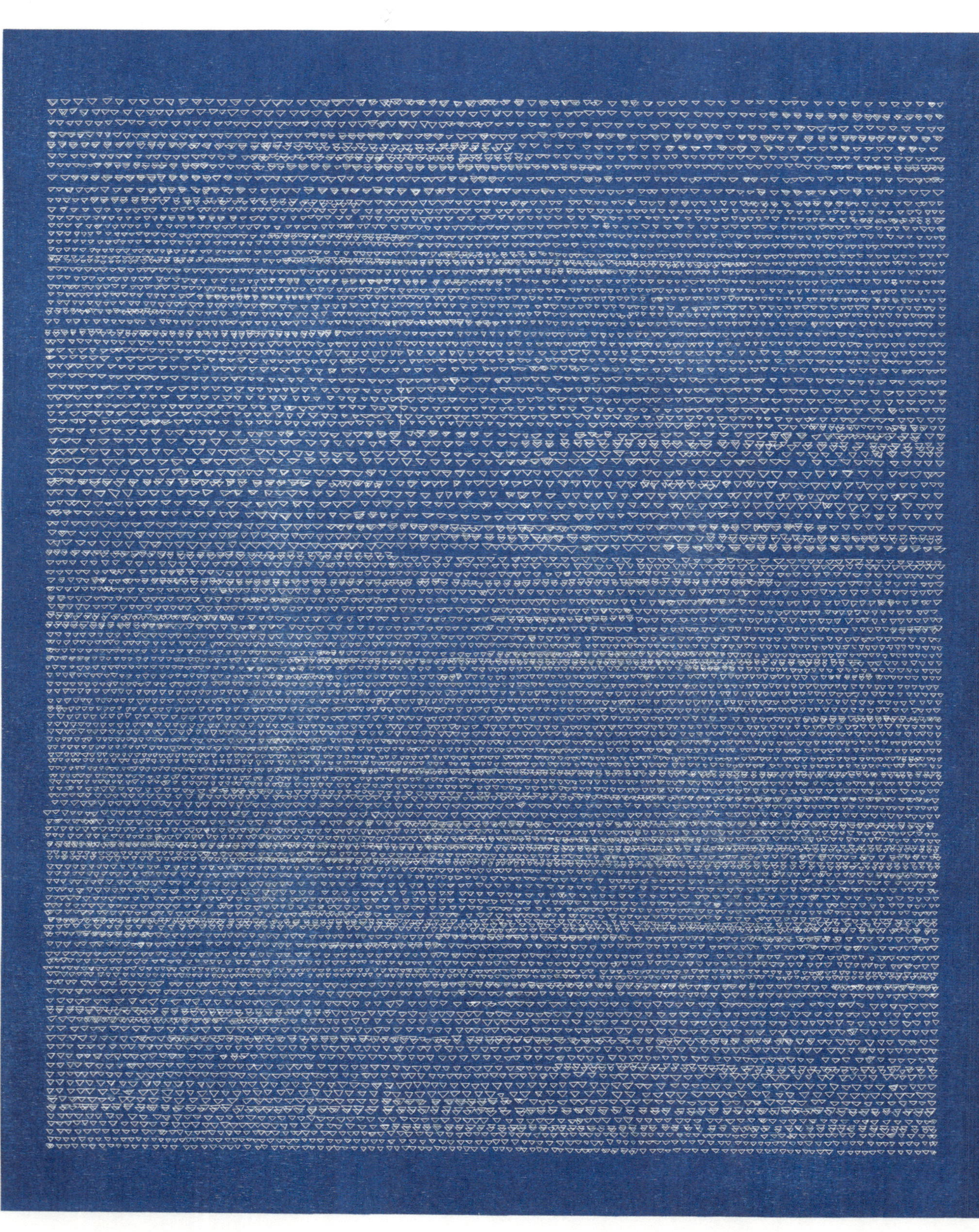

Woodbeds, brimming (among), 2021

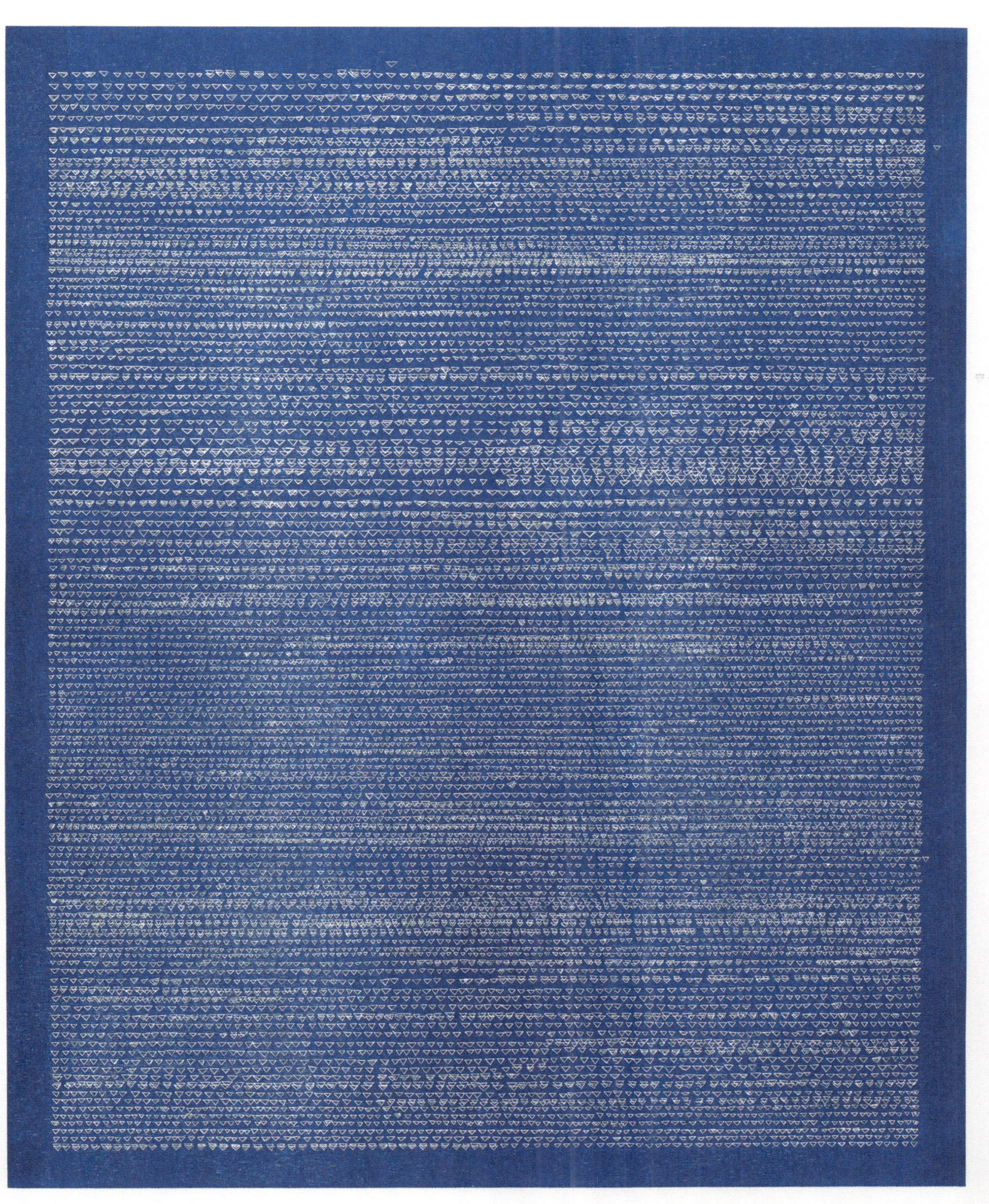

Woodbeds, brimming (to), 2021

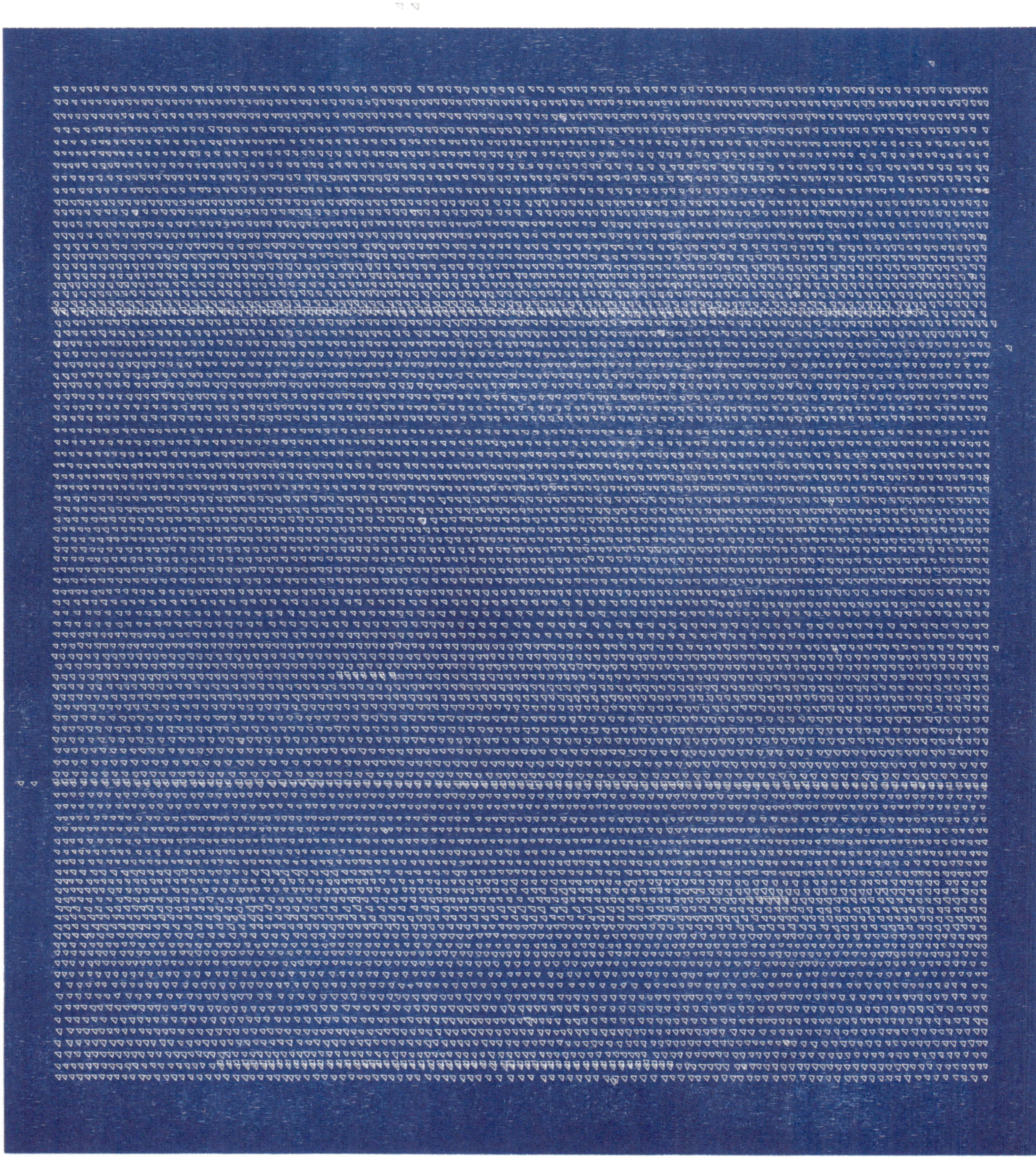

Woodbeds, brimming (down), 2023

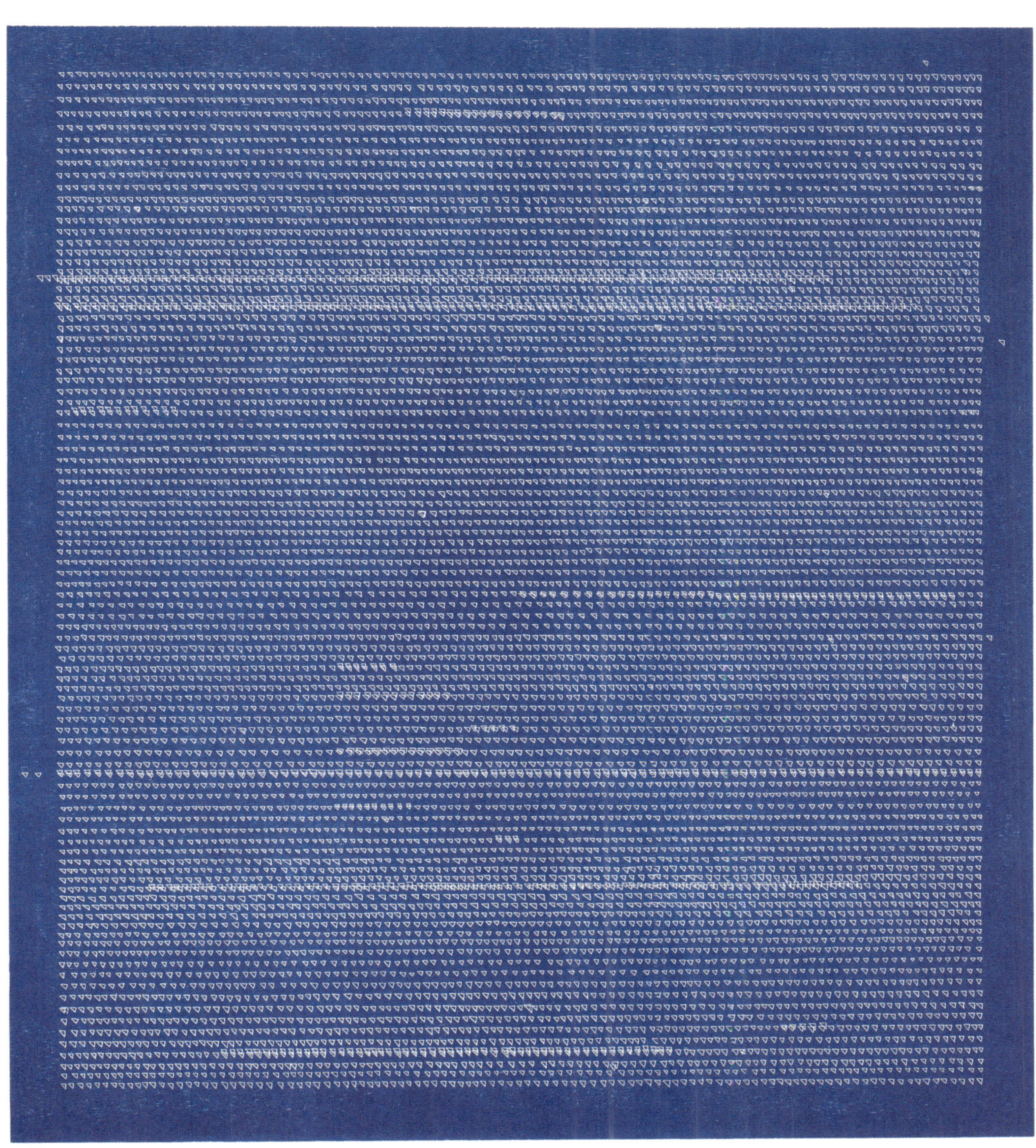

Woodbeds, brimming (come), 2023

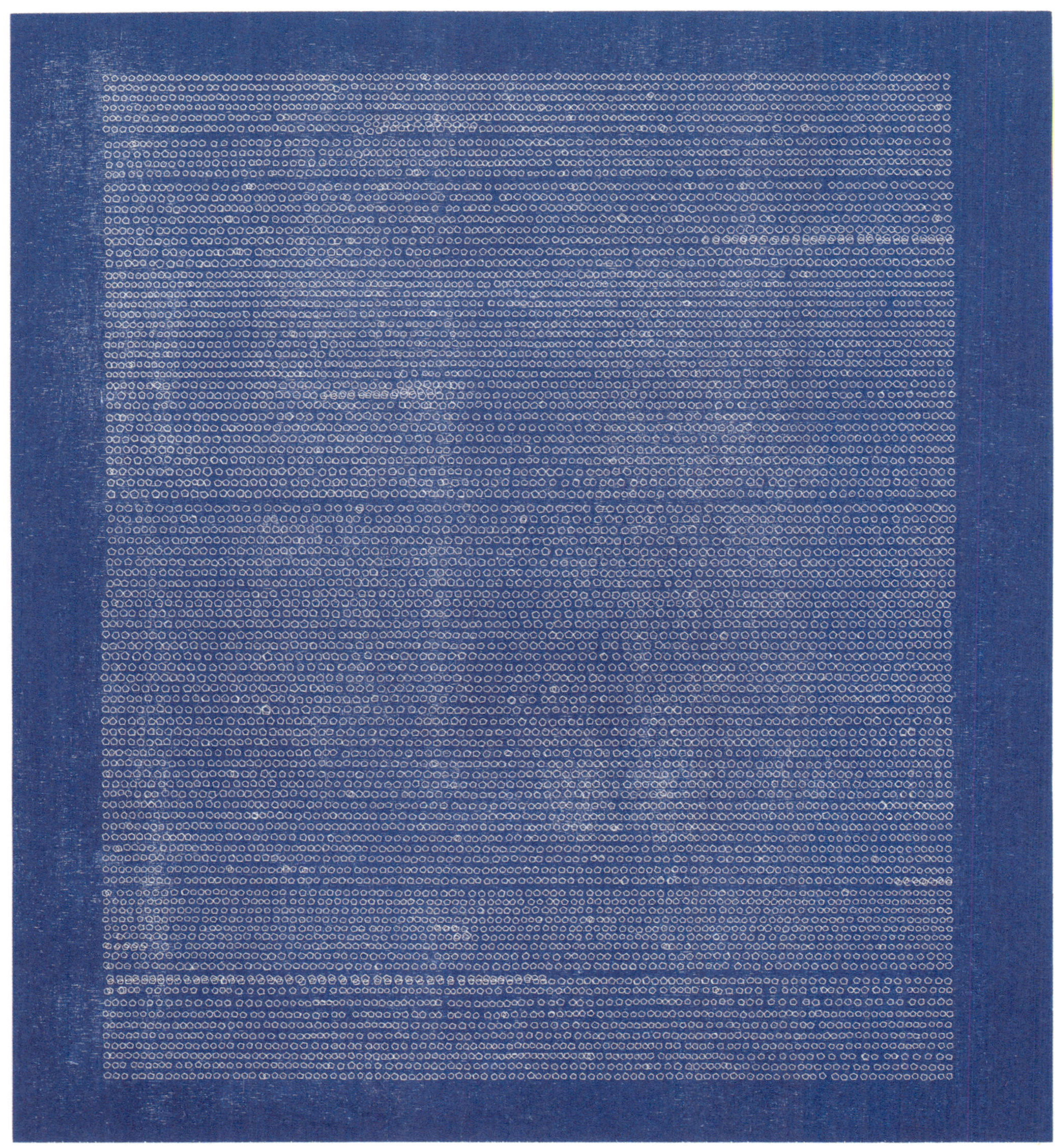

Woodbeds, brimming (soon), 2023

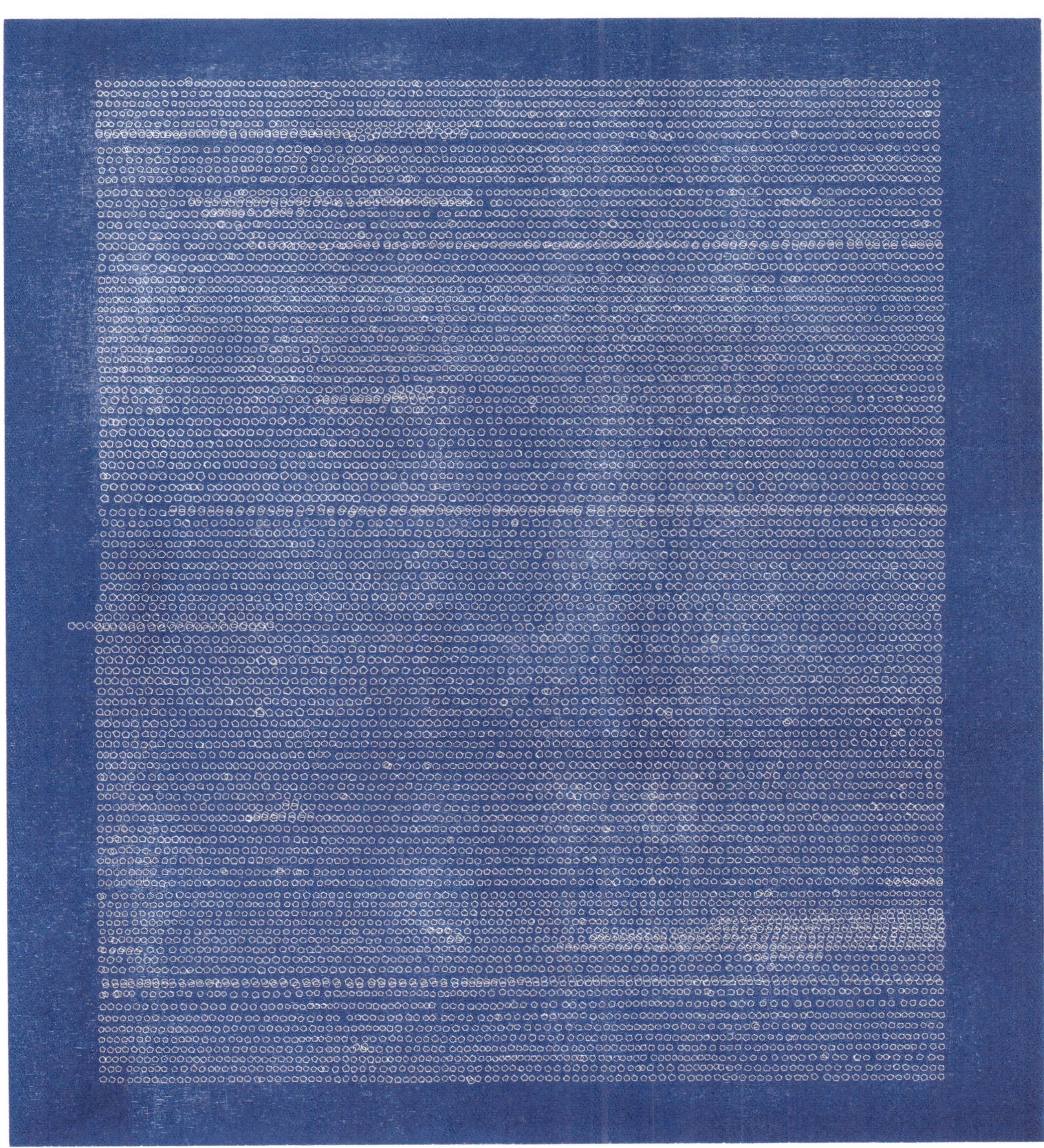

Woodbeds, brimming (turn), 2023

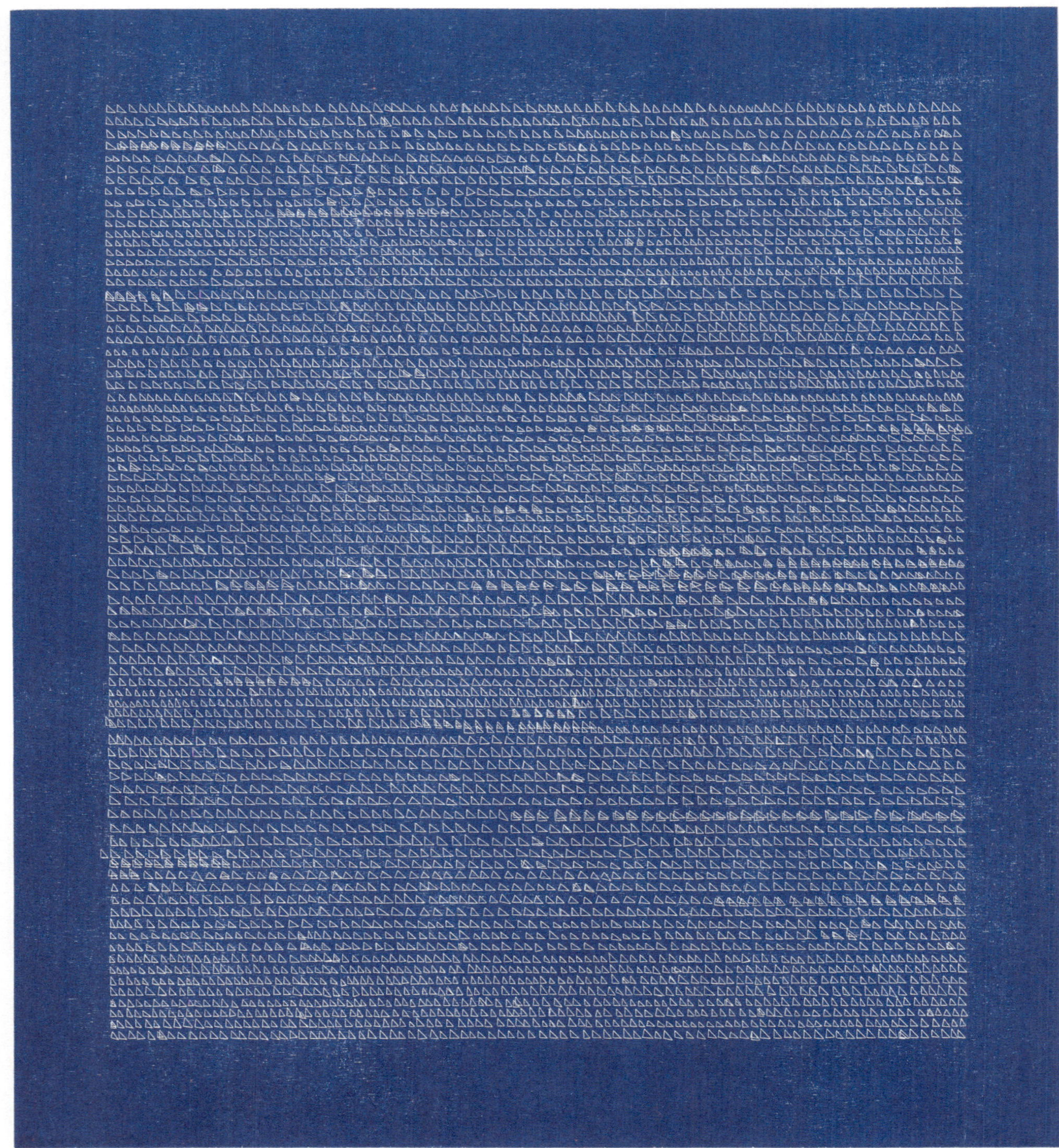

Woodbeds, brimming (in), 2023

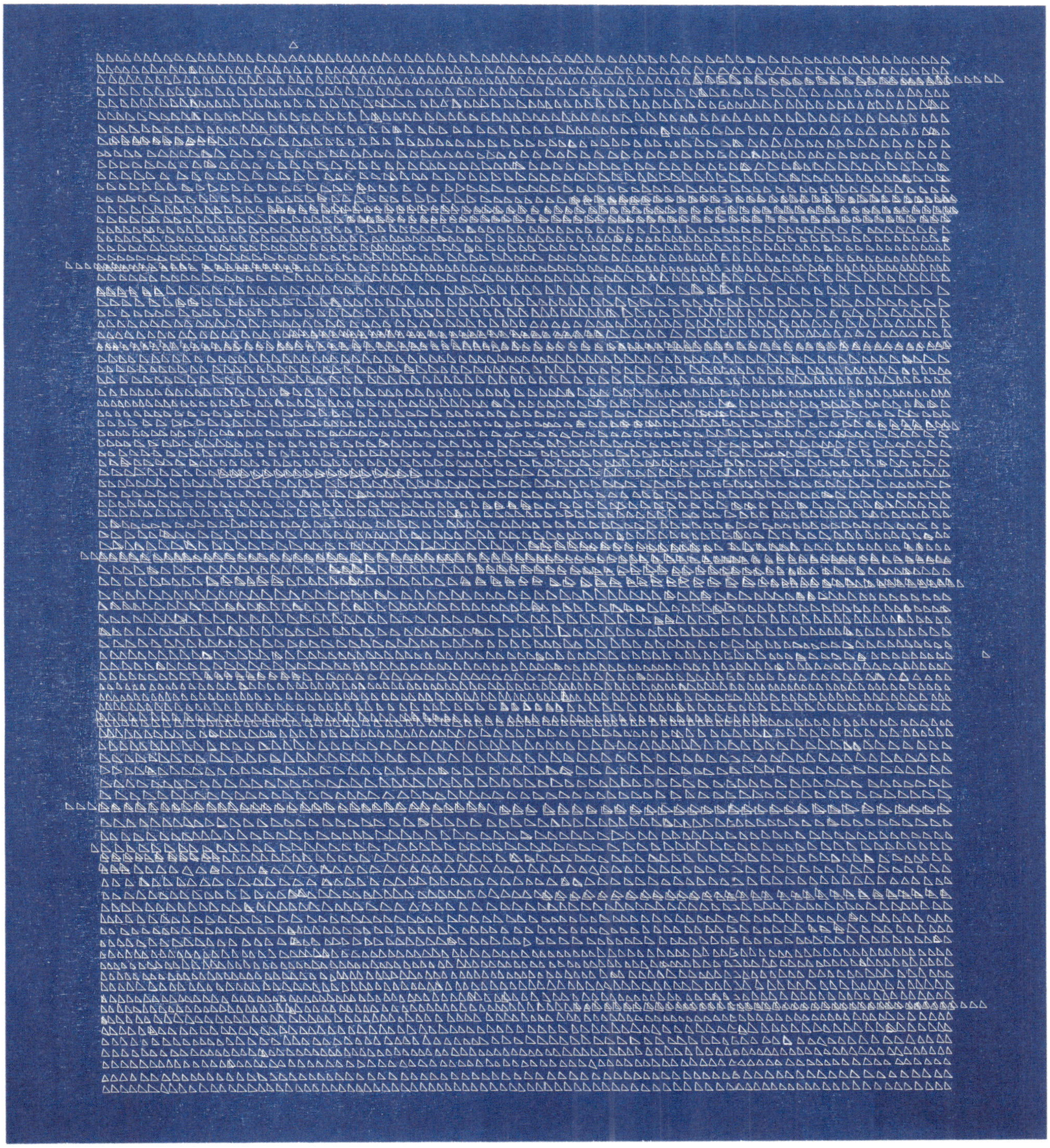

Woodbeds, brimming (full), 2023

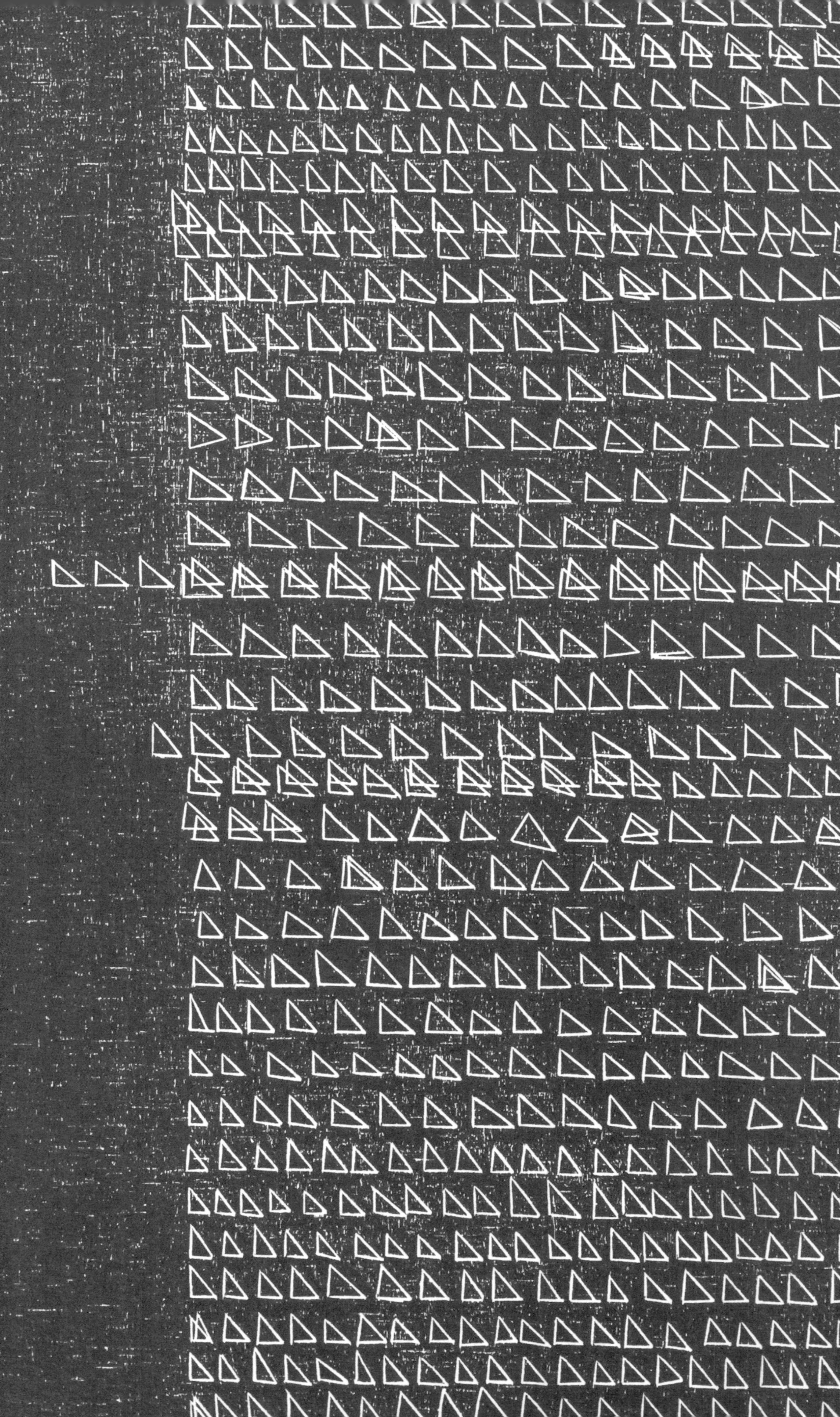

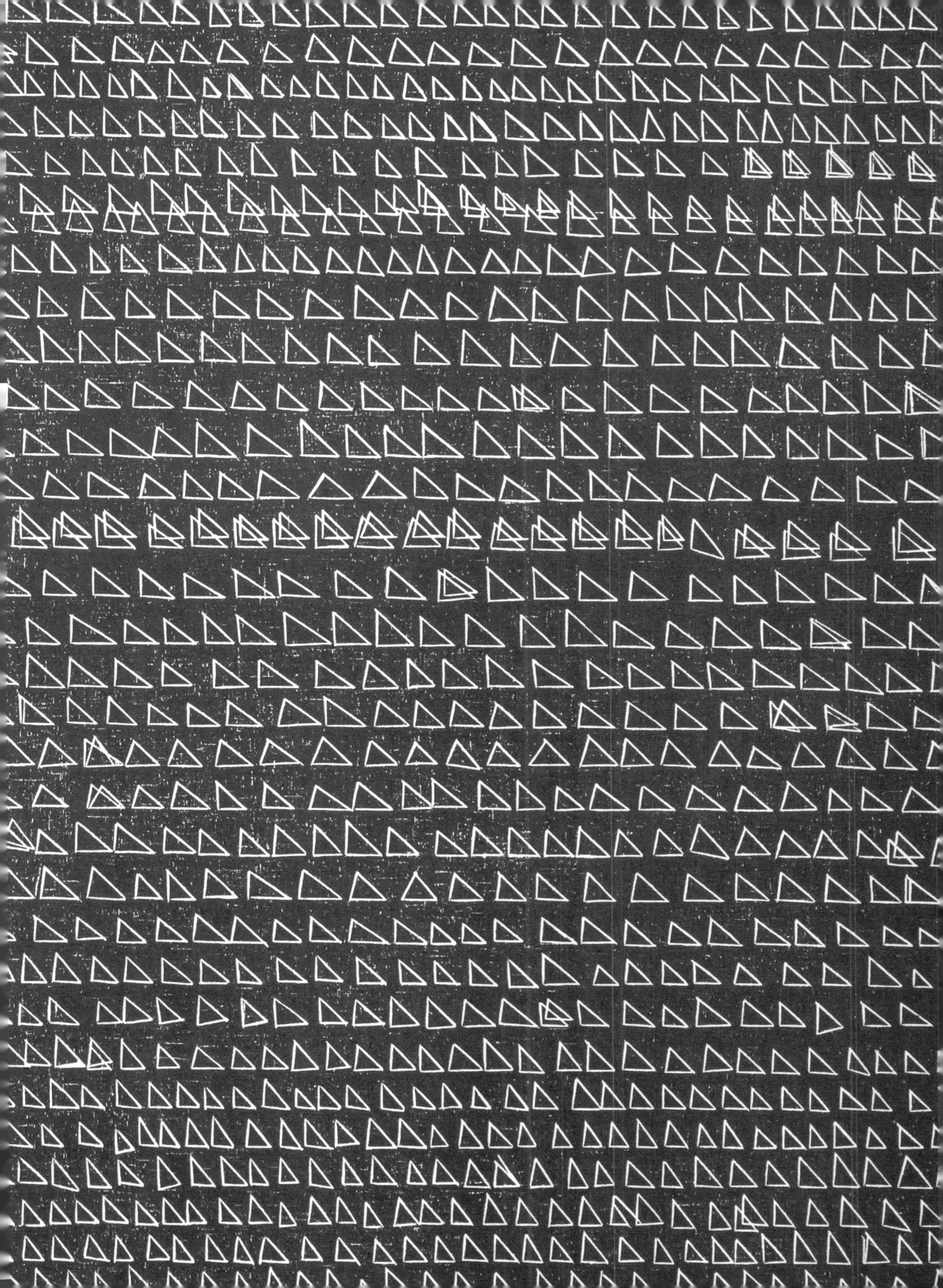

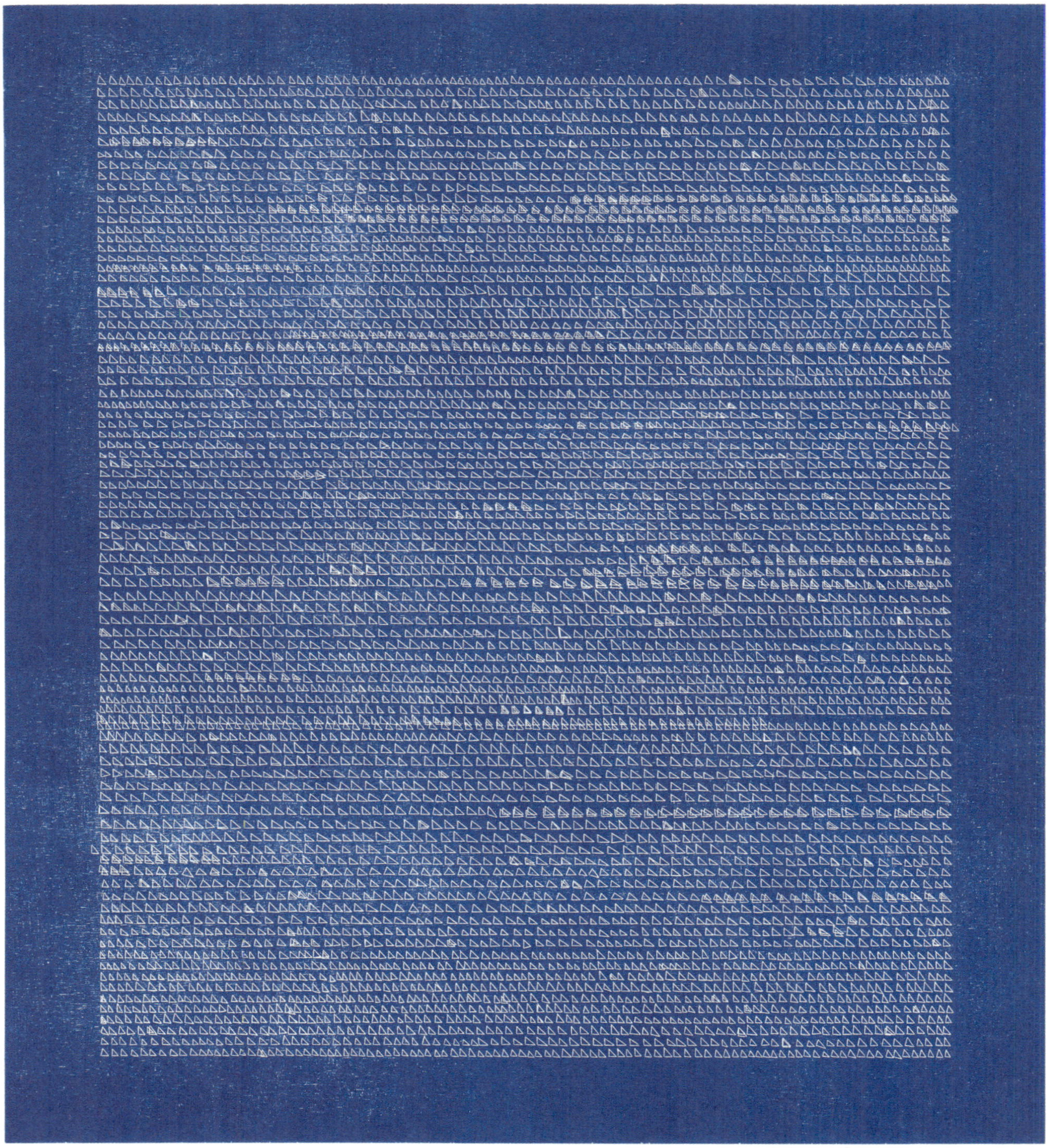

Woodbeds, brimming (back), 2023

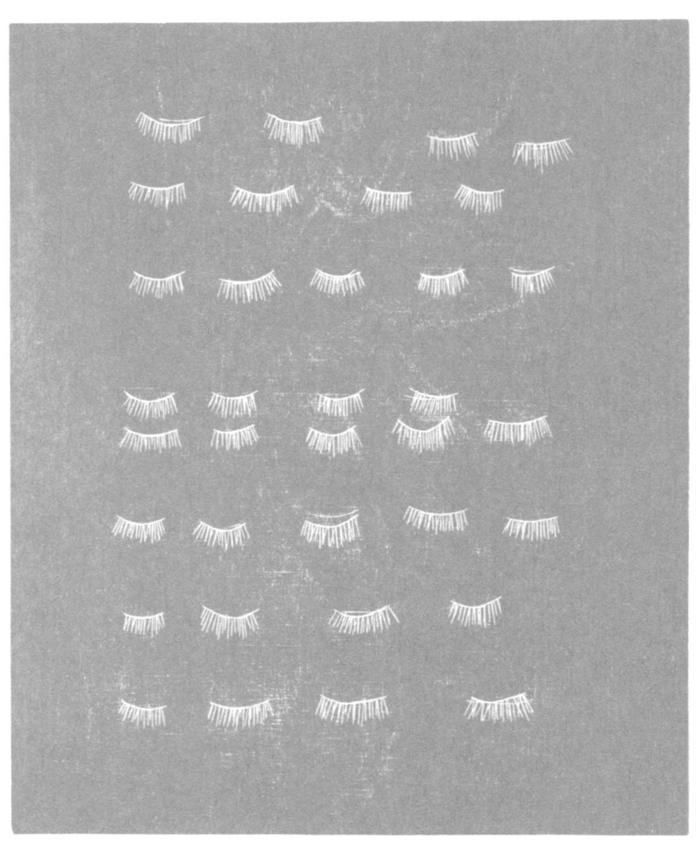

Cruising horizontal lines (silver), 2022

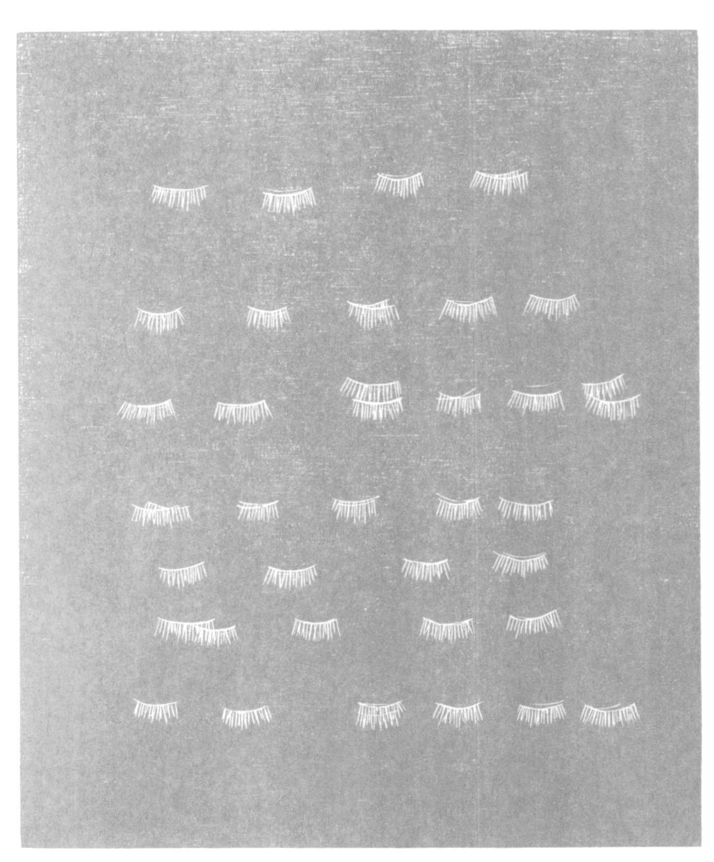

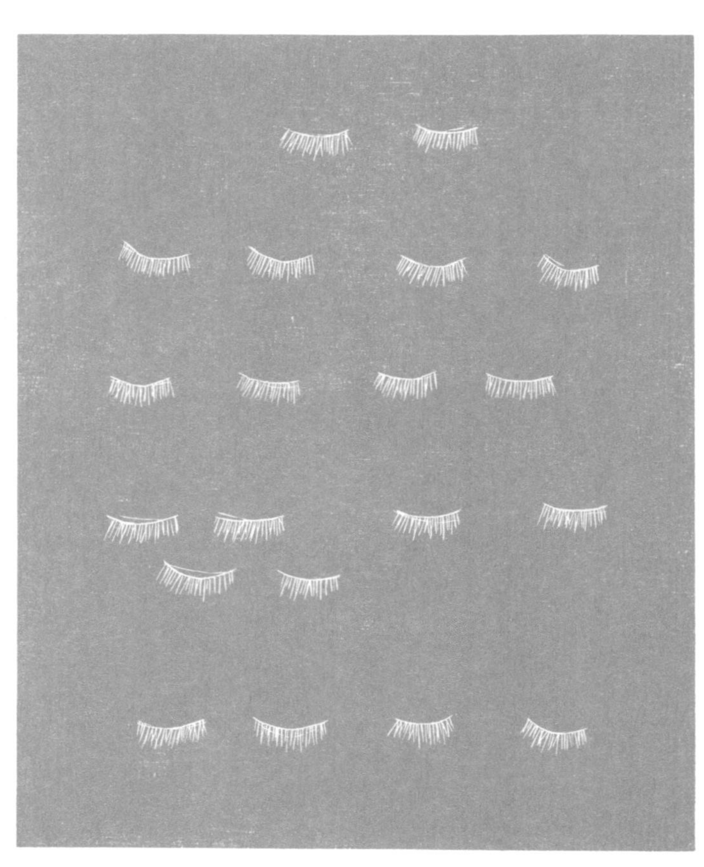

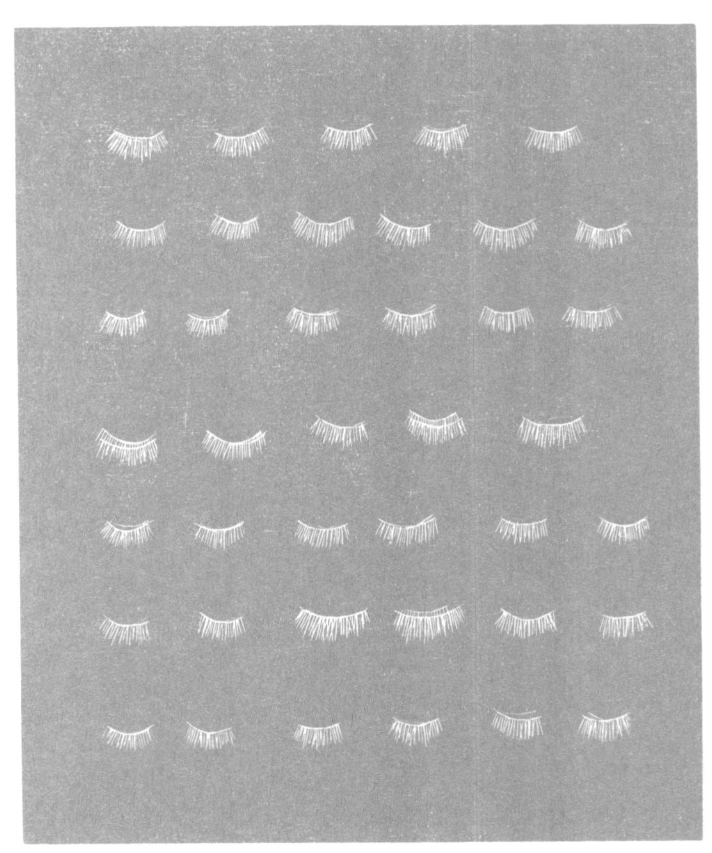

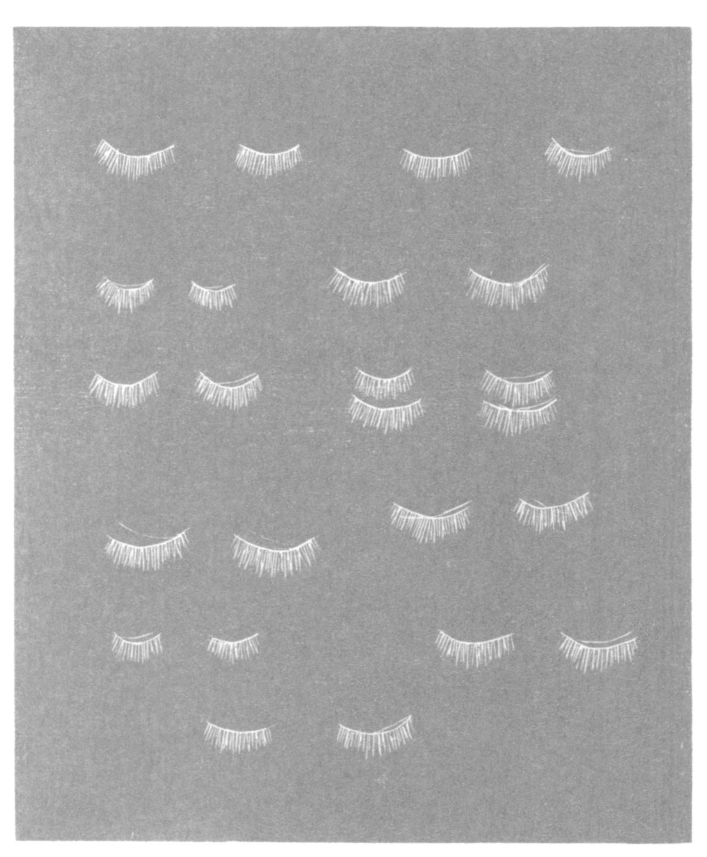

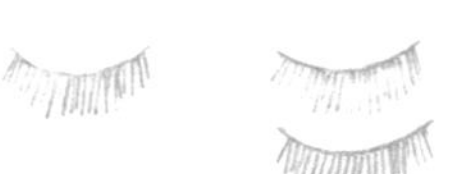

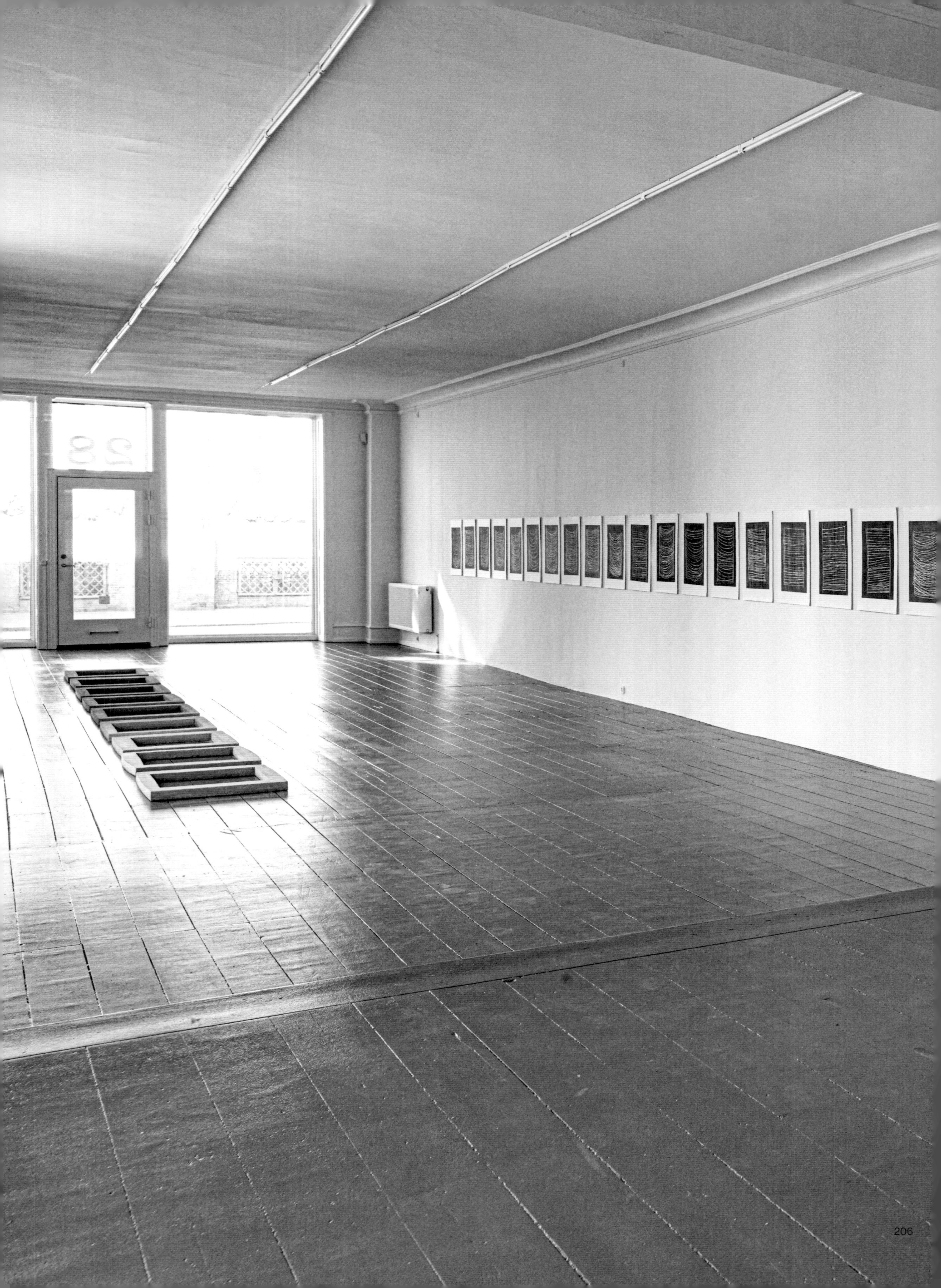

How to spell a sound that is physical, Aviskari Gallery, Copenhagen, 2015

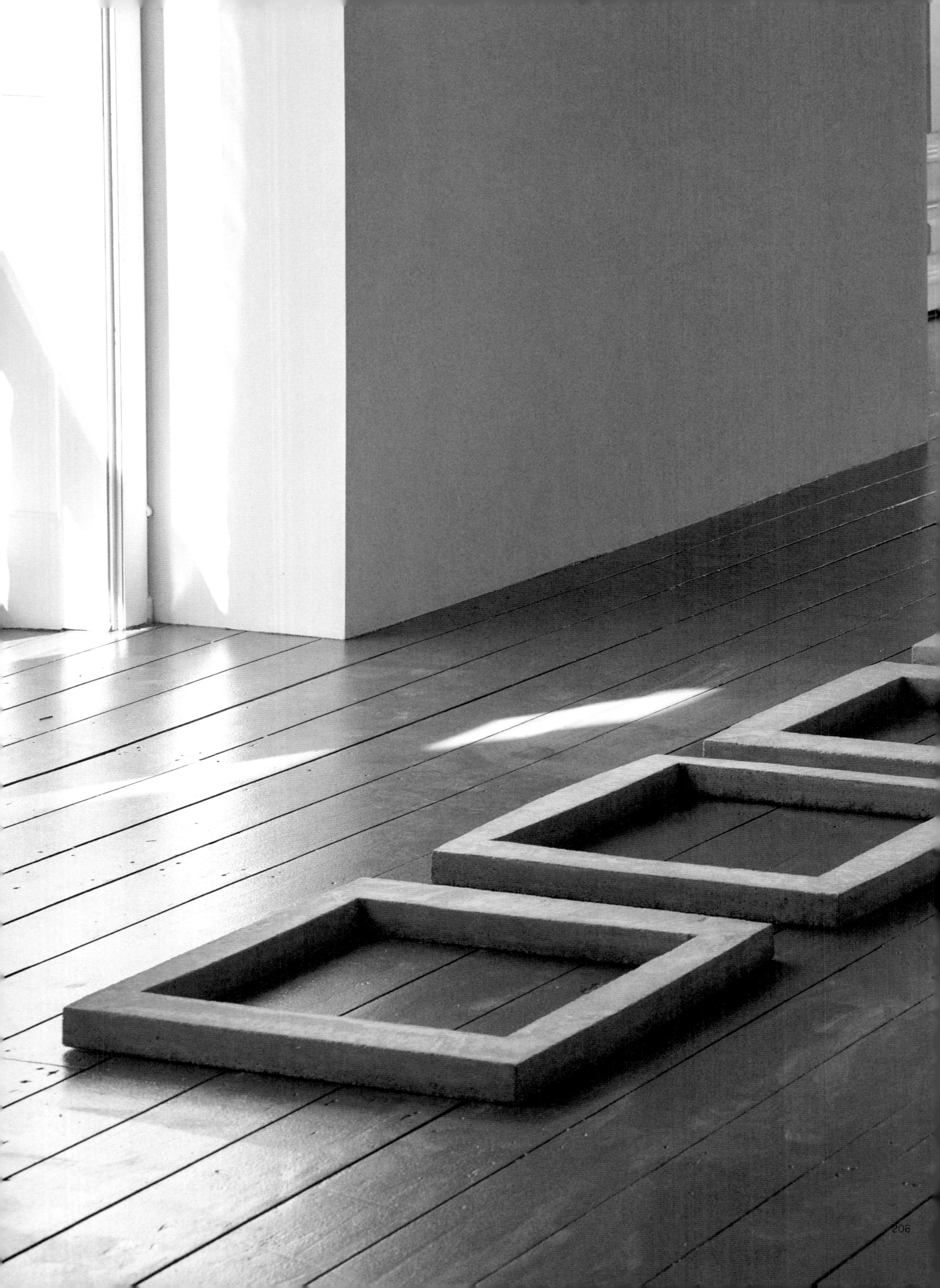

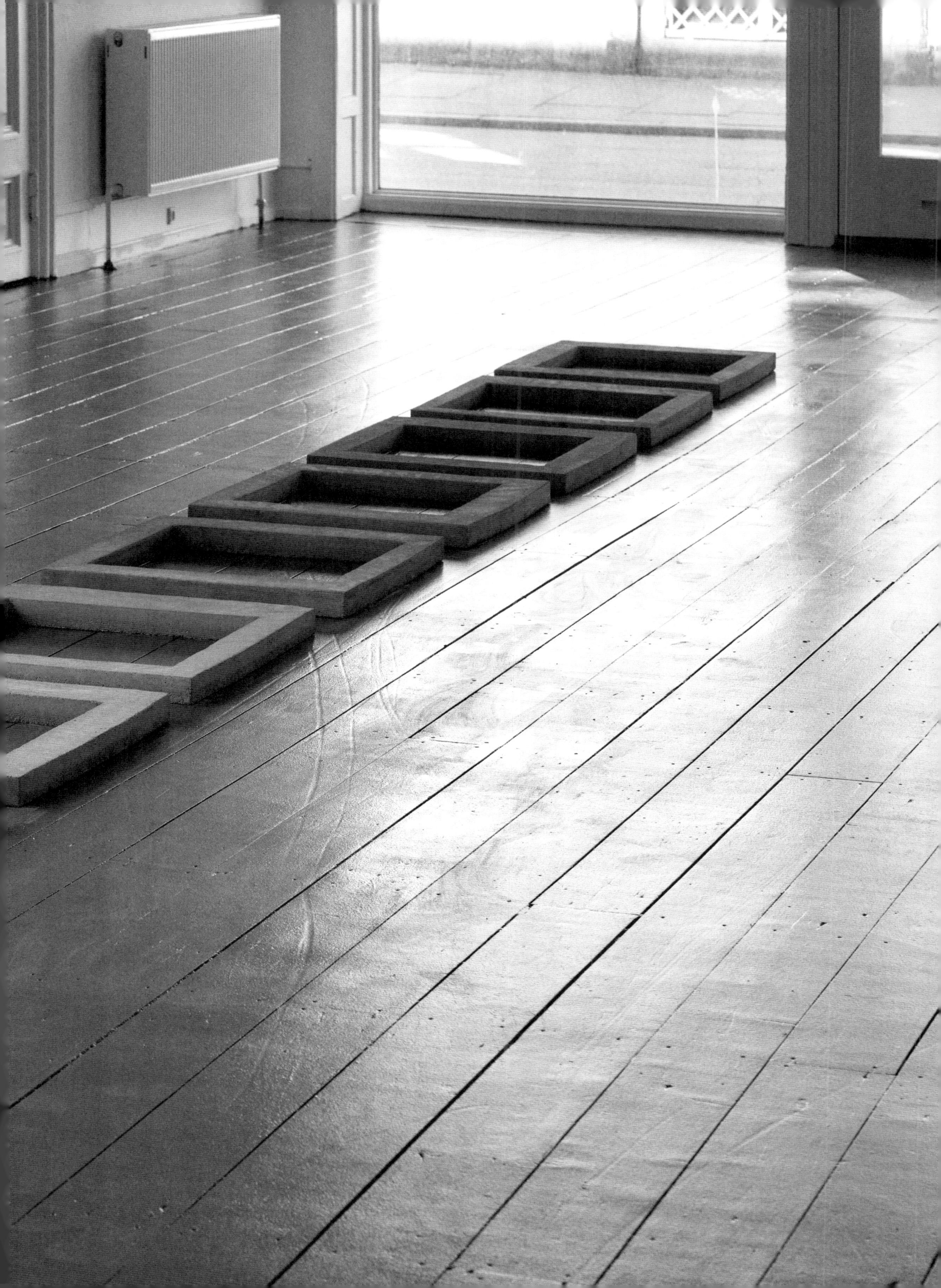

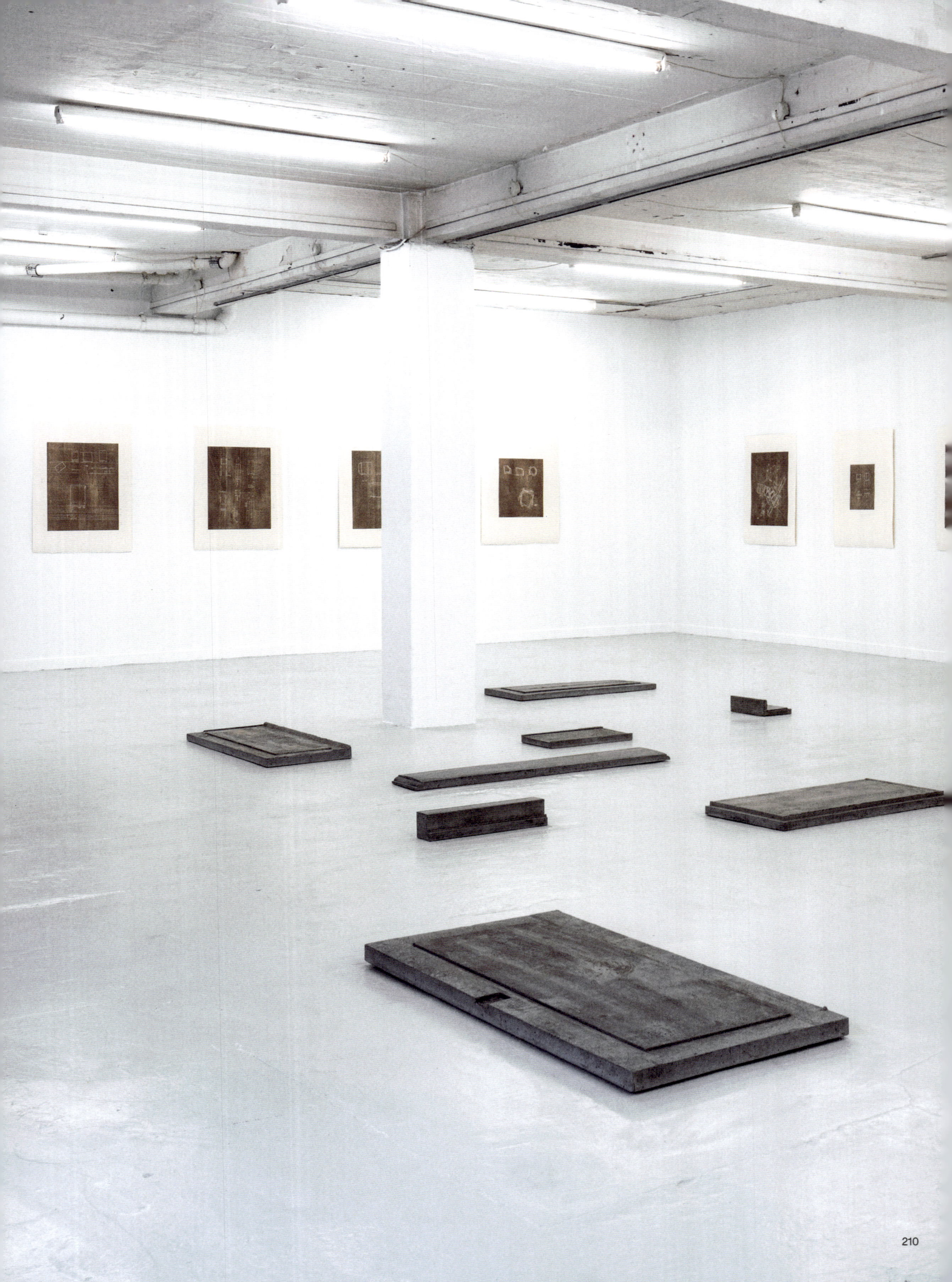

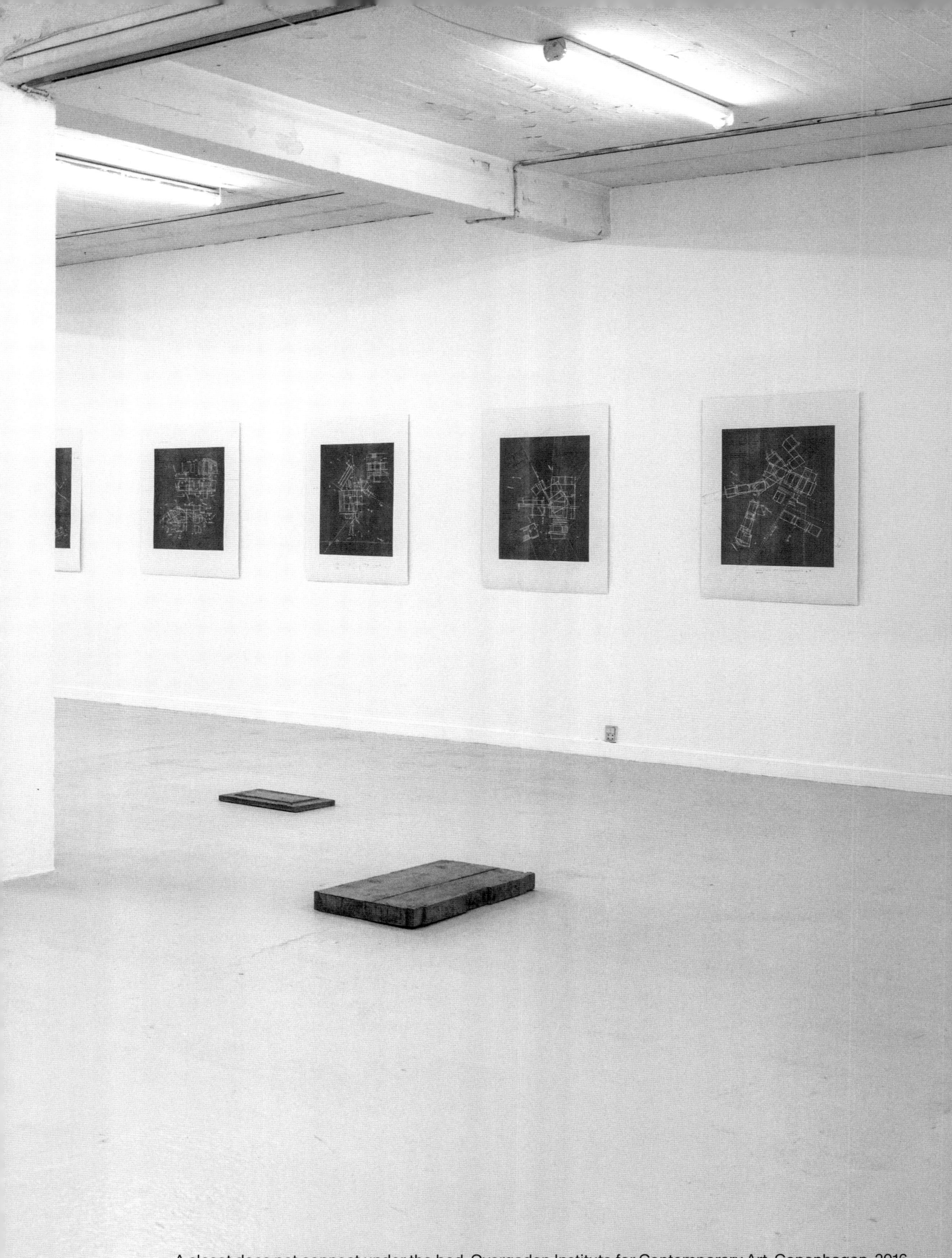

A closet does not connect under the bed, Overgaden Institute for Contemporary Art, Copenhagen, 2016

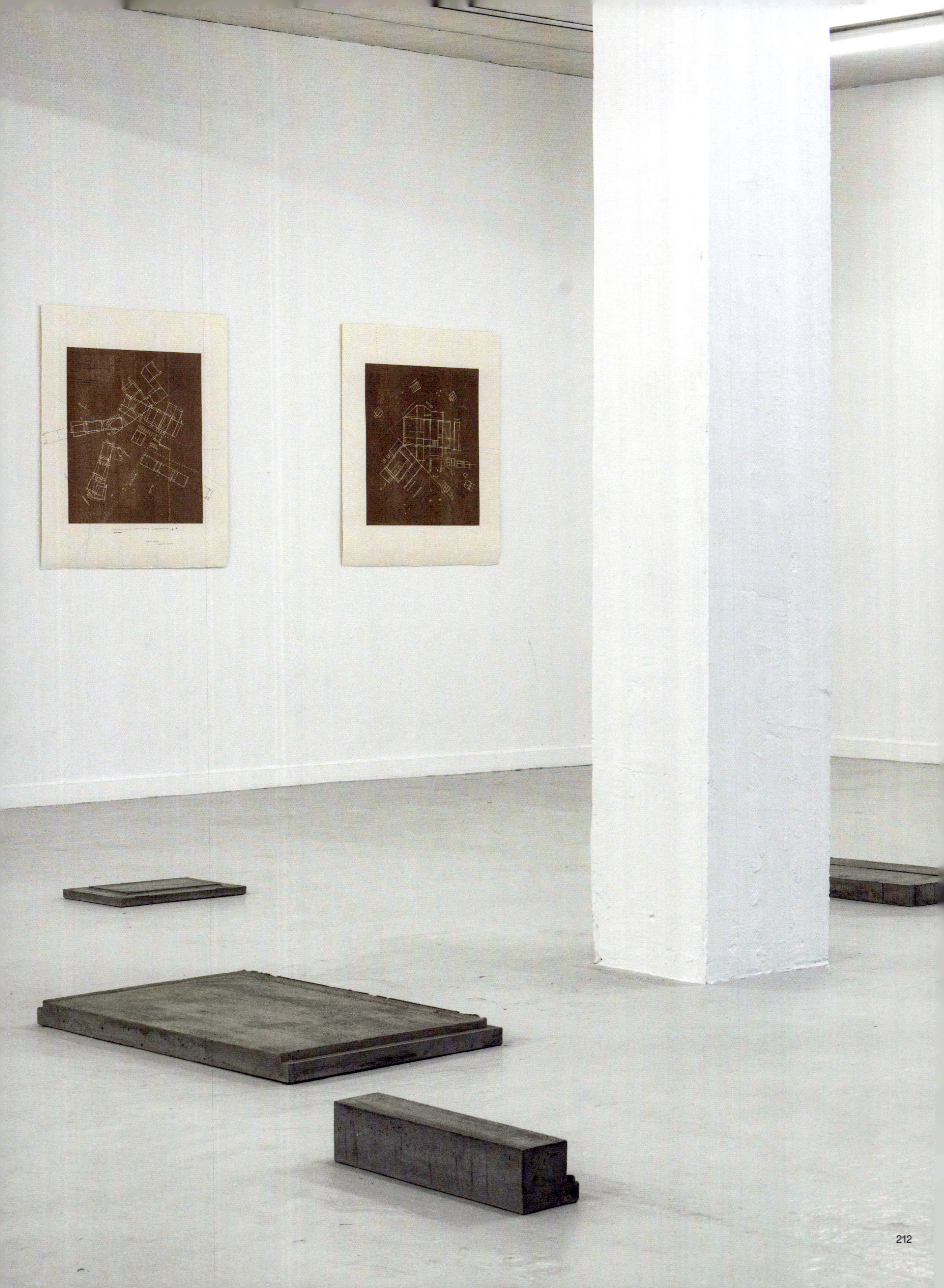

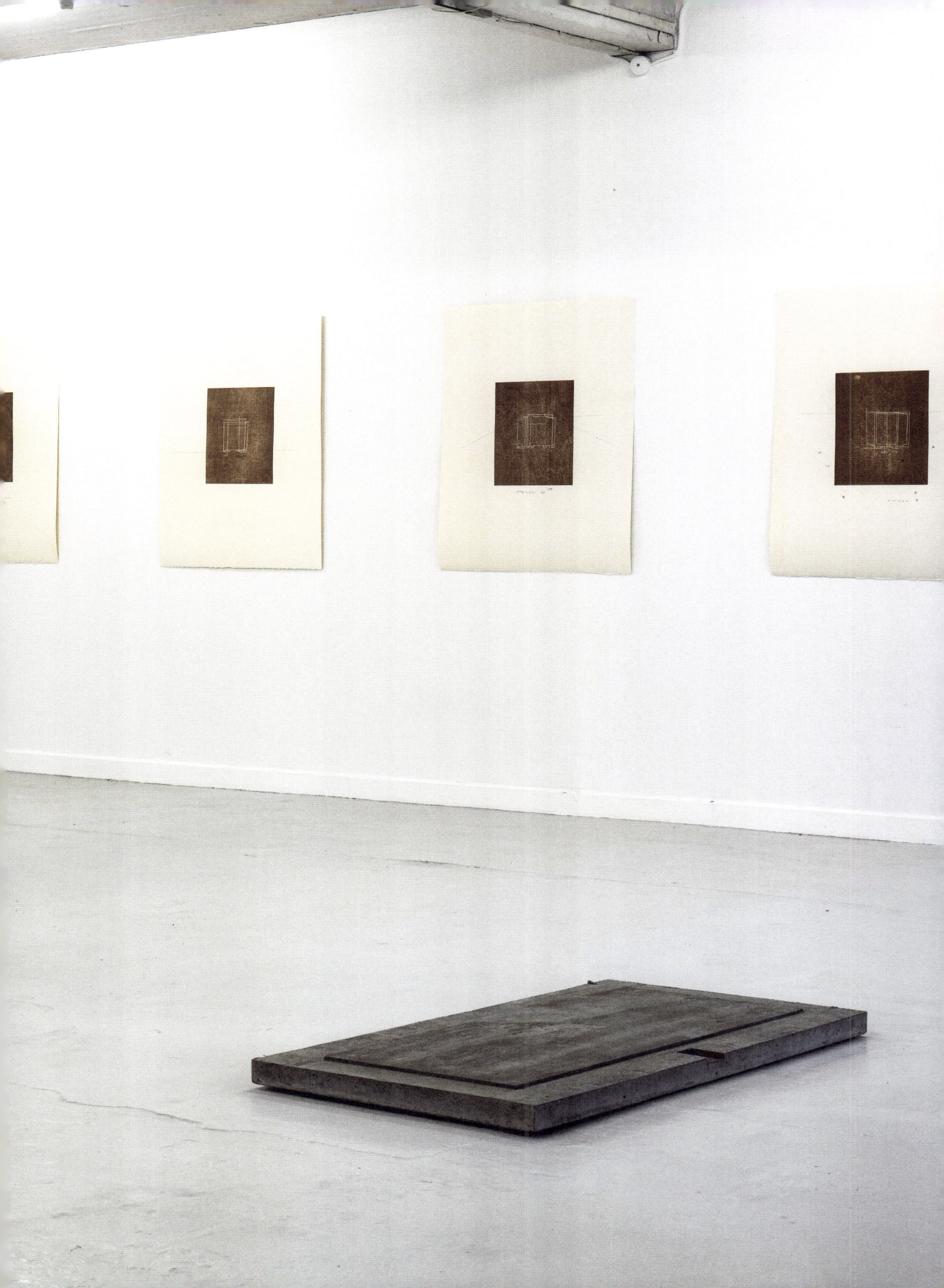

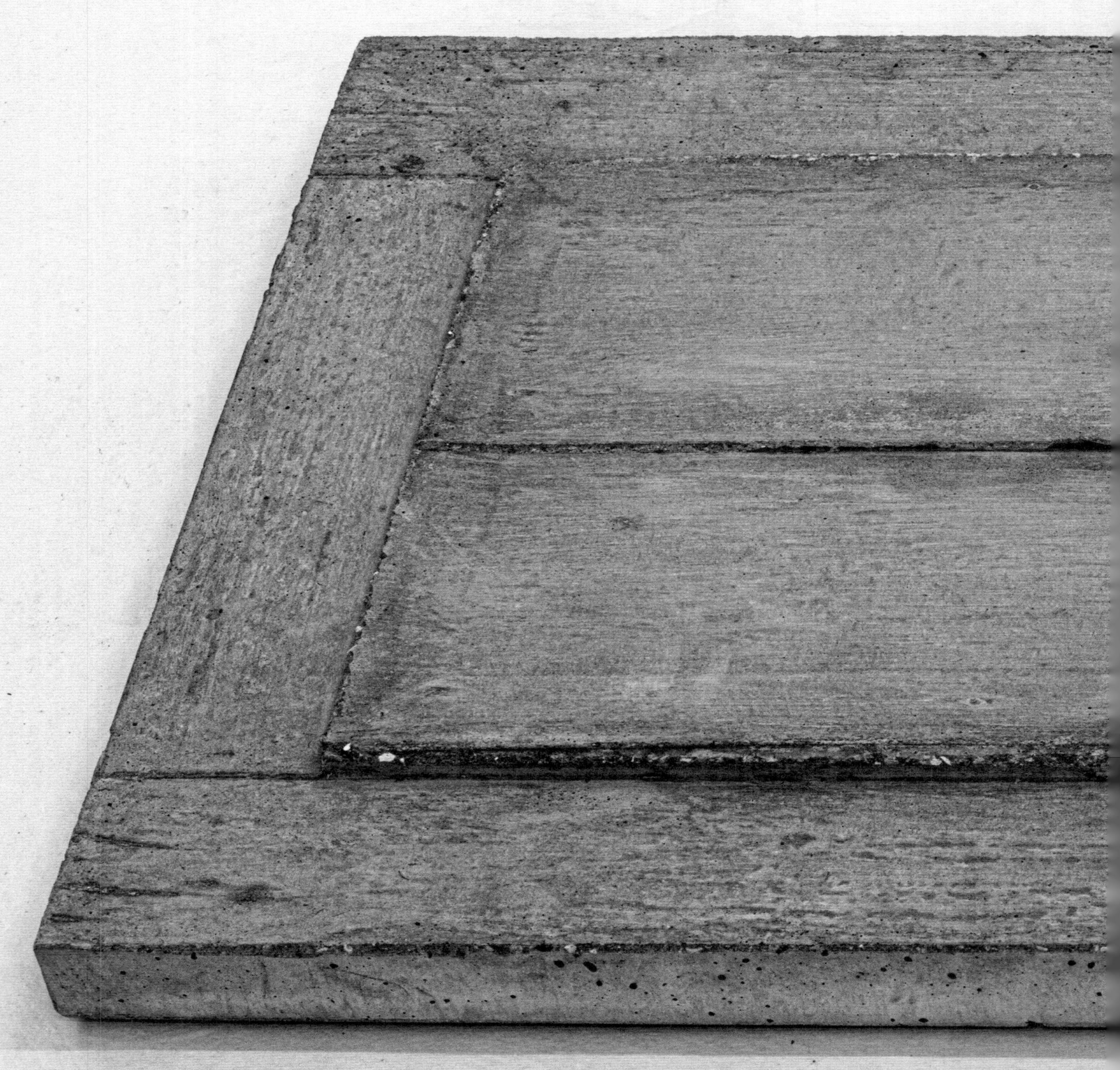

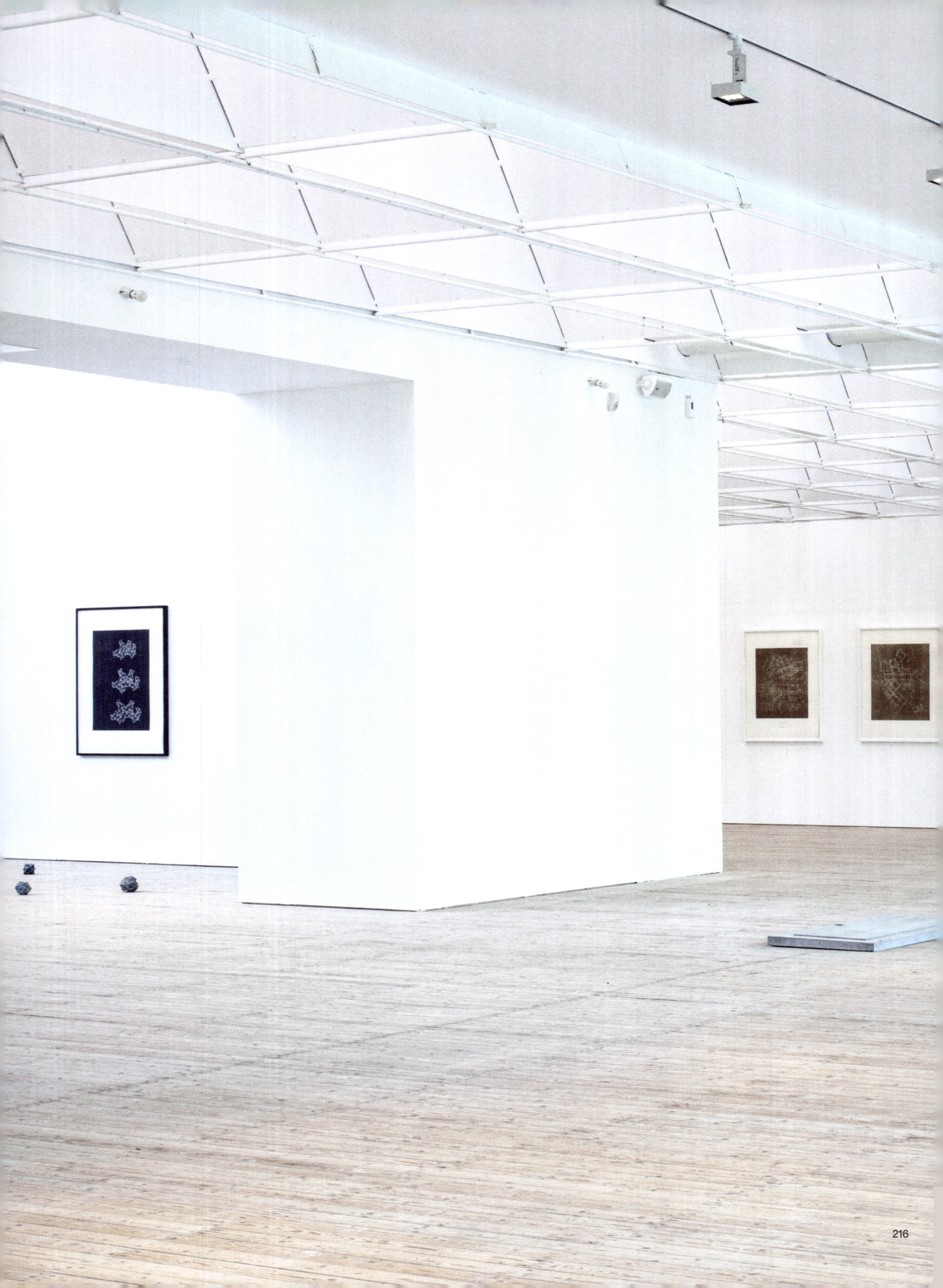

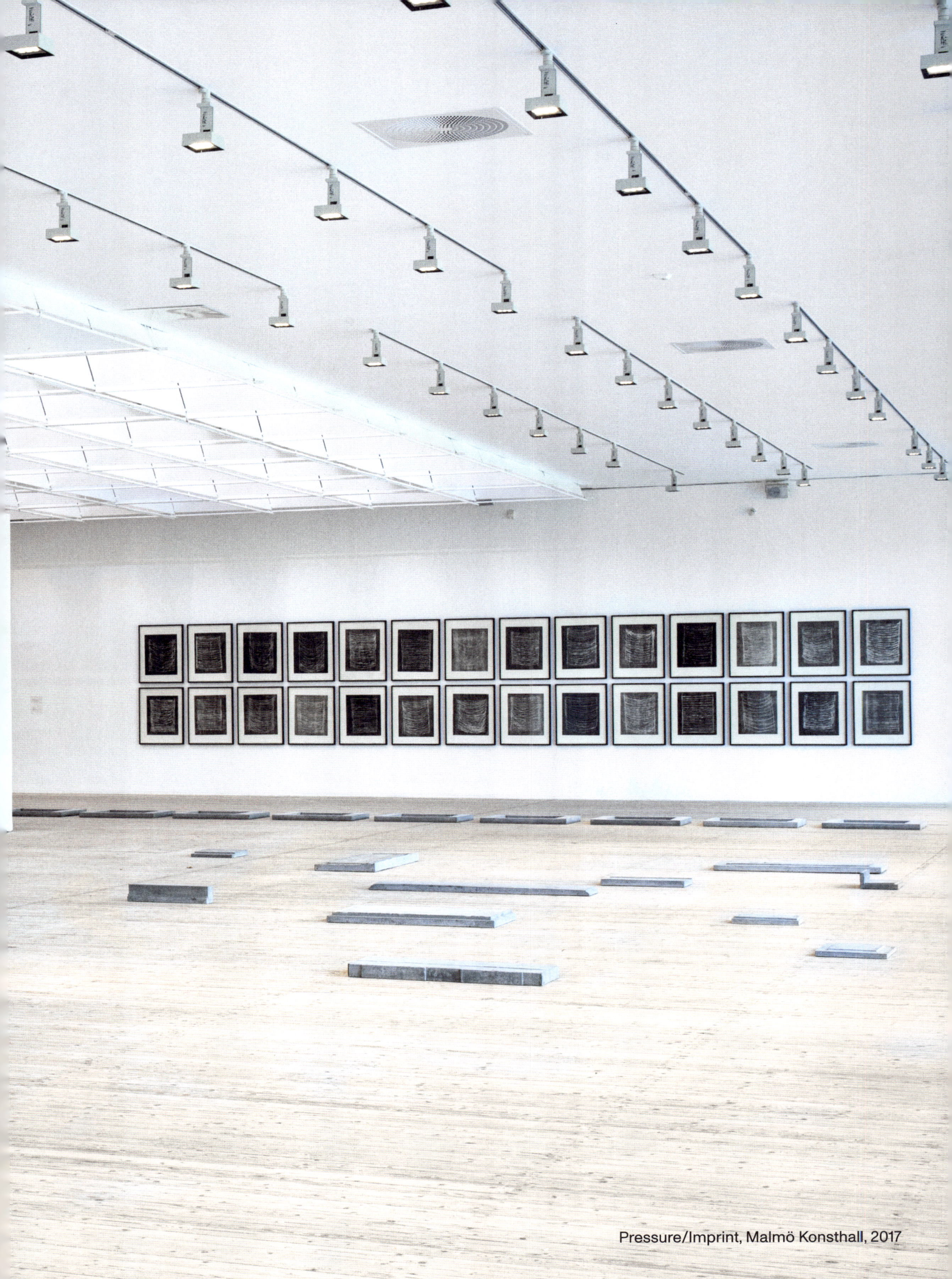

Pressure/Imprint, Malmö Konsthall, 2017

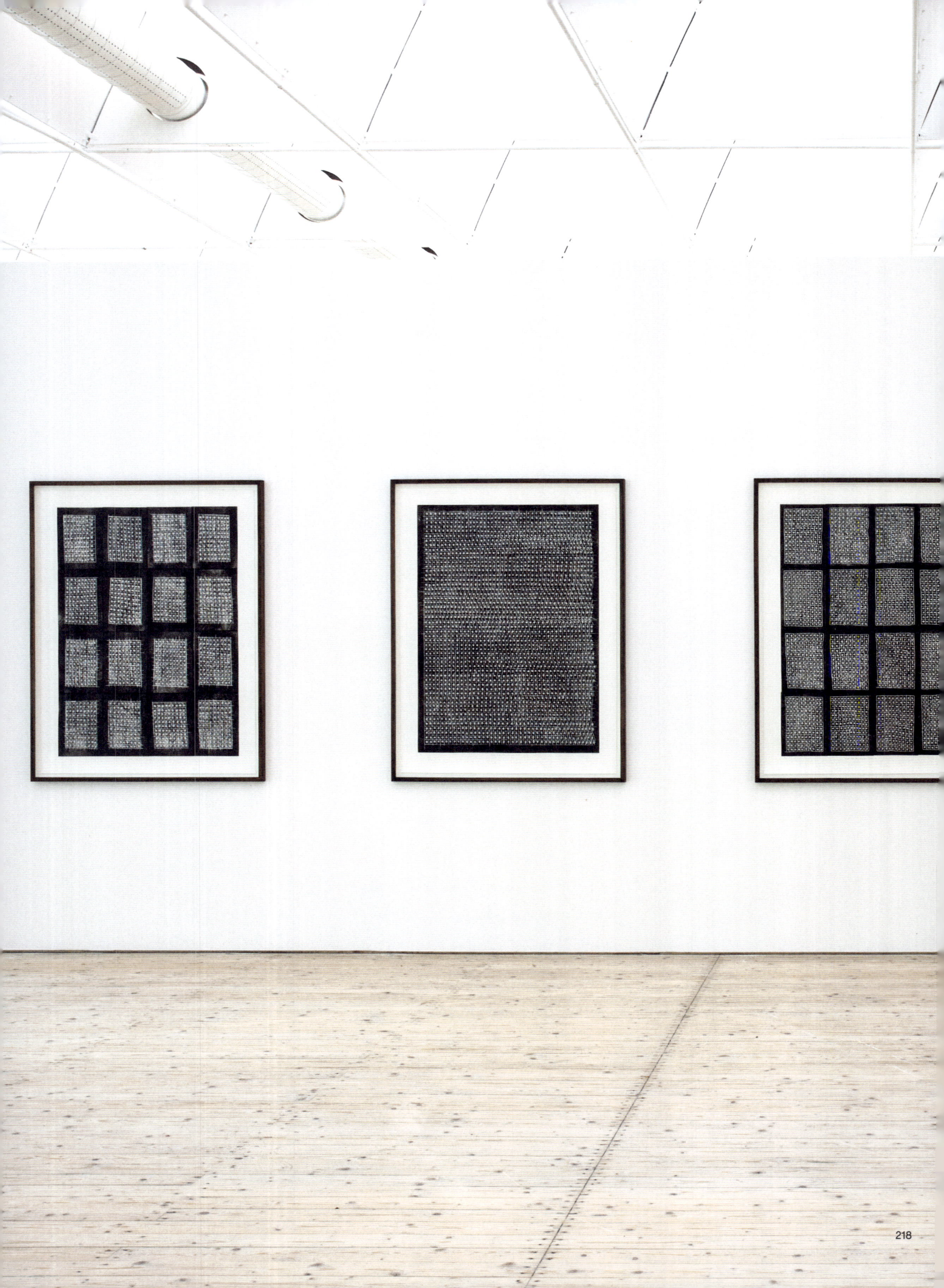

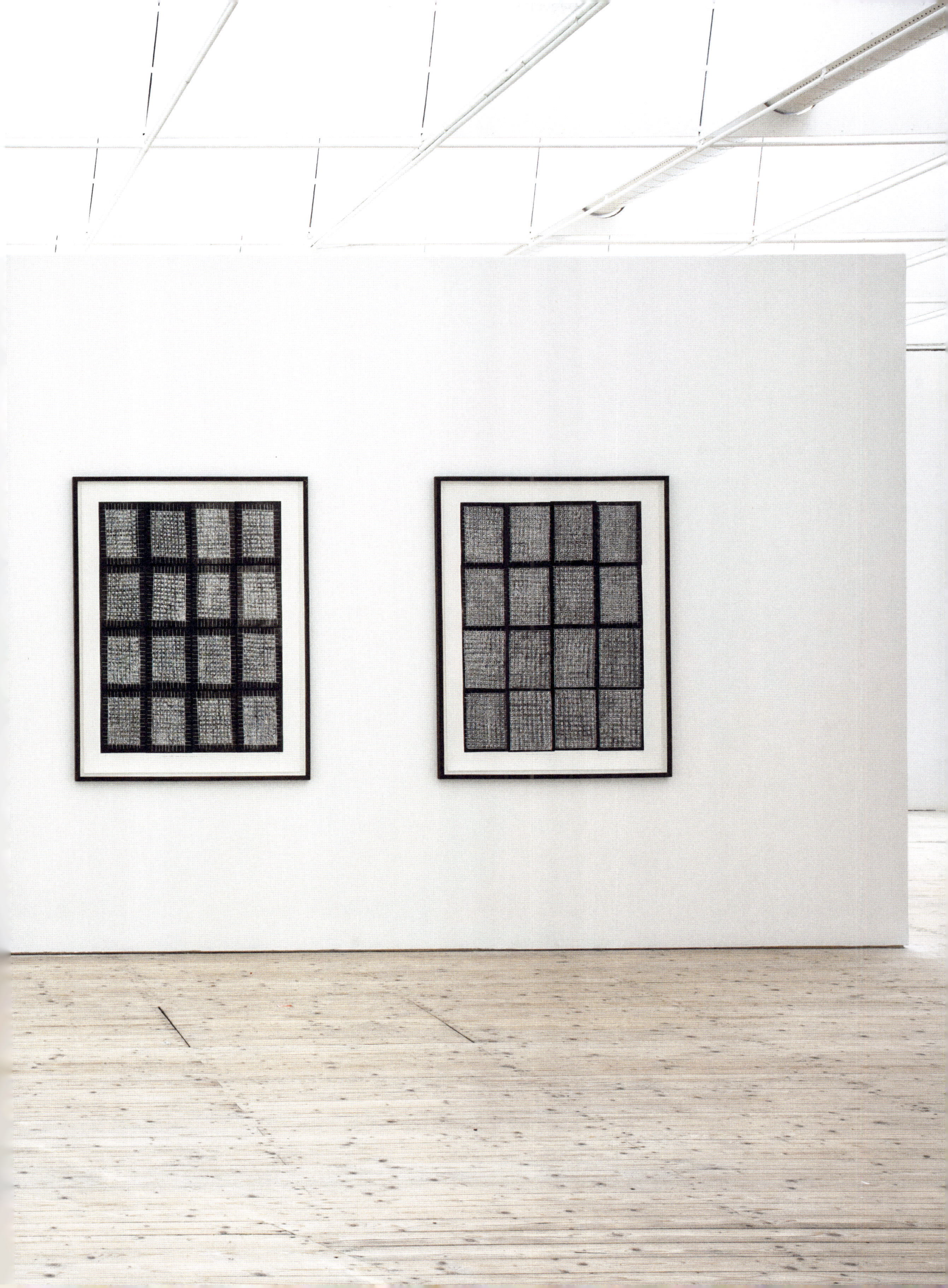

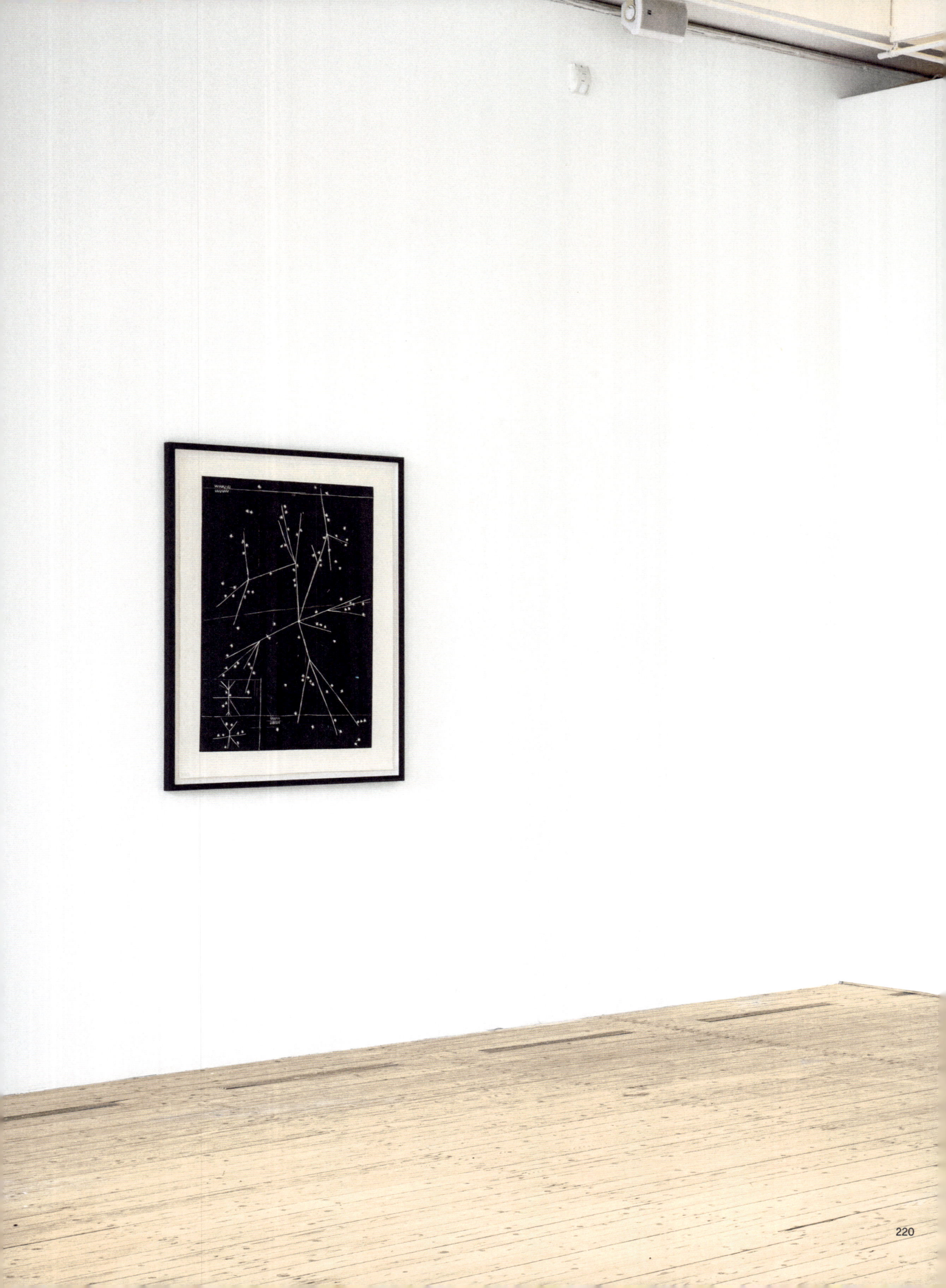

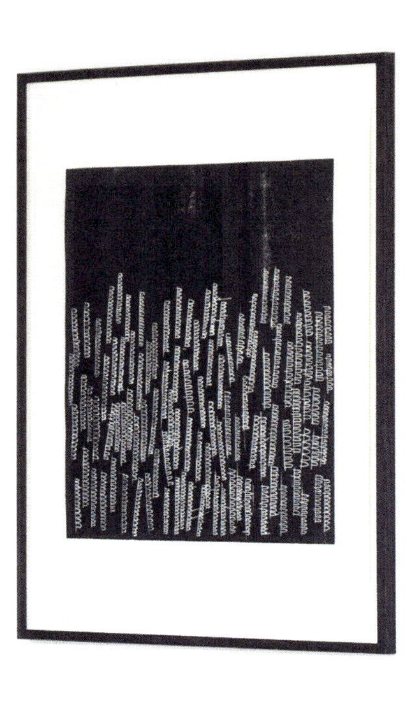
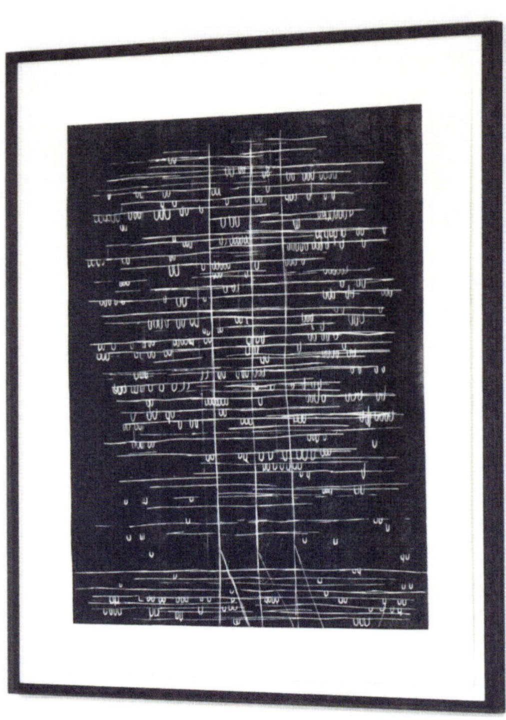

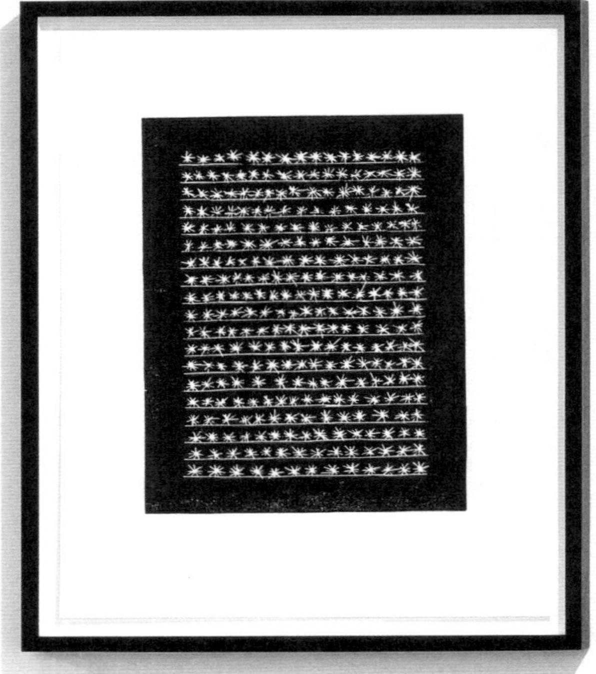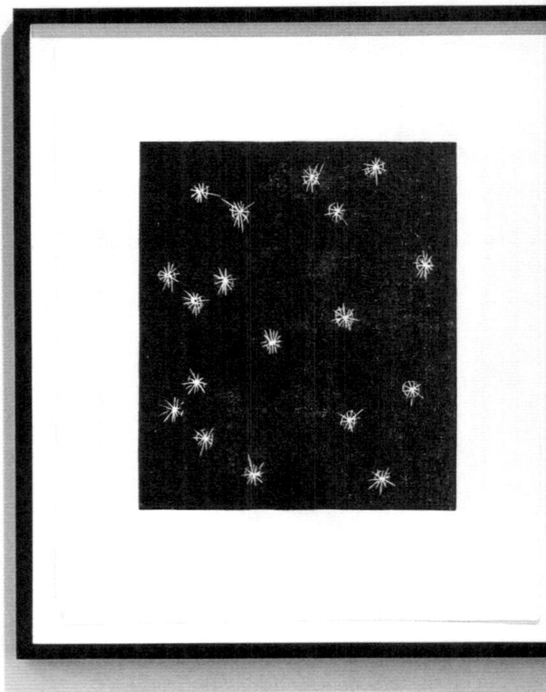

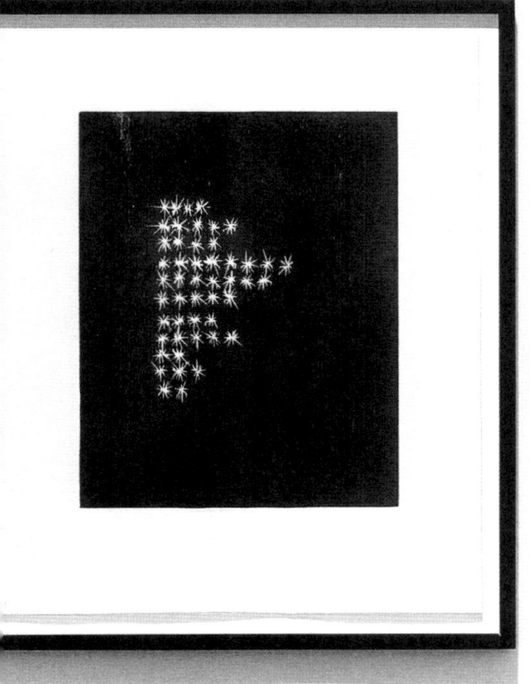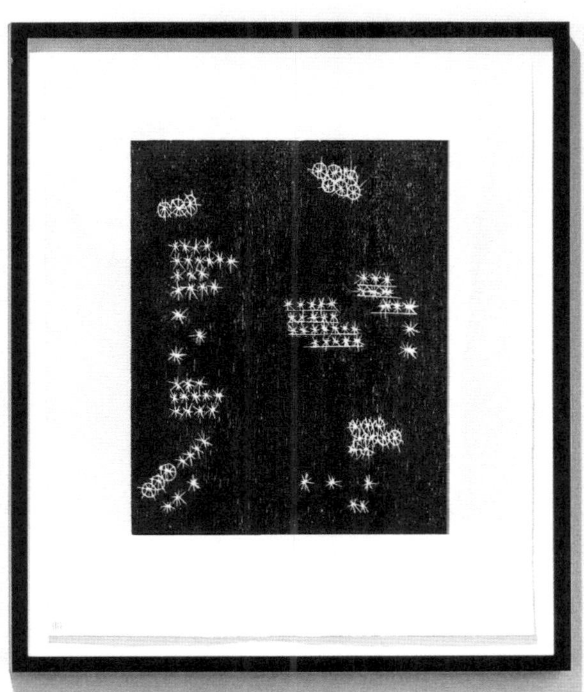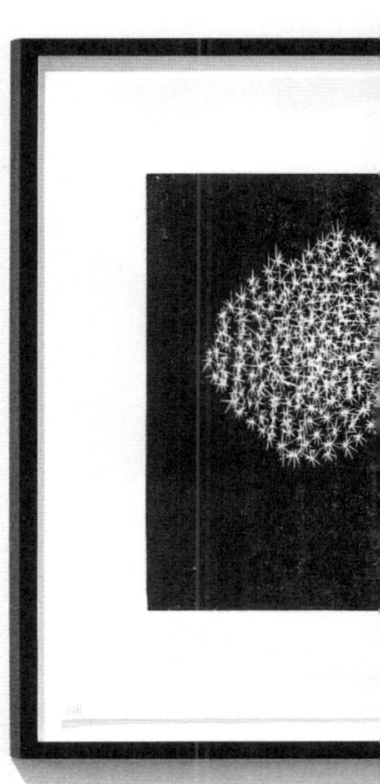

Now it is Light, Galeria Municipal da Boavista, Lisbon, 2018

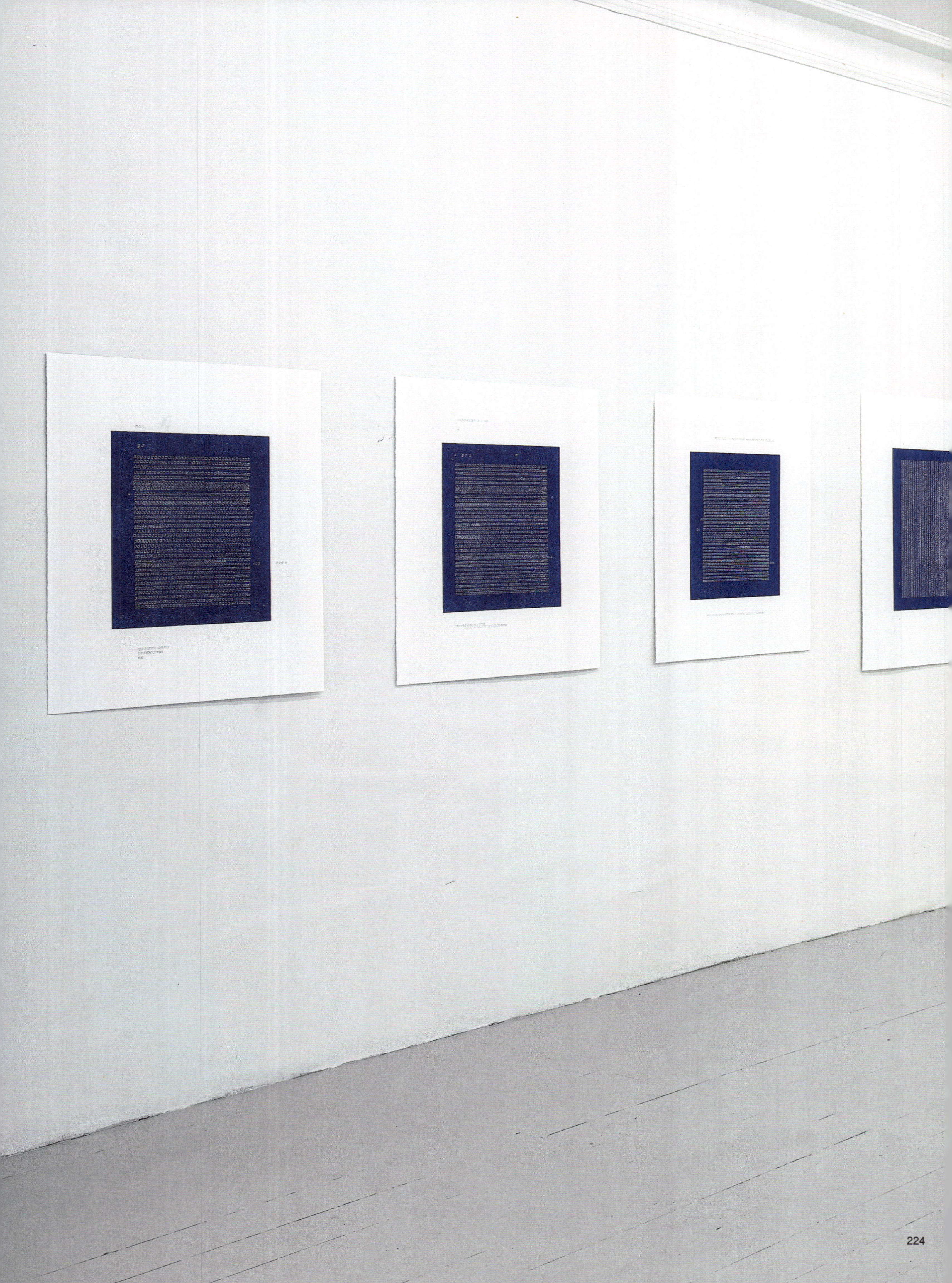

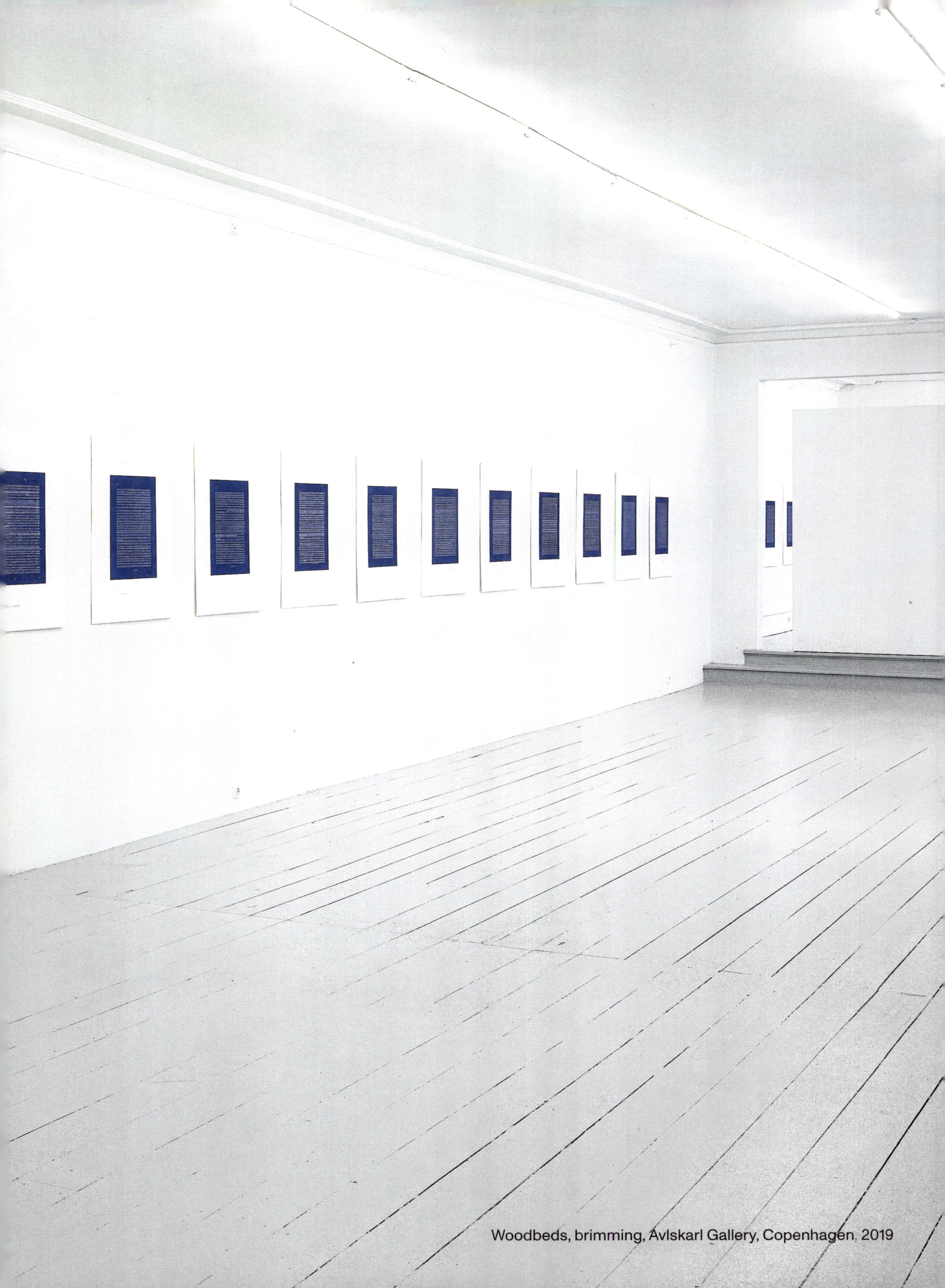

Woodbeds, brimming, Avlskarl Gallery, Copenhagen 2019

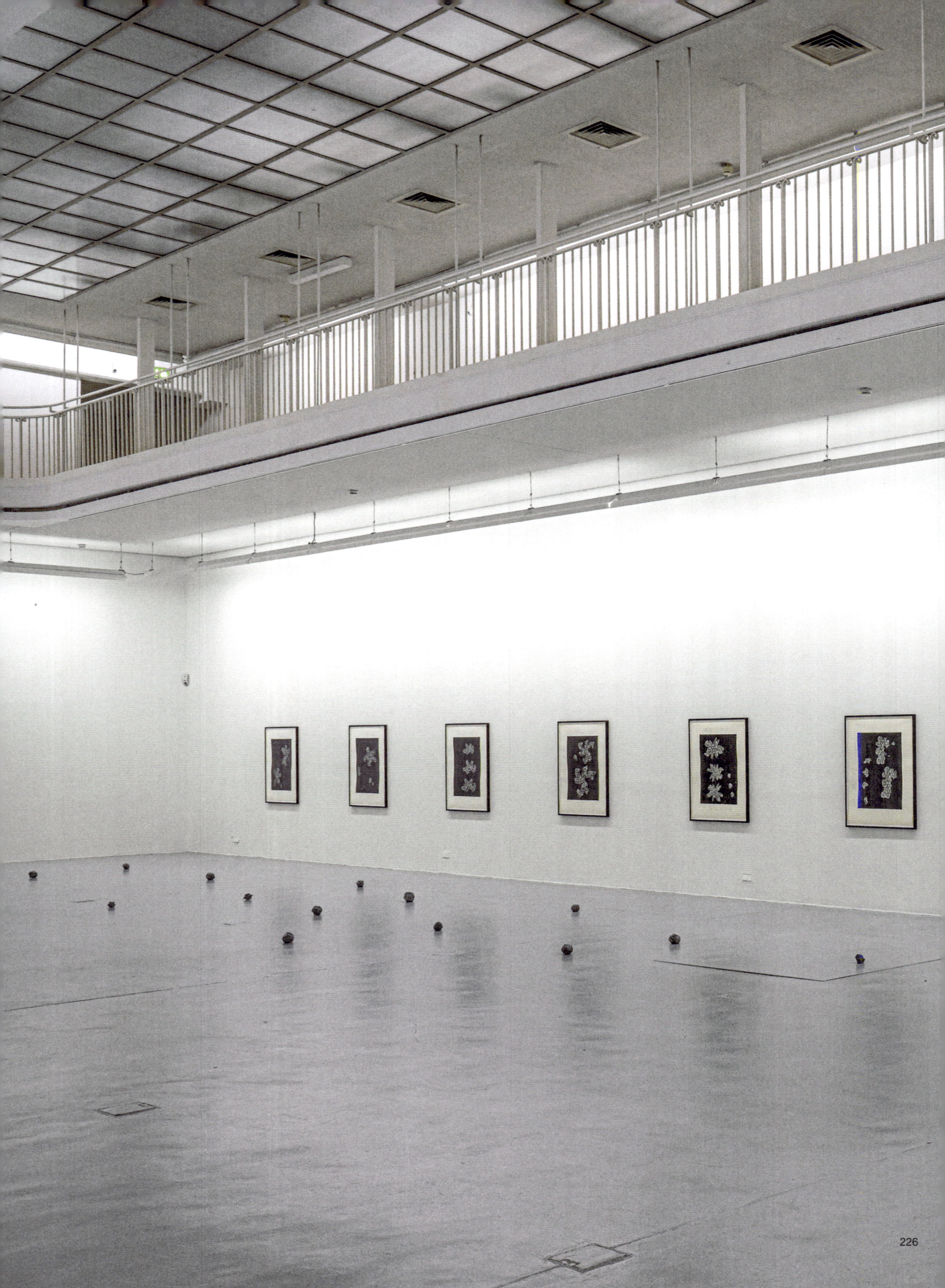

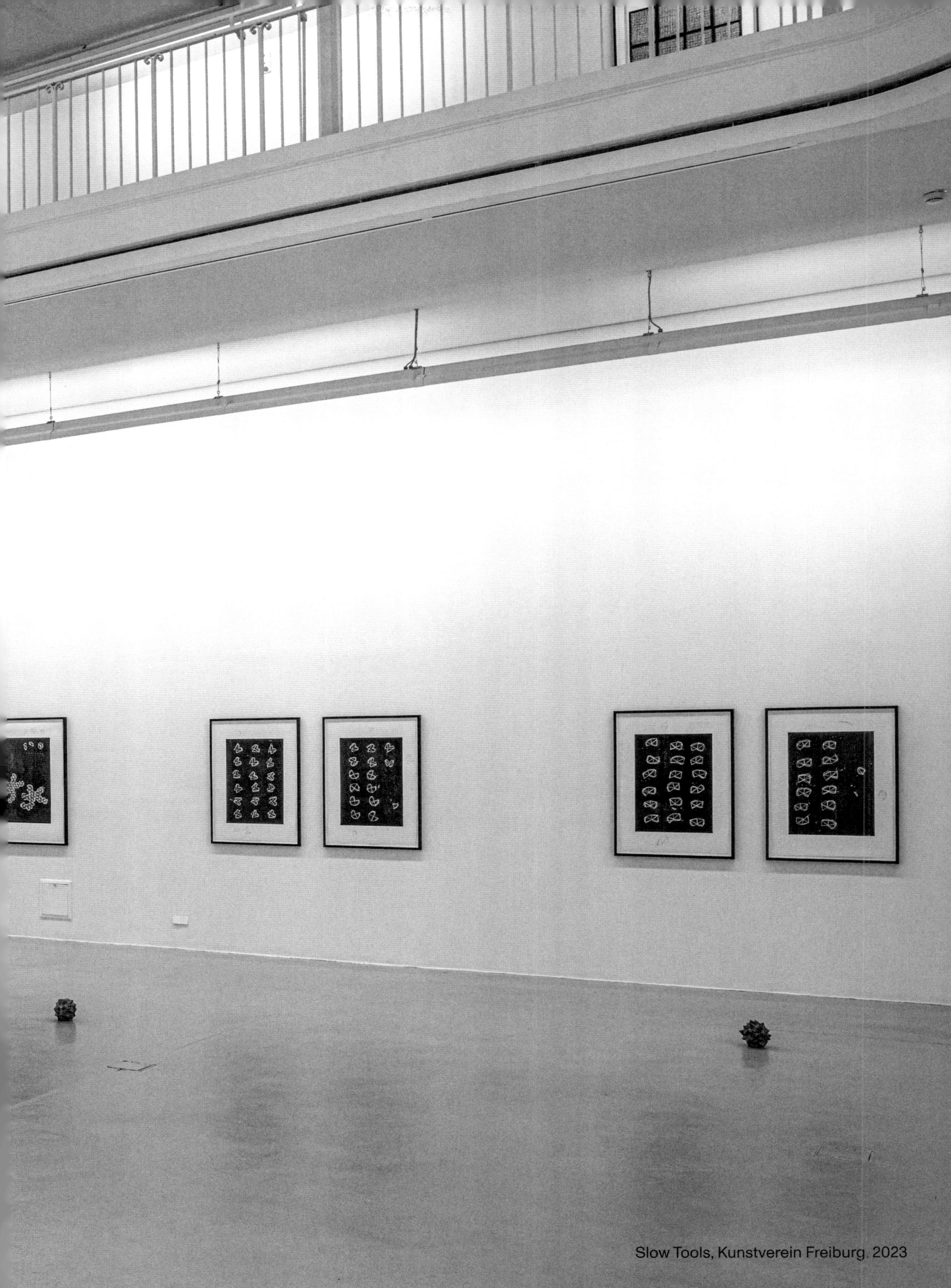

Slow Tools, Kunstverein Freiburg, 2023

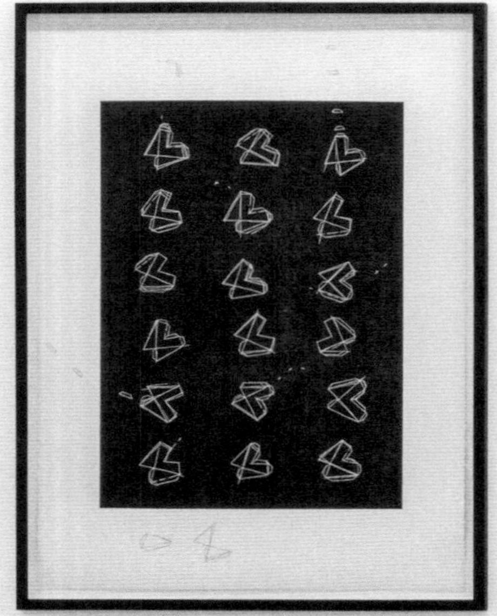
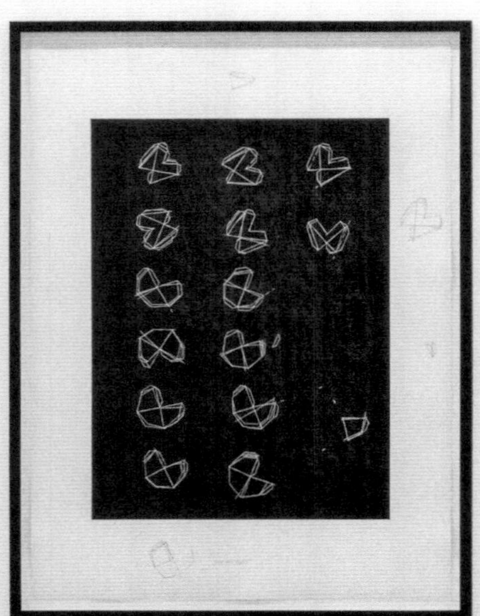
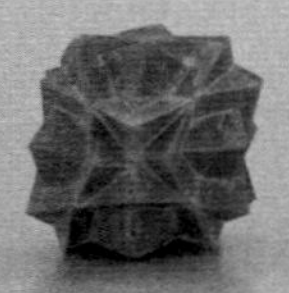

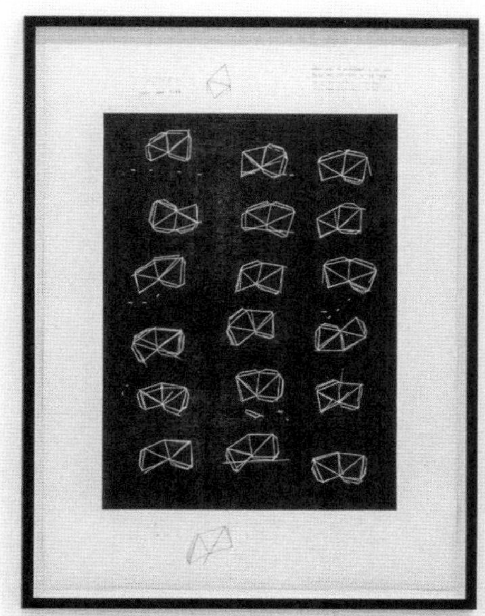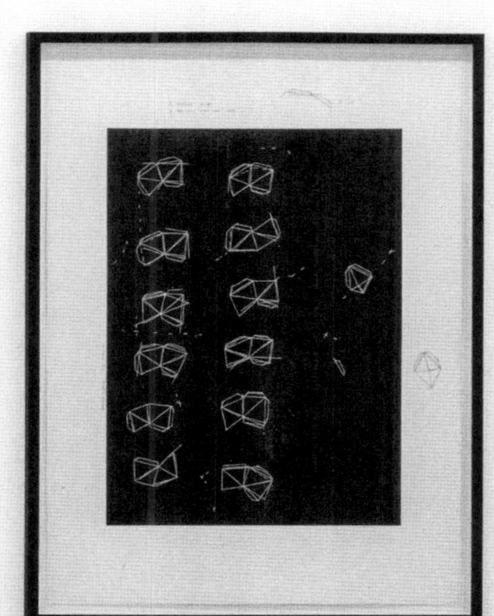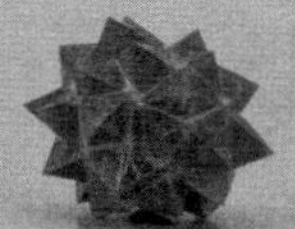

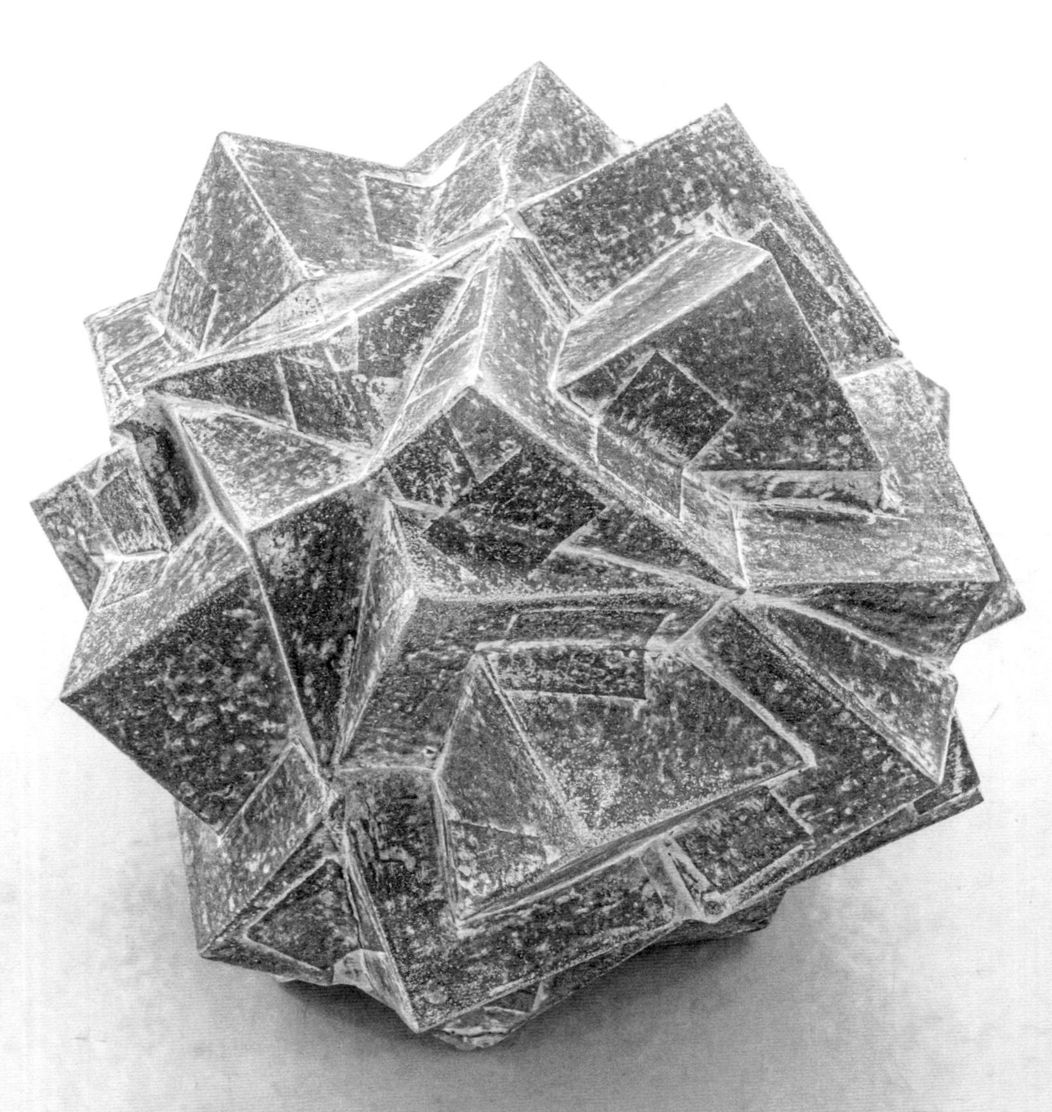

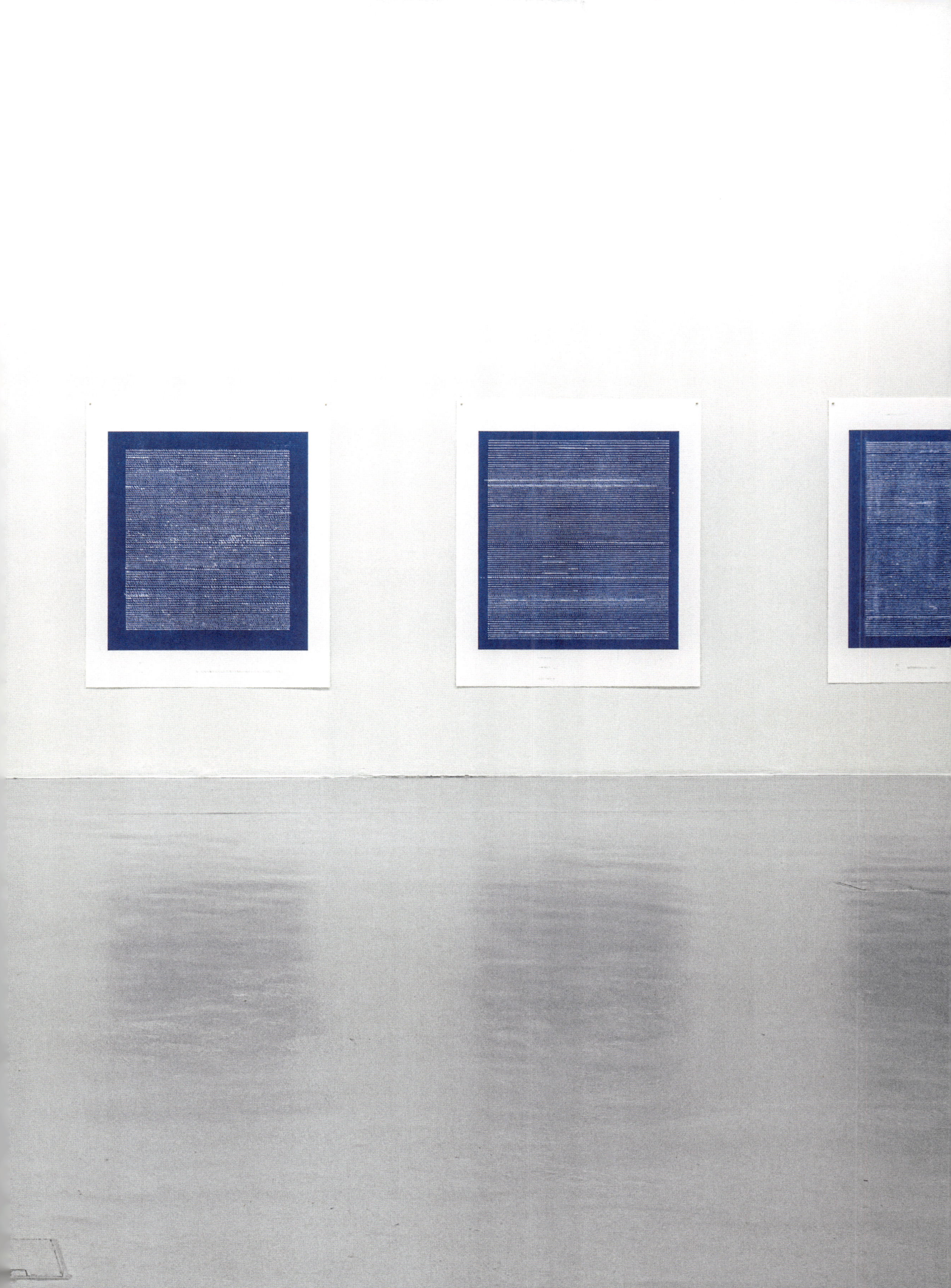

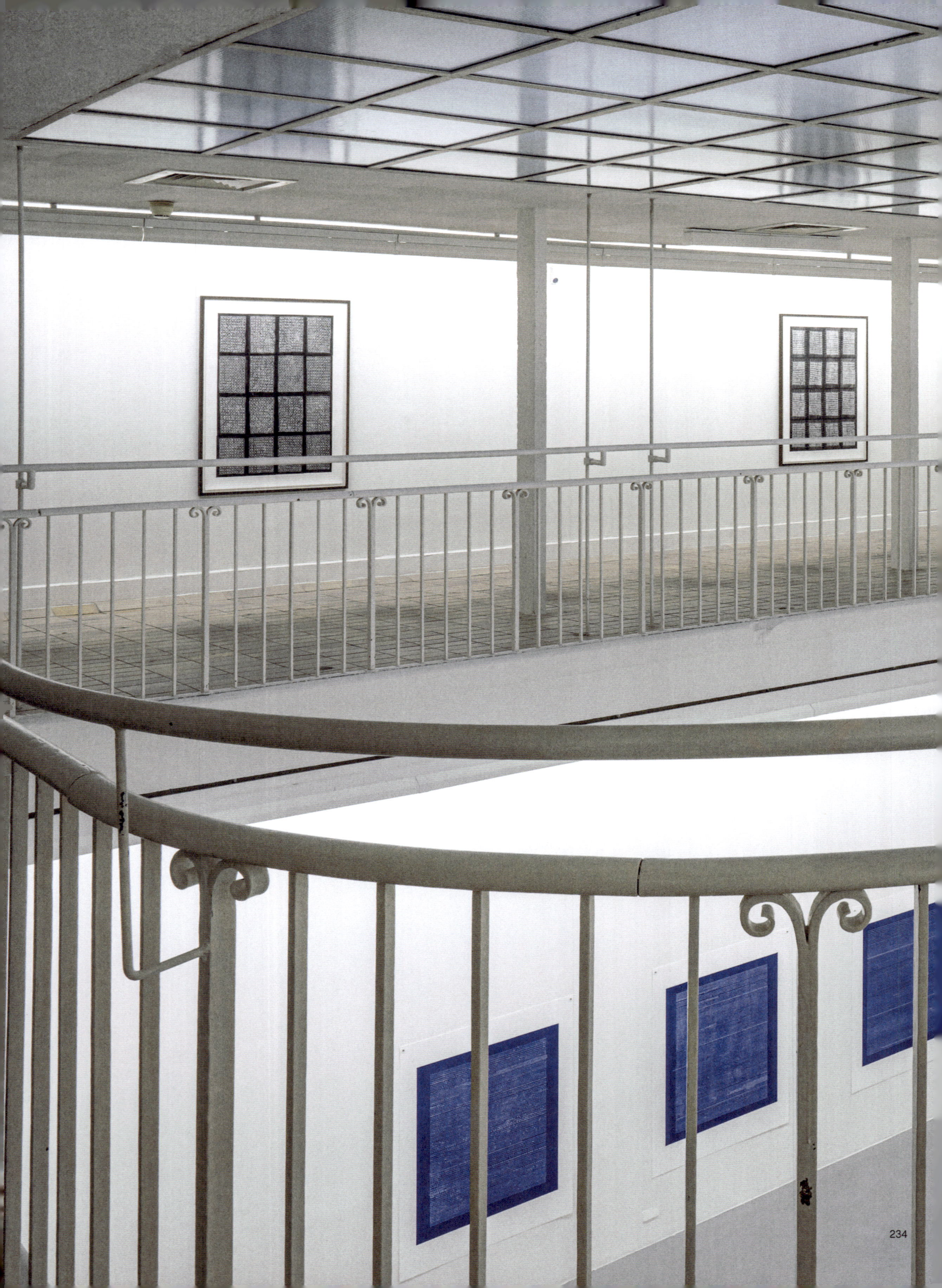

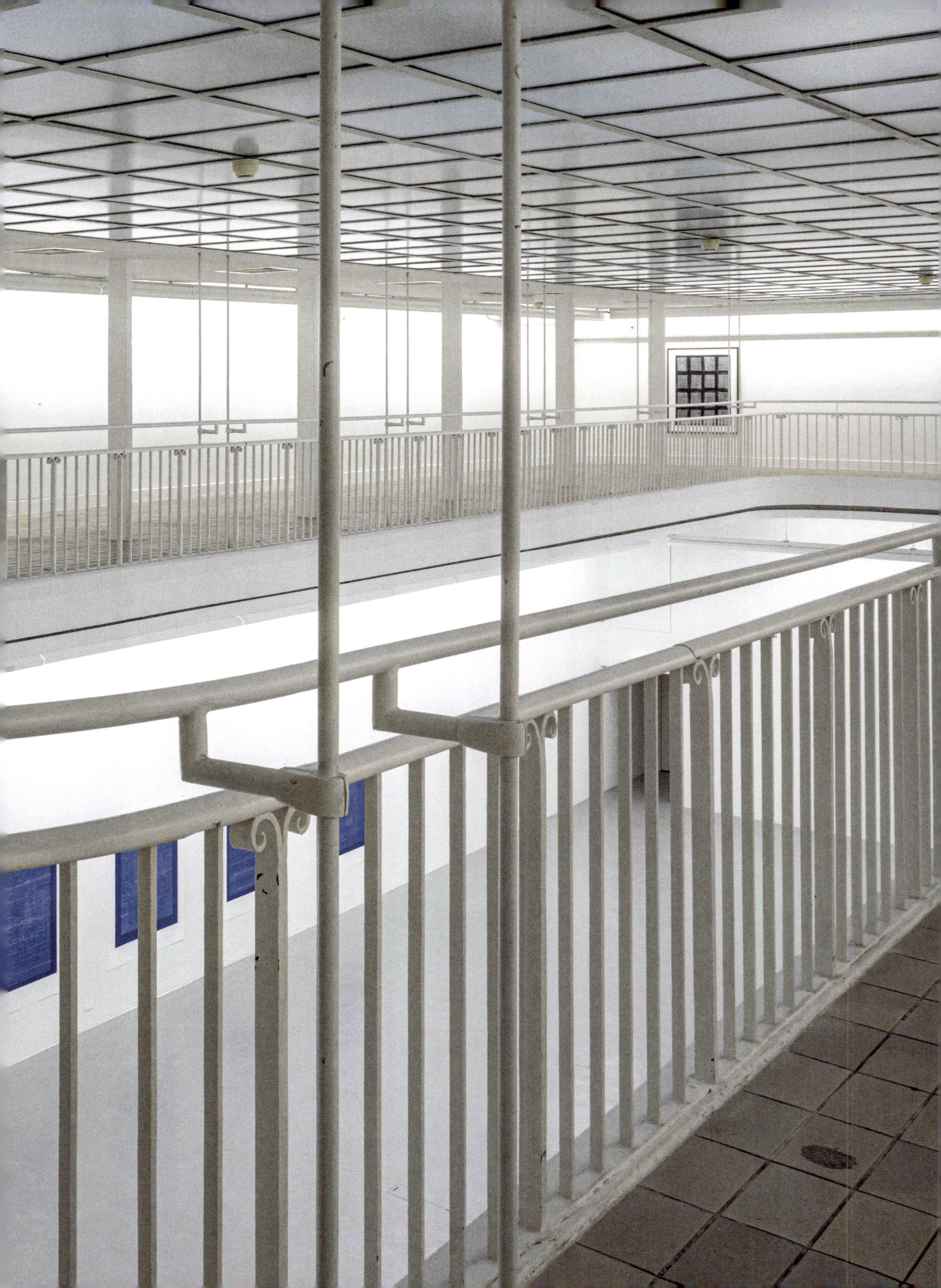

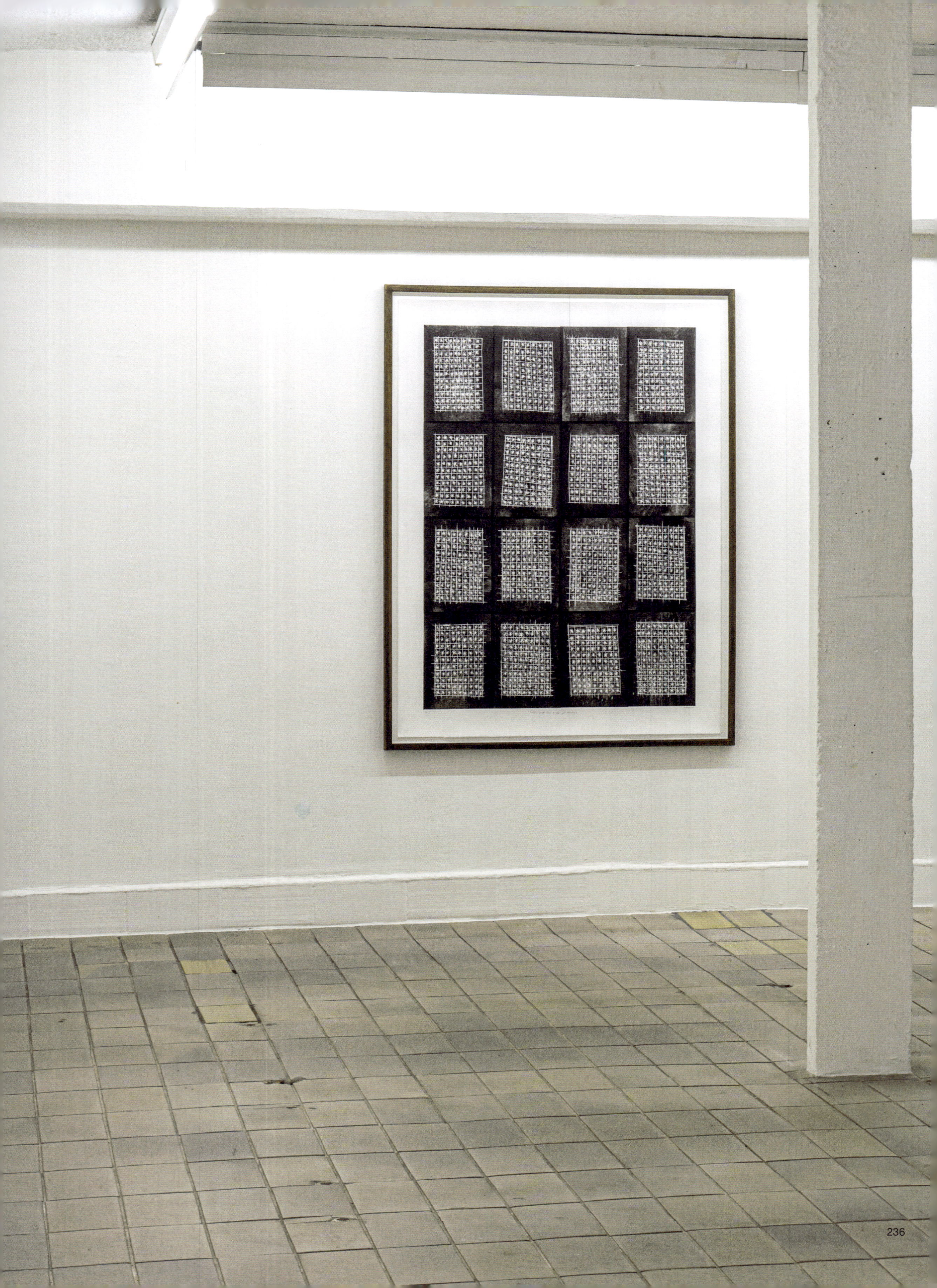

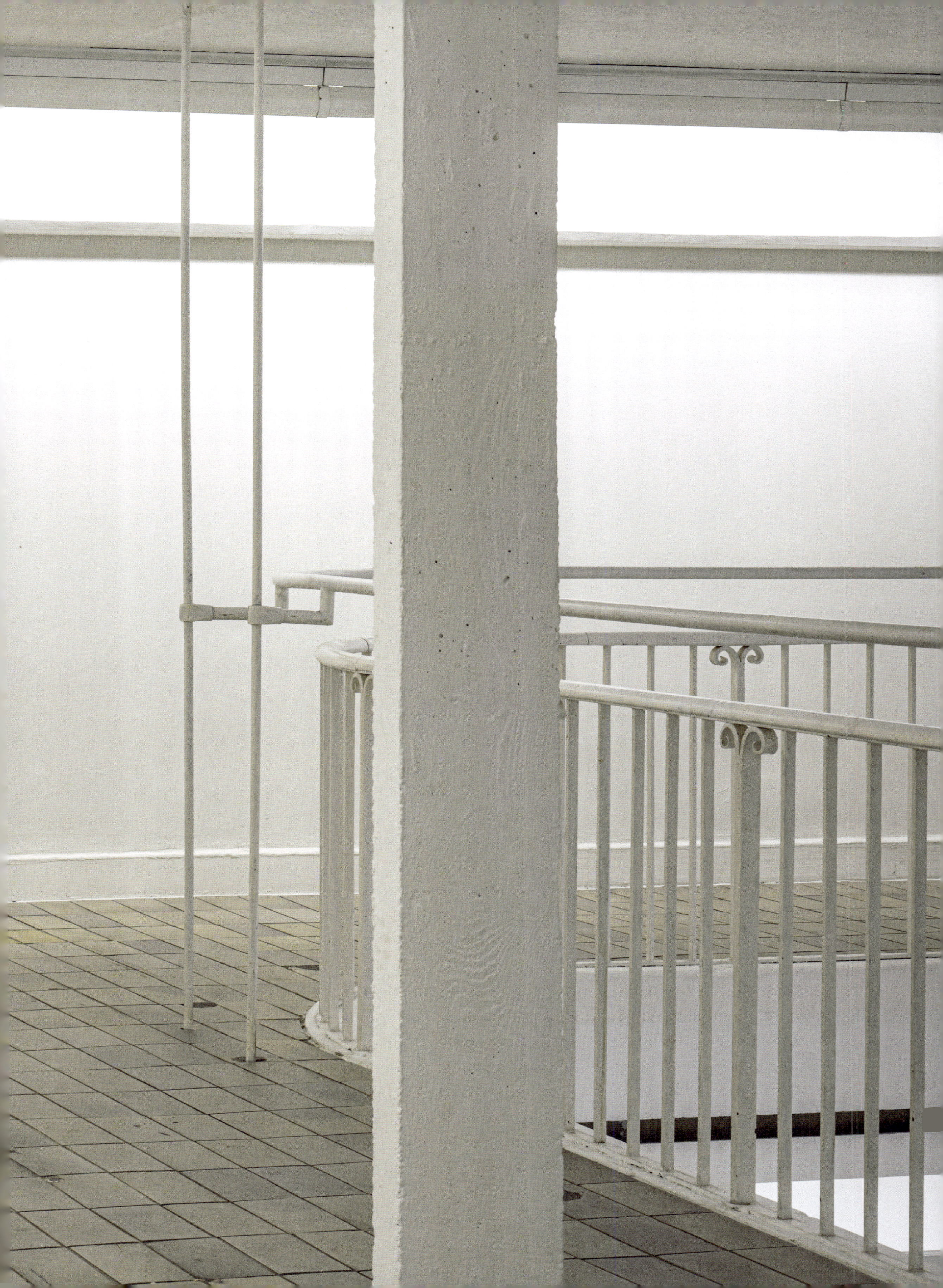

Relational Imprints: How I Love Ester Fleckner's Queer Abstraction
MATHIAS DANBOLT

How I love the backward belongings
How I love the collisions between the grid and the pulse
How I love the tradition as an improvised dress
How I love the combination of questions
How I love the wig and the humping of individuals
How I love that words can be negotiated like bodies and histories

How I love. Sentences starting with these three words are scribbled in
pencil across the upper margin of a monoprint in Ester Fleckner's series
of woodcuts, *Clit-dick Register* (2013–2014) (pp. 4–27). Like a chant or an
incantation, the sentences present declarations of desire, fascination, and
inspiration. Some lines verge towards the poetic and dreamlike. Others
bear semblance to an artist statement in describing a preference for aesthetic collisions, questions, and negotiations. Play with signs and signifi-
cation is also central to the image in the center of the print that pictures
hundreds of white signs in the shape of the letter U on a dark background.
The U-signs are organized in sixteen horizontal lines that increase in
size from small rows on the top to larger rows towards the bottom. Even
though the same form is repeated numerous times, the U's do not appear
standardized, as each line bears a trace of a hand having worked the
wood. This dynamism between seriality and singularity is also central to
the twenty-two monoprints that comprise the *Clit-dick Register* series.
While all of the prints stem from the same wood block, they are far from
identical, in part due to the different densities of ink used in the printing
process that make the backgrounds span from dark black to ash gray, and
in part due to the varied textual snippets written in the margins and on top
of the prints in both Danish and English.
    When seen from a distance, the prints with their distinct lines of U's
look like a concrete poem or a notation score for the sound of an in-
creasingly intense howl or orgasm. But the title of the series suggests a
shift in interpretive orientation from text and sound towards visuality:
Approached as a "clit-dick register," the prints appear as a visual record
of genital forms. "Clit-dick" is an ambiguous word that conjoins body parts
usually understood in binary terms. While the word "clit-dick" has been
used as a misogynist epithet for small dick or extraordinarily large clitoris,
the word also holds possibilities for referencing gendered multiplicity and
variety. This is also the case with the curvy U-shapes that can pass as
letters or breasts or tongues or dicks or clits or something in between.
Their formal simplicity resists easy identification and classification. Operat-
ing in the switch-point between representation and abstraction, repetition and difference, reading and sensing, *Clit-dick Register*'s concern for
nonconforming signs, words, and bodies represents one of the foundational tenets of what I see as Ester Fleckner's relational practice of queer
abstraction.
*

Like abstraction, queer is a fundamentally relational term. As art historian
David J. Getsy has noted, "one cannot be queer alone."[1] In their adjective
forms, both queer and abstract only take on meaning in relation to the
subject they are describing. To call something queer implies marking a
difference from something straight, linear, or normative. Similarly, abstract
describes a move away from representation, figuration, and transparency.
Approaching queerness and abstraction as relational terms means
letting go of ideas that some forms are intrinsically or essentially queer
or abstract. Instead, queerness and abstraction are best understood as
what Getsy describes as "capacities" that "are engendered by activating
relations—between forms, against an opposition or context, or (in the case
of complex forms) among the internal dynamics of their components."[2]
Considering the importance of asserting queer visibility in the history of

the Euro-American LGBT* movement, the turn towards abstraction could easily appear as a formalist retreat from the political. But if we understand queer politics as more than being "out and proud" and also about the work of reimagining relations of power, difference, and desire, this inevitably involves questions on the politics of form. As Getsy explains, "Queer existence is always wrapped up in an attention to form, whether in the survival tactic of shaping oneself to the camouflage of the normal, the defiant assembling of new patterns of lineage and succession, or the picturing of new configurations of desire, bodies, sex, and sodality."[3] Getsy's relational approach to what he terms "queer formalism" calls attention to how queer artists use abstraction to criticize questions around identity, representation, or iconography. Yet queer formalism is not only about critique but also about the desire to explore the creative potential in what he beautifully calls "the intercourse of forms." How do different forms "get on" with each other?

The relations activated by this intercourse of forms not only take place within the frame of the artwork but also involve those who engage with the work. Queer abstraction "stages new spectatorial possibilities," writes art historian Lex Morgan Lancaster in *Dragging Away: Queer Abstraction in Contemporary Art*.[4] Lancaster introduces the concept of "dragging away" as a framework for analyzing how queer abstraction "offers visual and material tools for queer resistance."[5] Referencing both the Latin root of the verb "abstract" (*ab*: away, *trahere*: drawing or pulling), as well as the queer performance tradition of drag, Lancaster pays special attention to how the "active, often unruly process" of abstraction works to hamper, obstruct, or slow down our interpretive operations in ways that emphasize the material and embodied experience of art.[6] In contrast to how modernist artists in the early twentieth century turned to abstraction in search of a universal language of transparent symbolism, Lancaster shows how queer artists use strategies of abstraction—from hard-edged geometry to glistening grids to bright colors to visual distortion—as aesthetic tactics to work against dominant representational logics of surveillance, visibility, and legibility. The artistic work of "dragging away from representation" thus holds potential in instigating per*form*ative processes that also drag us viewers "in multiple aesthetic, material, historical and political ways."[7]

Getsy and Lancaster's takes on queer abstraction offer inspirational perspectives for analyzing Ester Fleckner's work with letters, signs, and primary forms in their woodcuts and concrete sculptures. Returning to *Clit-dick Register* with these relational and embodied processes in mind, other aspects of Fleckner's formal politics come forth. The act of translating these works into words, for instance, makes me painstakingly conscious of the creative *and* coercive force in assigning names and categories to forms and figures in difference. Fleckner's visual vocabulary of abstracted U-shapes, which appear as letters as much as visual representations of body parts, not only complicate an easy "reading" of the prints but also suggest an ethical investment in the coexistence or intercourse of multiple frameworks of meaning-making including language, visuality, tactility, and embodiment. It is difficult to describe the unruly interplay between these elements without straightening them out, literally speaking, in the linear format of writing. After all, Fleckner does not provide any guide for how to analyze the prints, and the works work differently depending on the movements of my body. One needs, for instance, to be quite close to the prints to read the notes written in pencil in the margin.

But is "margin" really the right word to use for the white space surrounding the printed image in these artworks? Does this not risk implying a hierarchy between the center and periphery of the work, which risks positioning the written love notes as a *marginal* rather than as a coeval partner in the work's formal intercourse? When I pull back to get a better view of the printed image, the rhythmic variation between the seemingly similar U-shapes come to the fore. Despite the title's invitation to read the U's as a visual representation of body parts, to claim them as "clit-dicks"

would disregard the productive friction between the visual and textual
components of the image, including the title. The phrase *Clit-dick Register*
drags along associations to histories of violence perpetrated by medical
institutions against intersex bodies, trans*bodies, and other bodies whose
visual morphology have failed to match the shifting biopolitical doctrines
of the sex/gender-binary. Yet these heavy-hearted allusions clash with the
light-heartedness I see in the simple, almost childlike play with rendering
gendered and sexual forms that seem to signal how ridiculous it is to
reduce bodily difference to the form of a singular body part. A note scribbled in pencil at the bottom corner of the margin of a print in the series
points to these dynamics: "How I love the components of failure." While
the note does not explicate which standards or measures it loves to betray,
its appearance in proximity to the gender ambiguous U-shapes makes it
tempting to read it as a statement that flirts with the generative possibilities of failing to conform to normative taxonomies of gender, sexuality, and
language. Importantly, though, the note expresses a love of *components*
of failure, not failure per se. For how to love, or rather, who is able to love
falling between the cracks of *all* frameworks of recognition?

*

A desire for connection and belonging runs through Fleckner's series of
woodcuts titled *I navigate in collisions* (2014–2015) (pp. 41–57). The series
is introduced by a print subtitled *flyer* that includes a hand-carved text in
capital letters in white on an almost black background:

I NAVIGATE IN COLLISIONS
WOODCUTS BY ESTER FLECKNER
RELATION. YOU TALK IN A WAY ~~THAT~~ I DON'T KNOW BUT
THAT I'M MISSING. YOU TALK ABOUT BELONGING
DIFFERENTLY. I BIKE THROUGH THE CITY WITH MY EYES
CLOSED, OR ALMOST. I THINK ABOUT IMAGES ONE
CAN RECOGNIZE ONESELF IN OR NOT. I THINK ABOUT
FAMILY TREES. AND HAVING READ THAT IT DEMANDS
SYNCHRONICITY WITH THE PATTERNS AND RHYTHMS
OF A PLACE TO FEEL THAT ONE BELONGS. I WANT TO
HAVE A RELATION TO YOU AND UNDERSTAND THAT WE
ALREADY HAVE ONE.

The letter-like text addresses an unidentified "you"—a friend or lover?—
that the "I" seeks to get closer to. In linguistics, words such as "I" and "you"
are called shifters because their meaning shifts depending on the context
of the enunciation and reception. I'm often drawn to shifters such as "you"
in artworks that permit me to imagine myself in the position of the one
who is being addressed. Although I know I am not the "you" that is occa-
sioned by the text, since I first encountered this print, taped to the window
of the gallery C4 Projects in Copenhagen in 2014, I have felt a strong pull
towards the "you" in *I navigate in collisions* that first dragged me into the
gallery.[8]
    In contrast to the prints in *Clit-dick Register* that are based on the
same woodblock, the twelve prints in *I navigate in collisions* are all radical-
ly different. Yet they all appear to present alternative takes on the concept
of a family tree. Traditionally, a family tree is a visual representation of a
person's ancestry organized in a hierarchical order, where the hetero-
generational bloodline constitutes the roots of the tree's branches that
chart paternal and maternal lineages in successive strings of coupled
relations. By contrast, the visual diagrams presented in *I navigate in
collisions* are weird and wild, and seem to operate according to their own
queer logics that favor the rhizomatic structures of weeds or undergrowth
over the vertical form of trees. In *I navigate in collisions, 2* (p. 43), for instance, thin white lines stand out from a black-gray background and form
a precarious architectural structure that resembles an electrical tower or
a ship's mast more than a tree. A series of U-shapes hang side by side, like
bats, from the seven large parallel branches or beams affixed to the trunk

that balances on a scanty road. A similar structure appears in *I navigate in collisions, 3* (p. 46), but this time all of the U-shapes have fallen off the branches and float individually in space. In *I navigate in collisions, 4* (p. 47) the structure has grown and multiplied in all directions: Three parallel trunks are connected by countless overlapping beams that hold single or small clusters of U's in a complex web of connections. In several prints the U-shapes are accompanied by a small hand-carved sign that looks like a star or asterisk—or anus. When the *-signs made their first appearance in a series of prints entitled *Arguments for desire* (2013–2018) (pp. 28–39), Fleckner introduced them as "anus stars,"[9] and this beautiful term has saturated my view of star signs both within and outside of their work. If seen as indexes of bodies, the *-signs are as undecidedly gendered as the U-signs, and with a similar sexual potentiality.

The intimate constellations of unruly lines and erotic forms that appear across the print series *I navigate in collisions* chart alternative constellations of intimacy. This cartography of desirable connections points to a utopian territory of strange connectivities that I have a hard time fleshing out but that feels fleshy enough. By utopian I do not mean that *I navigate in collisions* presents political blueprints for the ideal organization of relational attachments, far from it. But confronted with these seemingly unrestrained and undomesticated charts, I become painfully aware of my limited ability to imagine a relational world beyond the gravitational pull of conventional coupledom that informs my own life as a married gay man living in a rainbow family with kids. How I love getting lost in the polymorphous perverse swarm of anonymous, gender-ambiguous figures that connect across these prints. Standing in front of the large diptych *I navigate in collisions, 8* (pp. 52–53), with its beehive-looking cloud of attachments where U meets U meets U in an assemblage of virtual intimacies, I cannot help but wonder how this world would work if the transmission of history and heritage, love, and economy were structured according to the logics of affinity and community rather than identity and family.

*

As you have probably realized by now, I do not pretend to write about Fleckner's practice from a "disinterested" or "objective" scholarly perspective. This has never been an option, as I have been hooked on Fleckner's practice since I first encountered their work more than a decade ago. Since then, I have not been able to stop thinking, talking, and writing about their work, hence, my approach draws on my expertise in art history mixed with the love of a fan and the critical intimacy of a friend.[10] Confessing to relational bonds in an essay like this could be seen as a break of protocol. The discipline of art history has had a long tradition of avoiding or hiding forms of affective attachments, as separation and detachment have been seen as foundational for upholding ideals of neutrality, impartiality, and objectivity. But just as critical distance is not a prophylactic for bias, partiality, or prejudice, critical intimacy is not necessarily an obstacle for scholarly practice. Emotional reactions—from desire and frustration to curiosity or love—are often what compels one to think and write in the first place, and physical and affective proximity can potentially give access to different perspectives and contextual frameworks. In the context of my take on Fleckner's practice, my approach is highly indebted to my long-term engagement in what we could call Copenhagen's queer scene, referencing the different but often overlapping arenas oriented around queer and/or LGBT* lives and politics, including bars, clubs, festivals, events, and even at times also art spaces. And it was also within the queer scene that I first encountered Fleckner's work.

In November 2012 Fleckner exhibited a series of small, mesmerizing photo-based collages at the queer feminist pop-up art bar *BarHvaViHar* at the queer performance institution Warehouse 9 in Copenhagen. Fleckner started the itinerant *BarHvaViHar* earlier that year together with Mette Clausen, Line Hvidbjerg, and Mo Maja Moesgaard, a group of fellow students at The Royal Danish Academy of Fine Arts. As a much-needed alternative to Copenhagen's straight, white male-dominated art scene, *BarHvaViHar* attracted a diverse crowd from the overlapping networks of people engaged in the DIY-inspired queer activist scene, that had developed in Copenhagen in the early 2000s, in addition to artists and academics working with queer art and performance. For me, who was struggling to finish a PhD in queer art history while mustering the courage to finally leave my then-boyfriend, *BarHvaViHar* felt like a safe refuge and energy boost. Its collectivist ethos not only provided a fertile site for seeing, sharing, and talking about queer feminist art, it also did so in a space that invited flirting and dancing. Beside working with the pop-up bar, Fleckner, Clausen, Hvidbjerg, and Moesgaard also organized a reading group at the art academy where art students and academics met to discuss new work by feminist, queer, and trans scholars such as Judith Butler, Jack Halberstam, Tobias Raun, and Sara Ahmed, to only mention a few. *BarHvaViHar* quickly became an important meeting place for people interested in developing new forms and formats to talk about the politics of gender, sexuality, and difference in our local context, and it was where I started my dialogue with Fleckner and their work—a dialogue that has continued to this day.

When Fleckner presented *Clit-dick Register* at their graduation show at Kunsthal Charlottenborg in Copenhagen in 2013, it was not difficult to see the relational imprints from these queer networks in the series. The experiments with gender-nonconforming signs and the textual notes clearly referenced the ongoing discussions on visibility, failure, and passing, taking place in queer and trans*-oriented spaces such as *BarHvaViHar* at the time. Yet *Clit-dick Register* did not *represent* or *document* these political debates but recast them in formal terms. This turn towards formalism allowed Fleckner to bring urgent questions being asked at the so-called margins of society into a mainstream art institution without contributing to the growing commodification and spectacularization of "difference" and "diversity."

*

The queer and trans* political dimensions in Fleckner's work may not be immediately available for viewers glancing at the prints for a minute or two in the gallery. But this does not mean that they are hidden from view. In contrast to historical as well as contemporary artists who work in contexts where exhibiting art with explicit queer content poses risks of criminalization, exclusion, or censorship, Fleckner does not use abstraction as a form of queer coding. After all, sexual and gendered body signs are often literally imprinted onto the surface of Fleckner's works, as in *Clit-dick Register* and *Arguments for desire*. Other series' address the conditions for public visibility and knowledge of sexuality and gender identity in slightly different terms, such as the prints in the series *A closet does not connect under the bed* (2016) (pp. 100–123), that deconstruct and disassemble the material and metaphorical idea of "the closet."[11] A similar resistance to the social expectation for transparency and recognizability of bodily difference can be found in a monoprint such as *Contraposer (Back-facing)* (2018) (p. 155), where constellations of small cubes create fragmented bodies that seem to turn their abstracted butts towards the viewer. The gesture of turning away can also appear in the prints *Cruising horizontal lines (silver)* (2022) (pp. 200–204) where numerous carefully carved eyelashes appear on a silver background. Whether alluding to closed eyes, withheld gazes, or make-up as an attention-grabbing cover, the prints rework the act of seeing and being seen in a shiny aesthetic that references exaggerated femininity in drag performance.

Fleckner's varied practice accommodates both forms of figuration and language that place bodies center stage, yet their prints are never straightforward. One needs to work to unleash the queer potential in these prints. As José Muñoz writes in *Cruising Utopia*, "to access queer visuality we may need to squint, to strain our vision and force it to see otherwise, beyond the limited vista of the here and now."[12] Even the most literal forms, like the stars that appear in multiple series, can be seen to function as "wildcard characters," akin to how asterisks are used in digital search engines to secure an open range of meanings.[13] Jack Halberstam's discussion of the use of the asterisk in trans*political contexts speaks not only to the stars in Fleckner's prints but to their use of abstraction more generally, "The asterisk holds off the certainty of diagnosis; it keeps at bay any sense of knowing in advance what the meaning of this or that gender variant form may be."[14] The recurrence of primary forms and signs in Fleckner's practice signals an ethical resistance to reducing the transition and transmission of meanings, bodies, and language to "a final form, a specific shape, or an established configuration of desire and identity."[15]

Nowhere is this investment in the process of seeing and sensing difference more evident than in the most recent works in the series *Woodbeds, brimming* (2019–) (pp. 158–198).[16] In the large-scale woodcuts in the series, printed in radiant blue, we are presented with white outlines of tens of thousands of small hand-carved geometric shapes that are lined up beside each other in successive horizontal rows, often with additional forms drawn in pencil on the perimeter of the printed image. The sheer size of the large prints in this series, with their insistent repetition of primary forms—from tiny down-pointing triangles to small right angled squares to rhomboids and trapeziums—overpowers me with a sense of awe *and* exhaustion. This concatenation of contrasting affective states can perhaps best be described with what cultural theorist Sianne Ngai, writing about the aesthetic of tedium in the poet Gertrude Stein's writing, terms "stuplimity." Evoking the sublime, the stupefying, as well as the stupid, Ngai uses the term stuplime to describe the way certain aesthetic forms can register "as at once exciting and enervating, astonishing yet tedious."[17] Ngai's take on Stein is helpful in this regard, for besides calling attention to the formal affinities between Fleckner and Stein, whose quotes appear in several of Fleckner's prints, Ngai's writing about stuplime aesthetics also puts pressure on the temporal dimensions in these artworks. Ngai argues that Stein's use of repetition creates a "slowdown of language" that shifts focus from formal differences to modal or *moody* differences centered around constantly shifting temperamental variations. When standing in front of *Woodbeds, brimming*, my astonishment at thinking about the time it must have taken to individually carve these minute forms is accompanied by a sense of exhaustion at the artistic labor as much as my limited ability for comprehending the abundance of repetition and difference.

Stuplime aesthetics do not describe a privileged political state to Ngai, since stuplime works, such as those of Stein, offer no progression, no release, and no transcendence. But stuplime artworks can "provide small subjects with what Stein calls 'a little resistance' in their confrontation with larger systems," writes Ngai.[18] I see "a little resistance" in Fleckner's approach to the abstract language of geometry in *Woodbeds, brimming*. The insistent modulation of primary forms in these prints pays little heed to geometry's standardized relationships between shapes and forms. In contrast to the tradition of seeing geometric abstraction as a universal language, Fleckner has instead turned geometric shapes into a malleable material for materializing difference.

It is precisely the formal unruliness that distinguishes Fleckner from some of the key modernist artists working with abstraction, such as the painter Agnes Martin (1912–2004) with whom they are often compared. There are surely visual semblances between Fleckner's patterns of geometric modulations in *Woodbeds, brimming* and Martin's famous grid paintings, for instance *Night Sea* (1963), with its individually painted blue rectangles carefully inlaid in a negative orthogonal grid. But while Martin and Fleckner share a dedication to the slow and meticulous craft of handmade image-making, the effects of their use of primary forms and repeated structures could hardly be more different. The smooth and calm surfaces of Martin's late paintings have often been described as "seamless" since it is "hard to see how she does what she does."[19] Fleckner, on the other hand, consistently brings the process to the front in their prints:

Words and signs are frequently crossed out in the prints, and the text fragments written in pencil often bear traces of having been erased or re-written. This embodied, processual transparency stands in stark contrast to Martin's impersonal brushstrokes and compositional defiance of explicit personal perspectives or singular vantage points.

Martin was in dialogue with the American uptake of Zen Buddhism at the time, and this shows in her visual orientation towards what art historian Jonathan D. Katz calls a "pictorial realization of equilibrium" where all visual elements are balanced by negating counterpoints.[20] Katz finds a queer or rather lesbian ethic in Martin's use of visual binaries that chronicles "difference within sameness."[21] The power of Martin's paintings lies, according to Katz, in the artist's ability to halt and seemingly transcend any dialectic or progressive movement within the binary structure they construct. The visual forms in Fleckner's prints, by contrast, do not hinge on the "tense stasis" in symmetric and balanced compositions. Instead, Fleckner uses abstraction to set signs, figures, and meanings in motion. The queer abstraction at play in prints such as *Woodbeds, brimming* chronicles difference differently than Martin's paintings, for the constellation of forms do not cohere around a binary logic of either/or but appear instead to operate according to the relational force of the conjunction "and." The shapeshifting triangles lined up in *Woodbeds, brimming (to)* (2021) (p. 187), for instance, read as geometric forms, *and* as references to symbols such as the pink triangle, *and* as representations of bodies, for instance a crotch, *and..., and..., and...*

While Martin's paintings flirt with the idea of freedom in transcending the powergame of identity, Fleckner's prints offer no release from embodiment and materialism—instead they work on reshaping a sense of the present, one form at a time.

*

"If at first you don't succeed, failure may be your style." The quote from the beautifully eccentric actor and writer Quentin Crisp is one of the starting points of Jack Halberstam's book *The Queer Art of Failure* (2011), where he makes a compelling argument about failure as a queer style that can be mobilized to refuse or resist the punishing norms that organize the measurements of success and failure in capitalist society.[22] Failure, like abstract and queer, is a relational term that can be used as a tactic for unlearning systems, disturbing expectations, and provoking new orienting points. As someone who has struggled with perfectionism my whole life—a problem intimately connected to growing up in a homophobic society that worked to install a kernel of shame into my sense of self— I find comfort in Fleckner's consistent work of bringing the often unruly and imperfect process to the front in their prints. The cross-out signs and snippets of texts that Fleckner chooses to leave in the prints not only provide a processual transparency to the non-linear process of making these works, these so-called errors also contribute to the overall function of the image.

It is precisely this uncompromising embrace of the irregular, the quaint, and the weird that have made me turn and return to Fleckner's practice, again and again, for close to a decade. Fleckner's persistent work on carving out space for the imperfect and uneven figures that fail to conform to normative standards functions as a training ground and testing site for my ability to imagine difference differently.

How I love being caught up in the relational intercourse of visuality, textuality, and tactility offered in these prints.

How I love the challenges they pose to me as a viewer and reader.

How I love how queer they make me feel.

Ester Fleckner: Woodcut as Resistance
JENNY GRASER

Woodcuts are the outcome of contact between two bodies: the printing
block and the picture support, which is often paper. The art historian
Jennifer Roberts compares the transfer process with a sensitive physical
act distinguished by engagement and disengagement, by presence,
contact, and intimacy, but also by loss, separation, and memory.[1] These
words resonate deeply in relation to the artistic practice of Ester Fleckner.
Since 2013, the year Fleckner graduated from the Royal Danish Academy
of Fine Arts in Copenhagen, the artist has been devoted to woodcutting as
a thread throughout their practice, and a tool for investigating questions
of gender and sexuality. After finishing their studies, Fleckner left their
native Denmark and moved to Berlin, drawn there by its queer and trans
scene. In 2018, Fleckner settled on the Danish island of Møn after purchas-
ing their own large-scale printing press. While they may have relocated
geographically, their focus on woodcut has remained.

WOODCUT: A PHYSICAL ACT

Wood is an organic material that reacts to its surroundings. Humid-
ity and temperature fluctuations have a direct effect on wooden printing
blocks. Changes in temperature can lead, for instance, to contractions
or expansions of the block that in turn distort the printed image. What is
more, a wooden printing block becomes elastic as soon as ink is applied
to it. The dampness causes the wood, unlike the copper plates of engrav-
ing and etching for example, to bend. And finally, owing to the individual
grain of the wood and any knotholes it might contain, every printing block
exhibits a uniquely uneven surface. In other words, every block exhibits
distinctive characteristics and is in a sense alive, thus resembling a body.

To make a woodcut, an image is cut into the printing block with a
knife or gouge. The block is injured but not destroyed; on the contrary,
here "injury"[2] is creation. The processing of the printing block—both the
cutting and the subsequent inking—takes Fleckner to the limits of what
is physically possible. Slowly, calmly, and with concentration, the artist
carves intricate compositions into the block after drawing them on transfer paper or directly on the wood. Their body not only leaves traces behind
on the wood as they cut into the block, but also as they ink it, a procedure
carried out manually by rolling ink onto the block's surface. During these
various stages, Fleckner and the printing block enter into a close and constantly changing physical relationship: the artist leans over the plate, turns
it several times, moves around it, and even sits on it. During this process,
the artist's body writes itself into the block.

The artist pulls several proofs to check whether the wood has ab-
sorbed the ink enough to achieve the desired degree of saturation. They
carry out the actual printing with their press—and not manually, as did, for
example, Swiss artist Franz Gertsch (1930–2022), who, in a time-consuming
process, rubbed the paper into the wood with a spoon to print woodcuts
measuring as much as two to three meters in size. When Fleckner inks
the block, pulls proofs on inexpensive paper, and then produces the small
number of final prints on higher-quality sheets, longer breaks are not
possible. This part of the production process must be carried out without
interruption to ensure that the desired intensity of color is achieved and
that the ink does not dry out on the printing block.

To generate both the proofs and final prints, Fleckner's process
unfolds over the duration of twelve to fourteen hours. During this labor-
intensive period, the artist becomes deeply acquainted with the printing
block down to tiny details. However, the final prints always contain a great
number of unknowns as the printing process is infused with an ongoing
loss of control.

FROM GRAPHIC BOOM TO ONE OF A KIND

Fleckner does not produce large editions, but mostly unique prints. In recent years, many artists working in printmaking—including with techniques that vary greatly from woodcut—have been producing smaller and smaller editions down to single copies. This tendency seems to be a reaction to what has been termed as the graphic boom,[3] an upsurge in printmaking taking place in the US and Europe in the 1960s, distinguished by large editions. This rise aimed to satisfy the aspiring art market by making prints available to a wider public at lower prices. In the 1970s, however, the printmaking market collapsed and interest in printed artworks rapidly declined.

During the boom, lithography and, even more so, screen printing were the mediums of choice for large print editions of several hundred copies. While woodcuts gained popularity throughout this period, they continued to be produced in a limited number of editions as they had before, regardless of the fact that the technique lends itself to printing up to a hundred sheets. Over time, though, the strong pressure of the printing press wears down the printing block and changes the image.[4]

The fact that present-day artists frequently decide to produce smaller editions or unique copies likely stems from a desire to increase the value of printmaking again. Yet it also reflects a shift in how printmaking is understood. Today, printmaking is no longer perceived and used primarily as a method of reproduction, but as an artistic medium on a par with painting, sculpture, and drawing. The fact that Fleckner primarily produces unique prints is a result of their extremely elaborate manual process, which makes the production of large editions impossible. What is more, the artist is not focused on the extensive dissemination of the same motif, but rather, on the ongoing development of their pictorial inventions.

INSISTENCE

After pulling the final prints from a printing block, Fleckner sometimes takes the same block in hand and resumes the cutting process. By adding further incisions, they change the image, and by repeating this process several times, they create a series of woodcuts consisting of continually modified compositions. In the series *Woodbeds, brimming* (2019–) (pp. 158–198) for example, the artist creates densely packed rows of triangles, squares, or pentagons, and organizes the shapes into horizontal rows that echo that of a text until the pattern covers the entire surface. These patterns have no center and no hierarchical structure. Each individual character, like each print in the series, is equal in status to the rest.

Every reworking of an already-used printing block means the loss of the previously cut image. At the same time, the predecessor is always also part of the new image. It is as if the past is constantly being embedded into the present. When the series *Woodbeds, brimming* is on view in its entirety, with each individual print beside the others, the artworks seem to be communicating. One print speaks to the other and the exhibition space fills with faint murmurs and soft whispers.

"Is there repetition or is there insistence,"[5] the modernist writer and avant-garde art collector Gertrude Stein inquired, "I am inclined to believe there is no such thing as repetition."[6] To go by Stein's words, which have inspired Fleckner deeply, repetition is not to be equated with replication but can instead be interpreted as insistence, and both variation and insistence are vehemently at work in Fleckner's art.

During the processing of the printing blocks, the artist exhausts both the wood's ability to withstand pressure and their own mental and physical resilience. The artist describes the cutting of the wooden block as a physical dialogue, a fight with the wood, stating "This cut could be both like a conflict or a fight with the material, a way of somehow speaking against something, but also of speaking in a different way."[7] This *discussion* is also steered by the respective wood type and its properties—how hard or soft it is, how pliant or resistant.[8] Fleckner used cherrywood for *Clit-dick Register* (2013–2014) (pp. 4–27), but usually works with printing blocks made of birch plywood as was chosen for *Woodbeds, brimming*.[9] In their processing of the printing plates, the artist is in dialogue with the wood's resistant qualities. Depending on the direction of the line, they work with or against the grain.

Georg Baselitz (b. 1938)—another author of extensive woodcut cycles—likewise works with the material as well as deliberately against it when cutting the wood. In his series *Women of Dresden I–V* (1990), he cut the lines of the motif—always an upside-down head of a woman placed centrally in the pictorial space—vertically, and thus against the grain of the wooden block, which ran horizontally. The resistive force of the wood made the lines' edges splinter and the contours jagged,[10] creating a restlessness that obscures the main motif and sets the beholder's inner eye oscillating. Whereas Baselitz used the idiosyncratic nature of the wood to explore questions regarding the abstraction of figurative motifs—that is, questions inherent to the images—Fleckner pursues a different goal in their contestation of the wood's resistance. Let us return here to the series *Woodbeds, brimming*. Of the many geometric shapes formed with fine lines and placed densely side by side, not a single one is identical to any other. The unpredictability of the wood does not allow for the precise replication of one and the same form, thus some unwanted differences occur among the cuts. At the same time, Fleckner consciously chooses to vary the sizes and shapes of the signs, often layering these forms. The artist uses birch plywood in particular because the hard material allows small details to be precisely cut. In the repetition and serial sequencing of a single geometric shape—the viewer experiences the ways in which one is different from the rest.

Besides the cut shapes, the specific characteristics inherent to each printing block also vary. The grain, the knots, and the knotholes leave traces behind in the printed image. Like artists before Fleckner such as Edvard Munch (1863–1944), the members of the Brücke in the early twentieth century, and later Joseph Beuys (1921–1986), Georg Baselitz, and Anselm Kiefer (b. 1945), Fleckner integrates the woodblock's physical properties into their compositions. Fleckner does not regard these aspects as limits. Instead, they emphasize the variety inherent to the wooden matrices. And although Fleckner's woodcuts do not adhere to a clearcut narrative or illustrate an explicit figurative motif, they have something to tell us: every living being is unique in character, expression, and physique.

BODY LANGUAGE

Fleckner is interested in the close relationship between language and the human body, a connection that ultimately informs their woodcut characters. The abstract shapes that the artist chooses for their woodcuts—stars, triangles, rectangles, and pentagons—frequently trace back to signs and symbols of Latin script, but also the human body—that is, individual extremities or organs in highly abstracted forms. The star-shaped signs in *Wooden Scripts (How I love your obscure), 1* (2015) (p. 90), for example, are derived in part from the asterisk on a computer keyboard. In the context of a text, this sign fulfills the function of adding a supplement or further explanation. Another reference for these signs is the human body, or, more specifically, the anus and its ring-shaped sphincter. It is no coincidence that Fleckner chose the anus as a motif. Few body parts are as politically charged: fraught with opinions, meaning, and joy, but also silence, shame, and violence.

Since their first woodcut series *Clit-dick Register*, instead of shying away from sensitive, shame-fraught topics, the artist has dealt with these subjects with the language of abstraction. In the abovementioned work, Fleckner arranged U-shaped crescents next to one another in countless rows. The prints spark associations with the text-based works of Hanne Darboven (1941–2009), for example, who outspread a kind of handwritten diary across hundreds of sheets and aimed to achieve as even a typeface as possible. Fleckner likewise conceives of their U-shapes as signs, as well as being representative of a multiplicity of genitals. And in choosing woodcut, Fleckner has decided on a medium that is itself based on a technique consisting of the simultaneous presence of opposing or binary characteristics. Thus, the final woodcut is an imprint of the elevated sections of the printing block—that is, everything that has not been cut away. In other words, a woodcut is based on an interplay between high and low, present and absent, light and dark, zero and one. Both are constantly present, and together bring forth the image. At the same time, abstract structures inherent in wood such as the grain or knotholes intersect within the composition and set the two-part system into vibration.

The artist conceives of their sign-based compositions as a form of writing that combines geometry and rigid systems with abstraction and poetry. "Words are marks and marks are words,"[11] declares American artist Harmony Hammond (b. 1944), with whom Fleckner's work is well-acquainted. Fleckner's words pick up on this thread, "Abstraction gives us an opportunity to rethink shapes and signs [that] we use all the time. It can function to deal with complex matters in a poetic and political way."[12] Reflecting on their abstract depictions of the body, the artist adds, "These small signs give me a way to consider how the language used to describe bodies so often fails in relation to gendered and sexual identities and categories. The simple forms create estrangements or 'abstractifications' of what is categorized and knowable in normative terms and understandings."[13]

Fleckner also touches on the limits of language through the text passages they carve directly into the wooden block or write in the margins of the sheets in pencil, as in *A closet does not connect under the bed* (2016) (pp. 100–123). In this body of work, the text reads, "How can I tell you without considering anxiety / pleasure / love // ~~How can I~~ // * *" Again and again, they erase or cross out writing and then add a new line. The corrections reflect the struggle to express a feeling or idea that language falls short of describing. For Fleckner, language's inadequacies and defectiveness possesses a value in its own right. "When I cross out words and sentences in my woodcuts, I don't consider the print to be a failure or any less perfect. Instead, [...] the print becomes a space to reflect on the failing relationship that exists between, for instance, the body and language. [...] I seek to stress and visualize a set of values that gives uncertainty and the unfinished a central position. That is also why I mostly do serial work. My prints reflect different attempts in the process."[14]

CHANGE OF PERSPECTIVE

"I think of the whole paper as my playground, not a margin with certain rules,"[15] Fleckner explained of their idiosyncratic approach to woodcut. Not limited solely to the printed zone, the artist supplements the printed image with handwritten notes or geometric forms drawn in pencil on the bright white periphery of an artwork's margins. Sometimes they add these markings after the printing process has been completed, sometimes before it has begun, which conflates the drawn and printed motifs.

When the artist draws, the figures flow directly from their hand to the paper where they are immediately visible. An image cut into a wood block, in contrast, remains hidden until the printing process is complete. Because the image must mirror and thus be cut into the plate in the reverse of the intended final version, the process of making the woodcut demands patience as well as the ability to reverse one's perspective. This may not seem as relevant for abstract compositions, however for text works, the need to reverse-orient is essential. The change of perspective correlates with Fleckner's perception of the world from a queer point of view. The artist asks, "What does it mean to feel different? What does it mean to have different experiences? [...] I tried to look at different systems in society from queer perspectives more than looking at queerness as a thing in itself. So for me queerness is very much about looking at the world, questioning it."[16] This questioning of perception is inextricably linked to Fleckner's approach to traditional woodcut, an approach characterized by crossing boundaries and breaking with norms. The artist treats the entire sheet, and both the recto and verso as the pictorial surface rather than only the printed section in the center. Drawing helps them occupy and appropriate the surface beyond the boundaries of the printed zone. Fleckner signs, dates, and numbers their woodcuts on the back rather than the front. This is not uncommon, but other artists make this choice primarily for aesthetic reasons—that is, so as to not sully the front with inscriptions. Fleckner's decision, however, is based on the desire to utilize the sheet to the fullest.

FROM PAPER SURFACE INTO SPACE

The geometric forms that occupy the picture planes of Fleckner's woodcuts extend beyond the surfaces of the paper into three-dimensional space through object-like works and installations. The series *A closet does not connect under the bed*, for example, is composed of twenty woodcut prints that were initially exhibited alongside twelve sculptural components (*Untitled* [2016]) (pp. 210–214). While the prints translate elements of disassembled closets into contour drawings and position them in varied relation to one another on a brown background, the sculptures are concrete imprints of old wooden closet parts. Star-shaped polyhedra with diameters of approximately 8–17 centimeters, also cast in concrete, accompany the woodcut series *All models are wrong, some are useful* (2017–2020) (pp. 126–143, 226–230). With their asymmetrical forms and visible tape marks, these concrete objects lack any semblance of perfection. In the respective woodcut series, the sculptures appear unfolded in different formations as white contour drawings against a black background. Though the ink is black, it is applied transparently, allowing the viewer to see the grain of the wood as part of the image. As a result, the organic material is part of the collision with the predictability of geometry. In this series too, the artist supplements the prints with fragments of text and drawings, written in pencil in the margins, addressing expectations and emotions around bodily appearance and ability. The notes on sheet no. 2 (p. 133) of the series read, "You were talking about appearing/ about polyhedrons / turning on sides to orient, rest / in four_ other dimensions." Those on sheet no. 8 (p. 143) include the words "There are no organs in a triangle / there are no organs in a triangle." Both series—*A closet does not connect under the bed* and *All models are wrong, some are useful*—moreover revolve around the opening of closed, confined spaces, which are disassembled and dissected.

Fleckner grants the viewers of the woodcuts and objects an immediate experience. The artist often presents the prints unframed when shown for the first time, placing the accompanying objects without bases in direct proximity to the paper works, encouraging them to be circumnavigated and closely contemplated from all sides. As three-dimensional objects, they enter into direct physical relationships and their compactness provokes intimacy.

POLITICAL ABSTRACTION

Fleckner's work activates the physical and political potential inherent to the woodcut. Though connections to early woodcutters, particularly of the twentieth century, are discernible, Fleckner is primarily indebted to artists working with a proto-feminist[17] or feminist approach to abstraction such as American painter Agnes Martin (1912–2004), German-American artist Eva Hesse (1936–1970) and American artist Hannah Wilke (1940–1993). These artists established a new pictorial language and approach to representation.[18] With the woodcut medium, and in Fleckner's own lexicon of abstraction, the artist expands on this legacy. Problematizing prescribed definitions of gender and the body, they explore the failures of rigid systems and narrow hierarchies, using woodcut as a lens for appreciating queerness and deviant ways of being. Thus, their abstract imagery is permeated by a political subtext, which is inherent to printmaking. In the words of Jennifer Roberts,"[...] pressure is a basic physical force that transfers images in printmaking but it also opens out onto social cognates like impression or oppression. Each of these terms, like pressure, denotes a specific form of intelligence and a specific area of sensitivity that allows for specific kinds of intervention in social and political life."[19]

In Conversation: Lex Morgan Lancaster with Ester Fleckner

This dialogue began in the summer of 2023, in connection with an on-line event for Ester Fleckner's solo exhibition Slow Tools *at Kunstverein Freiburg. The conversation continued online through autumn.*

Lex
Morgan
Lancaster

Ester
Fleckner

LML   For me, materiality is central to understanding how queer abstraction works (as a process or verb), and physical process also seems important for you. Can you talk about your use of the woodcut as a medium, and your material process?

EF   I am drawn to woodcuts for several reasons. The medium allows me to stay open and slightly out of control in terms of process, and to arrive at an abstract aesthetic. The cut line is rough and blurry, and wood imprints its own marks and structures onto paper. The technique is simple and immediate, and the physical resistance of the wood, as well as the printing process, allow for differences, errors, and unpredictabilities. My encounters with wood are intimate. My work begins with drawings, and then some of these drawings are transferred to wooden matrices. Through a process of cutting and printing, I develop compositions along the way. I print everything myself, and the printing process is as much a part of the work as the drawing and cutting. Making an artwork is an ongoing negotiation and material dialogue that often ends the way the work begins: I draw on the prints as a last step.

Performative moments of testing and experimentation become embedded into each work. For me, sketches and material investigations are closely related to queerness and how I work with abstraction because they challenge the recognizable, the finished, and the categorized.

LML   You have said that repetition and seriality are central for your work. What is it about the practice of repetition that yields alternatives that we might understand as queer?

EF   I am inspired by queer and trans theory to work with the concepts of movement, failure, refusal, changeability, and the unfinished. Terms that have compelled me to investigate different ways of working with woodcuts, where seriality and repetition have been central. Some of my series unfold by adding more cuts to the same wooden matrix between each print. *Woodbeds, brimming* (2019–) (pp. 158–198) is an example. Compositions begun in earlier works continue in the next, forging connections and collectivity, but also embracing differences between the pieces. The series is structured by repetition. I continue from a previous thread, while refusing and failing to make the same shape for an extended time. In other bodies of work like *How to spell a sound that is physical* (2014) (pp. 58–89), I use a new wooden matrix for each print and make variations on the previous composition.

I think of each work in a series as a suggestion, an attempt at the concept of trying again. No version is more final than the other. There is a sense of exploration related to Butler's thinking on gender performativity where language and repetition play a central role to the production of categorial binaries and the social implementation of gender norms. I try to work with repetition in ways that destabilize the meaning that signs and figures can carry from other contexts. Repetition can be frightening, but also used to enable openness and questions. When repeated imperfectly by hand in skew lines, layers, and grids through woodcut, the meaning and expression changes. Repetition (and difference) can enable sensitivity and insistence. But also humor. Or refusal. New tones, rhythm and poiesis can appear and represent queer feelings, desires, and relations.

LML   I'm wondering if you're interested in talking about the art historical relationships of your work to, say, Agnes Martin, and other legacies of abstraction and reference points you're engaging in? Your *All models are wrong, some are useful* (2017–2020) (pp. 126–143, 226–230), reminds me of Lygia Clark as well. I think about abstraction as a really loaded historical language, so I'd love to hear more about your queer attachment (or love-hate relationship, as you put it last time we spoke) with geometric abstraction especially, but also abstraction in general. How and why are abstract visual languages and models useful for you as a queer artist/an artist invested in queer politics? How might they also remain problematic, in ways we can't resolve?

EF   I think in some ways my strongest queer attachments are to queer and trans theory. The notion of failure according to Jack Halberstam inspired me early on to explore chaotic ways of knowing and unknowing, and to think about queerness as a position or space from which to question and refuse, rather than to seek inclusion or explain: to turn the gaze away from the marginalized body, and instead to look critically at conventional norms and structures. Queer and trans theory has given me primary inspiration to develop a practice where methods, processes, and materials are closely connected to political content.

My work often stages a collision with organizing systems and metaphors like the closet in *A closet does not connect under the bed* (2016) (pp. 100–123), the family tree in *I navigate in collisions* (2014–2015) (pp. 41–57), and gender binaries in *Clit-dick Register* (2013–2014) (pp. 4–27). I have found abstraction to be an alluring and innate visual language to represent queerness in alternative or extended ways.

Having said that, I feel a humble and broad connection to many art historical practices, particularly those that explore a queer and feminist approach to abstraction, form, and materiality. Agnes Martin's mode of combining contrasts of tight lines and systems with a sensibility, intimacy, and softness is powerful and dragging. The presence of the process, material qualities, and relationships between her works has always moved me.

My relationship to geometry is ambivalent. Through its strict formal language, geometry has historically dictated standards for bodies and their relationships to space and distance. I work with geometry through freehand drawing and woodcuts. The imprecision and repetition enter into a dialogue with the stringency and coherence of geometry. It's a way to make the geometry my own. In this way, the signs can also apply to moods, rhythms, breaks, and failures.

Abstract artwork touches me. Through materiality, form, spatiality, and color, abstraction addresses desire, emotion, and critique in ways that push us to think beyond simplified binaries. Abstraction can be an exploration of more open, chaotic, and poetic ways of representing not only a body, but also languages, intimacies, and relations.

You asked about the limitations of abstraction. The risk that artworks are understood relatively from person to person due to art historical legacies of abstraction, so political aspects can be disregarded, is something I think about often. Titles play an important role in my own way of underlining queer references and connections. Abstraction is not an alternative to direct representation for LGBTIQA+ politics. It can work as an addition. Visibility is important for movements and alliances. Abstract art can be the most powerful and touching, but it can also be overlooked. References can be very internal, but maybe that is an inevitability. Art requires curiosity and investment from viewers. For me, there is so much to unpack in abstraction as a strategy that the alluring aspects outweigh its risks and limitations.

LML   I would agree that abstraction and representation need not be in opposition, and also that every aesthetic language will have its potentials and its limits. The contingencies of spectatorship, the mutability of looks, are always at play—abstraction just makes this all the more apparent. You reminded me of what Barbara Hammer wrote in her essay on "The Politics of Abstraction," that abstraction insists on making the viewer active, and also opening a space for play.[1] It seems like abstraction is helping you to explore politics in different registers; for example, that the tension between your freehand exploration of form within a strict geometric system can act as a critique of closed binary systems while also opening space for something else to happen. I love that in some of your prints, little gestures seem to escape the central pattern or structure and wander off on their own to the edges of the page. You were already talking about the importance of queer failure and embracing a kind of chaos, so I wonder about the role that precarity, ephemerality, and intuitive process play in your work (both in terms of your making and how you think about the viewer's encounter). I think you've been circling around this already, but how and why is indeterminacy important in your work?

EF   Politics in different registers is a fine formulation. Precarity, ephemerality, and intuitive process are terms I value as points of orientation for my own work. They can point to vulnerability, gaps, complexities, and lived experience in relation to a specific concern. I test many variables within a frame or direction I give myself. I never work by intuition only, nor by strict concept alone, but prefer the combination of having a framework or starting point and moving playfully forward, often rubbing against the scaffolding. Some viewers read queer references immediately in my work, while others make more open readings about systems, language, and deviance. My own reflections and process drives the work, though I do think about how my interests and decisions communicate on many levels.

Indeterminacy is interesting in relation to abstraction and queerness. Indeterminable figures, signs, and visuals can express a gap or necessary complexity within an existing language and broader public mindset. Perhaps indeterminacy functions as an active term for me also. Like talking about queering something, it can be part of a work process to make something indeterminable, as a process of change, or a battle of ownership. I can use recognizable figures and signs in my works, but through abstraction and queering, the recognizable can be made insecure, thus questioning the stability of a figure and its usual context—similar to a process of destabilization mentioned earlier. Conditions and status of gender, sexuality, and relationships are often expected to be determined and clarified. Organizing structures are generally based on limiting discourse, definitions, and categorizations that link to a matrix with particular expectations for particular bodies. I think that indeterminacy can critically engage with such a matrix and help us to invent more open views of the body, gender roles, and beyond.

LML   I'm wondering, too, about your play with systems of language, or seemingly linguistic signs that also perform a drag on language through the kind of instability you were just talking about. Do you think of your work as a text, and if so, what kind of text is it? How does it operate? And I'm also wondering, how do you arrive at the sign systems that you're using? That is, are there particular signs that you find most generative or more open to play with?

EF   Many of my woodcuts mimic and reference text, words, and conversations. Dialogues move between the plates and the works in each series. It is exciting to investigate how language takes shape, in addition to where and how linguistic similarities arise and fall short. The power of language and the language of power, struggles over meanings, and the body's own language are respective preoccupations for me. It is through abstraction that I negotiate, dismantle, and challenge polarizing and biased communication.

In many of my works, the text may be an invitation into images, spaces, and conversations. Self-reflexive in form, these modes of ill/legibility address questions of community and formations of meaning, in addition to the stuff that falls through the cracks of language. My works *Clit-dick Register* and *Arguments for desire* (2013–2018) (pp. 28–39), for instance, are based on language and signs from the body. Clit-dicks, like U's, tongues, or genitalia, operate as texts and poetic images that explore communication about gender through linguistic and pictorial abstraction. The asterisk star, known as a sign on the keyboard referring to a footnote or the omission of letters or words, can be read both figuratively and abstractly, like stars and anus, creating room for new associations. It can be super banal—unpack-

ing meaning through repetition and letting meaning grow while retaining
its inherent simplicity. There is much that goes unsaid. Yet something
seductive arises through the changes formed through repetition.

Typically, I am preoccupied with a field of interest before ideas for artworks come.
At times I write texts often as part of researching a subject, and as a way of
creating a framework for a process. Some of my writing takes on a more
poetic character and fragments are incorporated into works or titles.

Gertrude Stein's writing and contributions to literature have been a great inspiration for my approach to investigating language. I admire her way of
breaking with the linear narrative within a single sentence itself. Her works
contain an enormous amount of humor and play with grammar, in addition
to the construction and breakdown of composition and narrative.

My series *How to spell a sound that is physical* was based on frustration and
recognition surrounding the challenge of communicating coherently
from A-Z. The crooked lines that cross and fail linearity became a way to
investigate how language and narrative can work in different directions
simultaneously. On each piece of paper, I first wrote different pieces of text
about navigating language with a pencil and then printed them over with
the woodcuts, so that it was completely random where the written text hit
or didn't hit the lines from the woodcuts. The printing colors have a great
deal of transparency in them, so that the pencil can be sensed or read
through the print. Inspired by Stein's work, it is a series that tries to depict
the possibilities and limitations of language and to express what language
can feel like.

In *Woodbeds, brimming*, basic geometric shapes act as a series of letters.
Exploring their inherent rigidity and reference to mathematics and architecture, I engage these figures through woodcuts in a direction where
presence and instability can enter. In *All models are wrong, some are useful*
woodcut prints depict unfolded polyhedrons in imprecise hand-drawings.
The prints relate to knotty and uneven concrete sculptures that are based
on the blueprints of woodcut graphics. The series resembles a parody of a
didactic demonstration, underscoring the relationship between geometric
ideals and material realization, model and reality, formula and form, and
the body and language.

I often follow a desire to collide, obstruct, and play with the signs I want to challenge. Cracks, openings and flirtations can make room for queerness
and other ways of talking about quirky, sometimes indefinable desires or
dreams.

LML The way you're pressing at the limits and excesses of language
points to the interpretive challenge posed by abstraction, and I appreciate how you make that part of the work by exploring language
and linguistic codes in relation to form. In this way, you seem to be
combining queer and trans thinking with conceptual approaches to
information systems—theoretical discourses that can be felt in and
through form.

I'm thinking especially about your works like *A closet does not connect under the
bed; All models are wrong, some are useful;* or *How to spell a sound
that is physical,* where the prints appear in strained relation to sculptural objects in the space. So then, we attempt to read the three-
dimensional geometric structures in relation to the images that
appear like diagrams—you were just describing the strained relationship between model and reality, or perhaps body and language.
Now I'm wondering about the affective register of this, because one
might see this more minimal and conceptual approach as austere
and even cold; and yet, you're thinking about bodies and desires.
Could you speak more to the relationships between the sculptures
and prints, as well as the embodied relationship we have to them
and the ways we might feel with them in space? What is generative
about exploring your core aesthetic concerns across these different
spatial registers?

EF In *All models are wrong, some are useful,* the prints and sculptures are
directly and conceptually connected: lines, mistakes, and errors mirror

each other. While both the print series *A closet does not connect under the bed* and the concrete installation *Untitled* (2016) (pp. 210–214) investigate the closet as an object as well as a metaphor, the relationship between the two bodies of works is less obvious. The prints depict abstracted construction drawings with different cabinet parts. There is no start, direction, or end to them. The installation *Untitled* consists of casts of twelve different interiors and exteriors of closets that are presented as fragments on the floor. While it might seem as though these parts form a single coherent object, neither the print series nor the installation function, together or separately, as instructions or models that form a functional closet.

The works address the metaphor of the closet which has an important but problematic role in queer history. The term "in the closet" is often used to describe that one is hiding, covering, or lying about one's sexuality and gender, in contrast to the societal norm of gendered and sexual transparency. On the other hand, the closet can also be thought of as a hideaway and temporary safe place in contexts where deviation from the norm is dangerous. However even in contexts where being LGBTIQA+ is somewhat accepted, we must also carry this furniture with us, ready to shoulder the burden of justifying, explaining, or correcting assumptions about our identities endlessly. I aimed to reflect on and question dominating constructions of normativity, in addition to the speech acts related to the closet metaphors, by literally working and reworking the form and function of a closet as a material object. In my casts and prints I do not directly represent or visualize queer bodies. I am instead interested in investigating the language and images that shape the construction of bodies. My focus on fragments and material imprints can hopefully provide an opening for another affective register in the work.

My first concrete installation was *Manoeuvring Overload* (2014) (pp. 206–209). I had made the *How to spell a sound that is physical* print series, and my thought was to cast some heavy and silly frames in concrete for them, that should lie on the floor. I made the outer dimensions of the casting frames according to measurements from a Danish standard pavement tile, 62.5 x 80 cm, and a smaller inner frame, so that the concrete work itself became an outline. Due to my lack of experience, the casting frames I used were too thin, causing the heavy concrete to push the frames to the sides. The sculpture became convex and crooked, a pleasant surprise that reflected my interest in failure. I continued this way, and made floor works from the errant tiles, *Manoeuvring Overload*. Similar to woodcut printing, errors that emerge during concrete casting become part of the object. If you want to change something, you must start again. Concrete is an industrial product used for the construction of buildings, formations intended for bodies to inhabit and to be enclosed within. I am interested in exploring concrete through processes in which its formal quirkiness and deviations connect to aspects of queerness, thus also investigating how identities are molded and constructed by material and spatial properties.

In addition to experimenting with concrete, in Danish there is a dated term for a masculine lesbian who is not deemed attractive according to the heteronormative male gaze, a "concrete lesbian" directly translated. In 2014, the year the work was made, this figure was shamed for her masculine appearance. Though the implications have changed by now, the (in)visibility that this figure can experience in a larger public, as well as the sex appeal she can represent in queer environments, interests me. Using this material is also a small queer gesture, and a reference to a mocked figure whom I appreciate.

LML I like this method of using casting to investigate social constructions and deviations in a material way. I get the sense that moving through the spaces with these concrete sculptures involves a maneuvering that makes us feel disoriented in relation to this deconstruction you're talking about. We would try, and fail, to visually construct a coherent structure out of these parts and the prints that seem like diagrams but don't work that way—so the failure that is so important to your process is also registering from the viewer's perspective.

In exploring both the interiors and exteriors of the closet as object, and thinking about this incredible formulation of the "concrete lesbian,"
you're pointing to the ways it is assumed that inside and outside
will always align, when it comes to identity categories generally
and especially those created to contain us. Your work both points
to the representational frames used to define queer and trans
bodies, and gestures toward their undoing—we might think here
with Jack Halberstam's take on architecture in relation to signifying
systems in "Unbuilding Gender."[2] In past art historical writing, there
have been some problematic ways of approaching abstraction as
though it were a kind of closet, a covering-over of difference, when
it has historically been used by queer artists. Do you think there is
something particularly queer about using certain models (such as
the geometry of the closet) against their own logic? Or a political
strategy of bringing something into visibility that was otherwise under the surface, in order to dismantle it? Can you say more about the
relationship between visibility and invisibility?

EF   With the use of abstraction as a visual strategy, the issues between visibility and invisibility are central. I have always found it difficult to directly
represent trans and queerness. They are capacious terms used in many
different ways, and visibility is much more than the body.

For me, visibility and invisibility can also be understood through the recognizable and the unrecognizable. Through the use of abstraction I can question
gender in a complex way, as embodied and something that cannot be
entirely legible through appearance. Visibility and invisibility can relate to
specific questions such as "which words are available to us?" and more
abstract questions like "what is visible and how is visibility expressed?"
Matters of in/visibility also point to how desires for queer relationships
can be visible to some and not to others. Visual queer codes and signs,
such as the handkerchief code, nail polish, earrings, etc. have been used
to create internal visibility and initiation. I guess many of us still navigate
partly through visual cues in public. Codes and appearances also point
to how abstraction—through form, colors, and materials—often carries
references and meaning in artworks.

Creating visibility around an object such as the closet or an architectural structure under the surface can be a useful approach to demand space for
more diverse bodily representation and queer navigation patterns.

Thinking of queer as a verb, rather than a noun, is useful. My practice is largely
grounded in unmaking, and rebuilding, to use Halberstam's excellent
terminology. I don't think we are at all finished with tearing down and
transforming all of the rigid establishments in language, architecture,
legislation, and beyond.

ENDNOTES

Relational Imprints: How I Love Ester Fleckner's Queer Abstraction
MATHIAS DANBOLT

1   David J. Getsy, "Queer Relations," *ASAP/Journal* 2:2, 2017, 255.
2   Ibid.
3   Ibid, 256.
4   See: Lex Morgan Lancaster, *Dragging Away: Queer Abstraction in Contemporary Art* (Durham & London: Duke University Press, 2022).
5   Ibid, 9.
6   Ibid, 11, 13.
7   Ibid, 9.
8   Parts of the analysis that follows are drawn from previous attempts at writing about this series, including Mathias Danbolt, "Fragments of Failure: A Conversation Between Mathias Danbolt & Ester Fleckner," *FRANK Conversations* (Oslo & Berlin: FRANK, 2015), and Mathias Danbolt & Ester Fleckner, "Intimate Constellations/Constellations of Intimacy: An Exchange on Navigating in Collisions," *Women & Performance: a journal of feminist theory*, 29:3, 2019, 303-331, DOI: 10.1080/0740770X.2019.1671102.
9   When a print from *Arguments for desire* was presented in the context of the art association Den Danske Radeerforening in 2018, Fleckner presented the star as an "anus star." This was picked up by art historian Rune Gade in his presentation of the print in the art association's magazine. See: Rune Gade, "Argumenter for begær—et træsnit af Ester Fleckner," *Den Danske Radeerforening – Medlemsnyt*, December 2013.
10 I borrow the term "critical intimacy" from art historian Mieke Bal who develops the concept in dialogue with the work of Gayatri Chakravorty Spivak. See Bal "Critical Intimacy," *Travelling Concepts in the Humanities* (Toronto: University of Toronto Press, 2002), 283-323. Yet, it is the writings of art historians such as Carol Mavor and Helen Molesworth that have taught me to value the mixture of desire, fandom, and love in the writing of art history. See in particular Carol Mavor, *Becoming: The Photographs of Clementina, Viscountess Hawarden* (Durham & London: Duke University Press, 1999), and Helen Molesworth, "Introduction," *Open Questions: Thirty Years of Writing About Art*, ed. Donna Wingate (London & New York: Phaidon, 2023), 13.
11 For a discussion of this series, see Mathias Danbolt, "Closet Constructs: Reflections on Ester Fleckner's *A closet does not connect under the bed*," Copenhagen: Overgaden Institute for Contemporary Art, 2016.
12 José Esteban Muñoz, *Cruising Utopia: The Then and There of Queer Futurity* (New York & London: New York University Press, 2009), 22.
13 Avery Tompkins, "Asterisk," *TSQ: Transgender Studies Quarterly*, 1:1-2, 2014, 26.
14 Jack Halberstam, *Trans*: A Quick and Quirky Account of Gender Variability* (Oakland: California University Press, 2018), 4.
15 Ibid.
16 The series *Woodbeds, brimming* contains both large and small prints. The prints made in 2019 are relatively small, with one larger print as the outlier, while the works in this series, made in 2020, 2021, and 2023 are all large format. My focus in this text is on the recent large-scale prints.
17 Sianne Ngai, *Ugly Feelings* (Cambridge & London: Harvard University Press, 2005), 264.
18 Ibid, 294.
19 Zoe Leonard, "A Wild Patience," *Agnes Martin*, eds. Lynne Cooke, Karen Kelly, and Barbara Schröder (New York & New Haven: Dia Art Foundation & Yale University Press, 2011), 79.
20 Jonathan D. Katz, "Agnes Martin and the Sexuality of Abstraction," *Agnes Martin*, eds. Lynne Cooke, Karen Kelly, and Barbara Schroder (New York & New Haven: Dia Art Foundation & Yale University Press, 2011), 186.
21 Ibid, 187.
22 Jack Halberstam, *The Queer Art of Failure* (Durham & London: Duke University Press, 2011).

Ester Fleckner: Woodcut as Resistance
JENNY GRASER

1   Jennifer Roberts, "The 70th A. W. Mellon Lectures in the Fine Arts: Contact: Art and the Pull of Print, Part 1: Pressure," posted April 25, 2021 at Harvard University, Cambridge, MA, video, 46:01, https://www.nga.gov/audio-video/mellon/mellon-2021-1.html.
2   Ibid.
3   On the so-called print revival or graphic boom, see: Christiane Lange and Nils Ohlsen, eds., *The Great Graphic Boom: Amerikanische Kunst 1960–1990* (Oslo & Stuttgart: Nationalmuseet & Sandsteen, 2017); Jenny Graser, "Eine 'Kampfansage' an das Informel: Die Druckgraphik der 1960r Jahre zwischen Avantgarde und Graphik-Boom," in *Freiraum der Kunst: Die Studiogalerie der Goethe-Universität Frankfurt 1964–1968* (Frankfurt am Main: Museum Giersch der Goethe-Universität, 2018), 32–49.

4   See: Georg Josef Dietz, "In Holz geschnitten, auf Papier gedruckt – Material und Technik des Holzschnitts," in *Holzschnitt: 1400 bis heute*, eds. Georg Josef Dietz and Christien Melzer (Berlin: Hatje Cantz Verlag & Kupferstichkabinett der Staatlichen Museen zu Berlin, 2022), 25, 21–27.
5   Gertrude Stein, "Portraits and Repetition," in *Lectures in America* (New York: Beacon Press, 1957), 166.
6   Ibid.
7   Avlskarl Gallery, "Ester Fleckner Interview," in conjunction with the exhibition *Woodbeds, brimming*, November 26, 2019, 10:42–10:51, https://youtu.be/DxRrRJGi-jE.
8   On this subject, see also: Georg Josef Dietz, "In Holz geschnitten, auf Papier gedruckt – Material und Technik des Holzschnitts," in *Holzschnitt: 1400 bis heute*, 21-27.
9   Ester Fleckner, email message to author, December 6, 2023.
10 See: Carl Haenlein, ed.,"Georg Baselitz – Gespräch mit Jean-Louis Froment und Jean-Marc Poinsot (Derneburg, Januar 1983)," in *Georg Baselitz: Skulpturen und Zeichnungen 1979–1987* (Hannover: Kestner-Gesellschaft, 1987) 51, 49–55.
11 Harmony Hammond, "Feminist Abstract Art – A Political Viewpoint," *Heresies: A Feminist Publication on Art and Politics*, 1977, 68, 66–70.
12 Macon Holt, "'There is a lot of queerness in nature,' an interview with Ester Fleckner," Blacklisted.dk, January 2019, https://esterfleckner.net/wp-content/uploads/2021/04/Blacklisted-Ester-Fleckner-Interview.pdf.
13 Mathias Danbolt, "Fragments of Failure: A Conversation between Ester Fleckner & Mathias Danbolt," ed. Sille Storihle, (Oslo: FRANK, 2021) 6, 1-8, www.academccessedie.edu.
14 Ibid, 4.
15 Ester Fleckner, email message to author, March 19, 2022.
16 Avlskarl Gallery, "Ester Fleckner Interview," 5:30–5:41.
17 For more information on Proto-Feminism, see "Proto Feminist Artists," The Art Story, accessed March 30, 2024, https://www.theartstory.org/artists/proto-feminist-artists/.
18 See: Eleanor Nairne, *Eva Hesse and Hannah Wilke: Erotic Abstraction* (New York: Rizzoli & Accuavella Galleries, 2020). See also: Annette Tietenberg, *Konstruktionen des Weiblichen – Eva Hesse: ein Künstlerinnenmythos des 20. Jahrhunderts* (Berlin: Reimer, 2005). For a broader overview, see: Christine Macel and Karolina Lewandowska, eds., *Women in Abstraction* (Paris: Thames & Hudson and Centre Pompidou, 2021).
19 Jennifer Roberts, "The 70th A. W. Mellon Lectures in the Fine Arts: Contact: Art and the Pull of Print, Part 1: Pressure."

In Conversation: Lex Morgan Lancaster with Ester Fleckner

1   Barbara Hammer, "The Politics of Abstraction" in *Queer Looks: Perspectives on Lesbian and Gay Film and Video*, eds. Martha Gever, Pratibha Parmar & John Greyson (New York: Routledge, 1993), 70–75.
2   Jack Halberstam, "Unbuilding Gender: Trans* Anarchitectures In and Beyond the Work of Gordon Matta-Clark," *Places Journal*, October 2018.

CONTRIBUTOR BIOGRAPHIES

MATHIAS DANBOLT is Professor of Art History at University of Copenhagen, Denmark. Over the last decade his research has focused on the politics of history and historiography in art and visual culture, with a special focus on queer, feminist, and decolonial perspectives. Danbolt is currently working on the contact zones between art history and colonial history in a Nordic context with an emphasis on memory politics, monuments, and art in public space. His latest publication is the anthology *Searvedoaibma: Art and Social Communities in Sápmi* (2024), co-edited with Britt Kramvig and Christina Hætta.

JENNY GRASER is a curator of contemporary art at the Kupferstichkabinett (Museum of Prints and Drawings) of the Staatliche Museen zu Berlin. Prior, Graser was a curatorial assistant and an assistant curator at the Städel Museum in Frankfurt am Main. She completed her PhD in Art History at Freie Universität Berlin and studied art, media studies, and modern history at the Braunschweig University of Fine Arts, the Technical University of Braunschweig, and Università degli studi Roma Tre in Rome. Among the several exhibitions that Graser has curated at the Kupferstichkabinett, she recently organized *Ruth Wolf-Rehfeldt. Like a Spider in a Web* (2022–2023).

LEX MORGAN LANCASTER is a scholar, professor, and curator who focuses on queer, trans, anti-racist, and crip contributions to the field of contemporary art. Their published essays and book—*Dragging Away: Queer Abstraction in Contemporary Art*—forge a queer formalist and materialist approach to the politics of abstraction. They are working on a second book focusing on trans approaches to abstraction and materiality. Based in New York City, Lancaster is Assistant Professor of Art History at The Cooper Union for the Advancement of Science and Art.

ARTIST BIOGRAPHY

The artistic practice of ESTER FLECKNER (b. 1983 in Aarhus, Denmark)
employs abstraction to challenge the recognizable, the finished, and the
categorized. Integrating queer and trans perspectives, their work addresses language, desire, and spheres of relation in open-ended and poetic
ways. Fleckner mostly works with woodcut printing—a simple, slow, and
physical technique that allows for differences, errors, and a loss of control.
Their practice expands from woodcuts to cast concrete sculptures, text
works, and drawings. Fleckner earned their MFA at The Royal Danish
Academy of Fine Arts in Copenhagen, Denmark and their MA in Gender
and Culture at Goldsmiths, University of London. Recent solo exhibitions
include *Slow Tools* at Kunstverein Freiburg, Germany (2023), *Bedfellows*
at M100, Odense, Denmark (2022), *Woodbeds, brimming* at Kunstplass
Contemporary Art, Oslo, Norway (2021) and Avlskarl Gallery, Copenhagen,
Denmark (2019), and *All models are wrong, some are useful* at Galerie
Barbara Wien, Berlin, Germany (2017), among others. Fleckner has been
awarded with grants from The Danish Arts Foundation, Aage og Yelva
Nimbs Fond, Den Hielmstierne-Rosencroneske Stiftelse, Ole Haslunds
Kunstnerfond, and was awarded the Art Brussels SOLO Prize in 2016.
Fleckner lives and works on Møn Island, Denmark.

Ester Fleckner is represented by

Barbara Wien
gallery & art bookshop
Schöneberger Ufer 65
10785 Berlin
Germany
www.barbarawien.de

Avlskarl Gallery
Bredgade 28
1260 Copenhagen
Denmark
www.avlskarl.com

LIST OF WORKS AND EXHIBITIONS

pp. 4–27
Clit-dick Register (English version)
2013–2014
Woodcut on paper, pencil
65 × 50 cm
Series of 22 unique works

p. 28
Argumenter for begær (Arguments for desire)
2013
Woodcut on paper
47 × 38 cm
Edition of 28, print made for Den Danske Radeerforening

pp. 29–34
Argumenter for begær (Arguments for desire), 2–5
2013–2015
Woodcut on paper
47 × 38 cm
Editions of 5

p. 30
Detail: *Argumenter for begær (Arguments for desire), 2*
2013–2015
Woodcut on paper
47 × 38 cm
Edition of 5

pp. 35–39
Arguments for desire (encore encore), 1–5
2018
Unique woodcut on paper
47.5 × 38.5 cm

p. 41
I navigate in collisions, flyer (English version)
2014–2015
Woodcut on paper
74 × 48 cm
Edition of 6

pp. 42–47
Jeg navigerer i kollisioner (I navigate in collisions), 1–4
2014–2015
Woodcut on paper
101 × 75 cm
Editions of 10

p. 44
Detail: *Jeg navigerer i kollisioner (I navigate in collisions), 2*
2014–2015
Woodcut on paper
101 × 75 cm
Edition of 10

pp. 48–50
Jeg navigerer i kollisioner (I navigate in collisions), 5–7
2014–2015
Woodcut on paper
101 × 75 cm
Editions of 5

pp. 52–53
Jeg navigerer i kollisioner (I navigate in collisions), 8
2014–2015
Woodcut on paper
101 × 75 cm each, diptych
Edition of 10

pp. 54–57
Jeg navigerer i kollisioner (I navigate in collisions), 9–12
2015
Woodcut on paper
101 × 75 cm
Editions of 5

pp. 58–89
How to spell a sound that is physical
2014
Unique woodcut on paper, pencil
68 × 52 cm
Series of 28 works
Collection the Danish Arts Foundation

pp. 90–99
Wooden Scripts (How I love your obscure), 1–6
2015
Unique woodcut on paper
123 × 90 cm

p. 92
Detail: *Wooden Scripts (How I love your obscure), 2*
2015
Unique woodcut on paper
123 × 90 cm

pp. 96–97
Detail: *Wooden Scripts (How I love your obscure), 4*
2015
Unique woodcut on paper
123 × 90 cm

pp. 100–123
A closet does not connect under the bed
2016
Unique woodcut on paper, pencil
104 × 80 cm
Series of 20 works

p. 125
Compounds of convictions
2017
Unique woodcut on paper
98 × 63 cm

pp. 126–127
Exhibition view: *All models are wrong, some are useful*
Galerie Barbara Wien, Berlin, 2017

Works:
All models are wrong, some are useful, 1–3
2017
Unique woodcut on paper, pencil, concrete
Woodcuts: 111 × 86 cm
Sculptures: 8–10 cm in diameter

pp. 222–223
Exhibition view: *Now it is light*
Galeria Municipal da Boavista, Lisbon, 2018

Works:
Argumenter for begær (Arguments for desire), 1–5
2013–2015
(pp. 28–34)

pp. 224–225
Exhibition view: *Woodbeds, brimming*
Avlskarl Gallery, Copenhagen, 2019

Works:
Woodbeds, brimming
2019
(pp. 158–179)

pp. 226–227
Exhibition view: *Slow Tools*
Kunstverein Freiburg, 2023

Works:
All models are wrong, some are useful
2017
(pp. 126–143)

pp. 228–229
Exhibition view: *Slow Tools*
Kunstverein Freiburg, 2023

Works:
All models are wrong, some are useful (copy and caress)
2020
Unique woodcut on paper, pencil, concrete
Two woodcuts: 100.5 × 73.5 cm each
Sculpture: 17 cm in diameter

All models are wrong, some are useful (solid pleasure)
2018
Unique woodcut on paper, pencil, concrete
Two woodcuts: 100.5 × 73.5 cm each
Sculpture: 17 cm in diameter

p. 230
Detail:
All models are wrong, some are useful (copy and caress)
2020
Unique woodcut on paper, pencil, concrete
Two woodcuts: 100.5 × 73.5 cm each
Sculpture: 17 cm in diameter

pp. 232–233
Exhibition view: *Slow Tools*
Kunstverein Freiburg, 2023

Works:
Woodbeds, brimming
2023
(pp. 188–198)

pp. 234–235
Exhibition view: *Slow Tools*
Kunstverein Freiburg, 2023

pp. 236–237
Exhibition view: *Slow Tools*
Kunstverein Freiburg, 2023

Work:
Wooden Scripts (How I love your obscure), 5
2015
(p. 98)

ESTER FLECKNER   I NAVIGATE IN COLLISIONS

Editors: Alison Karasyk Hines and Ester Fleckner
Text contributions: Mathias Danbolt, Jenny Graser, Lex Morgan Lancaster
Proofreading: Alison Karasyk Hines
Translation German to English (Jenny Graser's text): Judith Rosenthal
Graphic design: Anni's in collaboration with Ester Fleckner
Typeface: Monument Grotesk (Dinamo)
Paper: Munken Print White 18, 115 g. / Munken Lynx 300 g.
Lithography: Narayana Press
Bookbinding: Buchbinderei Büge, Celle

Frontcover: *I navigate in collisions, flyer* (English version), 2014–2015
Backcover: *Cruising horizontal lines (silver)*, 2022

PUBLISHED AND DISTRIBUTED BY
Mousse Publishing
Contrappunto s.r.l.
Via Pier Candido Decembrio 28,
20137, Milan–Italy

AVAILABLE THROUGH
Mousse Publishing, Milan
moussemagazine.it

First edition: 2024
Printed in Denmark by Narayana Press

ISBN 9788867496327
€ 30 / $ 35

The publisher would like to thank all those who have kindly given their permission for the reproduction of material for this book. Every effort has been made to
obtain permission to reproduce the images and texts in this catalogue. However,
as is standard editorial policy, the publisher is at the disposal of copyright hol-
ders and undertakes to correct any omissions or errors in future editions.

ACKNOWLEDGEMENTS
Ester Fleckner would like to thank: Bogg Johanna Karlsson, Anni's, Alison
Karasyk Hines, Mathias Danbolt, Lex Morgan Lancaster, Jenny Graser, Barbara
Wien, Isabel Podeschwa and all of the staff at Galerie Barbara Wien, Morten
Avlskarl, the staff at Avlskarl Gallery, Milena Høgsberg, Line Skywalker
Karlström, Sophia Baader, Mette Winckelmann, Helena Lindblom, Heinrich
Dietz, Line Hvidbjerg, and all of the photographers, collectors, and foundations
who supported this publication.

PHOTO CREDITS
Anders Sune Berg, pp. 4–27, 29–34, 41–123, 206–215
Nick Ash, pp. 35–39, 125–156, 184–187
Torben Eskerod. pp. 158–182, 200–204, 224–225
Marc Doradzillo, pp. 188–198, 226–237
Helene Toresdotter, pp. 216–221
Bruno Lopes, pp. 222–223
Sophia Baader, pp. 267–268

FINANCIAL SUPPORT
The New Carlsberg Foundation
The Danish Arts Foundation
Grosserer L.F. Foghts Fond

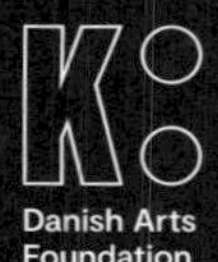

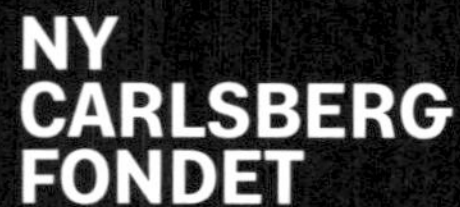

Ester Fleckner in their studio, Møn Island, Denmark, 2024

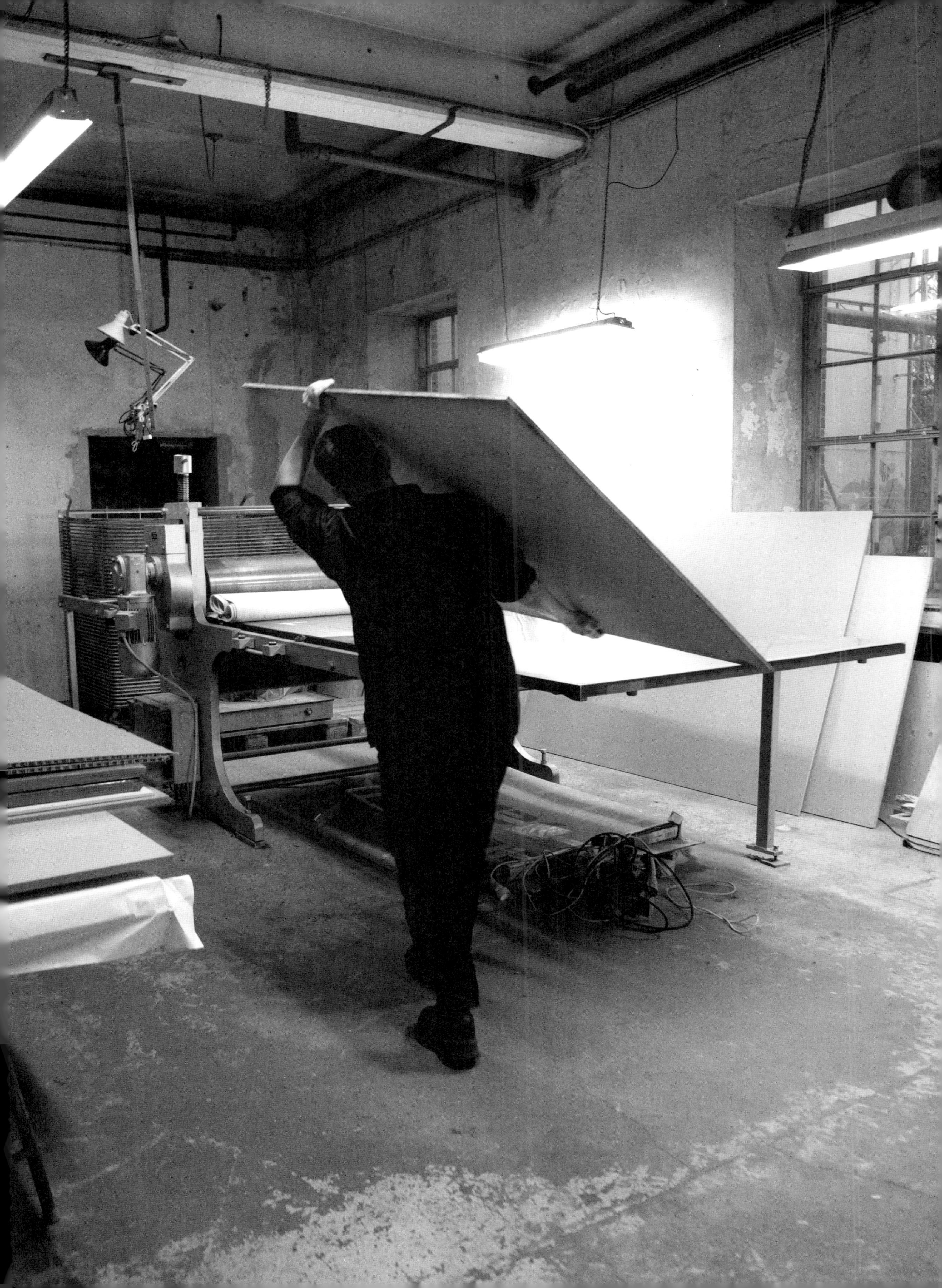

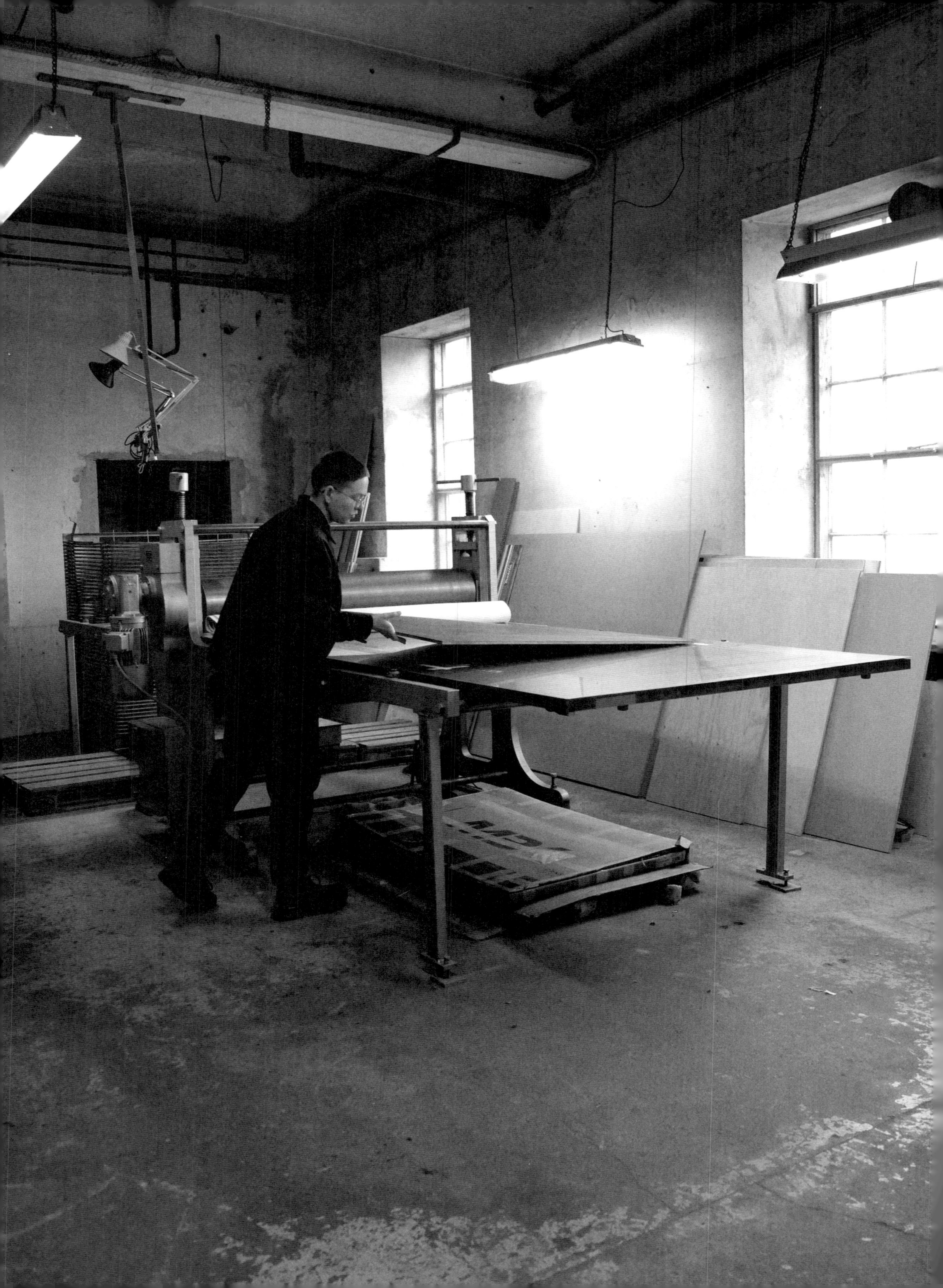